# Developments in British Politics 8

# Developments in British Politics 8

Edited by

Patrick Dunleavy

Richard Heffernan

Philip Cowley

and

Colin Hay

First published 2006 by
PALGRAVE MACMILLAN
Houndmills, Basingstoke, Hampshire RG21 6XS and
175 Fifth Avenue, New York, N. Y. 10010
Companies and representatives throughout the world

PALGRAVE MACMILLAN is the global academic imprint of the Palgrave
Macmillan division of St. Martin's Press, LLC and of Palgrave Macmillan Ltd.
Macmillan® is a registered trademark in the United States, United Kingdom
and other countries. Palgrave is a registered trademark in the European
Union and other countries.

ISBN-13: 978–1–4039–4842–7    hardback
ISBN-10: 1–4039–4842–9       hardback
ISBN-13: 978–1–4039–4843–4    paperback
ISBN-10: 1–4039–4843–7       paperback

This book is printed on paper suitable for recycling and made from fully
managed and sustained forest sources.

A catalogue record for this book is available from the British Library.

A catalog record for this book is available from the Library of Congress.

10   9   8   7   6   5   4   3   2   1
15   14  13  12  11  10  09  08  07  06

Printed and bound in Great Britain by
Creative Print & Design (Wales), Ebbw Vale

# Contents

# Acknowledgements

For this eighth edition of *Developments in British Politics* Andrew Gamble and Gillian Peele l ave left the editorial team. We thank them both for their splendid pas : contributions. We are delighted that both contributed chapters to this new volume. Philip Cowley and Colin Hay replace them.

As ever, our list of authe rs is entirely new. As the name of the series suggests, *Developments* foc ises its attention on up-to-date, cutting-edge developments in British poli :ics and we are enormously grateful to all our contributors for their expe rtise and their efforts. We are particularly indebted to them for meetin ; exacting deadlines that fell in a busy time in the academic year. We mus :, as is always the case, especially thank our publisher, Steven Kennedy. ! teven was given an award as Political Studies Association Publisher of the Year in 2004; he is, for us, publisher of every year in which *Development* ; appears. Thanks too to Brian Morrison for steering the book through t ie copy-editing and proof stages.

The volume editors and r ublisher would like to thank the Institute for Fiscal Studies for permissio 1 to reproduce Figure 15.1 from Emmerson, C. and Frayne, C., *Public S*, *ending* (2005).

*Patrick Dunleavy*
*Richard Heffernan*
*Philip Cowley*
*Colin Hay*

# Notes on the Contributors

**John Bartle** is Senior Lecturer in the Department of Government at the University of Essex. His most recent book is *Britain at the Polls 2005* (edited with Anthony King, Congressional Quarterly 2005).

**Sarah Childs** is Senior Lecturer in Politics at the University of Bristol. She is author of *New Labour's Women MPs* (Routledge 2004) and a co-author of the 2005 Hansard Society Report *Women at the Top*.

**Philip Cowley** is Reader in Parliamentary Government at the University of Nottingham. He runs www.revolts.co.uk. His latest book is *The Rebels: How Blair Mislaid His Majority* (Politico's 2005).

**Michael Cox** is Professor of International Relations at the LSE, Co-Director of the Centre for Cold War Studies at the LSE, and Chair of the European Consortium for Political Research. His most recent book is *Northern Ireland: A Farewell to Arms? Beyond the Good Friday Agreement* (edited with Adrian Guelke and Fiona Stephen, Manchester University Press 2005).

**Stephen Driver** is Principal Lecturer in the School of Sociology and Social Policy and Director of the Social Research Centre at the University of Surrey, Roehampton. His most recent book is *Blair's Britain* (with Luke Martell, Polity Press 2002).

**Patrick Dunleavy** is Professor of Political Science and Public Policy at the LSE. He is director of the LSE/Columbia MPA in Public and Economic Policy and Chair of the LSE Public Policy Group.

**Matthew Flinders** is Reader in Parliamentary Government and Governance and Deputy Dean of the Faculty of Social Sciences at the University of Sheffield.

**Andrew Gamble** is Professor of Politics at the University of Sheffield and author of *Between Europe and America: The Future of British Politics* which was awarded the Political Studies Association W J M Mackenzie Prize for the best book in political science published in 2003.

**Colin Hay** is Professor of Political Analysis at the University of Birmingham. He is either editor or author of: *The State* (with Michael

Lister and David Marsh, Palgrave Macmillan 2005), *Political Analysis* (Palgrave Macmillan 2002), *British Politics Today* (Polity Press 2002), *The Political Economy of New Labour* (Manchester University Press 1999) and *Demystifying Globalisation* (with David Marsh, Palgrave Macmillan 2000). He is a founding co-editor of the journals *Comparative European Politics* and *British Politics*.

**Richard Heffernan** is Reader in Government at the Open University and author of *New Labour and Thatcherism: Political Change in Britain* (Palgrave Macmillan 2001)

**Charlie Jeffery** is Professor of Politics and Co-Director of the Institute of Governance at the University of Edinburgh. He directed the Economic and Social Research Council's programme Devolution and Constitutional Change, which supported 38 projects on devolution at UK universities from 2000 to 2006. He writes on comparative territorial politics and multilevel governance.

**Samantha Laycock** is Lecturer in Public Policy at University College, London. Previously, she was Lecturer in British Public Policy with the Hansard Society at the LSE. She completed her doctoral thesis at the University of Essex.

**William Maloney** is Professor of Politics in the School of Geography, Politics and Sociology at the University of Newcastle. His main research interests are in the areas of interest group politics (internal and external dynamics), social capital, political involvement and non-participation. His next book is *Interest Groups and the Democratic Process: Enhancing Participation?* (with Grant Jordan, Palgrave Macmillan forthcoming).

**Tim Oliver** is currently completing a PhD in the Department of International Relations at the LSE. His thesis explores the changing nature of British foreign policy making.

**Gillian Peele** is Fellow and Tutor in Politics at Lady Margaret Hall, University of Oxford. She is author of *Governing the UK* (Blackwell 2004) and co-editor of *Developments in American Politics 5* (with Christopher J Bailey, Bruce Cain and B Guy Peters, Palgrave Macmillan forthcoming).

**Michael Saward** is Professor of Politics at the Open University. His most recent book is *Democracy* Polity Press 2003).

**Michael Smith** is Jean Monnet Professor of European Politics at Loughborough University. His most recent book is *The International Relations of the European Union* (edited with Christopher Hill, Oxford University Press 2005).

**Dominic Wring** is Senior Lecturer in Communication and Media Studies and a member of the Communication Research Centre at Loughborough University. He is author of *The Politics of Marketing the Labour Party* (Palgrave Macmillan 2004), co-editor of *Political Communications: The British General Election of 2005* (with J Green, R Mortimore and S Atkinson, Palgrave Macmillan) and Associate Editor of the *Journal of Political Marketing*.

# List of Boxes, Figures and Tables

## Boxes

## Figures

## Tables

## Chapter 1

# Britain Beyond Blair – Party Politics and Leadership Succession

PATRICK DUNLEAVY, RICHARD HEFFERNAN,
PHILIP COWLEY and COLIN HAY

In December 2005 the Conservatives' share of the general election vote intention in the MORI monthly poll touched 40 per cent for almost the first time since the autumn of 1992. Between 1992 and 2005, the party's score had typically languished in the range from 31 to 34 per cent and it had suffered three consecutive general election defeats with similar shares of the vote (with its share in 2005 up just 0.6 per cent on that in 2001). Put another way, the Conservatives for more than twelve years performed at a full ten percentage points less than their average general election score for the whole of the twentieth century, which was 44 per cent. Their apparent revival in December 2005 also saw them achieve a lead of over Labour (of 6 per cent) for almost the first time since 1992. The catalyst was, of course, the election of the previously little-known David Cameron as the new Conservative leader, triggering a 'honeymoon' period in public opinion. Famously such blips greeting new leaders tend to be evanescent, so in normal times not too much could be read into it.

But the circumstances were far from normal. For the first time since an aged Winston Churchill (eventually) bowed out of office to give the premiership to a long-frustrated Anthony Eden in 1955, the governing party was trying to secure the orderly transfer of power by agreement from an incumbent prime minister – this time Tony Blair giving way to a clear (but equally long-frustrated) heir apparent, Gordon Brown. The key difference lay in the fact that just before the 2005 general election Tony Blair had pre-announced his intention to 'serve a full third term', but not to stand again as prime minister at the succeeding general election, expected in 2009–10. This approach had never before been attempted in British politics. That Labour should go with it spoke volumes for its confidence that, since 1997, it had somehow become the 'natural' party of government. Blair's outstanding record in winning three successive general elections was matched by his extraordinary

1

significance for Labour as a party and as an electoral force. Assuming a 2009 election, Blair will have presided over a more than doubling of his party's total experience of office with a workable parliamentary majority. His going is widely anticipated for either May 2007 (his ten-year anniversary in power) or at most a year later in 2008 (Brown's last chance to acquire a record of his own as prime minister before a 2009 election). Inevitably it seems to signal a watershed in British politics, given extra salience by a possible Conservative revival. We discuss three key aspects – the implications for party system change, the contemporary role of leaders in politics, and the significance of the next few years for Britain's economic and social trajectory.

## Party system change

Political scientists who pored over the 1992 results before the Conservatives' autumn collapse in poll ratings following Black Wednesday were united in misconstruing the message. The initial academic reaction was to construe the Conservative's fourth consecutive victory as a sign of the party's continuing hegemony. Anthony King wrote that the UK had 'one major party, the Conservatives, one minor party, Labour, and one peripheral party, the Liberal Democrats' (King 1993, 224). The main British election study published its analysis of the outcomes as *Labour's Last Chance?* (Heath et al. 1994). A series of other publications and acres of journalistic comment argued that Britain had effectively become a one-party state, one in which the Conservatives looked set for indefinite rule.

There may seem far fewer dangers of similarly misconstruing Labour's success in winning most seats in the 2005 election, since the party suffered a loss of over 6 per cent of its previous vote and its majority fell from over 160 to a more assailable 66. Labour also regained power with the lowest share of the vote (and of the entire electorate) ever for a government with a secure Commons majority. Following the Conservatives' static vote share and Michael Howard's immediate resignation as leader, there seemed little prospect, either, of analysts overstating that party's future chances. The number of Conservative MPs increased by a fifth, the party won seats in all three countries of Great Britain for the first time since 1997 and the Tories almost entirely repulsed the expected assault on their seats from the Liberal Democrats. But Howard in fact got fewer seats than Michael Foot (who led Labour to spectacular defeat in 1983). Even in key seats where the Conservatives made gains against Labour this was mostly because the government's support drifted to other parties rather than because the Tory vote increased much. In parts of the country, the party's votes actually fell (Cowley and Green 2005). And in 2005 the

Conservatives achieved the r third-worst seats and votes outcomes for a century, beaten only by 2001 and 1997.

But perhaps the main d mension of uncertainty in assessing British party politics no longer l es in the ancient sport of forecasting the 'swing of the pendulum' be tween the top two contenders, so much as in working out the significanc e of different signals sent by voters in different kinds of contexts. Figure 1.1 shows four snapshots of different party systems, for Englar d outside London, and then for London, Scotland and Wales. The horizontal axis of the graphs shows each party's vote share at the 2005 general election, and the vertical axis shows their vote share at the last proportional representation (PR) election – which is the 2004 European Parliament election in England, the 2004 London Assembly elections, and the 2003 elections for the Scottish Parliament and Welsh National Assembly. (In the case of the last three systems, where voters have two votes under the Additional Member System, we take the parties' shares of the second or 'list' vote). For each party the plot shows the precise combination of vote shares in the two elections, the box around the data indicating the approximate size of the party's seat share. For example, Figure 1.1a shows that Labour got 30 per cent of the vote in the general election in England outside London, but only 20 per cent in the European election. Labour won 53 per cent of all English MPs in 2005, but only 22 per cent of the possible MEPs in 2004 – hence its seats box is rectangular with a long horizontal axis. By contrast, the Conservatives did better in terms of getting MEPs elected than n terms of getting MPs elected, so that their box is long in a vertical dimension.

The main point of Figure 1.1 is to show that the signals from voters in the two most recent contexts are significantly different and that the results in terms of seats vary sharply as well. In all four graphs the top two parties do better in the general election than in the PR election, where voters give more backing to third, fourth, and fifth parties who also go on to win more seats. The 'effective number of parties' for the PR elections here lies between 5.3 and 6.0 parties in terms of vote shares, but for the general election the variation is only from 2.7 to 3.6 effective parties.

How should we interpret these divergent signals of party performance? There is no consensus amongst political scientists, nor between the four editors of this book. For some scholars the general election results are clearly the more important or 'authoritative' ones, for three reasons:

- General elections involve the issues that most voters rate as the most important. Voters at this time are choosing between parties to help set

**Figure 1.1**   *The main parties' performance in votes and seats at the 2005 general election and the most recent proportional representation election, in Great Britain*

**(a) England outside London**

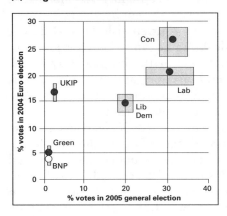

**(b) London**

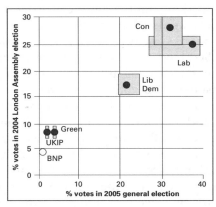

**(c) Scotland**

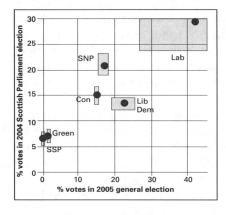

**(d) Wales**

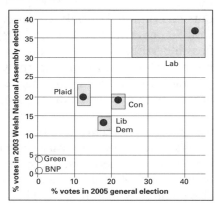

● Votes won by a party winning seats at one or both elections
○ Votes won by a party winning no seats
▨ Seats share at both elections

the big policy directions, and in the UK's system national politics remain dominant. So general elections show voters' most salient or 'primary' choices. In the other elections, covering 'secondary' issues and less important centres of power, voters might be more prone to indulge in 'luxury' choices, like protest voting or vote splitting.

- More people turn out to vote for MPs than for the PR elections, both confirming the first point above and meaning that the general election signals also draw on a much broader and more representative spectrum of voters' views.
- Parliamentary elections decide the overall constitutional direction – as witnessed by the fact that all the PR elections have come into existence since 1999 under Labour Hence what happens in Westminster is key for future directions. How the top two parties see their interests in these elections will determine what if anything happens to move the UK more decisively towards multiparty politics.

Other scholars take a different view, arguing that:

- Voters are constrained solely by the disproportional plurality-rule voting system used in Westminster elections to keep supporting the top two parties, when in fact the evidence shows that freed from constraint by PR systems they want to support a much broader range of parties. Hence it is Westminster voting that is 'inauthentic' or artificial, as people trying to not 'waste their vote' have to play games to get their message across to politicians.
- The turnout gap between general and PR elections has lessened sharply in recent years because of falling turnout at Westminster elections. The difference in Scotland was not very large between 2003 (49 per cent) and 2005 (61 per cent), while in Wales it was 38 to 62 per cent; in England 39 to 61 per cent; and in London 36 to 58 per cent.
- The trend to more fragmented voting in the UK is a long-run one. The first big growth in third and fourth-party support was in the mid 1970s, and has been broadly sustained ever since. A new growth of fourth and fifth parties has occurred since the 'coexistence' of PR and non-PR elections began in 1999. In 2005 there were more candidates from and votes for fourth and fifth parties in England than ever before. It seems unlikely that this trend will go into reverse. And at some point one of the top two parties will be forced by the pressure from voters alone to revise their self-interested support for maintaining the constitutional status quo.

One future possibility, much discussed in the past, but actually occurring very rarely in practice since 1945, is a 'hung Parliament' where no party at Westminster has an overall majority. In such a situation one option is a minority government, like those run by Labour from February to October 1974 and again from 1977 to 1979. The alternative is a coalition between two (or more) parties. A Lib–Lab government has run Scotland continuously since 1999. A shorter-term Lib–Lab administration ran Wales from

2000 to 2003. Less visible but equally important multiparty coalitions in the Greater London Assembly have sustained Ken Livingstone as Mayor of London since 2000. And Lib–Con and Lib–Lab coalitions run many councils with 'no overall control'. Previously anathema to the top two parties, a coalition government outcome *might* be more likely in 2009–10 than before for three reasons.

First, academic analysis shows that although Labour was badly weakened in 2005 the Conservatives still have a mountain to climb if they are to win outright in 2009–10. Assuming a uniform swing at the next election, to win most MPs (and hence have the right to try and form a government) the Conservatives need a swing of 4.8 per cent and a poll lead over Labour of 7.1 per cent. To win a bare overall majority and govern alone they need a swing of between 8 and 9 per cent. The last times a swing of that magnitude occurred to change the incumbent administration were in 1945 and 1997. Forthcoming boundary changes (due to be implemented before 2009) will help by reducing the number of low-population inner-city seats held by Labour, thereby redistributing representation to the suburbs and ex-urban areas where the Tories win more. But this will scarcely get them to the foothills of the mountain they must successfully negotiate. To win an outright majority they will need to beat Labour very substantially in vote share.

Second, the parties as well as the analysts have done the sums and the election arithmetic already indicates that the chances of a 2009–10 election producing a 'hung Parliament' are considerably greater than was possible at any post-war general election (Curtice et al. 2005). This recognition is likely to produce moves by both Labour and the Conservatives to court Liberal Democrat voters in order to try and attract their second preferences. The Tories will hope that Liberal Democrat voters will back them on a 'time for a change' basis in Labour vs Conservative marginals. One of the first acts of the new Conservative leader, David Cameron, was to appeal for Liberal Democrats to join him, proclaiming his 'liberal Conservative' credentials. Labour may want to repeat the offerings on constitutional reform which on some accounts played a large part in securing them Liberal Democrat support in 1997 and thus unified the previously divided 'opposition' votes to the Conservatives. Should Labour's electoral ratings further falter then an opening to the Liberal Democrats could look the more attractive to Gordon Brown the closer a crunch general election looms.

Third, coalitions or cross-party agreements might have been moved up the list of possibilities through the extensive recent experience of coalitions in the UK outside Westminster. Such two-party coalition administrations have been reasonably harmonious and generally either as effective or more effective than single-party control. The dawning of a more 'managerialist' poli ics also helps. With Cameron already proclaiming his commitment to 'big tent' politics this may be a dimension of British politics where the established governing 'ethos' of single-party control can begin to change.

## Leadership succession and political celebrity

The other great imponderal le of modern politics, and the focus of an enormous amount of attenti on in the 2004–05 period, has been the role of political leadership in the three biggest parties. We have already noted Blair's October 2004 decisi on to pre-announce that the 2005 election would be his last as premie r. The move, while temporarily preventing fevered speculation about the likelihood of Blair's replacement by Gordon Brown, neverthel ss made Brown's succession inevitable, prompting post-election bat les at the top and amongst different Labour factions in parliament over both the succession process and its precise timing. Blair's decision to qu it seemed for some to be underlined by the extent to which his leaderst ip and the baggage of the Iraq war visibly damaged his party's support in the campaign. After careful modelling to control for all other factors, analysis shows 'robust leadership effects ... the Prime Minister was clea ly a source of weakness for Labour' (Evans and Andersen 2005, 178). Blair's popularity subsequently went on a roller-coaster ride, first dipp ng in the election aftermath as vocal critics demanded that he go soon. It then bounced back after London's bid to host the 2012 Olympics wa successful and the prime minister was seen to give sure-footed leaderst ip in the aftermath of the July 7 terrorist bombings in London. Blair's poll ratings then dipped again as he first picked and then lost a battle with his own parliamentary party over a proposal to hold terror susp cts for 90 days without charge or trial and was then seen to yield signifi cant ground on Britain's rebate in the negotiations on the EU budget.

Meanwhile the Conservatives reached their third leader in two years. Michael Howard assumed the leadership in December 2003 without any rivals – he was the only ca ndidate when Tory MPs pushed out Iain Duncan Smith in a relatively bloodless coup. Howard then resigned the day after the general election in May 2005 to inaugurate a Tory leadership contest that ran unti December, creating a prolonged power vacuum that seemed at first o serve only to signal to voters a collapse of the Conservatives' efficacy l ut which in reality provided the party with considerable breathing spac e which allowed Tory MPs and the party membership to make a caref il choice of their new leader. The leadership contest itself fluctuated betw en initial elitist attempts to get a vote solely of Conservative MPs and an open (and in the end successful) democratic election of David Cameron by a clear two thirds of party members. The legitimacy boost this gave him, perhaps enhanced by the previous hiatus, then created the Tory bounce with which we started this chapter.

The Liberal Democrats entered the 2005 election under Charles Kennedy and achieved their highest number of MPs since the 1920s and their highest share of the vote since 1983. Most commentators judged this performance encouraging but unspectacular, and many Liberal Democrats, faced with an underperforming government and an unpopular primary opposition, considered it a lost opportunity. Immediately after the election under the party's rules there was an automatic re-election process for the leader. Kennedy was the only candidate and secured an apparently untroubled re-endorsement – only for serious worries about his leadership to re-emerge forcefully amongst his MPs (including his then deputy leader, Menzies Campbell) in late 2005 following the election of David Cameron as Conservative leader. As the Liberal Democrats' parliamentary presence has increased so tensions between the party's more left-leaning wing (led by Simon Hughes) and its more centre-right elements (led by Mark Oaten and perhaps Vincent Cable) have grown. Kennedy's efforts to tread a middle line, and his reduced visibility in the media, pleased no one in these push–pull conflicts (Rawnsley 2005). But privately many senior Liberal Democrat MPs were also worried about the extent of Kennedy's drinking, which they felt was seriously impeding his leadership. In January 2006, Kennedy was forced to make a statement in which he accepted that he had been struggling with a drink problem. He claimed that it was now 'essentially resolved' and called for a fresh leadership contest – in which he intended to stand – in order to re-legitimise his leadership. Two days later, however, and faced with the extent of opposition from senior members of his parliamentary party, he accepted that his position had become untenable, and stood down with immediate effect. On 2 March 2006 Menzies Campbell was elected as the party's new leader.

All this tri-party turmoil has focused attention on some longer-running academic debates about the role of political leadership in contemporary politics. For parties, securing the right person at the top is far more crucial than for a corporation. It is in fact more akin to a firm making critical 'brand development' decisions. The personal qualities of the party leader serve to embody in a walking, talking and changing presence the whole set of values, priorities and policies that the party stands for. The leader is someone who can (if successful) interpret policies in ways that become accessible to the enormous range of voters. This potential leadership effect applies across the board of issue and policy positions. And nowadays it is the focus of a whole smorgasbord of specialists' efforts. These are the special advisors, spin doctors, policy wonks, speech writers, public relations gurus, advertisers, opinion pollsters and morale boosters and protectors with which modern party leaders now surround themselves.

The likelihood of a Gordon Brown vs David Cameron vs Menzies Campbell contest by 2009 will shed light again on the three-dimensional triangle of leadership qualities demanded of modern leaders:

*Accessibility* Leaders must be telegenic, up-to-date in the way they communicate, and well-balanced and appealing in their personality and image. Contemporary voters seem to be searching for (or are at least increasingly encouraged to respond on the basis that they seek) a kind of political celebrity, someone whom they are comfortable to say to others that they support. Anthropologists speculate that the modern rise of a cult of 'celebrities' has deep roots in the loss of traditional tribal and community hierarchies, in which past centuries of humanity mostly grounded their sense of personal identity. A partial, fluctuating replacement is the modern 'star system' in which millions of people closely follow, identify with and discuss endlessly the fortunes of celebrities whom they have never met, allowing these new authority figures to influence how they dress, talk or have their hair done. Nowadays the leaders of the main political parties have to fit into this wider system if their fortunes are to prosper, as Tony Blair always pre-eminently understood.

*Trust* Citizens need to believe that what their political leaders say is true. Much of modern governance relies on 'nodality', the willingness of citizens and businesses to tell government things for free and also to pay special attention to the messages that government broadcasts back (Hood 1983). Without nodality and legitimacy, the quasi-voluntary compliance on which democratic governments inherently rely will begin to collapse. So anything that undercuts nodality has rapid and expensive impacts on government's ability to get things done. Labour's ruthless spinning momentum built up cumulatively from 1997 to the Iraq war in 2003. This played some considerable role in voters' consequent loss in confidence in this aspect of Blair's leadership, something which in turn played a large role in preventing him being the electoral asset in 2005 that he had been in 1997 and 2001. The consequences of overdoing government hype and spin did not stop with the leader alone. For instance, in late 2005 the government had to announce that the Office of National Statistics (ONS) would be established as a parliamentary agency completely outside the scope of ministerial control. This followed opinion polls showing that 64 per cent of citizens had no or poor confidence in the information that ONS was issuing.

*Strength*    The pervasive anxiety of citizens in modern civilisation is that it is now too complex (and perhaps the world too interconnected) for government to make a difference. To reassure the public that someone is 'running the show' and that 'the show is being run well', leaders have somehow to demonstrate their capability and experience to voters, especially their likely success in coping with crises and making difficult decisions. This is a very difficult trick for any opposition leader to accomplish. But Tony Blair did it in the mid 1990s by confronting and beating down established interests in his own party over Clause 4, Labour's legacy commitment to nationalising industries. Little wonder that Conservatives around Cameron anxious to emulate Blair are still searching for some analogous 'Clause 4 moment' that would allow their leader to accomplish the same trick.

Brown's leadership potential looks unchallengeable on at least one of the above criteria, namely strength and experience. Perhaps he could rate high also on the trust criterion, where his image of focusing on Britain first and foremost (especially in Europe) evokes positive reactions. His apparent success in running the national economy without overt recessions for eight, perhaps ten, years will also count with so-called 'pocket book' voters, concerned with economic stability and success (see below). But Brown looks highly vulnerable on the first criterion above, namely accessibility. He tends to come across as unapproachable or unsympathetic to many voters, and to gabble his speeches in a remorselessly intellectual way, perhaps even seeming dogmatic or overbearing in his approach.

Brown's future also still lies outside his own control, with no agreed date for Blair to step down and Blairite acolytes constantly floating stories in the press about the prime minister's own indispensability. Brown's rumoured 'succession plan' is supposedly being prepared under the supervision of Wilf Stevenson and the highly Brownite think tank, the Smith Institute. Rumours suggest that this plan apparently lays a great deal of emphasis upon Brown making rapid and far-reaching changes in the image and structure of government as soon as he becomes premier, imitating his speedy initial decision as Chancellor to grant monetary policy independence to the Bank of England. A 'big bang' start to Brown's premiership would be designed to establish that he is prime minister in his own right, and not just a long-serving second-in-command whose persistence has at last paid off. The elements of such a package are still vague. But some leaks suggest it will include a new constitutional settlement with more powers for devolved governments in Scotland, Wales and London; a new 'concordat' with local government (but in exchange for the abolition of two-tier local governments in county areas); and a national government focusing much more single-mindedly on just national, European and wider international issues instead of trying to micro-manage the wider welfare state as Blair and before him the Conservatives have both done.

Brown's internal position within Labour's ranks also looks unchallengeable now, but partly because Blair's now numerous critics have vested their hopes in Brown, imagining that he will be rather more traditional social democratic in character. The Blair critics also assume that Brown will be rather less trans-Atlantic and pro United States in his foreign policy choices. Neither stance in fact seems guaranteed. Brown has publicly declared that any government he leads will be Blairite, if not (as Blair would wish it) 'unremittingly New Labour'. And Brown, not Blair, was the architect and custodian of New Labour's fiscal and monetary prudence. He has not only backed, but been a principal advocate of, Labour's adoption and advocacy of enterprise, competition, flexible labour markets, public–private partnerships and PFI projects, financial incentives and strict fiscal discipline. As prime minister Brown is likely to retain tight control over the Treasury, appointing a favoured supporter as his successor as chancellor. Brown's political sensitivities have also always been more trans-Atlantic than European and he is less likely than Blair before him to be able to build a bridge between Europe and the US. Brown has spent his annual summer holidays in the United States for many years, has good connections with United States political elites, and may well disappoint the hopes of left-Labour MPs on this as on other dimensions. If these expectations are borne out, it remains to be seen how long Labour's likely honeymoon period with Brown will last.

Finally, Brown's future with Labour and with voters will also depend to some considerable degree on his deputy leader and Cabinet. Here he may find forces to balance out the youth–age problem he now has with Cameron. Labour's key 'next-generation' politicians seem likely to have quite similar personalities and track records to Cameron. David Miliband moved from policy advisor in 10 Downing Street to a seat in Parliament, rapid promotion to Cabinet minister, and towards certain prominence under Gordon Brown. Meanwhile Brown's own former advisors Ed Balls and Ed Miliband both began serving out 'apprenticeship norm' periods as new MPs in 2005, before ministerial office beckons in a future Brown administration.

Cameron's leadership potential is founded on almost the opposite foundations to Brown's, very high on accessibility and quite strong (initially) on trust, but very weak on experience. When Michael Howard decided to stay on as Tory leader throughout 2005 he was able to propel the little-known Cameron (and his close lieutenant, George Osborne, now Shadow Chancellor) into the Conservative front rank in the post-election

Shadow Cabinet reshuffle and give them greater exposure. Nonetheless, Cameron's initial candidacy for the leadership was widely seen in the media as a case of him positioning himself within the party for a future run at the leadership, five or ten years hence, rather than as a serious immediate bid. But his leadership hopes were transformed in the space of a week by his well-received campaign launch and party conference speech, and by the faltering campaign of the hot favourite, David Davis. Cameron soon eclipsed Ken Clarke as the favourite candidate of many pragmatic, more left-leaning Tory MPs, whilst Davis' campaign was derailed by a poorer performance than his rivals at a party conference 'beauty contest'.

The conventional wisdom admits that Cameron, like Blair before him, may be young, good on TV, vigorous, and keen to reform his party. But as such a new MP, with only four years in Parliament and no significant experience in a frontbench role before becoming leader, Cameron is also often presented as much more of a gamble for the Conservatives than Blair was for Labour in 1994. When they elected Iain Duncan Smith as leader in 2001 over Ken Clarke, the Tory membership opted for a candidate with no strong media qualities or parliamentary presence. By choosing David Cameron in late 2005 the Conservative members (albeit corralled by an enthusiastic news media) signalled a re-embracing of political efficacy, with add-ons. Cameron's actual experience of government in action comes from a spell as a special advisor to Conservative ministers in the mid 1990s. And his period of exile outside Parliament after 1997 before finding a seat was spent as the director of a public relations company. As Alastair Campbell has pointed out, the Conservatives, far from renouncing spin as they used to claim, seem instead to have elected a professional 'spinmeister' as their leader.

Cameron and his supporters are determined to travel light in policy terms. They want to give every public impression of their intention to move the Conservative party firmly to the centre, without alienating its core traditional constituency. In the short term this involves taking the fight to Blair (but particularly to Brown), avoiding having a series of detailed policies, and instead trying to redefine the image of the Conservatives – the 'brand'. This involves advocating a general disposition and putting forward a broad set of beliefs. It may well also involve confronting an old guard within the party in a style very reminiscent of the early days of the Blair leadership – confrontations that the leadership knows it can win and has the resolve to do so. As with Blair, Cameron might find that only by inflating the status of intra-party opponents can Tory modernisers then claim credit for having ousted them. Moreover, the new group in control knows that by winning it can demonstrate that the party has changed. There may be no single 'Clause 4 moment' (indeed, there was not really ever just one such moment in the creation of New Labour), but there will be several high-profile announcements in which the leadership picks a fight with its own party. Cameron's early commitments on increasing the number of women candidates and reforming the way that the party makes policy (in which the party chairman implicitly accused some of the party's own members of being 'fanatics') were early signs of this tactic. Others seem sure to follow.

This approach may sound superficial or contrived. But it also speaks to the heart of a central paradox of leadership – that an influential leader cannot be too far ahead of his/her desired followers, nor be too distinctive, nor so committed to a particular set of policies as to be unable to adapt to changing conditions. The leader's job instead is to estimate what is going to happen and then to 'surf' the ever-shifting moods of public opinion successfully enough to come out just ahead of their rivals and reach office. Here alone they acquire some limited capacity to fix or redefine outcomes and so to partly determine overall results.

## Economic prosperity and welfare state modernisation

The challenge for the Conservatives in search of an outright majority is to find some reason why the electorate might decisively reject Labour and embrace them instead. After all, the trigger factor that brought the Tories' poll support down so sharply in autumn 1992 and created Labour's opportunity to replace them was the mismanagement of a massive monetary crisis that resulted in Britain being forced to leave the European Exchange Rate Mechanism (ERM) and sent interest rates temporarily spiralling to as high as 15 per cent. But assuming that the enormously dislocating presence of the Iraq war in British politics has disappeared by 2009–10, and has not been replaced by any comparable source of problems (like internal terrorism), the political landscape does not contain any obvious bear traps for Labour of a similar size and scale.

Instead political debate s concentrated on relatively gradualist or managerialist debates about the best routes to achieving more economic prosperity and delivering modernised public services. The issues here are important ones but not easy ones on which any party in opposition can make much of an impression. Take the issue of economic growth levels, which in 2005 Gordon Brown first forecast at 3.0 to 3.5 per cent but which actually turned out to be at only half these levels at 1.75 per cent. To see how much this matters it may help to consider the magic formula of '70 divided by the growth rate', which tells you how long it will take for a country's national income to double. In the modern world, for instance, China is achieving year-on-year growth rates of 8 per cent, and so its national income is doubling every nine years. If Gordon Brown's initial forecast had come out right then UK national income would have been doubling every 20 years. But with the downgraded growth rate for 2005 it would take 40 years to achieve the same improvement in living standards.

Critics of Labour's record argue that since 1992 Britain's good headline economic performance has been driven by consumer demand. Britain has enjoyed a long consumption boom lasting for over a decade. It was fuelled first by rising stock market prices and, more recently, by rising house prices. Both served to boost consumption through the release of equity. Yet personal debts also rose, to historically unprecedented levels. Critics argue that the fragility of this approach could be exposed as never before as house prices stabilise and inflationary pressures (associated principally with oil prices) have started to build within the economy. If consumer spending carries on falling or stagnates, the peculiar growth dynamic of the British economy might unravel very rapidly and in a self-reinforcing spiral. If rising oil prices push up inflation then interest rate rises will be needed to control inflation. This change could only further depress the housing market, perhaps leading to negative equity, property repossessions, more declines in consumer demand and a regrowth of unemployment – previously at historically low levels under Labour. Externally the euro and the dollar might rise against sterling on the foreign exchanges, increasing the cost of imports and injecting further inflationary pressures into the economy.

Meanwhile the Chancellor has also borrowed heavily to finance a substantial public deficit produced by Labour's push to improve standards in health care, education and social security in old age towards more European levels of provision. Under its own economic 'golden rule' the Chancellor could thus be forced into putting up widely paid and highly visible taxes, as opposed to his previous alleged strategy of increasing only 'stealth taxes'. In such a context, critics argue that Gordon Brown's previous reputation for fiscal and monetary prudence could evaporate rapidly.

Government defenders and Brownites argue by contrast that the 2005 downrating of growth is an isolated blip in very difficult world conditions, conditions that in earlier times might have been expected to produce a real recession rather than just a growth slowdown. Brown's achievement in their view has been to preside over eight years of continuous growth, following on from two earlier years under the Major government, to create an unprecedented decade with no actual recessions.

Perhaps more worrying for Labour will be the public reaction to the outcomes of the government's incessant drives to improve the performance of the UK's welfare state. The underlying problem here is a kind of public opinion ambivalence that demands European levels of welfare state provision and government-financed infrastructures (for instance, in transport) while yet believing that somehow these can be provided with the United States' low levels of taxation. This is a circle that cannot be squared, although Labour hopes that if economic prosperity can be maintained it can somehow still be financed painlessly out of growth dividends. Public opinion has tended to respond positively but slowly to evidence of service improvements in health care and education, and to get just a little less downbeat and critical about transport. For Labour one danger is that these core issues for the party just move off voters' worry lists of salient issues, to be replaced by much smaller issues that for the moment look out of control (like the level of asylum seekers in the 2003–04 period). A more deep-rooted problem would follow if voters listen to the claims of Conservative media and think tanks (like the energetic body Reform) complaining that government-sector productivity levels have collapsed and that the increased resources lavished on the public services under Labour have been partly or even largely wasted. Labour has countered by launching the Gershon efficiency review, which aims to save £20 billion by 2008 and by backing proposals in the Atkinson Report to better measure government outputs and productivity. But proving that 'value for money' has been achieved will be no easy feat.

## Conclusion

In 2005 Labour was decisively advantaged by the electoral system, winning 55 per cent of Commons seats with just 35.2 per cent of the vote. While it took over 100,000 votes to elect a Liberal Democrat MP, and 44,000 to elect a Conservative MP, each Labour MP needed less than 27,000 votes. If anything like this advantage persists through to 2009–10 it will be a powerful insulation against outright defeat. But to ensure that this happens Labour needs to counteract a 'swing of the pendulum' effect that may strengthen with every passing year, unless the economy should significantly pick up, or unless a Brown government could somehow portray itself as a very different thing from its Blairite predecessors. Econometric analysis suggests that in the UK an incumbent government loses support at the rate of 0.1 per cent for every month it stays in office (Sanders 2005). This may not sound like much at first, but over a four-year (48-month) Parliament it means a decline of 4.8 per cent. This will have consequences for Gordon Brown, who will have been close to the centre of power for twelve years by 2009, and such a remorseless seepage of electoral support is a hard act to counteract. Still, the balance of probabilities must still be against a Conservative revival sufficient to topple Labour outright. Yet the context for the Brown–Cameron–Campbell leader battle will also be set by developments in the wider party system, including perhaps most critically the distribution of Liberal Democrat second preferences and whether the increasing fragmentation of the vote to other parties in the 2000 to 2005 period can be stabilised or reversed. What is certain is that Tony Blair's eventual departure from frontline British politics, Gordon Brown's long-awaited arrival in No. 10, along with the arrival of David Cameron and Menzies Campbell as opposition leaders will jointly mark a new era in British politics.

## Chapter 2

# The Blair Style of Central Government

RICHARD HEFFERNAN

Following the 2005 general election, having declared he would resign at some stage before the next general election and not seek a fourth term, Tony Blair's premiership began to edge toward its conclusion. Inevitably, his Commons majority having fallen from 179 to 166 to 66, it was suggested the prime minister was weaker than he once was, something typified by his first Commons defeat in November 2005 when MPs rejected a key plank in the government's anti-terrorism legislation. It made a change for Blair to be described as a weak prime minister. Previously his well-attested eagerness to lead his government from the front had prompted complaints of 'prime ministerial overstretch, the congenital disease of command premiers' (Hennessy 2000a, 390). Some went so far as to suggest that Blair's domination of the government and its ministers meant he was no longer a prime minister but had become a 'president' (Foley 2000; Poguntke and Webb 2005). One former minister, Clare Short, argued that there was 'no real collective responsibility ... no collective, just diktats ... Thus we have the powers of a presidential-type system with the automatic majority of a parliamentary system' (*Independent* 13 May 2003). Blair, unsurprisingly, dismissed all 'this president Blair rubbish', observing that similar claims had been made of other proactive prime ministers who 'tried to get things done'.

The idea that the prime minister is a president, an extension of the argument that he or she can be strong and authoritative, often reflects an informed and nuanced study of political leadership, particularly as presented by Michael Foley (2000, 2002, 2004). This notion of presidentialisation sits uneasily, however, with the core collegiality still found within central government. For instance Gordon Brown, Chancellor of the Exchequer since 1997, cannot be counted as simply a follower or subordinate of Tony Blair, let alone an acolyte or a functionary. Brown, Blair's ambitious heir apparent, has a political clout which, combined with the institutional power granted him by the Treasury's policy reach, makes him extremely influential across a swath of domestic policy issues.

17

Some say, such is Brown's remit, that Blair 'has been rather feeble about imposing his vision and his will. He has failed to make a reality of his ambition to take Britain into the single currency. He continues to struggle against ferocious resistance from the Chancellor to his agenda for public services ... This Government has never really been [a] presidency ... It has been a dual monarchy' (Rawnsley 2003). In short, Brown can, in certain policy areas, dominate Blair.

This is not to say that Blair has not been powerful and authoritative. Indeed, with the possible exception of Margaret Thatcher at her peak, Blair can lay claim to being the most predominant prime minister since 1945. Of course, Brown can be said to be the most predominant chancellor in that same period. He may be Blair's junior but both men, once very close allies, have had a fractious relationship which has often created a significant, troublesome fault line within the present government. Political disagreements between the two litter recent history, particularly when their policy differences have been exacerbated by the news media spotlight and are hyped by their respective supporters. These differences involve high and low politics, from euro entry to Brown's membership of the Labour Party NEC, health spending to junior appointments in government, but they mostly reflect an institutional rivalry born of the fact that Brown remains Blair's most likely successor and that he is very eager to succeed him.

The fact that Blair cohabits with Brown undermines claims that he is a presidential figure. Prime ministers and presidents are very different types of chief executive: each has leadership opportunities and constraints born of the fact that parliamentary systems have collective, collegial executives and presidential systems personalised, individualised executives. A prime minister's 'position can vary from pre-eminence to virtual equality with other ministers, but there is always a relatively high degree of collegiality in decision making' (Lijphart 1999, 3) while 'members of presidential cabinets are mere advisors and subordinates of the president' (ibid.). In the US presidential system, say, cabinet members defer to the president and are aware they serve only at his pleasure. The Blair–Brown relationship is not mirrored by George Bush and his Treasury Secretary, John Snow, nor was it shared by Bill Clinton and his Treasury Secretaries Larry Summers, Bob Rubin or Lloyd Bentsen. No US cabinet member could determine the president's policy against his will in the way Brown has been able to stymie Blair's policy preferences on, say, NHS reform and euro entry. It is also constitutionally impossible and politically inconceivable that any US cabinet member would angrily demand that the president resign and make way for him or her as Brown is alleged to have done of Blair (Peston 2005; Seldon 2005, 678).

The notion of presidentialisation reflects three interrelated – and important – factors which, in Foley's (2000) term, 'stretch' the prime minister, helping further empower him or her:

- the personal style of leadership of Tony Blair and that of Margaret Thatcher before him;
- the general media-led phenomenon of political personalisation, something that magnifies the prime minister, 'marginalizing other political actors to the periphery of public attention' (ibid., 293); and
- the hollowing out of political parties, something which places leaderships in firm control of their party's policy agendas and political direction.

The idea that the prime minister is a president, while highlighting the fact that the parliamentary chief executive is much more than 'just another minister', is challenged, however, by the core-executive model of British government. This model suggests that all central government actors and institutions, not just the prime minister, have some set of resources and that these confer different forms of power and authority (Dunleavy and Rhodes 1990; Smith 1999). As a result, for reasons discussed later, governing actors operate in a relationship of interdependence, something that prevents any one actor, even as powerful an actor as the prime minister, from exercising any form of total domination over government.

Of course, intragovernmental interdependence might ultimately confound all attempts at centralisation (Rhodes 1997), but, as Tony Blair's prime ministership demonstrates (and as the presidentialisation model points out), it can also prompt some degree of centralisation as government tries to overcome the perceived fragmentation – and the problems of policy delivery – that seemingly result. Tony Blair, eager to strengthen the governing hierarchy to better manage markets and networks, has strengthened the policy coordination of the Whitehall centre he leads, which he defines as his 'office, the Cabinet Office and the Treasury' (Blair 1998). It is this effort, the acknowledgment that fragmentation can limit the centre's ability to command, together with his authoritative and personalised form of leadership, that prompts the idea of presidentialisation, something that is often taken to be control freakery and as an autocratic style. The presidentialisation thesis, whatever its limitations, usefully reminds us of the need to account for the particular role of the prime minister within the core executive; to centre him or her, as it were, in the general study of central government.

## Government at the centre

Blair's Downing Street, still small compared with, say, the White House or the German Chancellery, exercises considerable political clout across British government. The Treasury under Brown comes close to its domination, but only in terms of domestic policy (Deakin and Parry 2000; Marsh, Richards and Smith 2003). It cannot match Downing Street in supporting or vetoing ministerial proposals across the board. Blair has endlessly tinkered with the Downing Street machinery as he has sought to expand his capacity to steer and coordinate the Whitehall machine. Downing Street itself, considerably revamped in 2001 by merging the private office and the policy unit, has been headed since 1997 by a Blair confidant, Jonathan Powell. It is currently subdivided into three directorates – policy, governmental relations and communications – and is presently staffed by a collection of civil servants, special advisors and consultants on secondment from the private sector. Senior foreign policy and European advisors, based in the Cabinet Office, report directly to Blair, not to the Foreign Office and Ministry of Defence, something further expanding the prime minister's reach (if not necessarily solidifying his grasp) within these policy areas.

The Blair government has built on past civil service reforms engineered under Margaret Thatcher and John Major, expanding the 'can do ethos', the administrative willingness to say 'yes, minister' rather than 'no, minister', pioneered by the Thatcher governments in the 1980s. Since 1997 the civil service has been headed by four cabinet secretaries, Robin Butler (inherited from John Major), Richard Wilson, Andrew Turnbull, and the present incumbent, Gus O'Donnell. This high turnover is largely explained by appointees having to retire at the age of 60. The civil service, according to Andrew Turnbull, 'no longer claim[s] a monopoly over policy advice. Indeed we welcome the fact that we are much more open to ideas from think-tanks, consultancies, governments abroad, special advisors, and frontline practitioners. In developing policy we not only consult more widely than we used to but involve outsiders to a far greater degree in the policy making process' (Turnbull 2005). With one in five senior civil servants now recruited from outside the service instead of being promoted from within, the past 15 years has seen the emergence of what Turnbull describes as 'a permanent civil service not permanent civil servants' (ibid.).

The civil service, so often criticised as being hierarchical and inflexible, an organisation devoted only to policy advice and administration, has thus been revamped in an effort to focus on policy delivery, subjecting services, particularly those provided by subnational agencies and actors such as education, health and law and order, to mechanisms such as cross-departmental working, so-called 'joined-up government', and centrally defined targets. In addition the government has announced plans (yet to be implemented) to further downsize the civil service, reducing its number by 104,000 of the present total of 466,000, with financial and personnel resources being pressed into the provision of front-line services.

The Blair government has also introduced significant changes in the topography of Whitehall. The rebranding of government, witnessed in the renaming of various departments, such as the Department for Work and Pensions (DWP) and the Department for Education and Skills (DfES), and the creation of new departments such as the Office of the Deputy Prime Minister (ODPM), the Department of the Environment, Food and Rural Affairs (DEFRA) and the Department for Constitutional Affairs (DCA), bears witness both to Blair's ambition to shake up Whitehall and to his inability to do so to his ultimate satisfaction. Such changes might well have been prompted by ad hoc, unorganised responses to political and short-term stimuli, rather than genuine attempts to reconstruct the administrative system, but they nonetheless indicate the government's willingness to try to make government better and more effective.

Blair's biographer, Anthony Seldon, suggests that the prime minister, being 'much more interested in – and better at – politics than management' (Seldon 2004, 343), has struggled to reform the Whitehall centre. As a result, he says, No. 10 and the Cabinet Office have 'seen years of almost Maoist "permanent revolution", with a bewildering number of changes of design to little effect' (ibid.). Such criticism is echoed by Peter Hennessy (2001, 2004). Nonetheless, Blair's administrative tinkering, prompted by his dissatisfaction with his existing policy leverage, has gone a considerable way to help establish an authoritative prime ministerial-led centre with Downing Street, together with the Cabinet Office, being revamped into a de facto prime ministerial department, 'an executive office in all but name' (Burch and Holliday 1999, 32).

Supporters of Labour's reforms argue that they provide Whitehall with an effective means of managerial intervention; critics argue that they are only a blunt and unsophisticated means of expanding a centralised control that is bound to end in tears. For the Blair government, however, extending choice and competition, part of the ongoing marketisation of public services, a process encouraging citizens to act as consumers, is seen as a means of reforming the state to efficiently and economically deliver public services. From this perspective, then, 'good government', defined as one directed by a strong and authoritative centre, has had three related objectives:

- pressing ahead with public-sector reform;
- securing improvements in public service delivery, particularly in health, education and crime prevention (the 'respect agenda'); and
- providing Whitehall with the authority to implement government policy.

Whatever its actual impact on service delivery and on achieving good government Blair's reworking of Whitehall, together with the reach of Brown's assertive Treasury, has meant that the British core executive as a whole is 'increasingly coordinated and coherent, and increasingly proactive and performance driven' (Burch and Holliday 2004, 20).

## The prime minister and the core executive

If the prime minister, even as influential and significant a prime minister as Tony Blair, is not as all-powerful a figure as some suggest, what then is the extent of his or her power? The major problem with the presidentialisation thesis is that, in addition to glossing over the core collegiality of the core executive, it crucially underestimates the degree of actual political leverage a British prime minister, compared to, say, a US president, can have over the legislature as well as the executive. It is hard to see how an authoritative prime minister such as Tony Blair, who heads up a powerful executive subject to less checks and balances than, say, its US counterpart, can be deemed *presidential* when being *prime ministerial* can often afford a wider authority and influence. This is because the prime minister's political influence reflects two phenomena:

- authority within the executive; and
- dominance over the legislature.

A president possesses the first resource, but given the independence of the legislature, which can be controlled by his or her political opponents, invariably lacks the second. In Britain, the executive as a whole, which cannot exist without a majority within the House of Commons, enjoys the second resource, yet the prime minister can – but may not – possess the first. The *prospect* of prime ministerial influence clearly begins with the executive's domination of the legislature, while the *opportunity* for prime ministerial influence is determined by the prime minister's ability to exercise influence within and over the executive (Heffernan 2005). Britain's parliamentary system creates a centralised government, should it possess a sizeable and reliable partisan House of Commons majority, as with Blair's governments, with a considerable degree of executive authority. Blair has headed a single-party government, elected under plurality rule, which largely dominates a reactive, asymmetrical, bicameral legislature.

The Crown prerogatives which enable the prime minister to appoint and dismiss ministers, allocate and reallocate portfolios, manage government business and oversee the machinery of government (Hennessy 2000b; Public Administration Committee 2003), place Blair at the heart of the government. They confer considerable influence over national, international and European Union policy, national security matters, government legislation, the civil service and control over the machinery of government (Burch and Holliday 1996, 83–102). Blair has such powers, by convention, not law, so long as he fulfils the following formal qualifications to be prime minister:

- being an elected member of the House of Commons, as MP for Sedgefield since 1983;
- being the leader of a political party represented in the House of Commons, as leader of the Labour Party since 1994; and
- being the leader of the political party with an overall majority in the House of Commons, heading up Labour majorities of 179, 166 and 66 since 1997.

These provide the tripod upon which Blair stands as prime minister. Should the first be lost or the second be relinquished (and therefore the third) the prime ministership is forfeit.

Blair's prerogative powers only relate to being head of the government and he has additional powers conferred by being leader of his party. The direction of the Labour Party is decided more and more by the parliamentary leadership, less and less influenced by the wider membership (Webb 2000; Katz and Mair 2002), something which further empowers the prime minister together with his most senior ministerial colleagues. Determining the direction of the party grants power over the direction of the government. This holds true even as party leaders have only a leasehold, not a freehold on the leadership and have 'authority so long as they retain the confidence of their parliamentary parties' (McKenzie 1964, 635). Being politically and electorally successful, delivering many of the policy and political goods the party desires, particularly winning support for the government's policy agendas and securing re-election, strengthens any party leader. Between 1997 and 2005 being a strong party leader has helped make Tony Blair a strong prime minister. The two roles are inextricably linked. Nonetheless, while Blair may have an enviable track record – and possess considerable political skills (and mostly have made wise use of them) – it is the political system, not simply his own abilities and powers, which largely determines what he can and cannot do as prime minister.

## Blair's prime ministerial authority

Tony Blair's potential to be a stronger element within his government owes much to his location at the 'core' of the core executive, something that reflects the 'asymmetrical power' model of core-executive behaviour identified by Marsh, Richards and Smith (2001, 2003). This can sometimes provide for a 'prime ministerial predominance' (Heffernan 2003a). Because the locus of key decision taking in British government continues to oscillate instead between the semi-monocratic (prime ministerial-led, not prime ministerial) and the oligarchic (inner cabinet-led), Britain does not easily fit into any of the usual categories of monocratic, oligarchic or collegial government found in parliamentary democracies (Andeweg 1997, 80). Of course the notion of asymmetrical power or prime ministerial predominance does not equate to an updated notion of prime ministerial government. Neither approach claims that there are no limits to prime ministerial power. As Tony Blair's relationship with Gordon Brown demonstrates, there are considerable limits. British government may never be wholly collegial, but it is never wholly monocratic.

Prime ministers are authoritative and powerful when they are able to propose policies to ministers and greenlight or veto policies ministers present to them. As the head of the government the prime minister is said to be 'first among equals'. This means he or she is:

- 'first' because he or she has the legal right to be either directly or indirectly consulted about all significant matters relating to government policy; but
- 'among equals' because their government includes semi-autonomous political actors, each of whom could replace the prime minister as head of the government.

Blair does not govern alone. No chief executive, whether prime ministerial or presidential, does so. Much policy enactment is both incremental and routine and it retains a strong departmental focus. The prime minister is, however, significantly able to lead ministers and direct the government. Over time traditional forms of collective action within British government have been gradually circumvented, limiting what was once a 'relatively high degree of collegiality in decision making' (Lijphart 1999, 3). Intragovernmental politics were structured around the supremacy of the cabinet before 1945, but characterised by the diminution of the cabinet a nd the rise of cabinet committees after 1945 (James 1992). Since 1980 he full cabinet has been in eclipse and the power of committees has been diminished. Andrew Turnbull, cabinet secretary 2002–05, observ :s that in '1975 cabinet met 56 times and received 146 memoranda. By 1990, Mrs Thatcher's last year, cabinet met 40 times and received only 10 papers. Most of the formal decision making had been moved eitl er to cabinet committees or to ad hoc groups under the prime minister's chairmanship. In 2002 ... cabinet met 38 times and received 4 papers and 1 presentation ... and [in 2004] 38 times and receiving 9 papers and 23 presentations' (Turnbull 2005). The full cabinet, as another former cabinet secretary Robin Butler also makes plain, 'doesn't make decisic ns' (Johnson 2004) although it occasionally has 'presentations' made to it. Its demise reflects the rise of informal forms of government, lar;;ely centring on the prime ministerial-led centre, intradepartmental networks and ad hoc ministerial meetings. Indeed, between 1997 and 2005 it is impossible to cite a meaningful collective decision that has been taken by the full cabinet by a truly collegial means. The exception n ay be the fully supported decision in 2003 to embrace the London Olymp ic bid.

The 2003 intervention in Iraq, while discussed in cabinet some 23 times in 2002–03, was man aged by an ad hoc war cabinet that circumvented existing cabinet and ministerial committees (Butler 2004). Postwar military engagements before Blair, most notably the 1982 Falklands War under Thatcher, had usually been run by a formal war cabinet, a ministerial subcommittee cf the full cabinet, to which regular reports were made and key decisions referred for ratification or discussion. In 2003 Blair's 'war meetings' comprised Blair; the Secretaries of State for Foreign Affairs, Defence a nd International Development, respectively then Jack Straw, Geoff Hoon and Clare Short; and Blair's Chief of Staff, Jonathan Powell, Directors of Communication and of Political Relations, Alastair Campbell and Sally Morgan, and his Foreign Policy Adviser, David Manning. This made it a prime ministerial, not a cabinet committee. The full cabinet did not receive papers on Iraq, only sometimes note verbal reports of decisions taken, and it was never invited to take any form of vote or reach an open and agreed collective decision (Butler 2004). Of course, because those ministers who strongly disagreed with the Iraq policy, most notably Robin Cook and (eventually) Clare Short, resigned from the government, it can perhaps be assumed that all other ministers happily supported the policy Blair and others laid down.

With the demise of collegial government comes the reinforcement of the centrality of the prime minister within the formal and informal networks that organise ministers and officials. The management of the Iraq crisis is only one example of Tony Blair's informal style of government. His habit of working from the centre with and through his advisors and hand-picked ministers on key issues has been criticised, particularly by a number of former senior civil servants (Hennessy 2005a). This form of 'government by sofa' – a reference to Blair's habit of conducting meetings in his sparse and small Downing Street office – has been caricatured as 'Tony's denocracy' (Seldon 2004). Blair has been openly dismissive, if not scornful, of past forms of cabinet government, decrying the idea that a cabinet meeting could 'go on for two days and you had a show of hands at the end' (Foster 2005, 164). After the 2005 election Blair dramatically reworked the cabinet committee structure, establishing new committees charged with pursuing his policy priorities, particularly health, education, crime and anti-social behaviour, which he usually chaired himself. Usually, however, urgent government business is expedited outside and around cabinet committees, often enacted by responsible ministers working with and through Downing Street, with cabinet committees being used to work up agreed policies and to prepare future policies.

Of course Blair's changes to the dispatch of business built on past changes. They make much of the long-established fact that as government has become less collegial, ministers take less of an interest in the work of other departments. While they publicly cheerlead for the government they accept that they have hardly any impact on policy matters beyond their own department. Since Margaret Thatcher, bilateralism, which sees ministers working with and through the prime minister and his or her staff, has become a key means of enacting government business. While cabinet committee deliberation still helps forge policy – particularly in thrashing out difficult or complex detail – bilateral negotiations between relevant ministers, involving the prime minister or his or her key staff, often prefigure such deliberation, so presetting the agenda or agreeing a common line (Lawson 1992, 128).

The impact of bilateralism is to disaggregate the government and configure a set of networks outside traditional structures. Ministers participate in these networks only if they have a departmental interest in the policy under discussion or are invited to do so by the prime minister. As the former foreign secretary, Robin Cook, reflected, '[a]s with so many meetings called by Tony, he [takes] great care to square the key players on the central decision' (Cook 2003, 148). Those ministers not privy to policy deliberations are obliged, contrary to the tenets of collective responsibility, to support decisions they have not influenced. Hence, with few exceptions, Patricia Hewitt, the Secretary of State for Health, say, is rarely willing or able to impact decisions involving John Reid, the Secretary of State for Defence, and vice versa. Tony Blair is, however, able to influence such decisions. He helps reaggregate the disaggregated government, something that locates the prime ministership at the centre of the loop, making the prime minister and Downing Street the principal node of key core-executive networks.

Why, asked the former Chancellor of the Exchequer, Nigel Lawson, do ministers put up with this and other forms of prime ministerial-led bilateralism? '[S]pinelessness or careerism may be adequate explanations for some, it will not do for all' (1992, 129). Instead, he argues, because ministers are each preoccupied with their own department, it will be 'highly convenient ... [and] comforting for them to feel that all they need to do is strike a deal with the prime minister and not have to bother overmuch about persuading their other colleagues' (ibid.). Of course, because future preferment is all too often a by-product of hewing to the party line, ministers tend to defer to the prime minister, particularly if they are ambitious or are weak (or when they are both). Those who find themselves in disagreement with Blair's preferences usually bite the bullet and keep silent, perhaps privately indicating their discontent through off-the-record briefings to favoured and discreet journalists.

As a result, given the extent of Blair's intragovernmental authority, leastways before his power began to wane after 2003, the conclusions of ministerial 'meetings at which Blair was not present – except in areas [Chancellor Gordon] Brown dominated – became only recommendations [presented to] Blair, unless he was uninterested in them, or they seemed unimportant, when they would be allowed to stand' (Foster 2005, 167). Indeed, given that, according to Robin Cook, Blair 'avoids having discussion in cabinet until decisions are taken and announced to it (*Sunday Times* 5 October 2003), ministers found that the best way to forward a major proposal was to win Blair's support by 'squeeze[ing] a meeting into the prime minister's crowded and ever changing diary, and [only succeeding] if what he [sic] proposed was what Blair wanted to hear' (Foster 2005, 168). An 'increasing tendency for business to flow to the prime minister's office and for ministers to feel the need to consult Number 10 before launching significant departmental initiatives' (Burch and Holliday 1996, 31) may therefore predate Tony Blair, but it has certainly considerably increased under him.

## The limits to prime ministerial authority

Blair, in common with all prime ministers, has always to carefully negotiate the various obstacles thrown up in the path by Parliament, specifically his own parliamentary party, opposition politicians, electoral opinion and the pressure of events. In addition, the government has to carefully manage the House of Lords, which often involves negotiating with the Conservatives and (particularly) the Liberal Democrats and winning them over. Of course, governments are more likely to be reactive then proactive, having to firefight crises and respond to problems. For instance, when embarking on his second term in June 2001 Tony Blair had no idea he would be – in the light of September 11 – proposing military action in Afghanistan and Iraq. He has consistently had to organise his priorities, such are the policy demands that crowd in on him. In opposition he suggested that 'education, education, education' would be the priorities of his government, but in office he has had to focus on other issues, most notably on public service reform, criminal justice issues (now renamed the 'respect agenda'), the Northern Ireland peace process, and, inevitably, international policy and prosecuting the war on terror.

If the 'scale and heterogeneity of government responsibilities are too great for any one individual to comprehend' (Rose 2001, 16) then the sheer impacts of events and the pressures of time place enormous demands upon any prime minister. For instance, in addition to the routine administrative demands expected of any prime minister, Blair had to simultaneously contend in four weeks in June–July 2005 with several issues, each of which separately offered a considerable challenge. These included dealing with the French and Dutch rejection of the proposed Constitution of the European Union, which entailed ensuring that the June European Council agreed a 'pause for reflection' in regard to ratification; fending off French demands for an end to the British rebate on the EU budget; assuming the presidency of the European Council; assuming the chairmanship of the G8, which involved preparing for and chairing the Gleneagles summit, tabling proposals on African debt relief and climate change; travelling to Singapore to lobby for London's successful bid to host the 2012 Olympics; and then, tragically, having to manage Britain's response to suicide murder on and under the streets of London.

Such pressures are not unusual. Robin Cook reported that in the first week of September 2002 Blair had 'flown to Johannesburg to make a big speech; returned overnight and the next day given a major press conference in Sedgefield; flown to Spain the very next day to attend the wedding of the daughter of prime minister Aznar. On Saturday he flew to the US and back for a face-to-face meeting with Bush, and on Sunday he went to Balmoral for his annual residence with the Queen' (Cook 2003, 200). Blair himself, while given to little public introspection about being prime minister, has said the job 'is utterly relentless. You are dealing with a multiplicity of issues the whole time. And the decision making process stops with you. That's an amazing thing – when every decision stops with you' (*New Yorker*, 2 May 2005, 87). Not all decisions stop with Blair, obviously, but it is rather telling that the prime minister should imagine that they do. Of course, important, non-routine decisions are made by Blair or, as significantly, by Downing Street staffers acting on his behalf.

Any prime minister, in addition to being a multitasking individual, has also to contend with the critical spotlight thrown by an ever more intrusive and aggressive news media. Tony Blair perhaps knows this better than most. The media's predilection for 'process stories' – discussion about happenings behind the scenes – rather than policy outcomes, both magnifies and facilitates disagreements within government. This is particularly so when a journalistic pack is in full pursuit of a story, witnessed numerous times in the past eight years, most recently in the case of the 2004 and 2005 resignations of David Blunkett, the events following the 2003 suicide of the weapons inspector David Kelly or the 2002 furore over Cherie Blair's association with a noted conman, Peter Foster. Not for nothing has Blair ruefully remarked that life in government is a 'constant barrage of attacks' (*Observer* 6 March 2005). How a prime minister is perceived is seen as being vital to their success, so the news media, which both provides and interprets political news, is both resource and obstacle, a friend and an enemy. If the prime minister benefits from favourable media attention in good times, he or she suffers from critical media attention in bad times. Tony Blair's endless ambition to be spun centre stage means he has been suitably placed to accept praise, but it has also meant that he has been subject to ferocious criticism.

Even while grappling with the pressure of events and the demands of the news cycle Downing Street has still to manage Tony Blair's base of support, both within the Labour Party and among the electorate at large. Lacking the security of tenure offered, say, a US president, Blair has always gently (sometimes, not so gently) to manipulate his parliamentary party through patronage and wise use of the payroll vote, those Labour MPs who are ministers or parliamentary private secretaries and who have therefore to support the government or else resign or be sacked from their post. Blair has also sometimes to compromise (or back down) in anticipation of parliamentary reaction. His government entered perilous parliamentary waters when Labour rebellions cut Blair's parliamentary majority to 17 on NHS reform in 2003, to 5 in a vote introducing university tuition fees in 2004 and to 14 on bringing in control orders to curb the activities of suspected terrorists in 2005. In November 2005 Blair lost a Commons vote on the length of time suspected terrorists could be detained without being charged. Clearly, parliamentary rebellions – or the very real threat of such rebellions – inevitably limit the prime minister's freedom of manoeuvre and can require government to make concessions to or reach compromises with its backbench critics.

All prime ministers have therefore to keep a substantial majority of their MPs sweet. Usually, a sufficient majority of them are always publicly sweet even when they are privately unhappy. This cannot, however, always be assumed. Even the most abject worm may one day turn. In this regard, although several of his predecessors were turfed out of Downing Street when losing the confidence of their MPs, most notably Margaret Thatcher, Blair's prime ministerial tenure was remarkably secure in 1997–2005 despite him having amassed a number of personal enemies and political critics from within his own parliamentary party. He has reportedly only seriously contemplated resigning at one point, a period in mid 2004 which found him at a low personal ebb, and his October 2004 announcement that he would serve only a 'full third term' and not seek a fourth owed little to grumblings from the usual anti-New Labour leftists and certain fervent champions of the Chancellor, Gordon Brown. It was seemingly prompted by the acknowledgement that – contra Thatcher – he could not aspire to 'going on and on and on' and would have to step down at some stage. Indeed, not a substantive or serious Labour voice was raised against Blair's continuing leadership in his first term and for most of his second term. Although his position was considerably weakened in that second term, leastways in comparison to his unassailability in his first, something which owed much to fallout from the intervention in Iraq, no serious campaign was waged against him.

Prime ministers operate within a set of structured governmental bureaucracies and have to work with and through senior ministers and civil servants. A core intragovernmental collegiality is a principal constraint on prime ministerial power. Blair, able to effectively manage policy areas of interest to him, has often been a poor manager of government. His government reshuffles have too often been hasty and ill-thought-out, particularly in 2002 and 2003, when Blair late in the day decided to create a Department of Constitutional Affairs instead of a much larger Ministry of Justice and seemed not to know what to do with the Scottish and Welsh Offices. Blair knows that he cannot just appoint anyone he wants to cabinet and has to sensibly sometimes appease powerful could-be foes, balance party factions and recompense loyalists and friends. Factors any prime ministers have to take into account in promoting individuals to cabinet include their:

- ability;
- reliability/suitability;
- seniority;
- gender;
- popularity/party standing;

- political and policy record in previous posts; and
- loyalty/agreement with government policy.

Another factor, party balance, the minister's location on the left or the right of the parliamentary party, is of far less significance than it once was, principally because party factions are less important and party leaders are far more in control of the party than previously was the case.

All prime ministers are constrained – to some degree – in the appointments they make. They accordingly find themselves surrounded by friends and by rivals, by stronger and weaker ministers, prime ministers in waiting, and even, as John Major embarrassingly declared, by ministerial rivals they would term 'bastards' (Seldon 1997, 390). Having to identify talent while rewarding able loyalists is something that Blair has not been particularly good at, indicating his impatience with the niceties of collegial government. For instance, one minister, the able loyalist John Reid, has often not been put to best use, having been shuttled around the government, being variously Minister of Transport, Leader of the House of Commons, Secretary of State for Scotland, for Northern Ireland and for Health before ending up Secretary of State for Defence in 2005.

Popular and authoritative ministers who enjoy a political base independent of the prime minister exert a significant leverage on him or her through the government and the party. If elements of the cabinet constrain the prime minister against his will then Tony Blair cannot be remotely likened to, say, a US president. All political leaders have their freedom of manoeuvre restricted by what their party and the public will permit and what real-time events allow. Blair has eagerly kicked against such constraints, and has been remarkably successful in governing against the ingrained wishes and instincts of the Labour Party, but he has still to work with and through his ministers who can assert their own preferences and sometimes protect their interests.

The collegial imperatives imposed by powerful ministers can sometimes be circumvented, but only temporarily, never permanently. This is because ministers (and particularly senior ministers) have institutional resources denied the prime minister, among them (Marsh, Richards and Smith 2001):

- a professional, permanent and knowledgeable staff;
- expert knowledge;
- relevant policy networks;
- time;
- information; and
- an annual budget.

All are devoted to a limited policy area, whereas the prime minister is obliged to range across all policy areas, cherrypicking those that either take or require his or her interest. Much routine policy work is channelled through departments and carried out by agencies. As a result a great deal of day-to-day executive politics, which is not collective but rather segmented, is still constructed around individual ministers and officials who control routine department-based administration. While the prime minister can successfully assert his or her preference, compromise can also often be the name of the game. Blair has successfully directed and instructed ministers, but he has sometimes had to coerce, cajole or entreat his colleagues to pursue some matter. On other occasions the prime minister has to qualify or abandon his or her preference.

## The Tony Blair–Gordon Brown axis, 1997–2005

A prime minister is number one in government while the Chancellor of the Exchequer is usually, not always, the acknowledged number two. The present chancellor, Gordon Brown, is, however, widely expected to follow Tony Blair in Downing Street once Blair departs sometime during the 2005 parliament. Some chancellors, most recently Norman Lamont, find themselves outranked by other colleagues, lacking either the political seniority or the general gravitas that should place the chancellor in the front rank, but most rank among the serious contenders to replace the prime minister should he or she fall (or be pushed) from office.

Gordon Brown's institutional base is weaker than Blair's but he lays claim to significant resources, not least those that arise from the institutional power of the Treasury. His policy purchase largely arises from the Treasury's responsibility for the management of macroeconomic policy and control of the public purse. It also largely results from 'the comprehensive spending review and their detailed public service agreements which give the Treasury a degree of control over departmental policy outcomes of a kind previous chancellors could only dream of' (Hennessy 2000a, 389). The stated policy objectives of Brown's Treasury (HM Treasury Departmental Report 2003) –

- [m]aintaining a stable macroeconomic framework;
- maintaining sound public finances;
- quality and cost effectiveness of public services;
- increasing the productivity of the economy;
- expanding economic and employment opportunities;
- maintaining an efficient tax and benefit system;
- high standards in public finance;

- fair and efficient financial services; and
- promoting international financial stability

– grant him a finger in numerous domestic, if not foreign policy pies. Brown's political base within the Labour Party enhances his institutional base and vice versa. His extended policy reach owes much to his standing as Blair's de facto deputy, someone infinitely more powerful and influential within government than the nominal deputy prime minister, John Prescott.

Blair and Brown's collective policy purchase, when they are working in tandem, is often extraordinary, particularly in helping pre-process pending decisions. In the most glaring example, Bank of England independence, only two other ministers knew about the decision before they were told about it. Not only was the cabinet not consulted but it had yet to convene when the decision was announced (Hennessy 2000b, 480–1). Similarly, successive comprehensive spending reviews, run by the Treasury in tandem with Downing Street, have exerted the power of the Blair–Brown centre over departments, albeit mostly with the willing connivance of the ministers affected.

Nowhere has the prime ministerial–chancellorial lock on key policy development been plainer, however, than in regard to Britain's policy toward euro membership. Blair, should it be politically possible to join, is a convinced supporter of membership, but Brown is much less enthusiastic. A compromise position between the two was hammered out in the late summer of 1997, supporting membership in principle, but only at such time as the benefits of entry would be seen to outweigh the costs. Five economic tests, devised by Brown and his allies, would be applied by Treasury officials to determine when that time would be. In summer 2003 – and to Blair's dismay – the Treasury assessment determined the time was not right to even further consider entry. Rebuffing Blair's attempts to retain the option of deciding on entry in 2004, Brown adopted his favoured policy of euro 'procrastination and postponement' (Scott 2004, 228), arguing that the assessment was set in technocratic stone and could not be altered. As was now customary, it was only when Blair and Brown came to their compromise that other members of the cabinet were consulted. Ministers were not permitted to directly influence the debate, let alone actually collectively decide the matter. Certain pro-Blair ministers (and pro-European confidants such as Peter Mandelson) had some input into the process, principally by unsuccessfully urging Blair to front-up to Brown, but all other ministers were merely spectators of the decision. The vast majority, however, were simply sent the 1,982-page economic assessment (in the case of the blind minister, David Blunkett, converted into some 300 hours of audiotape) and invited to be briefed by Blair and Brown about the decision they had taken (ibid.).

Professional jealousies have frequently divided Brown from Blair, not least in regard to Blair's exasperation at what he sees as Brown's effrontery and Brown's sense of amour propre and his ambition to succeed Blair sooner rather than later. Such personal differences less often find a policy edge, however. Both Blair and Brown have been at the heart of much of the New Labour project. Blair's responsibilities clearly range wider than Brown's, not least in terms of foreign affairs, health, education and crime policy, while Brown has been able to use his institutional base to exert some influence over transport and welfare. Both have to play some role in developing European policy. With Blair having indicated his intention to step down as prime minister 'having served a full parliament' it seems at present a racing certainty that Brown will succeed him. No date for Blair's departure has been agreed – and may not even have been privately set – but Westminster gossip currently suggests that the prime minister will go, and Brown thereby presumably succeed, some time in 2007. Time alone will tell. Whatever the future brings for Blair and Brown the relationship between the two – if nothing else – clearly demonstrates the pitfalls encountered in trying to describe Tony Blair as a president.

## Conclusion

British central government, having to govern with and through a variety of state and non-state actors, has sought to establish a strong executive presence. This, naturally, has its problems particularly when a focus on delivery, say, makes ministers managers, not politicians. Tony Blair, by his own admission, has had to 'learn to be prime minister'. For him 'doing politics' was one thing, managing the government another. When his then cabinet secretary, Richard Wilson, told him in 2001 that he had 'never managed anything' Blair pointed out that he had 'managed the Labour Party'. Wilson's reply, that Blair 'never managed them, you merely led them. There's a big difference' (Seldon 2004, 629), perhaps pointed to a weakness in his style of political leadership. Nonetheless, in terms of running the government, setting its agenda, its tactics and strategy, Blair's Downing Street has largely led from the front, working in tandem (but often separately) with Brown's Treasury and, in vote seeking terms, in harness with the Labour hierarchy.

It is, as Marsh, Richards and Smith suggest, 'extremely difficult to establish a generalisable model of patterns of [prime ministerial] intervention. What is clear is that whether a prime minister intervenes depends on a range of variables including salience, external context, the status of colleagues, personal interest, the critical nature of issues and the nature of the department and policy' (2001, 110). Prime ministerial power, which can be influential and wide-ranging, is also often marginal. It is always provisional. Government and its actors are always at the mercy of real-world politics.

The prime minister – and the government he or she leads – invariably finds him or herself at the mercy of a variety of political, electoral and social factors that are either under or beyond their control. Blair, stronger and more popular, say, in 2000 than in 2005, was more authoritative earlier in his premiership than later. A prime minister leading a party in 1997 with a majority of 179 and a share of the vote of 44 per cent is inevitably stronger than one in 2005 with a majority of 66 and 35 per cent. All prime ministers and most politicians eventually discover they have a shelf life. Even if Enoch Powell overstated his case by claiming that 'all political careers end in disaster', no modern-day politician can expect to remain in office forever: not Margaret Thatcher, who was able to maintain her grip on Downing Street for eleven and a half years, nor even the formidably able Tony Blair.

## Chapter 3

# Making Parliament Matter?

PHILIP COWLEY

In late 2005 the newspaper columnist Simon Heffer wrote an article for the *Daily Telegraph*, to celebrate his return to the paper after ten years away. In it, he criticised many of the changes that had taken place in the intervening decade: 'John Major was Prime Minister', he wrote, 'but apart from that things have got worse' (26 October 2005). In Parliament, he lamented Labour's decision to remove most of the hereditary peers from the House of Lords, on the grounds that whereas we used to have a House of Lords that was a 'proper revising chamber', one which defeated the government 'with alarming regularity', it was now 'full of the personal friends of the Prime Minister, or of donors to his party'. And he observed that the House of Commons of 1995 'had yet to adopt that posture of slavishness and ineffectuality that now characterises it'.

Such writing may win prizes for style – as all-encompassing whinges go, Heffer's was beautiful to read – but it gains few for originality: it is now commonplace to moan about the weakness and ineffectuality of Parliament, and to bemoan its decline. But most importantly of all, such a piece wins no prizes for accuracy. For, *pace* Heffer, both the House of Commons and the House of Lords have become more, not less, important in the last decade. And all the signs are that they are set to become more important still over the next decade.

## Parliament in perspective

Those who think that they are being somehow radical by pointing out that Parliament plays a marginal role in the making of policy are in fact being astonishingly conventional. More than 80 years ago Lord Bryce's influential study (1921) argued that all parliaments were in decline. Most studies of the role of Westminster since then have concluded that it is at best of marginal or sporadic importance in the making of policy (Norton 2005). Indeed, as Hugh Berrington (1968) has shown, even the so-called Golden Age of Parliament in the mid-nineteenth century was not quite as brilliant as is traditionally thought. By the late 1970s, one study went so far as to describe British politics as 'post-parliamentary' (Richardson and Jordan 1979), by which they meant that public policy was formulated in segmented consensus-seeking policy networks, each network consisting of the relevant organised interests and executive units; once formulated, policy was presented to Parliament, where because of strong party discipline and exaggerated government majorities it was almost always accepted. As a description of the formal reality of parliamentary life, this is a perfectly valid description. It is (and long has been) extremely rare for governments to see their measures defeated within Parliament; even minor amendments are very unlikely to be passed unless supported by the government. Public policy is made outside of Westminster; it is then given effect by Westminster. There is nothing new about this. Critics of Parliament who bemoan its marginality are being about as novel as someone who complains about the new-fangled motor car.

But it is a mistake to assume that marginal or sporadic influence on policy is the same as no influence. Parliament may not make policy, but it does constrain (and occasionally prod) government. All but the most technical of decisions are affected by some considerations of party management. John Major, for example, was forced to tack and trim for the entire five years from 1992 to 1997, most obviously over Europe, where his freedom of manoeuvre was limited by Conservative Eurosceptic MPs, but also in a range of other areas – such as Post Office privatisation – where the government withdrew or modified policies in the face of parliamentary opposition. Similarly, despite enjoying a large majority (between 1997 and 2005), and despite a relatively disciplined parliamentary party (between 1997 and 2001), the Blair government has also been willing to enter into behind-the-scenes negotiations with its parliamentary critics in order to defuse rebellions (Cowley 2002). As Ronald Butt's magisterial work *The Power of Parliament* (1967) shows, this is merely the continuation of a long tradition of backbenchers managing to influence government through overt or covert pressure.

Even if Parliament usually plays this limited role in policy making, there are issues where its role is far more significant – so-called 'free votes', those on which the party managers do not provide instructions for their MPs, covering such topics as embryo research, capital punishment, euthanasia, gun control, homosexuality and hunting (Cowley 1998). Here, the executive remains (ostensibly) neutral and the issues are left to parliamentarians to decide. As a result, rather than being peripheral, the legislature, and the legislators within it, becomes central. The formulation of British public policy as a whole may be post-parliamentary but when dealing with issues of conscience it remains firmly parliamentary.

MPs and Parliament also matter for symbolic reasons. Who cares if Joe Bloggs, ordinary Labour Party member, moans about the things that the government is doing (at times it appears that Labour Party members are never happier than when moaning about the things that the government are doing)? But if Joe Bloggs MP says something that deviates from the party line, then that is something else entirely. It is a 'split', in which Bloggs is inevitably presented as 'slamming' the government. Few members of the British media follow US President Herbert Hoover's injunction that 'honest differences of views and honest debate are not disunity. They are the vital process of policy making among free men.' As one Labour whip argued, 'other than policy failure, the most damaging thing that can happen to any British government is division and disunity.' Parties that want to appear united need their parliamentarians to be united. Parliament also plays an important symbolic role in legitimating policy (Judge 1993), with the process of parliamentary approval making policy predominantly made elsewhere seem legitimate and acceptable.

More recently, however, Parliament – and the centralised British state in general – has faced a series of broader constitutional challenges, beginning with the EEC (and its various later incarnations), and (most recently of all) taking in the lopsided process of devolution and the Human Rights Act (Riddell 2000). This has led to debates about the extent to which the 'Westminster model' of government is still applicable in British politics, debates with which this volume is replete. Yet it is possible to overstate the extent to which these have changed Parliament's de facto function, as opposed to its de jure potential. In Scotland, Wales and Northern Ireland, the impact of the Westminster Parliament has been reduced by devolution (albeit suspended in the case of Northern Ireland at the time of writing). This, though, still leaves England, which is (to put it mildly) a not insignificant part of the United Kingdom, and which is still governed directed from Westminster. In reality, most of the shifts in power as a result of these constitutional changes – to sub- or supranational bodies, such as the EU – were not shifts in power away from Parliament – since de facto Parliament had never been in control of them before – but from the London-based executive. They were in other words shifts in power from Whitehall, not Westminster. And much of the evidence from the last decade has seen a modest, but important, reversal in Westminster's fortunes vis-à-vis Whitehall, as will become clear throughout this chapter. There has also been a further growth in the amount of work MPs do in their constituencies and on behalf of their constituents.

## The constituency face

In October 2004, and anticipating the coming into force of the Freedom of Information Act in January 2005, the House of Commons authorities for the first time published details of the expenditure claims made by each MP. It revealed that MPs claimed a total of just over £78 million in allowances and expenses between April 2003 and March 2004, an average of £118,000 per MP. This was up £5 million on the previous year, and a rise of almost 50 per cent on the £57.5 million claimed in 2001/02. By October 2005 that figure had risen to just under £81 million, an average per MP of £123,000.

Entirely predictably, the media worked themselves up into a lather of contrived moral indignation, with newspapers depicting MPs as a 'bunch of thieving, fiddling, wasteful, good-for-nothing, feather-bedded spongers', languishing in the Palace of 'Wasteminster'. Most headlines talked of MPs getting their expenses on top of their salary. But anyone giving the figures even a cursory glance could see that most of the expenditure was not 'expenses' in the way that the phrase was normally understood. Most of the money went on staff costs (around £71,000 on average), with most of the rest of it eaten up by paying for office space, plus stationery and travel expenses. As Stephen Pound, Labour MP for Ealing North, said: 'This is not about filling our boots. This is not about trousering a lot of money. This is about the money it takes to do the job.'

The majority of the 'expenses' were being spent on the ever increasing constituency work of MPs. As the Liberal Democrat Archy Kirkwood put it: '[MPs] now deal with issues, and communicate in ways unheard of a few years ago. They require more back-up staff, more computer resources and more allowances to enable them to travel back and forth to Parliament, living away from home for days at a time, while keeping in touch with the problems and issues of their constituents' (BBC Online 22 October 2004).

Even the least constituency-focused MPs of today pay more attention to their constituents than any MP of 40 or more years ago. One Labour MP elected in 1945 famously told of his first visit to the constituency after the election. He was met by a top-hatted station master who asked whether he would be making his annual visit to the constituency at that time of the year. Another was such an irregular visitor to the constituency that his successor, a man called George Darling, was selected as Labour candidate on what was then a radical promise of quarterly visits to the constituency.

The growth of the constituency role of MPs dates back to the 1960s (Norton and Wood 1993), but the large influx of MPs elected since 1997 have been especially constituency-focused. A survey of the 1997 intake found that 86 per cent ranked 'being a good constituency member' as the most important role of an MP, compared to just 13 per cent who thought 'checking the executive' was the most important task. More recent research found a similar concentration on the constituency (Healey et al.

2005), albeit not always as the most important task (Hansard Society 2001, 142). This manifests itself in a variety of ways. MPs are now:

- more likely to live in their constituencies. Fifty years ago, MPs may have visited their constituency occasionally, but few lived there. Nearly all MPs now have a home in the constituency. They are also increasingly likely to have come from the constituency; high-profile cases of favoured candidates being 'parachuted' into constituencies by the leadership obscure the extent to which – especially on the Labour side – local candidates are increasingly being chosen to fight elections;
- more likely to maintain staffed offices in their constituency, and to hold regular 'surgeries' – akin to those held by GPs – where voters can raise issues of concern to them;
- more likely to spend time in the constituency. One of the purposes of the recent reforms of the timetable in the House of Commons (see below) was to allow MPs to spend more time away from Westminster. Many MPs now arrive in the constituency late on Thursday or early on Friday, and remain there throughout the weekend, departing for Westminster on the following Monday (or sometimes Tuesday). This means that some of them are now spending more days of the week in the constituency than at Westminster;
- more likely to receive mail – mostly still letters, but with an increasing amount of e-mail as well – from their constituents. A study in the 1950s found 12–20 letters a week (Richards 1959); by 1967, that had risen to 25–75 letters a week from constituency sources; and by 1986, the figure was 20–50 a day, of which half were from constituents. By 2003, the Palace of Westminster was receiving 12.5 items of mail a year, of which 10 million were for the Commons, an average of around 15,000 per MP. 'What in 1986 was the highest figure in the range of mail received by MPs was, by 2003, the average amount' (Norton 2005, 182);
- more likely to be writing to their constituents, both in response to the letters received, but also – increasingly – in proactive attempts to engage with voters. The latter activity is governed by strict parliamentary rules around what is and is not allowed, but many MPs are pushing these rules to their limit (and, in one or two cases, beyond), by responding to voters' letters or other contacts with regular updates. The average figure for postage costs in the 2004/05 financial year was £3,813, but 44 MPs spent over £10,000 on postage. The highest figure was £38,750.

The rise of the constituency role of MPs is very much double-edged. It is liked, and appreciated, by voters. Surveys of voters show that they rank constituency work as the number one priority for MPs: looking after constituents is what they think MPs should be doing. It is one reason why although public satisfaction with Parliament waxes and wanes, public satisfaction with voters' own MP has remained almost constant over the last decade. The majority of voters who write to their MPs say that they are satisfied with the response. (This is similarly one reason why voters tend to be more likely to say that they think their MP is doing a good job than think Parliament as an institution is doing a good job.) MPs themselves will also frequently say that they value the interaction with voters – some describe it as the most fulfilling part of their job – and some also claim to find it useful in alerting them to policy failures and problems. Much of the impetus for some of Labour's often-criticised drive against 'anti-social behaviour', for example, came from Labour MPs' experiences in constituency surgeries, where they were faced with cases which seemed to them to be unacceptable but where the police claimed to be unable to act. The rise of the constituency role is thus both useful in keeping MPs engaged with the public, and providing what the public say they want from their MPs. Yet it is also very costly, both in terms of staff and office costs (which then leads to criticism of MPs' supposed lavish lifestyles) and in terms of MPs' time. By 1996, it was estimated that MPs were spending almost 40 per cent of their time dealing with constituency-related work (Power 1996). That figure has almost certainly risen recently. The danger is that this work becomes so all-consuming that it prevents MPs properly fulfilling their other duties – scrutinising the government, examining legislation, and so on – because MPs are so focused on the parochial that they have no time for the national picture, let alone the international (Power 1998).

## Voting in the House of Commons

One central part of the criticism of the Westminster Parliament is the discipline MPs exhibit in their voting. This is nothing new:

- In 1878, for example, in *HMS Pinafore,* W S Gilbert wrote one of the most scathing criticisms of the party discipline for which today's MPs are always criticised: 'I always voted at my party's call | And I never thought of thinking for myself at all.'
- In 1946, the Conservative MP, Christopher Hollis, wrote in his *Can Parliament Survive?* that on most votes it would be 'simpler and more economical to keep a flock of tame sheep and from time to time to drive them through the division lobbies in the appropriate numbers'.

- In 1966 Samuel Beer was driven to remark that 'when one makes a statistical study of party voting, the figures are so monotonously 100 per cent or nearly 100 per cent it is hardly worth making the count.'

By the end of the nineteenth century, party votes – those in which 90 per cent or more of the members of one party vote one way, facing 90 per cent or more of the members of the other principal party – were the norm in the House of Commons (Lowell 1924). That practice continues today, and in this the British House of Commons is similar to most other parliaments in Western Europe; indeed many have much higher levels of party discipline than those seen at Westminster (Owens 2003).

There is a widespread belief that discipline has strengthened at Westminster in recent years, as a result of the rise of the so-called 'career politician', the MP who comes into the Commons without having done a substantial 'proper' (by which is meant non-political) job beforehand (Riddell 1993). This had led, so the argument goes, to politicians with little experience of the real world as it exists outside of the rarefied atmosphere of Westminster and Whitehall, and who are afraid to speak their minds for fear of damaging their career prospects. In fact, the reverse is true. The rise of the career politician has coincided with a *revival* in backbench independence, not a decline, with the result that British MPs in recent years have become *more* rebellious and independent-minded, not less.

Backbench discipline in the House of Commons was at its peak in the 1950s and early 1960s when the Commons was full of all those supposedly 'independent-minded' MPs. There were two sessions in the 1950s – two whole years – in which not a single Conservative MP defied their party whip even once (Norton 1975). Every division in the House of Commons in those two years saw complete unanimity amongst the Government's backbenchers. Today's whips would be green with envy at the thought of such behaviour. Backbench cohesion began to weaken in the late 1960s and 1970s, at exactly the same point as those much-derided career politicians began to enter Westminster in such numbers.

The most recently completed parliament, between 2001 and 2005, was noteworthy for both the frequency and size of the backbench rebellions that took place. Labour MPs defied their whips on a total of 259 occasions, more than in any other post-war Parliament except that of 1974–79. But the Wilson/Callaghan government of 1974–79 lasted for five parliamentary sessions, whereas the second Blair government consisted of just four. Measured as a percentage of the divisions (votes) to occur in the parliament, the period from 2001 to 2005 saw Labour backbenchers rebel in 20.8 per cent of divisions, more than government backbenchers in any other parliament since 1945 (Figure 3.1).

**Figure 3.1** *Percentage of votes to see rebellions by government MPs 1945–2001*

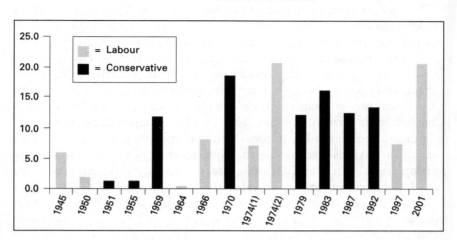

Some of the revolts, such as those over University top-up fees or foundation hospitals, were especially large, and the rebellions over the Iraq war – the largest of which saw 139 Labour MPs vote against their whip in March 2003 – were the largest rebellions by MPs of any governing party on any type of policy since modern British party politics began (Cowley 2005). They shattered all existing records:

- the 93 Liberals who had voted against Gladstone's proposals for Home Rule in June 1886;
- the 95 Conservatives who had defied the Major government over aspects of its post-Dunblane firearms legislation in February 1997;
- the 110 Labour MPs who had rebelled in July 1976, during the passage of the (now long-forgotten) Rent (Agriculture) Bill.

To find a larger rebellion than the one on Iraq, you have to go back to the Corn Laws in the middle of the nineteenth century. Then Robert Peel had seen two thirds of Conservative MPs vote against their own administration with just a third backing him in the division lobbies. But since then – since the beginnings of modern British politics, in other words – there had been nothing to match the Iraq revolts.

To return to Simon Heffer's specific example from the introduction to this chapter – his comparison of 2005 with 1995 – during the 1994/95 session, government (Conservative) MPs were rebelling in around 8 per cent of divisions in the Commons. The figure for government (Labour) MPs in the session of 2004/05 was 39 per cent. So, the supposedly supine

Labour MPs were rebelling more than four times as often as they did a decade ago.

The government managed to survive the period from 1997 to 2005 undefeated on a whipped vote in the Commons, but it did so both because for eight years it enjoyed the largest single-party majorities since 1935 and because it was frequently willing to negotiate with its back-bench critics, giving policy concessions to them, in order to stave off defeat. Only those who have a very limited understanding of the concept of political power focus solely on the number of times a government is defeated in the division lobbies. Those with a more sophisticated under-standing of politics will also focus on the numerous policy retreats. This was most obviously seen with the government's policy over University top-up fees where the final policy was markedly different from that which the government first introduced (Cowley 2005).

Crucially, one of the key factors that had kept the government unde-feated – the size of its majority – changed in May 2005. The official line from the Labour Party on election night, and afterwards, was that their smaller Commons majority of 66 (effectively 71 since the Sinn Fein MPs don't take up their seats) would 'concentrate the mind' of Labour MPs. The bloated majorities enjoyed since 1997 had allowed Labour back-benchers to rebel without giving much thought to the consequences. With a smaller majority, so the argument went, Labour MPs would have to exercise more self-discipline. Such a view was widely accepted by many observers, who would point out that the government's majority was larger than in most post-war parliaments, and – a comparison the Prime Minister himself would use – was larger than the majority of 44 with which Mrs Thatcher had managed between 1979 and 1983.

Yet in mid November 2005, just six months into Labour's third term, the government crashed to two defeats in the Commons during the Report Stage of the Terrorism Bill (Kelly et al. 2006). What many observers – and, indeed, the Prime Minister – had failed to take into account was the extent to which backbench rebellion had become so commonplace between 2001 and 2005. What one whip described as 'the threshold of rebellion' had been crossed by most Labour MPs (Cowley 2005, 4–5). Two further defeats followed in January 2006.

This does not mean that there will necessarily be a string of Commons defeats during the 2005 Parliament, not least because a government defeat is rarely the aim of disgruntled backbenchers (one reason why it is pointless simply to study the number of defeats). Most Labour MPs still see a defeat of their own government as an admission of failure – both a failure on their part to persuade the government not to do something silly, and a failure on the part of the government to listen. Most – all but a handful of the most disgruntled and bitter – have no desire to see their

---

**Box 3.1    What happens when the leadership changes?**

Recent experience shows us that any new Labour leader will enjoy a brief honeymoon with his (no one expects the next Labour leader to be a woman) backbenchers – as both John Major and Jim Callaghan did when they assumed the leadership of their party. Major's initial period as prime minister from November 1990 through to the election in 1992 saw just limited and sporadic backbench revolts, with his parliamentary party in this period being the most cohesive in the division lobbies that it had been at any point throughout the 13 years of Conservative government from 1979 to 1992. There was a similar effect when Callaghan took over from Wilson in 1976. Callaghan was elected Labour leader on 5 April 1976, and did not suffer a Commons defeat as a result of Labour backbench dissent for ten months, despite the perilous state of his majority.

But both examples also indicate that any honeymoon effect can be short-lived. Major's honeymoon with his backbenchers ended with the Maastricht Bill in 1992, which saw the most serious and sustained campaign of intraparty dissent in the Conservative Party's post-war history. Callaghan's ended in February 1977, with a defeat on the Scotland and Wales Bill, the first of 18 defeats that he was to suffer as a result of backbench dissent – twelve of them also over devolution, defeats that reshaped the legislation as a result, and ultimately led to the government losing a vote of confidence in 1979 (Cowley 2005).

---

government brought publicly to heel in the division lobbies. But the government is going to have to be more conciliatory with its backbenchers if it is to avoid future defeats.

## Commons modernisation

A further (misguided) criticism of Parliament comes from those who have complained about the process of Commons 'modernisation', undertaken by Labour since 1997. (Less noticed, there was also a similar package of reforms in the House of Lords.) Part of the problem in analysing the extent to which modernisation of the Commons has taken place is that the phrase itself is largely meaningless. As Richard Rose (2001) noted, the term 'shows a preference for what is new rather than what is old, and for change against the status quo. But it does not identify what direction change should take.' As a result, it means different things to different people (Wright 2004). For some, it was about making the

Commons appear more modern, stripping away some of the more anti-quated procedures and practices. Others wanted to make the Commons more efficient, changing the hours and making the passage of legislation more predictable. Others wanted to make the Commons more accessible, more open to the public. Yet others wanted to make it stronger, 'shifting the balance' – a much-used phrase – between the Commons and the executive.

Partly because of this terminological inexactitude, the story of Commons modernisation in the period of the Blair government has been very mixed. Of the first 15 substantive reports published by the House of Commons Modernisation Committee between 1997 and 2001, only two contained proposals to help enhance the power of the Commons in relation to the executive (Norton 2005). The others were designed for cosmetic or tidying-up purposes, or for the convenience of Members. As one observer argued, although many of the changes introduced by the committee were desirable in themselves, '[t]he basic questions of scrutiny and accountability – of power – have not been addressed' (Riddell 2000). This critique remained true of many of the later reforms (Cowley and Stuart 2005). Much depended on the agenda of the Leader of the House, the person who chairs the Commons Modernisation Committee. Blair's first two office holders, Ann Taylor and Margaret Beckett, were fairly executive-minded, and unwilling to do anything that might cause the Commons to become more assertive against the executive. The high point of modernisation came following the appointment of Robin Cook as Leader of the House in 2001. His appointment followed shortly on the heels of a series of influential reports which urged further reform of Parliament, such as the Hansard Society's Commission on Parliamentary Scrutiny, which published the well-received *The Challenge for Parliament – Making Government Accountable* (2001).

Despite the favourable intellectual climate, and his own considerable skills, Cook struggled to get all of his reforms through, facing opposition not least from the Government whips' office (who were afraid of losing too much control of the legislative agenda) (Cook 2003). Cook's attempt to reform the way that select committee members were chosen, for example, narrowly failed, after allegations that the whips had been working behind the scenes to undermine support for them (Kelso 2003). Yet in two separate sets of votes in 2002, he still managed to pilot through a more comprehensive set of reforms than would have seemed possible a year before – and far more than had been achieved in the preceding four years (Box 3.2). They generated a letter to *The Times* (5 November 2002) from Michael Ryle, a former parliamentary clerk and one of the founders of the academic Study of Parliament Group, who argued that the reforms brought 'almost to completion the most systematic package of parliamentary reforms for 100

---

## Box 3.2  Key modernisation reforms 2001–05

- Payment for select committee chairs, to try to develop a parliamentary career path as an alternative to becoming a minister.
- Ending the sessional cut-off, allowing Bills to carry over from one session to another, thus stopping the legislative logjam which routinely occurs at the end of each parliamentary year.
- More topical Parliamentary Questions, and answers to written questions to be provided during the recess.
- Changes to the parliamentary timetable: for the first time there would be a House of Commons calendar (to be announced a year in advance) that would allow MPs an extra week to work in their constituencies; and the Commons would return earlier from its summer recess.
- Changes to the parliamentary day, with constituency business given precedence on Fridays, in order to better enable MPs to connect with their constituents.
- More bills to be published in draft form, thus allowing for earlier and routine prelegislative scrutiny.
- A more regular use of time limits on backbench speeches.
- An earlier start to Prime Minister's Questions at noon on a Wednesday, instead of 3pm, in order to generate better media coverage.
- More of an effort to connect with the public by improving public access to Westminster, including on Saturdays.

---

years'. His letter ended: 'As a campaigner for parliamentary reform for more than 40 years, I can now retire happy.'

Although not technically a part of the 'modernisation' reforms, there was also the Prime Minister's decision to appear before the Liaison Committee – the committee consisting of the chairs of the other select committees – twice a year for a meeting of two and a half hours at a time, during which he is quizzed by the MPs in depth. Each session covers a different theme or set of themes, with the Prime Minister knowing in advance the themes to be covered but not the exact questions. It represented a significant advance in the scrutiny of the Prime Minister; it was the first time for 65 years that a Prime Minister had been before a select committee – and it will now be very difficult for any future Prime Minister to refuse to attend such meetings. It is also difficult to think of any other world leader who would appear, alone and unaided, before their senior parliamentarians for two and a half hours.

If nothing else, the process of modernisation showed that it was possible to reform the House of Commons. The idea that the institution is pickled in aspic is clearly false. 'The changes that have been implemented stand as a tangible correction to those who assert, wrongly, that Westminster is a fossilised institution, unable or unwilling to adapt itself to changed circumstances' (Brazier et al. 2005). But with the benefit of hindsight, it is possible to be slightly more sceptical than Michael Ryle's valedictory letter to *The Times*.

Whilst Robin Cook showed the impact that a reformist Leader of the House could have, it also meant that his absence – following his resignation over the Iraq war in 2003 – led to the process of modernisation slowing down, and, in some cases, even going into reverse. His immediate replacement as Leader of the House was John Reid, although he was barely in post before being moved on again to be Secretary of State for Health. Reid was in turn replaced by Peter Hain, who combined the role with being Secretary of State for Wales. Under Hain, the process of modernisation continued, but with none of the intellectual verve brought to the subject by Cook, and without any great enthusiasm.

Hain's period as Leader of the House did see some of the earlier reforms bedded down by being made permanent as well as seeing yet further reforms to public access (where most of his energies went). This period also saw the partial reversal of one reform, following MPs' complaints about the new hours, especially those involving a late ending on Mondays, followed up by an early start for committees on Tuesday mornings. As a result, the hours were partially reformed again in January 2005, with the hours of business on Tuesday reverting to those that had existed prior to October 2002: 2.30pm to 10pm.

The impact of several of the other reforms has turned out to be peripheral at best:

- Little in the way of meaningful legislative business has been conducted in the new two-week period in September (it was dropped in 2005, and appears unlikely to return).
- The new carry-over facility has been restricted to a very small number of bills, with most sessions ending in a now-familiar legislative ping-pong between the Lords and the Commons over key government bills.
- The innovation of prelegislative scrutiny – a favourite of parliamentary reformers for years – has proved less than entirely satisfactory. Several bills that had gone through the process, such as the Gambling Bill or the Mental Capacity Bill, exploded into exactly the sort of partisan controversy that prelegislative scrutiny was supposed to avoid. Peter Hain was to remark privately that the reformers' zeal for prelegislative scrutiny had somewhat naively reckoned without the intervention of party politics.
- For a bill to receive prelegislative scrutiny remains very much the exception rather than the rule. It is nowhere near becoming a norm of parliamentary life.

It was also unfortunate that the process of modernisation ceased to be a cross-party initiative in any meaningful way. Many of the reforms in the 2001 Parliament were driven through the Commons using the bulk vote of the Parliamentary Labour Party (albeit on free votes), supported by very few opposition-party MPs. Probably the most important of any of the reforms in terms of its impact on the legislative process was the automatic timetabling ('programming') of legislation, which meant that each bill went through a prearranged timetable of debates. This had begun in the 1997 parliament but was only made permanent in 2004. The vote to make programming of government bills permanent saw not a single Liberal Democrat or Conservative MP vote in favour. This did little to weaken the suspicion that many of the reforms were not aimed at improving the scrutiny of government.

Although many of the reforms made Parliament more efficient and several made it more open and accessible (and almost by definition, they all made it more 'modern'), it is possible to argue that few of the reforms did much to strengthen the capacity of the legislature to hold the executive to account. The authors of one study of the modernisation process argue that 'modernisation-as-efficiency has had more success than modernisation-as-scrutiny' (Brazier et al. 2005). In other words, the Commons has become more efficient in what it does, but it has not necessarily become much stronger or more effective as a result.

## The House of Lords

The House of Lords is one of the most misunderstood parts of the British political system. It was Walter Bagehot (1867 [1968]) who wrote that 'the cure for the House of Lords (is) to go and look at it', and those who don't know about its more recent history – especially those who cling to political orthodoxies learnt 30 years ago – see it merely as one of Bagehot's 'dignified' parts of the constitution: a weak and feeble upper chamber, packed full of old men (and a few old women), who have good lunches and who frequently fall asleep whilst listening to debates, but who have almost no impact on policy. Such a view has been exacerbated by the alleged 'packing' of the Upper House by Labour-supporting peers frequently described as 'Tony's Cronies'.

Some of this critique is undoubtedly true. At 68, the average age of peers is high (ironically, it got slightly higher as a result of the removal of the hereditary peers, since some of the hereditary peers were quite young) and it won't take an observer in the gallery of the House of Lords long to spot a peer who *has* fallen asleep during a debate. Moreover, the process of House of Lords reform was not Labour's finest hour in government. It

## Box 3.3   House of Lords reform

The first Blair term saw the government enact what it called Stage One of Lords reform. The House of Lords Act 1999 removed all but 92 hereditary peers from the Lords. Further reform was to be left to a second stage, preceded by a Royal Commission (the Wakeham Commission) which duly reported early in 2000.

The publicly stated intention was to deliver Stage Two of Lords reform during the 2001–05 Parliament, but this failed to materialise. The government's initial proposals, contained in the White Paper *Completing the Reform* (2001), were for a removal of the remaining 92 hereditary peers, and for just 20 per cent of the Upper Chamber to be elected. That plan fell beneath a combination of parliamentary opposition (especially from Labour MPs) and opposition from some within Cabinet (especially Robin Cook). Instead, a joint committee of MPs and peers was appointed to draw up a series of options for reform, which would then be subject to free votes in both Houses, with the government then introducing legislation in the light of these free votes.

In February 2003, the Lords rejected all of the elected options, coming out in favour of a wholly appointed Chamber by a margin of three to one. But on the same day the Commons managed to reject *all* of the available options for reform. The option that came nearest to succeeding – an 80 per cent elected Chamber – failed by just three votes. The reasons for this embarrassing outcome – with the Commons unable to choose a single outcome – included (Maclean et al. 2003):

→

consisted (Box 3.3) of a compromise followed by a hapless White Paper followed by a U-turn followed by a farce followed by another U-turn. By 2005 Labour had still not fully implemented its manifesto pledges to make the House of Lords more 'democratic and representative' (1997) or 'representative and democratic' (2001).

Yet the focus on the somewhat botched debate on Lords reform – and the ongoing discussion of future options for reform – has tended to obscure the way the Lords is now actually functioning. The renaissance of the House of Lords can be dated back to the 1960s, following both the introduction of life peerages in 1958 and the failure of Labour's 1968 attempt to reform the Upper Chamber (Baldwin 1985). As a result, peers began to attend the Lords more regularly, and the Lords began to behave in a more assertive way. From a chamber that had almost fallen into abeyance in the 1950s, the Lords now sits for longer than it ever did before, and in some years it sits for more days during the year than does the Commons (Norton 2005).

Labour's (partial) reform of the House of Lords has also usually been

→
- the Prime Minister's public rejection of any elected element in the Upper House, which persuaded some Labour MPs to follow suit, not least because they did not want to be out of touch with their leadership;
- the behind-the-scenes behaviour of Labour whips, many of whom were opposed to an elected element in the Upper House, and who privately lobbied some Labour MPs to 'support Tony';
- the failure of supporters of an elected element fully to coordinate their support; if all those who had voted for a largely elected House of Lords had coordinated their forces around one single option they would have won the vote;
- a small group of four MPs – enough to have made the difference between 80 per cent succeeding or failing – got confused, and voted the wrong way by mistake.

The government's initial reaction was to announce that it intended to introduce a House of Lords Bill to remove the remaining 92 hereditary peers – thus leaving a fully appointed House, the option that had been most heavily rejected in the votes in February 2003 – but in March 2004, faced with the parliamentary reality of trying to enact such a bill, it announced that it would not be introduced until the next Parliament.

Labour's 2005 manifesto included a pledge to remove the remaining hereditary peers, and then 'allow a free vote on the composition of the House' (Labour Party 2005, 110). It did not, however, also pledge to introduce a bill subsequent to that free vote. The manifesto also included pledges on reforming the internal procedures of the Lords, in order to expedite legislative business.

part of more recent complaints about Parliament's marginalisation (as in the remarks by Simon Heffer with which this chapter began). By removing most of the hereditary peers, the government, critics argued, was emasculating the one remaining check on its dominance of Parliament. For example, of the first 53 defeats the government suffered in the Lords after 1997, all but six occurred as a result of the votes of the hereditary peers. And so, the argument went, remove the hereditary peers and you remove any effective opposition.

In fact, as was clear within a year or two of the House of Lords Act 1999 coming into effect – and as a handful of people did point out was likely (Cowley 2000) – the exact opposite occurred. The pre-reform House of Lords, conscious that its legitimacy was limited by the presence of so many hereditary peers, frequently practised a self-denying ordinance, pulling back from many confrontations with the government. But with the hereditaries largely gone, those peers that remain have seen themselves as more legitimate and have become more assertive than

**Figure 3.2**   *Average number of government defeats inflicted in the House of Lords per year 1975–2005*

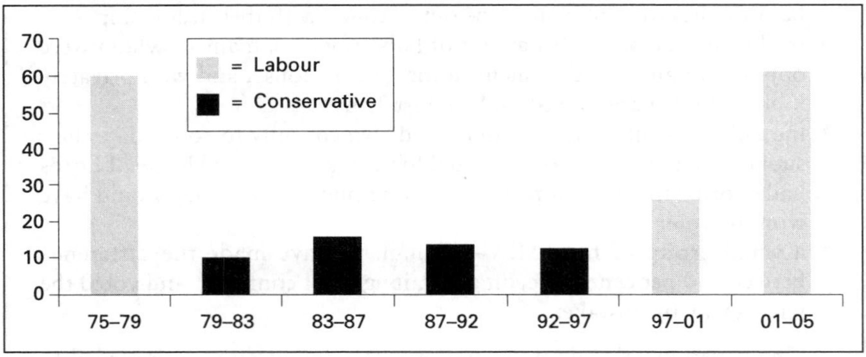

before. If the government hoped it had created a poodle of an Upper Chamber, then it was very much mistaken.

The full consequences of reform became increasingly clear during the second Blair term. The 2001–05 Parliament saw the government defeated on 245 separate occasions. This was more than double the number of defeats (108) in the first Blair term. The comparison with the preceding Conservative governments was particularly stark (Figure 3.2). The (mean) average number of Lords defeats per session during the extended period of Conservative government between 1979 and 1997 was just over 13. The (mean) average for the 2001 Parliament was just over 61. In other words, the Lords were defeating the Labour government of 2001–05 more than four times as often as they defeated the Thatcher and Major governments, and more than twice as often as they had defeated the first Blair government. This was also more than they had been defeating the Labour government of the 1970s.

These defeats ranged across almost every major piece of government legislation, and as the 2001 Parliament progressed, the Lords became more intransigent and less willing to give way, with the result that the sight of a bill pinging back and forth between Commons and Lords became commonplace at the end of a parliamentary session. This was most obvious during the passage of the Prevention of Terrorism Bill, just before the 2005 election, when the Lords resisted several clauses in the bill, and it shuttled back and forth between the Lords and the Commons for almost 29 hours (Cowley and Stuart 2005b) before a compromise was worked out between the two Houses. This, however, was merely the most high-profile of a number of stand-offs throughout the Parliament, such as over foundation hospitals, jury trials and the pensions bill (Cowley and Stuart 2005b).

Of the two Houses of Parliament, therefore, it has been the Lords that has been more of a block on the government in recent years. Government ministers preparing legislation for its passage through Parliament knew that they faced a more serious test in the Lords than they did in the Commons, and ministers routinely resisted giving too many compromises whilst a Bill was passing through the Commons in order to be able to offer placatory gestures to their Lordships (Cowley 2005).

The extra problems which the government faces in the Lords is sometimes ascribed to the greater sagacity of peers, their greater wisdom, and their increased independence of thought. In fact, the parliamentary parties in the Lords are no less cohesive than those in the Commons (Norton 2003). The difference – and it is a crucial one – is that in the Lords no one party holds a majority. Despite Labour increasing its membership in the Lords throughout the Blair years (its supposed 'packing' of the Lords) the government remains permanently in a minority position (Table 3.1), with fewer than one third of the votes of peers. In order to win votes in such a 'hung' chamber, the government needs to persuade at least one of the other party groupings to support it. Indeed, in an irony not lost on members of the Upper Chamber, its composition currently better reflects the pattern of votes cast at the last general election than does the Commons (Russell and Sciara 2006). The process of Lords reform since 1999 has thus created a more representative second chamber, one which is permanently hung, and one which is willing to stand up to, and regularly defeat, the government of the day.

There are signs that the Lords is becoming yet more assertive still. Shortly after the 2005 election, the Liberal Democrats announced that they would no longer be abiding by the Salisbury Convention, the convention dating back to 1947 which guarantees that the Lords will not block legislation promised in a government's election manifesto. The

**Table 3.1**   *Party composition of the House of Lords 2005*

| Party/Category | N | % |
|---|---|---|
| Conservative | 208 | 29 |
| Labour | 210 | 29 |
| Liberal Democrat | 74 | 10 |
| Crossbenchers (i.e., non-party) | 192 | 27 |
| Others (inc. Bishops) | 37 | 5 |
| Total | 721 | 100 |

*Note*: Correct as of 1 November 2005

Liberal Democrats argued that when the Lords better represented the electorate than did the Commons, there was no longer any justification for the Commons automatically getting its way (Russell and Sciara 2006); Lord McNally, the Liberal Democrat leader in the Lords described the 'continual plea to the Salisbury Convention' as 'the last refuge of legislative scoundrels'. Given that the Liberal Democrats frequently act as the swing voters in the Lords, determining government victory or defeat, this means that the government will face even more difficulties getting its legislation through the Lords in future.

Even more significantly, when a Conservative government returns to power at Westminster, it too will face this permanently hung, and increasingly assertive, second chamber. No future Conservative government will inherit the overwhelmingly Conservative Upper Chamber of the past. There is still a legitimate debate about the extent to which the Lords *should* be elected, and whether (as a result) the Lords should be yet more powerful. That dispute is one which has been fought out within the Labour Party for the last few years, between those who feared an Upper Chamber which made it harder for a Labour government to enact its legislation and those who wanted a more democratic composition, even if it made the Lords stronger and as a result caused more problems for the government (Russell and Sciara 2006). That debate will continue over the next years, especially under the party's new leadership. It has similarly been a debate within the Conservative Party, which in 2002 committed itself to a largely elected second chamber, called the Senate, only for the majority of Conservative MPs and peers then to vote against that option in February 2003 (Cowley and Stuart 2004). A Cameron leadership may well reopen this debate within the party, only to find opposition from within the party's ranks at Westminster.

This debate, though, should not obscure the fact that the Lords in recent years has become increasingly powerful and assertive, not less. Compared to, say, 50 years ago the transformation is remarkable. Then, the Lords had almost atrophied, and Westminster was effectively a unicameral legislature. Now, it is a system of asymmetric bicameralism, but one in which the weaker chamber has become increasingly strong and assertive over the last decade.

## Conclusion

Complaining about the weakness of Parliament is not a recently invented pastime; it has, rather, been a popular participatory activity for at least the last 100 years, if not longer.

Much of this criticism is valid. Parliament remains a marginal actor in the policy process. There has been a plethora of reports published in recent years which have suggested reforms that would better enhance the ability of Parliament to stand up to the executive. Few of these proposed reforms have been introduced. The various reforms of the Commons since 1997 have modernised the institution, and improved its efficiency, but they have done little, if anything, to strengthen it. Even if one does not buy the arguments put forward by some of more vehement critics of the process of modernisation – mostly, though not solely, Conservatives – that the process of modernisation has reduced the ability of the Commons to stand up to the government, it is hard to make a realistic case that it has strengthened it.

Yet by many other criteria, things are now much better than they used to be (Ryle 2005). MPs are now increasingly focused on the needs of their constituents, spending an amount of their time dealing with their constituents' needs which would have been unimaginable 50 years ago. Although valued by constituents, this is not without its risks, of which the most serious is that MPs lose sight of the national picture. Sorting out Mrs Miggins's pension may be laudable and rewarding (to both Mrs Miggins and the MP) but if it prevents proper scrutiny of forthcoming legislation on pensions reform, which will affect millions of Mr and Mrs Migginses in the future, it is less useful.

But despite the lack of any major positive internal reforms to the Commons, and despite the risks of MPs taking their eyes off the national picture, the Blair government – and particularly in the period 2001–05 – resulted in a partial rebirth of Parliament. Almost none of this was intentional on the part of Blair or his immediate circle. The House of Lords Act 1999, for example, was not intended to result in the far more assertive body that it created – but it did. Similarly, it was not the wish of the government that its backbenchers, routinely dismissed as weak and feeble when they were first elected to government, should become increasingly rebellious during the second Blair term – but they did, with the result that they now constitute one of the Labour leadership's most serious headaches, and a real impediment to the legislative programme that Tony Blair would like to enact in his remaining years as Prime Minister.

## Chapter 4

# Political Parties and Party Systems

SARAH CHILDS

On the surface, the 2005 general election appeared to be business as usual. It was a contest between the big three political parties, primarily between the big two, at the end of which Labour won a decent-sized majority, the Conservatives came second and the Liberal Democrats came third. Nothing new there. Yet such a headline account is misleading. Away from the national stage, and the focus of the Westminster village, things looked rather different: in Scotland and Wales the nationalists remained significant players; in Northern Ireland, the battle was between and within the nationalist and loyalist parties with the oldest established unionist party, the Ulster Unionists, vanquished by the Democratic Unionists; and even in England smaller parties, such as the United Kingdom Independence Party (UKIP), the Greens, the British National Party (BNP) and Respect contested significant numbers of seats. Indeed, three mainland constituencies saw MPs returned who were not standing for one of the more established parties; an independent, Peter Law, taking the Labour stronghold of Blaenau Gwent, the expelled Labour MP George Galloway standing for Respect and unseating Labour's Oona King in Bethnal Green and Bow, and Richard Taylor, elected again for Kidderminster Hospital and Health Concern. Some 10 per cent of the vote at the 2005 general election went to parties 'other' than Labour, Conservatives and the Liberal Democrats, and the two main parties gained marginally over two thirds of the vote. Largely masked by the workings of the electoral system, this more complex political terrain suggests many of the orthodox conceptions of British politics in the post-war period may no longer be tenable.

The era of two-party politics may not be quite dead but at the Westminster level it is kept alive by the continued existence of the single-member plurality system (SMPS). Indeed, rather than talking about a British party system (singular), it is now necessary to recognise that Britain has multiple party systems (plural). Moreover, running alongside this fracturing of the party system, there have also been striking changes in the internal structures of British political parties. By analysing the structures and rules that determine policy making, the selection of party leader and the recruitment of parliamentary candidates, it becomes clear that the relationship between party members and party leaders is one of interdependence. Those who classify British political parties as purely 'elite-driven' or 'top-down' are missing much of the reality of modern British party politics. A further aspect of British party politics which is often overlooked (and which this chapter also discusses) is its gendered nature, the extent to which women and women's concerns have been incorporated into political discourse.

## Britain's party systems

Those with a longer historical perspective are well aware that having a multiplicity of parties in British politics is nothing new. Significant third parties (especially the Irish Nationalists prior to the partition of Ireland) and coalition or minority governments have been far more frequent than is often realised (Searle 1995). During the immediate post-war period, however (and certainly up to 1970), British party politics was often considered the archetype of a two-party system. British politics (Northern Ireland excepted) was dominated by two major parties contesting elections across the whole country in order to form a single-party government. In broad terms, there were:

- parity of power between the parties;
- parties governing consecutively rather than concurrently (although the Conservatives managed one extended period of rule between 1951 and 1964);
- parity of support;
- duopoly of support;
- duopoly of representation;
- nationwide patterns of competition;
- centripetal patterns of competition.

Between 1945 and 1970 the Conservative and Labour parties received over 90 per cent of votes while the average gap between their respective shares of the vote was only 4 per cent; MPs from the two main parties constituted at least 90 per cent of all MPs; competing nationwide, both parties sought to position themselves close to, and gain the support of, the median voter.

This model began to break down in the 1970s as a result of class and partisan dealignment and the emergence of post-materialist issues (such as environmentalism and gender equality) and the question of Europe, which cross-cut the traditional party divide. The post-1974 re-emergence of the Liberals (later transformed into the Liberal Democrats) saw the erosion of the old two-party duopoly, even as the Conservatives (under Thatcher and Major) and Labour (under Wilson, Callaghan and Blair) continued to monopolise control of government. In addition, a by-product of New Labour's post-1997 devolution settlement was the establishment of a variety of new subnational political institutions elected via proportional representation (see Table 4.1). This, given that the new institutions were elected by means other than SMPS, further helped to transform British party politics.

To better capture the multiple party systems in the UK it is useful to draw distinctions between different political arenas (the electoral, legislative and executive) and different levels of jurisdiction (the local, regional, national and European) (Webb 2000). Only at the national level (Westminster) and in respect of the executive arena (and to a lesser extent the legislative arena) can it be reasonably claimed that there is life left in the British two-party system. Even here, and notwithstanding the increasing damage caused to it by a dealigned electorate and the party targeting of seats, it is only Westminster's electoral system that protects the two-party system (Webb 2003). For example:

- The 2004 European elections saw MEPs elected from seven parties: Labour, Conservative, Liberal Democrat, SNP, PC, Greens, and UKIP.
- The 2003 Scottish elections resulted in a Scottish Parliament with representatives from seven parties, and a now well-entrenched Labour–Liberal Democrat coalition government in a polity dominated by Labour in Westminster elections.
- Elections to the Welsh Assembly since 1999 have so far resulted in three different types of government: as well as a one-party majority government, there has also been a minority government and a coalition government.
- Elections to the Greater London Assembly saw members returned from five political parties – Labour, Conservatives and the Liberal Democrats, plus the Greens and UKIP, with the BNP only just failing to win a list seat despite gaining 4.9 per cent of the vote.
- Independent candidates have also been directly elected as mayors, including the local football team mascot (H'angus the Monkey) in Hartlepool (although he in fact proved to be relatively popular and was later re-elected under his own name), and the ex-Labour MP Ken Livingstone in the first London mayoral election (who then rejoined Labour before the second contest).

Britain in 2005 had, then, not a single party system but multiple ones, operating at different levels. Dunleavy (2005) terms these 'overlapping

**Table 4.1**   *Electoral systems in the UK*

| Level of jurisdiction | Type of electoral system | Brief explanation |
| --- | --- | --- |
| Westminster | Single Member Plurality System (SMPS) | Single-member constituencies from which candidate gaining plurality of votes is elected |
| Scottish Parliament | Additional Member System (AMS) | 73 MSPs elected using SMPS, with an additional 56 chosen from regional lists to ensure reasonable proportionality |
| National Assembly for Wales | Additional Member System | 40 AMs elected using SMPS, with an additional 20 chosen from regional lists to ensure reasonable proportionality |
| Northern Ireland Assembly | Single Transferable Vote (STV) | A preferential voting system in which voters rank candidates; votes from elected or eliminated candidates transfer to the voter's next favoured candidate. In Northern Ireland, each of the 18 Westminster constituencies elects six MLAs |
| Greater London Assembly | Additional Member System | 14 AMs elected using SMPS, with an additional 11 chosen from a London-wide list to ensure reasonable proportionality |
| Mayoral | Supplementary Vote | Voters indicate a first and a second choice; if no candidate gets 50 per cent based on first preferences, all but top two candidates are eliminated and their second preferences counted |
| European elections | Regional List system (STV in Northern Ireland) | Eleven regions, each electing between three and ten MEPs; candidates are chosen from regional lists in proportion with their party's votes in that region |
| Local elections (England and Wales) | Simple Plurality | Usually SMPS (as above), although some wards have more than one member |
| Local elections (Scotland and Northern Ireland) | Single Transferable Vote | A preferential voting system in which voters rank candidates; votes from elected or eliminated candidates transfer to the voter's next favoured candidate |

party systems', in which there are up to five or six serious contenders for seats each staking out their own distinct ideological positions. Leaving aside the three main parties, nationalism, Euroscepticism, anti-asylum/immigration and anti-Muslim sentiments, socialism and ecologism are reflected in the various nationalist parties, UKIP, the BNP, Respect and the Scottish Socialist Party, and the Green Party.

None of this should be overstated. For example, despite its well-publicised success in Bethnal Green and Bow, Respect stood in fewer than 30 Westminster constituencies in the 2005 election. Outside of a handful of seats it gained a derisory share of the vote. For every seat like Bethnal Green, there were several others such as Hove, Neath, or Dorset South, in each of which it gained under 300 votes. Similarly, although the BNP managed some very impressive vote shares in individual seats – 17 per cent in Barking, 13 per cent in Dewsbury – results that compounded their success at the local level – they remain relatively weak in terms of party membership and organisation. Though they fielded over 100 candidates and managed an average of 4.3 per cent where they stood, this only constitutes 0.7 per cent support overall. Moreover, parties still perform differently in different types of electoral contests. UKIP's performance in the 2004 European elections, aided by the former TV presenter Robert Kilroy-Silk – in which they gained some 2.7 million votes and returned 12 MEPs – persuaded some (including Kilroy-Silk himself) that he had a chance of breakthrough on the national stage. Yet, when Kilroy-Silk stood for his newly created party, Veritas, in the 2005 general election in the Derbyshire constituency of Erewash, he came fourth, gaining under 6 per cent of the vote. Even in European elections (when the two main parties polled marginally below half of the votes) Labour and the Conservatives still gained 26.7 and 22.6 per cent of the vote compared to parties like the Greens with 6.3 per cent or UKIP with 16.1 per cent. Regardless of whether one thinks the electoral system is propping up the two-party system at Westminster, it is still thus propped up, and in the most important of the various political arenas. Put bluntly, elections to the House of Commons matter more than the election of the Hartlepool mayor.

It is clear, however, that something is happening. The party systems of the UK have become more fragmented, more diverse, and more eclectic in recent years, a trend that is unlikely to be reversed. Indeed, future developments may exaggerate the process. All post-1997 political institutions are elected by some form of PR and any moves to an elected House of Lords – either wholly or partially elected – would more than likely also involve PR, giving the other parties increased representation in the Upper House. Changes for the Commons seem less likely, with the Conservatives historically antithetical to PR, and, at any rate before the election of David Cameron as the Conservative leader, showing no signs of changing position on the issue. Labour's official position is not encouraging for reformers and its 2005 election manifesto merely promised to review the existing PR electoral systems in practice, with the vague claim that a referendum 'remains the right way to agree any change for Westminster' (without specifically promising to have such a referendum in the 2005 parliament). The best hope for reformers from within Labour is the possibility that a Brown-led government would push for PR (perhaps a watered-down version of electoral reform like the Alternative Vote) as part of an attempt to rebuild links with the Liberal Democrats, but any such move would face serious internal opposition from those within the party who wish to retain the extant electoral system for Westminster.

Of course, the absence of PR at Westminster does not mean that the main political parties can ignore the changes wrought by PR elsewhere. The various PR elections have helped institutionalise the other political parties, providing them with both resources and legitimacy that they lacked before. In several political arenas beyond Westminster (excluding local government) the more established political parties must now compete (in both policy and campaigning terms) against an unprecedented range of political parties in a variety of different electoral contexts, aware that the electorate are prepared to vote for different parties in respect of those different electoral contexts.

## The main five parties

Tony Blair preannounced his (eventual) retirement from being prime minister some seven months before the 2005 general election – declaring publicly that it would be the last election he would contest as party leader – and Michael Howard announced his resignation the morning after the general election. As a result, the 2005 parliament began in the certain knowledge that the leaders of the two main parties would not be contesting the next general election. Charles Kennedy's resignation in January 2006 made it a hat-trick of new leaders. But as well as changes – real and potential – in personnel, all five main parties are also undergoing serious internal debates about the future policy direction of, and interparty competition between, the parties.

### The Labour Party

For Labour, the key question is whether the party can renew itself whilst in government in order to be electorally successful at the next general election. There is also the (related) question of whether the leader who succeeds Blair, widely assumed to be the Chancellor, Gordon Brown, will entrench or else reposition the party away from the positions adopted by New Labour since it came into office in 1997. Whilst Labour's third consecutive victory in the 2005 general election was unprecedented in the party's history, the election also revealed worrying signs of voters deserting the party, its vote down more than five percentage points from 2001, a drop of eight percentage points since 1997. This occasioned an ongoing debate within the party about its future electoral strategy, a debate which was itself revealing in the extent to which political reality is now explicitly multiparty. There were those within the Labour Party – like Ken Livingstone – who argued that because the party had lost voters to the left (broadly defined) – with voters defecting to the Liberal Democrats, the Greens and Respect – the obvious response would be to reposition the party to the left in order to win back those voters. Yet others – notably the ex-Cabinet minister and Blairite Alan Milburn – pointed out that the seats that Labour need to keep in order to maintain a majority in the House of Commons were predominantly former Conservative seats, nearly all won in the landslide of 1997. These, so the argument went, were unlikely to be held by repositioning the party to the left. At the same time, other MPs – like Jon Cruddas, the MP for Dagenham – argued that Labour's policy agenda and campaigning strategies designed to win middle-class swing voters in marginal seats were allowing the BNP to mobilise white working-class voters who felt disenfranchised in its safe seats. In other words, serious voices argued that Labour needed to move back to the left, to stop voters moving to the right. The reality – an uncomfortable reality for Labour – is that all of these analyses are correct. To remain electorally successful, Labour needs to regain the support of those it has lost on the left, whilst also holding on to former Conservative voters. This is an extremely difficult balancing act.

Renewing whilst in Government is a difficult task for political parties, but it has been done before and in recent memory. The Conservatives managed it in 1990, when John Major replaced Margaret Thatcher as leader, and Major led the party to its fourth successive election victory in 1992. The change in leadership (and one or two attendant changes in policy) then had the effect of transforming the party's fortunes with the voters (Crewe 1996), helping secure the party's electoral victory in 1992. Then fewer voters blamed the Major government for things that they thought were wrong, blaming instead the Thatcher government, which they saw as distinct, despite the two governments being of the same party and involving many of the same personnel (Sanders 1993). However, the comparison is not exact. Prior to his election as prime minister, John Major was still a relatively unknown political figure, at least to the electorate, to whom he appeared to represent something new. Should the new Labour leader turn out to be Gordon Brown, he will not be such a radical new face and the effect of a change in Labour's leadership might not be as pronounced as was the case with the Thatcher-Major transition.

Comparing a likely Brown premiership with Major's premiership is apposite in a further way. Although Margaret Thatcher was Prime Minister for eleven years, it was the seven-year premiership of John Major that really embedded many of the Thatcherite reforms into the British polity. Although Tony Blair is always said to be keen to create his political legacy in policy terms prior to his departure from Number 10, it will in fact be his successor, most probably Gordon Brown, who will determine whether the Labour Party realigns itself permanently as a party of the centre or whether it shifts back to the left (Webb 2002). The various clashes between Brown and Blair – and their two 'camps' – have often been portrayed as being a clash of personalities. At times, however, they were differences of policy and of underlying ideology. Brown accords a higher role to the values and ethos of the public services rather than envisaging the state simply as a purchaser of services (Toynbee and Walker 2005). Yet, those who envisage (or hope for) a significant move towards old Labour economic policy or an interventionist state under Brown are likely to be disappointed; Brown believes that the appropriate role for the state remains very much on the supply side: ensuring an educated, skilled and flexible workforce and a stable and attractive economy.

The debate about the future direction of the Labour Party is not helped by the extent to which its record in government is more complicated than many simplistic caricatures suggest. A good example have been the various issues on the liberal–authoritarian axis, as well as security and civil liberties issues associated with the war on terrorism. To many on the left, the Blair-led government has looked to be illiberal, with the government seemingly siding with an agenda more suited to the socially conservative *Daily Mail*. Such critics point to the introduction of anti-social behaviour orders (ASBOs); more prisoners and longer prison sentencing; imprisonment of terrorist suspects for an extended period without trial; and, the bête noire of many liberal-left/libertarians, the proposal to introduce ID cards. Yet the reality is more complicated than this. At the same time as Labour has introduced such socially conservative policies, it has also pursued liberalising measures. These include such reforms as gay and lesbian rights, including the lowering of the age of consent, allowing same-sex couples to adopt, and introducing civil-partnership rights. There was the downgrading of cannabis from a Class B to a Class C drug, the liberalising of both gambling and licensing laws (the latter often described as '24-hour drinking', but usually entailing little more than an extra hour or two at most licensed venues) and legislative measures on domestic violence, forced marriages and female genital mutilation. None of these policies were inspired by the *Daily Mail* – and several saw opposition from that very paper.

## The Conservative Party

At the 2005 general election, despite making its first advance in winning seats since 1983, the Conservative Party found itself having effectively stood still for three elections. In terms of share of the vote, 2005 was the third-worst Conservative performance for 100 years, beating only 1997 and 2001. In parts of Britain (such as the North of England), the Conservative share of the vote even fell at the 2005 election. In other parts (the Midlands or Scotland) it went up microscopically (Cowley and Green 2005). Michael Howard's resignation, coupled with his failed attempt to reform the rules for electing the party leader, meant the party was effectively in stasis between June and November 2005, although it then benefited from the high profile given to the leadership contest.

That contest was carried out according to the rules introduced under William Hague's leadership. The parliamentary party chose two candidates, David Cameron and David Davis (knocking out Liam Fox and Ken Clarke); Cameron and Davis then went forward to a membership ballot of the extraparliamentary party. This high-profile leadership contest was a debate about the qualities of the candidates (who was more electorally appealing, the better speaker, more voter-attractive), but also on what was to be the Conservatives' response to the string of defeats suffered in 1997, 2001 and 2005. The key division was between the socially liberal wing (championed especially by David Cameron) and a more socially conservative grouping (headed by Liam Fox, but also by David Davis). Very crudely, this division also mapped onto those who advocated a comprehensive modernisation of the party (Cameron) and those who believed – like many in the Labour Party did in 1992 – that 'one more heave' would be sufficient to win the next election (Davis, Fox). Ken Clarke represented a more socially liberal, one-nation candidacy, albeit that he was personally largely uninterested in reform of the party.

In the event, the party ended up overwhelmingly endorsing David Cameron, widely seen by pundits and the public alike as the candidate with the most radical views about the future direction of the party. Although David Davis, widely regarded as being on the right of the party, had begun as the clear front-runner, his campaign had faltered once the contest began in earnest and the bandwagon of the young and telegenic David Cameron began to roll. Although Davis led the first round of MPs' voting (see Table 4.2), his level of support was lower than had been expected and it then fell between the first and second parliamentary ballots, the very opposite of the momentum needed to stave off the Cameron challenge. Amongst other things, Davis had been harmed by a widely publicised focus group conducted for BBC *Newsnight* by the US pollster Frank Luntz, which showed Cameron warmly received by most voters, and by a poor speech that Davis made at the 2005 party conference. These combined to produce serious doubts about the extent to which he would be able to communicate with the electorate. Cameron, by contrast, had delivered a highly praised speech which he had memorised in advance, in which he had appeared to be both confident and charismatic.

The figures for round two of the contest (Table 4.2) appear to show Cameron as the runaway winner of the contest on MPs' votes. Such figures are, however, slightly misleading. Had the contest been decided solely by the MPs, there would at this point have been a final ballot, from which Liam Fox would have been eliminated. As his supporters were predominantly on the right of the party, many of them would have been likely to have supported David Davis in any run-off between him and David Cameron. Whether this would have been enough to have secured majority support for Davis amongst the MPs is uncertain, but it means that the parliamentary party was broadly evenly split between those willing to support the more 'modernising' candidate, Cameron, and those willing to support the more 'traditional' candidate, Davis. The Tory membership, however, were much more supportive of David Cameron and he won the leadership comfortably, winning 68 per cent of the votes to 32 per cent for David Davis.

This was ironic because before the contest began it had been widely assumed that the conservative grassroots of the Conservative Party were much more likely to support a right-of-centre candidate than the MPs.

**Table 4.2**   *Conservative leadership election 2005*

| Candidate | MPs | | Party members |
|---|---|---|---|
| | Round 1 | Round 2 | |
| David Cameron | 56 | 90 | 134,446 |
| David Davis | 62 | 57 | 64,398 |
| Liam Fox | 42 | 51 | |
| Ken Clarke | 38 | – | |
| Total | 198 | 198 | 198,844 |

Indeed, Howard's proposed reform of the way the leader is chosen was to restrict members of the extraparliamentary party to a consultative role where they would indicate a non-binding preference between candidates who had received the support of at least 5 per cent of the parliamentary party. Many observers saw this as an indication that MPs did not trust their party membership to choose an electorally attractive leader, and it was frequently said that the party needed to restrict the right of the grass-roots to be involved in the leadership election if ever a moderate candidate was to be elected leader. In the event, while Howard's proposals were not approved (despite the support of the majority of MPs and senior party members, they failed to garner the winning two-thirds margin needed), the result of the Cameron–Davis ballot proved the opposite to what was feared: the party in the country was more willing to vote for a centrist candidate than were the MPs. Battered by three heavy, successive electoral defeats, Tory activists overwhelmingly plumped for David Cameron, the most inexperienced candidate, but the one widely considered to be the more electorally friendly.

Cameron was keen to play down any comparisons with Tony Blair in public, despite claims that he himself had made the comparison ('the heir to Blair') in private. Despite the superficial similarities between the two leaders (both telegenic, relatively young, privately educated Oxford graduates with a desire to radically reform their party), there were also important differences. Blair had been an MP for eleven years before he became leader, whereas Cameron had only four years under his belt. Blair, an experienced and confident parliamentary performer, had held senior posts within his party, including Shadow Energy Secretary, Employment Secretary and Home Secretary, where he had demonstrated his ability successfully to take on elements within his party resistant to reform. Cameron was much more of an uncertain quantity – a greater gamble for his party – than Blair had been in 1994. It was a comment on the seriousness of the Conservatives' electoral plight that in 2005 enough of them were prepared to take that gamble in the search for electoral salvation.

### The Liberal Democrats

On the face of it, the Liberal Democrats had a good general election in 2005, increasing their parliamentary representation to its highest level since 1923. A more hard-headed analysis, one shared by many Liberal Democrats, was, however, more critical. Put simply, the party had fought on two flanks – against Labour and the Conservatives respectively – but only won votes and seats on one flank: from Labour. The problem for the Liberal Democrats was that they had to defend themselves against – and win seats disproportionately from – the Conservatives. Yet occupying the radical centre, being, inter alia, pro-higher taxes, anti-Iraq war, pro-European, pro-environmentalism and in favour of social liberalism meant that it was always going to be easier for the Liberal Democrats to attract disillusioned Labour voters rather than Tory voters. As a result, whilst the Liberal Democrats managed to take some seats off Labour – including one or two quite spectacular gains such as Manchester Withington, Hornsey and Wood Green, and Cambridge – they failed to take many of their target Tory seats. Many Liberal Democrats therefore saw their best result for more than 80 years as a missed opportunity. This was one – although only one – of the reasons behind Charles Kennedy standing down in January 2006.

A significant grouping within the Liberal Democrat parliamentary party is now pushing for the party to move towards (or, as some of them would put it, back to) more free-market liberal traditions (Laws and Marshall 2004). The problem for the leadership with such a strategy is twofold. First, any such move would face opposition from much of the party's grassroots membership. Such opposition was demonstrated at the 2005 party conference when frontbench proposals to part-privatise the Royal Mail were voted down by the grassroots. Just as Charles Kennedy did, so Menzies Campbell (elected in March 2006) will have to carefully to manage tensions between his grassroots and his parliamentary party. Second, the Liberal Democrats are trying to reposition them-selves politically at the exact same time as we may expect other parties, particularly the Conservatives, to be doing the same. This could create a particular problem for the Liberal Democrats, who might find them-selves squeezed between a centrist Conservative Party and a centrist Labour Party.

## The nationalists

Both the Scottish National Party (SNP) and Plaid Cymru (PC) had simi-lar trajectories at the devolved level between 2001 and 2005 when both lost seats, in the elections to the Scottish Parliament and the Welsh Assembly in 2003 (a loss of eight for the SNP and five for PC respec-tively). At the 2005 general election the SNP made modest gains, appar-ently revitalised by the return of Alex Salmond as their leader, but the new PC leader, Ieuan Wyn Jones, was compared unfavourably to his more popular and charismatic predecessor, Dafydd Wigley, and PC expe-rienced a net loss of one Westminster seat. Looking to the next set of devolved elections both parties need to contend with new positions. Weakened by its electoral losses at Holyrood the SNP's ability to oppose the Labour–Liberal Democrat coalition is lessened. In Wales PC is facing a Labour Party led by the popular Rhodri Morgan who is intent on putting clear red water between Labour in Cardiff and Labour in London.

## Cartel or cadre?

Characterisations of the organisation of political parties trace them through different stages of development (Webb 2000). First came the emergence of *cadre parties* in the early nineteenth century (elitist organisations with origins in parliamentary alliances and with restricted local organisation). Second came their gradual transformation into *mass-membership parties* from the late nineteenth century onward. Third came the further transformation of the mass party, with an interest in a targeted section of the electorate, into *catch-all parties* – 'ideologically lite' – which seek support beyond their natural class base and with leadership autonomy from the activist grassroots. Fourth, more recently, came the *electoral professional* parties, effectively modern cadre parties (Webb 2000); elite-driven, top-down parties, lacking a genuine membership base and seeking to maximise their potential vote by targeting the 'national interest', undertaking opinion polling and engaging in political marketing (Heffernan 2003b, 126). Fifth, some commentators suggest that such electoral professional, modern cadre parties are becoming what are called *cartel* parties (Katz and Mair 1995); parties that are heavily interpenetrated with the state – not least through extensive state funding – and which engage in interparty collusion, thus making it difficult for new parties to emerge.

The last model, although widely cited in the literature on political parties, currently has little purchase in Britain. For one thing, there is not (yet) extensive state funding and, although the parties benefit from some indirect resources from the state (limited mail shots at elections, free television election broadcasts) and some direct funding (resources given to opposition parties in parliament), this remains limited by comparison with most Western European countries (Fisher and Clift 2004). Moreover, if one defining purpose of cartel parties is that they operate a de facto cartel to stop other parties emerging – in the same way that business cartels would collude to prevent competition – then recent events suggest they have not been very successful. The growth of other parties throughout Britain in the last decade hardly suggests a terribly efficient cartel, stifling new competition.

The fourth model – the modern cadre party – appears at first sight to fit British political parties relatively well. All the parties have a much-reduced membership; all seek voters beyond their traditional core; and all make extensive use of professional marketers, pollsters and professional campaigners. Yet on closer examination, even this model does not quite describe the realities of modern British party politics. In particular, the leaderships' continued desire to acquire new party members and the resulting power balance between party members and leaders severely limits the extent to which the parties fulfil the criteria of a modern cadre party (Russell, A 2005, 353).

## Party members

The era of British mass parties is clearly over. Notwithstanding a short-term increase of 40 per cent between 1994 and 1997, the Labour Party's membership had declined from just over 400,000 members in 1997 to around 200,000 in 2005. The Conservatives have seen a similar decline from 400,000 in 1997 to just over 250,000 at present, whilst the Liberal Democrats had nearly 83,000 members in 1999 but a membership of roughly 73,000 by the time of their leadership contest in early 2006. Such declining numbers are not the result of any conscious decision on the part of the political parties themselves. Parties still actively seek members – not least for reasons of effective governing, legitimacy, party funding and campaigning (Seyd 1999). Of the various possible explanations for the decline in party membership in the UK over the last 40 years (see Table 4.3), supply-side, not demand-side, factors predominate.

Because of limited state funding Labour, the Conservatives and the Liberal Democrats are reliant on donations (Fisher 2004). In 2003 the Labour and Liberal Democrat parties received 34 per cent and the Conservatives 56 per cent of their income from donations (Electoral Commission 2004). This dependency, whether it is Labour's relationship with the trade unions (reportedly worth £6 million per year) or donations from wealthy individuals to all parties, is frequently associated in the public mind with sleaze and corruption, notwithstanding the transparency afforded by new regulatory legislation, not least the Political Parties, Elections and Referendums Act 2000 (PPERA, see Table 4.4). Most parties would much rather enjoy a larger membership base, thus making them less reliant on such donations (Seyd 1999).

In addition to their financial worth, members are also needed for campaigning. A raft of academic studies using a range of methods – analysing local members' activism (Seyd and Whiteley 2004), surveying local constituency agents (Denver et al. 2004), or evaluating constituency spending (Johnston and Pattie 2003) – all agree that local campaigning makes a difference, both raising turnout and affecting party performance. With more elections to fight than ever before, an electorate with fewer

**Table 4.3**   *Supply- and demand-side factors accounting for the decline in party membership*

| Supply-side factors | Demand-side factors |
|---|---|
| Partisan dealignment (voters feeling less strongly attached to political parties) | National rather than local campaigning by political parties |
| Decline in trade union membership | Use of marketing and modern communication methods |
| Competition from other organisations – especially single-issue pressure groups | Corporate donations to political parties |
| Time pressures (the work/life balance) | Donations from wealthy individuals |
| Women's greater paid employment | |
| Decline of working-class communities | |
| Suburbanisation | |

*Sources*:  Adapted from Seyd and Whiteley (2004); Webb (2000)

**Table 4.4**   *Main provisions of PPERA 2000*

Donations must not be anonymous

Donations must come from individuals on the UK electoral register and/or a company carrying out business in the UK, trade unions or another UK party

Registered parties must compile quarterly donation reports and publicly declare donations of £5,000+ to central and £1,000+ to subnational units

Registered parties must submit weekly donation reports during elections

Maximum expenditure for a party contesting all seats in mainland Britain is £19.23 million

partisans, and lower turnout, political parties need members willing to campaign, irrespective of whether that means actually delivering leaflets or sitting in offices telephoning potential voters (Denver et al. 2004). This need is particularly acute for parties with fewer financial resources, such as the Liberal Democrats, but it is an ever-present one for all of the parties.

## Party structures and policy making

Yet, despite wanting to attract more members, party leaderships remain wary of giving their membership too much power. The underlying theme (often unsaid, but ever-present) of most discussion of internal party structures and reform is the uneasy trade-off between involvement and exclusion; attempting to give the party grassroots membership enough involvement to keep them satisfied, but not too much. As mentioned above, a similar trade-off was demonstrated in the 2005 Conservative leadership contest. Some in the leadership doubted whether the grassroots membership had the political judgement to choose the most electorally successful candidate, but the grassroots resisted this move, demanding more of a say in the running of their party. In itself, the process for the selection of the Conservative leader is a good example of how the supposed centralisation of political parties is more nuanced than it is sometimes portrayed as being. Rather than there being a process of ongoing centralisation, recent reforms have extended the franchise. First, the Conservative leader was chosen merely by consultation among party elites (the so-called 'magic circle'). Second, he or she was chosen solely by MPs (from 1965 through to 1997). Third, he or she is elected – where the election is contested – by a membership ballot once Conservative MPs have whittled the shortlist down to two candidates (from 2001 onwards).

Something similar is true in the case of the Labour Party, despite complaints about ever-increasing centralisation. Reform of Labour's structures predates Blair and affected the composition and role of the party conference, the selection of the leader and parliamentary candidates, and the powers of local parties. Most of the reforms completed in the late 1990s were neither initially instituted by the leadership nor had a clear-cut effect of empowering the leadership. While the empowering of ordinary members at the expense of activists (perceived to be more extreme than the leadership) might have been attractive to the party leadership, Labour's two big changes – the reduction in the formal role of the trade unions and the rolling out of individual-member democracy by the introduction of 'one member one vote' (OMOV) – in practice created new, if different, constraints for the leadership (Russell, M 2005).

Labour's 1997 'Partnership in Power' established a two-year rolling programme of policy formation. In the first year, membership submissions and input from external organisations and individuals are considered by policy commissions. In the second year, these are fed into the National Policy Forum (NPF) before going to a Joint Policy Committee, the National Executive Committee and then the party conference.

'Alternative positions' in NPF policy documents are put to a vote at the conference. Critics argue that this process has reduced intraparty democracy and resulted in disillusioned, previously active party members leaving the party (Seyd 1999). The NPF agenda is said to be 'heavily influenced by frontbench parliamentary elites'; initial policy drafts derive from ministers; party officials facilitate discussion and have 'considerable interpretative powers' over reports; and the NPF meets in secret prior to the party conference (Webb 2000). Indeed, several pieces of high-profile government legislation, such as that on foundation hospitals, tuition fees, education reform and anti-terrorism measures, have raised questions about the lack of any links between the NPF and government policy.

Meg Russell argues, however, that the NPF 'created important new sites of dialogue between leaders and members, institutionalizing contact between Labour ministers and ordinary members', at the same time that it 'formalized the powers the leaders already held' (Russell, M 2005, 7, 130). Reforms in 2003 that allow up to eight 'highly contentious issues' to be debated at the party conference are another example of changes with which the leadership would not be best pleased. She also points out that the system is far from stable. The 'Warwick Accord' (2004) between the party and trade unions shows the continuing power held by the unions as well as demonstrating the potential for an anti-leadership alignment between the unions and other party critics (such as the Campaign for Labour Party Democracy).

On paper, the Liberal Democrats are the most internally democratic of the three main British parties. It is a federal party, organised on the basis of the principle of subsidiarity and with the biannual conference as the sovereign policy-making body. Delegates with voting rights are sent from each local party, Westminster MPs, Scottish MSPs and Welsh AMs, officers of the party and prospective parliamentary candidates. However, even among the Liberal Democrats, this formal mapping of power in the party is challenged by the growth in the relative power and potential tensions between the party's grassroots and the leadership. Crucially, the parliamentary party is said to have 'de facto power of veto over the design of policy' and professional party workers – such as the chief executive, Lord Rennard – are critical players in the making of policy (Russell and Fieldhouse 2005). The defenestration of Charles Kennedy in January 2006 came about not because of any pressure from the grassroots – indeed, it was widely believed that he might have won any contest conducted amongst the party's wider membership, despite his acknowledgement of his drink problem – but because enough of the party's MPs withdrew their support from him, thus making his position untenable.

## Choosing more diverse parliamentary candidates

The right to select candidates for Westminster is widely recognised as an incentive that party members value and one which they will robustly defend. At the same time, the party leadership has good reasons to try to limit their autonomy. One such reason is the parties' professed desire to increase the number of women and black and minority ethnic (BME) MPs elected, something which appears unlikely to occur without central party-leadership intervention. The significant and rapid increase in the number of women elected to Westminster since 1997 is best explained by the Labour Party's use of what used to be called 'positive discrimination', what is now described as 'equality guarantees', and in particular their use of all-women shortlists (AWS). In 1997 and 2005 Labour used AWS to select women candidates, with the result that they increased their number of women MPs. In 2001, they did not – the procedure having been declared illegal by an industrial tribunal – with the result that the number of women MPs fell, for the first time since 1979 (Table 4.5). The Sex Discrimination (Election Candidates) Act 2002 allowed such measures again, hence their renewed use in 2005 (Childs 2003).

Selections involving AWS are, by their very nature, top-down initiatives. For the 1997 general election half of all seats defined as winnable on a 6-per-cent swing and half of all vacant Labour held seats would be all-women shortlists; for the 2005 general election (and barring exceptional circumstances) half of Labour's early-retirement seats and all those seats where the sitting MP retired after December 2002 would be AWS.

The power of Conservative local associations in the selection of parliamentary candidates had remained relatively undiminished despite substantial reforms initiated from the centre (such as competency tests for aspiring candidates), in all elections that have taken place since 2001

Table 4.5   *Use of AWS by the Labour Party for Westminster MPs*

| Year | Total number of women MPs | Number of Labour women MPs | Number of Labour women MPs selected for that election on AWS |
|------|------|------|------|
| 1992 | 60 | 37 | – |
| 1997 | 120 | 101 | 35 |
| 2001 | 118 | 95 | – |
| 2005 | 128 | 98 | 30 |

(Childs et al. 2005). There were a few signs of change, even before David Cameron's election to the leadership. For 2005, a small number of constituencies selected their candidates through American-style primaries in which, irrespective of whether they were open (where anyone in the constituency who registered could participate) or closed (where only Conservative members could participate) the selectorate was extended beyond the normal party selectorate. More importantly, in the party's City Seats Initiative (CSI), groups of would-be MPs were selected by Conservative HQ to undertake city-wide campaigning, only to be subsequently selected by local associations for individual constituencies. At the same time, the centre's impotency beyond these pilot schemes remained clear. When the local party was left to make its own choices the local selectorates chose the same old candidate type – white, middle-class and male (contra, Garnett 2004). Forty-one BME candidates and 116 women candidates were selected by the party but of these only two BME and 13 women candidates were selected in Conservative-held seats. Almost David Cameron's first substantive act on becoming party leader was to attempt to change this – expressing his intention to make the public face of the party more representative of modern Britain, not least by taking steps to increase the number of Conservative women and BME MPs. He ruled out AWS during the course of the leadership election, but instead chose to implement a 'priority list' (the 'A' list) for Conservative-held and target seats, consisting of an equal number of men and women, along with a proportion of BME candidates. The Liberal Democrats faced the same dilemma about central intervention. Charles Kennedy had been explicit in his advocacy of equality guarantees for women but he was unable to convince his party. Menzies Campbell faces the same problem.

More generally, the gendered nature of the British party system has yet to be fully acknowledged. Gender effects are present in parties' ideologies, structures, in their strategies to win women's votes as well as in processes of candidate selection. They are also evident in the interactions within and between parties (Lovenduski 2005). Over the last decade or so, Britain has witnessed a significant feminisation of party politics – the integration of women *and* women's concerns and perspectives into politics – albeit one that is currently asymmetric between the different party systems, institutions and parties: women presently constitute just under 20 per cent of the House of Commons and 50 and 40 per cent respectively in the new institutions in Scotland and Wales (Table 4.6). There has also been a significant shift of power from men to women in the Labour Party, because of both internal party sex quotas and the use of AWS (Russell, M 2005, 124). As a result, women's concerns and perspectives have moved from the margins

**Table 4.6** *Women's numerical representation in British politics*

| Institution | Percentage of women |
|---|---|
| National Assembly for Wales | 50 |
| Scottish Parliament | 40 |
| GLA | 36 |
| European Parliament | 24 |
| Westminster | 20 |
| Northern Ireland Assembly | 17 |

towards the centre of the political agenda, in part a reflection of the interest in, and actions of, gender-conscious women MPs (Childs et al. 2005). Issues such as maternity leave, flexible working, a national child care strategy, citizens' pensions and the work/life balance are concerns over which the parties now compete, but which were largely ignored a generation ago.

## Conclusion

The British party system can no longer be classified as a two-party system. Multiparty systems operate in the electoral arena in all jurisdictions, while multiparty systems are evident in the legislative arena (subnational and European) and executive arena (Scotland and, recently, Wales). Only the executive arena at Westminster remains largely indifferent to these changes, protected as it is by the continuing effects of the SMPS electoral system. Even at Westminster, however, the presence of smaller parties (such as the BNP, UKIP, Greens and Respect) in the electoral arena indicates that a more competitive and open arena may well be emerging. Beyond Westminster, in elections to the Scottish and European Parliaments, the Welsh and London Assemblies, voters, when faced with various proportional systems of voting, are making different political choices, and supporting a broader range of parties than those effectively offered up for Westminster in its SMPS elections (Dunleavy 2005).

Interparty relations of competition between the main British political parties vary according to the electoral context within which they are competing at any particular moment. In addition to Labour, the Conservatives and the Liberal Democrats, nationalist parties are key actors in Scotland, Wales and Northern Ireland and in certain elections the smaller parties can sometimes punch above their apparent weight. In short, the number of significant British parties now ranges between five and seven depending on the electoral context. As election-fighting machines, and there are more elections to contest than ever before, political parties remain dependent upon membership, despite all the talk of national campaigns, call-centres and innovations such as e-campaigning. Yet the parties face an ever-decreasing number of members. A consequence of parties' desire for members – for whatever reason – is that the sought-after members have the potential for leverage.

Trying to capture the ideological terrain of British interparty competition in the UK is a complicated matter. Not only are there clear limitations in placing the political parties on a single left–right ideological dimension, the issue remains problematic even when using two dimensions. Where do you put a party (such as the current Labour government) that favours ID cards but has introduced legislation and practices to deal more effectively with domestic violence? Moreover, notwithstanding micro-level debates over policy direction between and within parties, the three main parties seem to be eschewing grand political ideology and traditional narratives in favour of 'common-sense' managerialism. They might be right to do so if parties are only to be judged on their ability to deal with 'complex political and economic issues facing the country', rather than receiving votes on the basis of ideological support as some electoral research suggests (Clarke et al. 2004). But at the same time, support for some of the smaller parties – such as the Greens, BNP or Respect – seems to suggest a desire for more ideologically based politics. The result is that British party politics is currently entering one of the most intriguing and unpredictable periods since the end of the Second World War.

# Chapter 5

# Elections and Voting

JOHN BARTLE and SAMANTHA LAYCOCK

Winston Churchill's advice to those entering politics was that they had 'to foretell what is going to happen, tomorrow, next week, next month and next year. And to have the ability afterwards to explain why it didn't'. The same advice could safely be offered to anyone attempting electoral analysis. General election outcomes are always easier to describe than to explain – and they are also much easier to explain after the event than to predict before they take place.

Such tasks have been made more complicated in Britain by the changing rules of electoral politics. Many of the nostrums of the post-war period apply no more:

- The link between class and voting is now weaker than ever before.
- Partisan identification – the extent to which an individual 'identifies with' a particular party – has weakened considerably, to the point where some dispute it exists any longer, if it ever did.
- The effect of the Single Member Plurality System (SMPS) electoral system used at Westminster has become increasingly difficult to predict before an election, and it is noticeably more exaggerated in its effects.
- Elections have become increasingly localised (itself one reason why the effects of the electoral system are harder to predict), with local factors having an increasing effect on the outcome in a seat.
- Voters are increasingly willing to vote for parties other than the main two, the Conservatives and Labour. For every three votes cast in the 2005 election, for example, one went to Labour, one to the Conservatives, and one to one of the other parties.
- And turnout – something rather complacently taken for granted for much of the immediate post-war period – is now a major source of concern for politicians, having fallen to record lows in the last two elections (Electoral Commission 2004).

All of these effects were demonstrated clearly in the 2005 general election. They were, however, merely evidence of trends that have now been clear for several elections (King 2006).

Attempts to explain (or account for) general election results often fail to distinguish between two very different analytical questions:

- Why did the parties gain that share of the popular vote?
- Why did that share of the vote translate into that particular share of seats?

The difference between these two questions has been especially important in recent elections, because of the increasingly exaggerated effects of the electoral system. As a result, what in post-war terms would be seen as relatively poor election results (like Labour's in 2001 or 2005) can generate large or very large majorities in the House of Commons (Dunleavy and Margetts 2005).

In the case of the 2005 election, there is also a third question. Why, despite widespread attempts to increase turnout, did turnout remain relatively low, at just 61 per cent, up just two percentage points on the historic low point of 2001? It was not just that there were more non-voters than supporters of the Labour Party; but at 39 per cent of the electorate, non-voters outnumbered supporters of the winning party by almost 2 to 1. Out of every five members of the electorate, one voted Labour, one voted Conservative, one voted for one of the other parties – but two did not vote at all. This chapter considers each of these three questions in turn, before considering the overall state of electoral politics in Britain.

## The 2005 election results

Labour won the 2005 election with just 35.2 per cent of the popular vote (down 5.5 points compared with 2001) (Kavanagh and Butler 2005). This was the lowest share of the vote won by any governing party since 1923, and the lowest share of the popular vote of any party to gain a majority since 1832. Given the relatively low turnout of 61 per cent, it meant that Labour commanded the support of just 21 per cent of the electorate, another record low for a winning party.

Both the Conservatives (32.3 per cent, up 0.6 points) and the Liberal Democrats (23.0 per cent, up 3.6 points) made some improvement on their 2001 performance but not enough to seriously threaten Labour. Just as significantly, 'other' parties increased their share of the vote to 10.4 per cent, up by one percentage point, despite both the major nationalist parties in Great Britain (the Scottish National Party and Plaid Cymru) losing votes. Support for the Greens rose from 0.6 to 1 per cent and support for the British National Party from 0.2 to 0.7 per cent, though neither won a seat. There were also relatively strong performances by Respect and UKIP.

**Table 5.1**   *British general election results 1945–2005*

| Party | Average % vote | | | % vote |
|---|---|---|---|---|
| | 1945–70 | 1974–92 | 1997–2001 | 2005 |
| Conservative | 44.8 | 41.7 | 31.2 | 32.3 |
| Labour | 46.8 | 35.2 | 42.0 | 35.2 |
| Liberal Democrat | 7.1 | 20.0 | 17.8 | 22.1 |
| Others | 1.3 | 3.1 | 9.3 | 10.4 |

In 2005, therefore, the electoral tide turned against Labour, but it did not flow strongly in the direction of the Conservative Party, the only other party that could have reasonably been expected to form a government.

The assessment of any party's election performance is based on comparisons and, as Table 5.1 shows, it matters considerably which elections are used as reference points. Labour's share of the vote in 2005 was 11.6 points lower than its average for the general elections between 1945 and 1970 (an era of two-party politics). Its performance was, however, the average for the era of two-and-a-half party politics between 1974 and 1992. Viewed from this perspective, Labour has some reason to be pleased. But compared with the last two elections (when Labour averaged 42 per cent) and the pre-election opinion polls (in which it averaged 38 per cent) the party's performance was less impressive.

The Conservatives' share of the vote, however, was disastrous by almost any standard. They polled 12.5 points less than their 1945–70 average and 9.4 points less than between 1974 and 1992. Over the last three consecutive elections, the Conservatives have failed to secure more than one third of the vote. The Liberal Democrats, like Labour, had mixed feelings about the election outcome. Their vote was 15.9 points higher than the average for 1945–70 and three points higher than the average between 1974 and 1992. But they had entered the 2005 election with some of the best polling figures in a generation and expected to gain momentum in the campaign. In the event, they added just a couple of points and only ten more seats than in 2001.

The steady rise in the support for the 'others' may be just a short-term consequence of disillusionment with Labour, an unpopular opposition and individual issues – such as asylum seekers and Iraq – which boosted the support of parties. But it may also be that voters have got into the habit of voting for small parties in the increasing number of elections fought under different (and sometimes more proportional) systems (the European Parliament, Welsh Assembly, Scottish Parliament, Greater London Authority and the elections of mayors).

**Table 5.2**    *Votes and seats at the 2005 general election*

| Party | Votes % | Change % | Seats | Change in seats 2001–05 |
|---|---|---|---|---|
| Conservative | 32.3 | +0.6 | 197 | +33 |
| Labour | 35.2 | –5.5 | 355 | –47 |
| Liberal Democrat | 22.1 | +3.8 | 62 | +11 |
| Others | 10.4 | +1.0 | 31 | +3 |

Interpreting any election result is, however, complicated by the effect of the electoral system. Table 5.2 shows how these vote shares were translated into seats in the House of Commons. Labour's 2.9 percentage point lead was converted into a substantial overall majority of 66 seats. The Conservative 0.6-point increase produced a net gain of 33 seats, but the Liberal Democrats' much more impressive 3.9-point gain translated into just eleven extra seats.

## Explanations of voting

There are essentially three ways of thinking about voting behaviour (Box 5.1) (Denver 2003):

- sociological models, which examine the relationship between social characteristics and vote;
- social-psychological models, which examine the relationship between voters' partisan self-images and vote;
- issue-voting models, which examine the relationship between voters' preferences and the vote.

In practice, most analysts do not subscribe exclusively to one model. Sociologists, for example, accept that voters' preferences are not solely determined by their social characteristics and that issues can have some unique effect on vote. Social psychologists concede that voters' self-images are rooted in their social characteristics and that contemporary issues can pull voters away from their long-term allegiances. Advocates of issue-voting models similarly accept that voters' preferences are rooted in their social characteristics and that voters may adopt policy positions simply because they are advocated by 'their' party. Accordingly, most explanations of voting behaviour draw on a range of factors.

## Box 5.1   Models of voting

*Sociological models* posit that membership of social groups leads voters to become aligned with particular parties (for example, that the working class tends to vote Labour). In some cases, that attachment is because parties share the norms or values of that group; in other cases the association between group and party is the result of exposure to biased information that leads voters to form favourable or unfavourable impressions of parties.

*Social-psychological models* assume that parties are important 'groups' in their own right and that many voters form a general enduring image of themselves as 'being Conservative' or 'being Labour'. This then results in an enduring emotional attachment to a party which persists through time. This partisan self-image (or party identification) is the joint product of self-images and stereotyped beliefs about groups. Once formed, these alter slowly and, accordingly, so does party identification.

*Issue-voting models* treat voters as if they were consumers and votes as if they were instruments to influence political outcomes. Voters are assumed to choose parties on the basis of what provides them with the most utility. Voters calculate the likely costs and benefits of voting for particular parties on the basis of their positions on enduring and current controversies, past performance, prospective competence, and the qualities of their leaders. Such models correspond more closely to traditional democratic theories than the previous two models – with voters making a conscious and reasoned choice between parties – but they should be treated with caution. There is a tendency for survey respondents to 'rationalise' their support for parties by bringing their responses into line with their behaviour. When asked 'Which party is best at managing the economy?' respondents may reason (consciously or not), 'I vote Tory, so it must be the Tories,' in which case vote causes recorded preference, rather than vice versa.

## Sociological and social-psychological evidence from 2005

It is easy enough to see evidence of sociological models at work in the voting at the 2005 general election (Table 5.3). There was, for example, a striking correlation between age and vote, with young voters being much less inclined to support the Conservative Party than older voters. Only 22 per cent of those aged 18 to 24 voted Conservative in 2005 but this rose to 40 per cent among those aged over 55. Ethnicity was also a powerful influence. Fifty-six per cent of non-white voters gave their vote to Labour, compared with 37 per cent of white voters. And despite speculation

**Table 5.3**    *Social characteristics and the vote 2005*

| Category | Con | Lab | LD | Lab lead over Con |
|---|---|---|---|---|
| Male | 31 | 38 | 23 | +7 |
| Female | 34 | 37 | 21 | +3 |
| 18 to 24 | 22 | 40 | 31 | +18 |
| 25 to 34 | 23 | 46 | 25 | +23 |
| 35 to 44 | 22 | 48 | 23 | +26 |
| 45 to 54 | 35 | 36 | 24 | +1 |
| 55 to 64 | 41 | 30 | 22 | −11 |
| 65 plus | 40 | 36 | 18 | −4 |
| White | 34 | 37 | 22 | +3 |
| Non-white | 19 | 56 | 22 | +37 |
| Home owner | 46 | 27 | 20 | −19 |
| Mortgage holder | 26 | 43 | 23 | +17 |
| Council tenant | 16 | 55 | 19 | +39 |
| Left school at 15–17 | 34 | 39 | 20 | +5 |
| Left school at 18 | 30 | 45 | 20 | +15 |
| Left school above 19 | 35 | 34 | 26 | −1 |
| Still in education | 9 | 34 | 54 | +25 |
| Self-employed | 55 | 28 | 14 | −27 |
| Salariat | 36 | 34 | 23 | −2 |
| Routine non-manual | 39 | 33 | 21 | −6 |
| Foreman | 29 | 39 | 24 | +9 |
| Working class | 21 | 51 | 20 | +30 |
| Trade union member | 25 | 48 | 21 | +23 |
| Public sector | 29 | 39 | 25 | +10 |
| Private sector | 34 | 38 | 21 | +4 |
| Church of England | 43 | 34 | 17 | −9 |
| Catholic | 32 | 43 | 23 | +11 |
| Muslim | 14 | 50 | 33 | +36 |

*Source*: Data from British Election Study 2005

among commentators that 'women had fallen out of love with Blair' and might defect en masse from Labour, Table 5.3 suggests that men and women behaved in similar ways in 2005, as they did in 2001 and 1997: Labour's relative appeal among women continues to be a reason for its success compared with 'Old Labour'.

As in every other election, there were also clear differences in the vote preferences of the social classes. The Conservatives enjoyed a substantial 27-point lead among the self-employed and Labour had an equally large 30-point lead among the working class. The self-employed, however, constitute a very small group and the working class a declining proportion of the population. Moreover, although Labour still enjoyed a substantial lead amongst the working class, it was also the group that swung most to the Tories in 2005. Thus, among the electorate as a whole, class voting was probably weaker than at any previous election. Similarly, trade union members and public-sector employees are much less likely to vote Labour than 30 years ago. The process of 'class dealignment' – first noticed in the 1970s, and by which the links between social class and voting had begun to fracture – has continued unabated (Clarke et al. 2004).

Although religious adherence is in decline, it continues to have some influence on individual vote decisions. Catholics remained disproportionately pro-Labour, whilst members of the Church of England favoured the Conservatives just as in most previous elections. Muslims have traditionally provided Labour with strong support, but switched in substantial numbers to the Liberal Democrats in 2005; fully one in three Muslims voted for that party. This switch was undoubtedly caused by the Iraq war, which was strongly opposed by most Muslims. It is difficult to tell, however, whether the war will lead to a permanent shift in the allegiances of Muslim voters.

Yet despite such dealignment, social characteristics should still be taken seriously: demographic and social trends influence what we might call the size of a party's 'natural electorate'. If those groups that support Labour are becoming more numerous then, other things being equal, this should benefit it. Yet although some social changes (such as immigration) may have benefited Labour, most (such as the ageing of the population, the reduction in the size of the working class, the decline in trade union-ism, and the spread of home ownership) should have benefited the Conservatives. This makes Labour's recent electoral success all the more remarkable. It also suggests that, although there is a relationship between sociology and vote, that relationship can change. Parties are not prisoners of social change.

There has also been considerable evidence over the last 30 years of a decline in what is called 'partisan alignment' – the extent to which people see themselves as being of one party or the other. In the 1960s, 1 in 20 voters was a 'non-identifier'. By 1997 this had increased to 1 in 10. By 2005, it had increased to 1 in 5. Moreover, even among the smaller proportion of identifiers, the strength of identification has declined. In the 1960s, around 4 out of 10 identifiers expressed a 'very strong' sense of identity. By 2005, this had fallen to 1 in 10. Voters are, therefore, simply less partisan today than they were 40 or 50 years ago, with the result that parties can now rely on a very much smaller portion of 'all-weather' support in each election.

## Issue-voting evidence from 2005

The decline in both class and partisan alignment over recent decades has meant that issue voting has become increasingly important in British elections. However, such issue voting is more complicated than it may seem at first – it takes many different forms, from retrospective judgements about the government's performance, to views on the leaders – and the effect of many of these different types of issue voting is usually less dramatic than many commentators believe.

### Labour's record

The basis of the famous phrase that oppositions don't win elections, governments lose them, is the idea that voters pass a retrospective judgement on the performance of the incumbent government. By 2005, Labour had been in power for eight years, and voters were able to treat the election as a 'referendum' on the government's performance.

As Table 5.4 shows, the public gave Labour relatively good marks on the economy and dealing with terrorism (around a half of all voters thought that it did 'very' or 'fairly' well on these issues). The first of these

**Table 5.4**    *Evaluations of the Labour government 2005*

| Issue | % saying government handled problem very/fairly well |
|---|---|
| The economy | 55 |
| Terrorism | 45 |
| Education | 38 |
| NHS | 34 |
| Taxation | 27 |
| Crime | 27 |
| Iraq | 21 |
| Pensions | 20 |
| Rail | 14 |
| Asylum | 9 |

*Source*:  Data from British Election Study, 2005

is one of the most remarkable features of the 2005 election. Historically, the Conservative Party has been thought the party of economic competence. Indeed, until September 1992, the Tories almost always led Labour on this issue. Since then, Labour has been thought the more competent party in managing the economy, and – by May 2005 – the economy was Labour's strongest policy area (King 2006).

But voters were much less happy with Labour's record on the public services, including the NHS and education, and on crime, where it was widely judged to have failed to deliver on its promises. Its record on asylum was even worse. A mere 9 per cent of voters thought that Labour had done 'very' or 'fairly' well on this issue, and when voters were asked to choose a word to describe their feelings about asylum, 37 per cent first chose 'uneasy', 19 per cent 'disgusted' and 17 per cent 'angry'. Perhaps not surprisingly given this, support for the anti-immigration BNP increased in many Labour seats with a large immigrant community.

Views on policies like those in Table 5.4 did have an effect on the way people voted. Even once the influence of partisan self-images has been removed, evaluations of the government's performance on crime, education, tax and rail were still significantly related to the decision to vote Labour or Conservative. Views of the government's record on taxation, in particular, strongly differentiated between support for the Labour and Conservative parties – with those who approved of Labour's record on tax voting for the government, those who disapproved being more likely to vote Conservative. Since evaluations of Labour's performance on all these issues were disproportionately negative, they thus reduced Labour's vote share in 2005.

But most surveys also suggested that the public services, particularly the NHS and education, were among the two most important issues to voters, and no matter how badly Labour was thought to have performed on these issues, it was still the preferred party of most voters. When ICM asked voters which party was best able to handle various problems, Labour invariably led the Conservatives: it had a 13-point lead on the NHS and an 11-point lead on education. And evaluations of which party was best able to handle 'the most urgent problem' were also powerful predictors of vote, net of all prior factors. As a result, although the public did not greatly approve of Labour's record in many areas of policy, this did not harm the party as much as it might have done, because voters still thought Labour would be better at dealing with what they saw as the key issues facing the country.

Surprisingly, retrospective evaluations of Labour's record on the economy did not appear to influence the choice between Conservative and Labour, though prospective evaluations of economic competence did (see below), whilst evaluations of Labour's performance on Iraq, education, terrorism, rail and pensions helped discriminate between Labour and Liberal Democrat voters. Again these issues must have caused a significant number to support the Liberal Democrats, because evaluations of Labour's performance (with the exception of its stance on terrorism) were negative.

In other words, different issues pushed voters to the different opposition parties, but dissatisfaction with Labour's performance must account for a large part of its 5.5-point fall in vote share.

### The Iraq war

One particular dissatisfaction that many voters had was the decision to go to war in Iraq. The Iraq war had complex effects on the 2005 election. Reservations about the war had a direct effect on Labour support. For example, analysis of the British Election Survey (BES) data makes it clear that Labour's conduct of the war caused many voters to switch to the Liberal Democrats. Iraq was clearly a factor in the loss of Bethnal Green and Bow to the Respect Party and in the large reductions in Labour's share of the vote in some seats (such as Birmingham Sparkbrook and Small Heath and Birmingham Hodge Hill) with large Muslim populations. But further electoral damage was inflicted by the indirect effects of the war. Cabinet and backbench dissent on the issue made the party appear disunited and the disaffection of party activists reduced the

**Figure 5.1**    *Ratings of parties in opinion polls 2001–05*

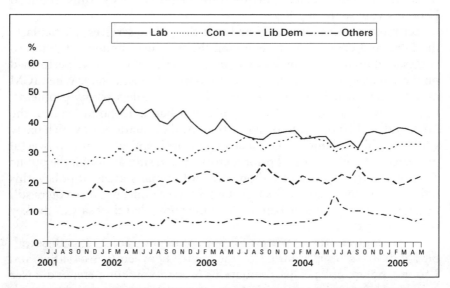

*Sources*:  Gallup, YouGov, ICM, MORI, Populus, CommRes, Live Strategy, NOP, BPIX

intensity of campaigning. These indirect effects may have been just as important as the direct effects on vote decisions.

## Prospective evaluations of economic competence

Voters look forward as well as back, and Labour's record with the economy over its eight years in government – unemployment had fallen, inflation was under control and interest rates were at very low levels – fed into evaluations of future competence. When voters were asked which of the two major parties was best able to manage the economy Labour emerged as the clear winner (by 45 to 35 per cent, according to the BES). Statistical analyses suggest that this factor powerfully influenced individual vote decisions in 2005. Those who thought that Labour would be best at managing the economy were far more likely to vote for the government than those who did not, even after removing the effect of party identification and retrospective evaluations of Labour's performance. More than any other short-term factor, prospective evaluations of economic competence helped Labour to victory in 2005. Again, this feature of the election – Labour being helped by judgements about their competence – is in danger of being taken for granted (both by the party, and by many commentators). It is, however, historically remarkable.

## Leaders and leadership

Tony Blair was widely believed to have been a considerable asset to Labour in both the 1997 and 2001 elections, being preferred by most voters to both John Major and William Hague. By 2005, however, Blair's personal appeal had diminished, and as Table 5.5 shows, evaluations of Blair were mixed. Respondents to the BES were asked to rate each leader on a scale from 0 to 10 on a range of traits. Blair's highest rating was for 'competence' (5.7) and his lowest for 'trustworthiness' (4.2). These ratings were,

**Table 5.5**    *Evaluations of the party leaders 2005*

| Trait | Average mark out of 10 | | |
|---|---|---|---|
| | Blair | Howard | Kennedy |
| Competent | 5.7 | 5.0 | 5.0 |
| Likeable | 4.7 | 4.4 | 4.9 |
| Responsive | 4.8 | 5.0 | 5.0 |
| Trustworthy | 4.2 | 4.3 | 4.7 |

*Source*: Data from British Election Study 2005

however, comparable with those of the other party leaders. Michael Howard, the Conservative Party leader, was thought to be less competent than Blair (5.0), and almost as untrustworthy (4.3). Indeed, overall, despite being much criticised, Blair came out slightly ahead on the ratings of the party leaders; and when pollsters asked respondents to choose who would make the best prime minister, then despite the criticisms of him, Blair enjoyed a healthy lead (by 15 points, according to ICM).

Statistical analyses suggest that evaluations of a leader's trustworthiness were a powerful predictor of the vote in 2005, even controlling for other variables. However, since both major party leaders were considered almost equally untrustworthy it is difficult to believe that this had much impact on vote shares. Thus, while Blair might have had a major indirect impact on the election by the government's perceived failures to improve the public services and the decision to go to war, he may not have pushed many to vote Conservative. Charles Kennedy, however, may have had more of an effect on the Liberal Democrat vote. The third party's leader became increasingly popular as the election went on (his likeability score increased from 4.9 to 5.5) It is possible that voters may have switched to the Liberal Democrats as a result of these favourable impressions. Any effect, however, was probably quite small and this did not prevent disaffected Liberal Democrat MPs from forcing Kennedy out as leader in January 2006.

## The image of the Conservative Party

Given the relative unpopularity of the government by the time of the 2005 election, there was the potential for the Conservative Party to make considerable electoral gains. That that potential was not translated into reality was due to public perceptions of the party. Even by 2005, eight years after leaving office, the Conservatives remained one of the most unpopular oppositions in British history. Their party image was almost uniformly less attractive than that of Labour. YouGov, the internet pollsters, found that 48 per cent of voters thought the Tories seem to 'appeal to one section of society rather than the whole country' and 45 per cent agreed that the party seemed 'stuck in the past'. Other polling evidence suggested that the party was associated with groups such as the 'rich', 'professional and business people' and 'people who live in the country' (King 2006). Large majorities did not think that the Tories were close to the poor, the working class, ethnic minorities and – most remarkably of all, given that the party used to enjoy relative success amongst them – women. Even when specific Conservative policies, such as their plans to reduce the council tax for pensioners, were popular, voters simply failed to 'connect' with the party.

Thus even when voters were dissatisfied with the government – as many of them were – many of them did not feel that they could support the main opposition party instead. This helps to explain why the sizeable shift in votes away from Labour went to both the Liberal Democrats and the plethora of other parties, and not to the Conservatives.

## From modest plurality to comfortable majority

Yet all of this is only the first part of an explanation of the election outcome. All the factors listed above helped Labour capture the support of marginally more than a third of those who voted. Yet this modest plurality of votes enabled them to capture 55 per cent of seats, and generated a comfortable majority in the House of Commons.

It is not enough simply to respond that the difference between the shares of seats and of votes was caused by the way the SMPS electoral system worked, since the electoral system has worked in different ways at different times, producing electoral outcomes that are more or less proportional, and which favour one party or the other (Johnston et al. 2001). In the immediate post-war period, for example, the electoral system tended to favour the Conservative Party; in more recent elections it has favoured Labour.

In 2005, the electoral system rather generously rewarded the Conservatives' somewhat meagre net gain of just 0.6 percentage points with an additional 33 seats, while grudgingly rewarding the Liberal Democrats, who gained 3.9 per cent, with just 11 net gains. Moreover, Labour's modest lead was translated into a comfortable majority of 66. The reasons for this pattern are complex.

The Conservatives were advantaged by there being more Labour/Conservative marginal seats than Labour/Liberal Democrat marginals. So as Labour's vote fell, it lost seats to the Conservatives, but not to the Liberal Democrats. The Liberal Democrats also gained a lot of additional votes in safe Labour seats that they were extremely unlikely to win. More important, though, is the efficiency with which Labour wins seats. The reasons for the pro-Labour bias in the current operation of the electoral system are as follows:

- Labour-held seats have smaller populations (67,000 electors on average) than Conservative seats (around 73,000), so Labour needs fewer votes to win a seat.
- Welsh constituencies are smaller (55,800) than those in England (70,200). Labour is strong in Wales and so gained an advantage.

- Scottish constituencies are still smaller than English constituencies (65,300) even after the reduction in the number of Scottish seats. Labour is stronger in Scotland and again therefore has a small advantage.
- Labour seats also see lower turnouts (an average of 58 per cent in 2005) than do Conservative seats (65 per cent), so again it needs fewer Labour votes to win a seat.
- And the performance of other parties is also important. The Liberal Democrats won 43 seats where the Conservatives came second and only 18 where Labour came second. As a result, Labour did not 'waste' votes coming second in many Liberal Democrat seats.

As a result, it took around 27,000 votes to elect a single Labour MP, 44,000 to elect a Conservative and 100,000 votes to elect a Liberal Democrat.

Labour were also helped here by the influence of tactical voting. According to the BES, fully 17 per cent of Liberal Democrat voters thought of themselves as tactical voters, compared with just 8 per cent of Labour and Conservative voters. While Labour's record on Iraq, education and the NHS might have strengthened their preference for the Liberal Democrats, it still appears that Liberal Democrat identifiers were more likely tactically to vote Labour to stop the Tories than Tory to stop Labour. This is illustrated by responses to YouGov's so-called 'forced-choice' questions, which asked voters how they would vote if they were forced to choose between the Labour and Conservative parties. In 2005, Labour had a 17-point lead (52 to 35 per cent) in response to this question, so that many Liberal Democrats must have been persuaded to vote Labour to stop a Tory candidate from winning.

There is, however, no iron law that the electoral system will always operate in Labour's favour. As recently as the 1980s, the Conservatives benefited from the electoral system and it is entirely possible that the system may operate to their advantage again in the future. Improved targeting of constituencies, coupled with the gradual disillusionment with Labour may mean that the Conservatives become the second choice of many Liberal Democrats. Tactical voting to remove Labour MPs might then cut into Labour representation.

Moreover, the body charged with drawing up the constituencies, the Boundary Commission, will report in 2007 and will inevitably recommend the abolition of some (Labour) seats to reduce the variations in constituency size that have emerged as people have moved from declining (Labour) areas to prosperous (Conservative) areas. This too will reduce the pro-Labour bias in the operation of the electoral system (although there are no plans to reduce the number of Welsh seats so that element of pro-Labour bias will continue). And minor party wins may advantage Labour less in future. The

Liberal Democrats are now second in many Labour seats in the North and may begin to threaten Labour in its heartlands.

The fact that Labour has benefited from the electoral system in recent years is therefore no reason to expect the party to continue to benefit from it.

## Turnout

Turnout in the 2005 general election was 61.3 per cent. This was the second-lowest turnout of any election since 1918, only marginally better than the record low of 2001.

Turnout rose by 1.5 percentage points from 59.8 to 61.3 per cent in 2005. The failure of turnout to increase any further was all the more striking because a new system of rolling registration had been introduced, which should have made the electoral registers a more accurate reflection of who was eligible to vote. Furthermore, the rules relating to postal voting had been relaxed and it was easier than ever to vote without physically going to the polls. Indeed, it is possible that without these changes to electoral procedure there would have been a further decline in participation.

Yet again the three basic models outlined above provide different insights into the drop in participation (Clarke et. al. 2004).

Sociological models would suggest that participation is influenced by voters' individual social characteristics (primarily the resources they have at their disposal) and also group norms that predispose people to turn out to vote. Those who have the ability to understand politics (the better educated, for example) are more disposed to turn out than those who find it difficult to understand politics (the less educated). Similarly, those who develop a network of social contacts are more likely to be subject to norms of participation compared with the socially isolated; the denser the networks, the more powerful the stimulus to vote.

Yet sociological models cannot provide plausible explanations of the decline in turnout. Indeed, according to sociological models of participation turnout should actually be increasing. After all, more voters have the resources to understand politics, simply because they are now (on average) older, better educated and have more access to the media. One of the continuing paradoxes of electoral participation is that more educated voters are more likely to vote, yet overall rises in education have not led to an increase in (and indeed have seen a fall in) electoral participation. About the only demographic trend that should be leading to a lower level of turnout is the increase in the ethnic minority population (members of ethnic minorities tending to show lower levels of participation) but this increase has been under way for some time and can hardly explain the sudden decline in turnout that occurred in 2001. Similarly, those who have speculated that the decline in turnout is the product of a more fractured, less communal, and more individualised society cannot explain the recent sharp fall in turnout.

There are similar problems in trying to explain the fall in turnout as resulting from the process of partisan dealignment. Although there is clearly a relationship between dealignment and a decline in turnout – since partisans are more likely to vote than those with no alignment – it can only explain why turnout has trended down over a long period of time. The strength of partisanship declined from the mid 1970s onwards, but turnout did not fall markedly until 2001.

Issue-voting models assume that votes are the result of choices based on calculations of expected costs and benefits. The problem with this approach, however, is that rational individuals are unlikely to vote at all in most elections (as explained in Box 5.2). This aside, issue-voting models can still help explain much of the variation in turnout. In particular, turnout should be higher the more there is at stake in the election and the closer the expected election outcome. There is certainly some evidence for this, with those who live in marginal seats being more likely to vote, either because they feel more decisive or because they are more likely to be targeted by the parties. Indeed, one cause of the decline in turnout may have been the steady decline in party membership and party activism. Research has shown that local

---

**Box 5.2    Why it is irrational to vote**

Attempts to explain voters' behaviour by way of their preferences run into one logical hurdle. Logically, it is irrational for almost any of us to vote. Any rational voter would calculate the difference that having their favoured party in power might have on their welfare and then multiply this by the probability that their vote will alter the election outcome. In most large-scale elections this probability is almost non-existent, so the expected benefit arising from their vote is tiny. It is likely that the costs of voting (even if just measured in time, shoe leather and so on) exceed any expected benefit. The net benefit from voting is, therefore, negative and a rational voter would abstain.

This paradox has generated an enormous academic literature, with people attempting to explain why it could still be rational to vote (Dowding 2005). Some analysts therefore believe this argument makes all rational or issue-based explanations of the vote implausible.

campaigns stimulate turnout (Denver et al. 2004). The fall in the membership of political parties means that on election day 2005 there were probably fewer people involved in ordinary campaign activity (canvassing voters, staffing polling stations, and displaying posters) than ever before.

Attitudes towards elections are also associated with turnout. Those who believe that it is one's civic duty to vote, who have an interest in politics, and who believe that they can influence politics are all more likely to vote. Those who believe that voting is a waste of time or that it is too much effort to vote, on the other hand, are less likely to vote. These findings are hardly earth-shattering, and moreover, few of these variables have changed dramatically over time. Levels of interest in politics, for example, are now just as high as they were 40 years ago. The only noticeable change has come with the drop in people believing it is their duty to vote.

Since it is so difficult to explain the decline in turnout by reference to long-term factors, it is tempting to suggest that the reduction in participation is a consequence of more immediate political circumstances. It may simply be the unique combination of circumstances in the early twenty-first century (Allen 2006). In both 2001 and 2005, a less-than-popular government faced an even more unpopular Opposition, advocating broadly similar world views. Most voters (and most of the media) thought that the less-than-popular government would win all the same. These hardly seem to be the sort of circumstances to prompt people to participate in elections!

## What lies ahead?

### Labour

Despite the drop in its share of the vote and its number of seats in 2005, Labour continues to enjoy a number of key electoral advantages as it looks ahead to a potential fourth victory (Crewe 2006). For example, it continues to be able to draw on the disproportional backing of several groups which help provide the party with a bedrock of support:

- Black and Asian voters remained strongly with Labour in 2005 despite the government's decision to take Britain to war in Iraq. To be sure, many Muslim voters withdrew support for Labour but the party remained first choice even among this group.
- Labour appears to have closed the 'gender gap', by which women (numerically superior to men) traditionally favoured the Conservatives.

- Younger voters were less likely to vote Labour than in 1997 or 2001, but they remained more likely to vote Labour than for any other single party. In any event, the young are a small (and decreasing) proportion of the electorate.
- Despite talk of the middle classes deserting Labour in 2005 as a result of 'stealth taxes' such as national insurance, the non-manual Labour vote held up well; if anything, it was Labour's traditional working-class vote – disproportionately located in seats which are Labour strongholds and thus less vulnerable to electoral loss – that seeped away.

Labour also continues to enjoy a substantial lead in terms of voters' enduring party identities, and Labour policies, particularly their commitment to high-quality public services, appear to be more in tune with public sentiment than any alternative approach. The British economy has, to date, remained strong and, given the party's new-found reputation for economic competence, this too has helped Labour.

None of this, however, is set in stone:

- Given how important economic success has been to Labour's record in government, any economic recession could badly damage Labour's reputation and cause voters to re-evaluate the Conservatives, thus removing Labour's new-found advantage.
- Just as Labour reversed the traditional gender gap, there is no reason why it could not revert to its historical pattern, with women becoming likely to support the Conservatives again.
- Surveys of public opinion continue to suggest that voters are still prepared to pay more taxes for better services, but support for higher spending and taxes has fallen dramatically in recent years, as voters feel their money has not produced the promised improvements in services. This shift in the public mood suggests that Labour is running out of time to put public services right.
- Although the Liberal Democrats didn't win very many seats in 2005, one effect of their increased vote was that they are now second to Labour in many traditional 'heartland' seats. This means that Labour may fight the next election on two fronts, both against the Tories in its marginal seats and against the Liberal Democrats in its more traditional seats.

Blair's decision to step down as Labour leader before the next election provides Labour with both opportunities and problems. In 1997 and 2001 he was widely thought to have been a considerable asset to the party. Labour would, however, have won these elections almost as well under other leaders. Yet by 2005 his appeal had faded and his personal unpopularity was a factor, albeit a small one, in reducing Labour's majority. Gordon Brown, Blair's likely replacement, was widely regarded as more competent and more popular than the prime minister at the time of the 2005 election, and there was then a hope that a combination of Blair's removal, Brown's leadership and the sheer lapse of time from the Iraq war, would freshen the party's appeal, and thus provide him with a window of opportunity to win a fourth term. However, opinion-poll figures after the 2005 election – and especially after David Cameron became Conservative party leader – presented a rather different picture, showing that Brown was far from the electoral asset that he had appeared to be prior to May 2005. It is best to be careful about such hypothetical opinion-poll questions – which ask respondents to say how they would vote if X was leader instead of Y – but it is safe to say that the assumption that Brown would be a definite electoral asset as Labour leader is at least questionable. Once Blair has gone, Labour may miss the 'Blair effect'.

### The Conservatives

Many Conservatives were pleased with the outcome of the 2005 election. They should not have been. The party made little headway in its share of the vote and the party's poor performance among the young (where it is the third choice of voters) is particularly worrying. Indeed, given the gradual increase in the size of the middle class, the continued drift of people to the South of England and the steady rise of home ownership, the party's failure to increase its share of the vote by more than 0.6 points was all the more remarkable.

The party's strategic problem is how to broaden its appeal, while retaining its core vote among older voters. This is a considerable, but not insurmountable, challenge. Simply making the party look more 'modern' and less angry about recent social trends (immigration, sexual behaviour and so on) might help – hence David Cameron's comment, on being elected leader, that he 'loved his country as it is, not as it was'; but this will not be enough on its own.

It is frequently said that in order to broaden its appeal, the Conservative Party must reach out to ethnic minorities and young people. Whilst doubtless desirable (both electorally and intrinsically) this will be difficult for the party to achieve, not least because both groups have long been largely antipathetic to the party. Moreover, both groups are small; one, the ethnic minorities, is growing in importance (albeit still small); the other, the young, is reducing in size. Far more important for the party, therefore, is to regain the support of groups such as women and the middle class who once constituted its core supporters. Not only must it win back these groups from Labour but it is also facing stiff competition for these groups from the Liberal Democrats.

The biggest hurdle the Conservatives face, however, is the effect of the electoral system. It is perfectly possible to imagine the Conservatives outpolling Labour at any general election in 2009/10. It is, however, very difficult to imagine them winning enough seats to form a government because of the current operation of the electoral system, which remains biased against them. Prior to the boundary changes due in 2007 this bias means that, assuming a uniform swing, the party will need a lead of 7.1 per cent over Labour if they are to become the largest party in the House of Commons. It will need a lead of 11.9 per cent to gain a bare majority of just one seat in the Commons. The sort of swing that they need has only been achieved twice in the post-war era, on both occasions by Labour, in 1945 and 1997. It is, therefore, possible – but highly unlikely.

## The Liberal Democrats

Since the creation of the Liberal Democrats in 1988, the party has made steady progress in increasing its share of the seats in parliament (up from 22 to 62), but its vote share has fluctuated between 17 per cent (1997) and 22 per cent (1987 and 2005), and has not yet hit the levels achieved by the SDP–Liberal Alliance in 1983 (25 per cent). The Liberal Democrats made substantial progress in 2005, but it was far from being the long-awaited breakthrough. This, and Kennedy's post-2005 performances, combined with rumour about his 'personal problems', most notably a drink problem, led Liberal Democrat MP to force Kennedy's resignation from the leadership in January 2006. But the problems the Liberal Democrats face go far wider than their leader. The real stumbling blocks to the Liberal Democrats achieving wider electoral success at Westminster are:

- the lack of support of key groups;
- the lack of a clear identity;
- the operation of the electoral system.

Whereas Labour can call on the working class and the Conservative Party on older voters, the Liberal Democrats have no such core support. The only group that seems significantly more disposed to the Liberal Democrats than any other party are the university-educated. In time, this group may constitute an important electoral group but their support is unlikely to be decisive. There are also signs that younger voters are attracted to the party but whether this is merely protest voting against Labour over tuition fees and Iraq or whether this is part of a longer-term trend remains to be seen.

Weakening voter identification with the Labour and the Conservative parties benefits the Liberal Democrats, but it now also benefits other parties such as the Greens, Respect, UKIP and the BNP. Moreover, dealignment is a mixed blessing for the Liberal Democrats; they may be successful in attracting disaffected voters but they find it difficult to keep them. This explains, in part, why the Liberal Democrat vote has fluctuated rather than progressively increasing over time.

Another problem for the Liberal Democrats is the lack of a clear identity. In voters' minds the Liberal Democrats lie somewhere between Labour and the Conservatives on a left–right spectrum. In 2005 some felt that the party was positioned somewhere to the left of Labour by advocating a 50-per-cent tax on earnings over £100,000. Others felt that the party was closer to the Conservatives on the issue of choice in the public services. The policy review announced in the aftermath of the general election may result in a more distinctive programme but only if due consideration is given to which groups might constitute core supporters and where the Liberal Democrats stand in relation to other parties.

Before the 2005 election the party's main competitors were the Conservatives (predominantly in the South of England). The large reduction in the Labour vote in some areas means, however, that after the 2005 election the Liberal Democrats are now also within striking distance of a whole clutch of Labour seats in urban Britain. This presents the party with a major strategic dilemma: if it moves to the left in an effort to attract former Labour voters it risks alienating voters in seats that it currently holds in the South.

What the party really needs, of course, is electoral reform at Westminster. This almost certainly depends on a hung parliament in which the Liberal Democrats constitute the balance of power. This outcome looks increasingly possible after the 2005 election. Even if the Conservatives recover they are unlikely to recover enough to form a government on their own. In the circumstances of a hung parliament the Liberal Democrats may be able to negotiate electoral reform as a price for their support in any coalition government. In other words, the Liberal Democrats' future electoral success depends on growing dissatisfaction with Labour and a rejuvenated Conservative Party. Their fate is not in their own hands. Paradoxically, however, the Liberal Democrats may find themselves losing seats at the next election and yet acquire more influence both in the next parliament (as coalition makers) and in subsequent elections (as one of the increased number of possible coalition partners in a more pluralistic party system). David Cameron might be well advised to start making approaches to the Liberal Democrats in order to open the door to post-election negotiations. Of course, if none of this happens we will gladly follow Churchill's advice and explain why it didn't...!

# Chapter 6

# Political Participation Beyond the Electoral Arena

WILLIAM MALONEY

Much of the contemporary concern about a 'crisis of participation' has been catalysed by growing distrust of politicians and democratic institutions and by low and falling electoral turnout. Both phenomena have been directly correlated to the growth of citizen disenchantment and political disengagement. As documented in a plethora of surveys over the last ten years or so trust in government, political parties and politicians is low compared to other state institutions such as the police and courts (see below for further details). In addition to this, turnout at the 2001 and 2005 general elections was 59.8 per cent and 61.3 per cent respectively – down from an average of 76.5 per cent in elections between 1945 and 1997 (with the high point being 83.9 per cent in 1950 and the low 71.4 per cent in 1997). In other elections turnout has also been low – for the Scottish Parliament elections in 1999 and 2003 it was 58 per cent and 49.4 per cent; the Welsh Assembly in 2003 it was 38.2 per cent; the 2004 London mayoral election it was 36.4 per cent; the London Assembly it was 36 per cent; and for the European Parliament in 1999 and 2004 it was 24 per cent and 38 per cent. Finally, between 1973 and 2004 average turnout at English metropolitan council elections has been below 40 per cent. It should be noted that declining turnout is not a peculiarly British phenomenon – many advanced democracies are subject to this 'pathology'. Nevertheless, the data on trust and turnout have fuelled a sense of 'crisis' among the political class and some quarters of academia.

While elections are crucial for political legitimation there is more to democracy than the occasional vote. Arguably a vibrant democracy requires citizens to be involved on a more regular basis than simply at election times. If they are not, then Rousseau's question, '[A]re the people of England free only once every five years when choosing whom they will be subservient to?' would continue to resonate. In fact, citizens participate in a variety of ways: by political-party or interest-group membership; by signing petitions; by writing to, faxing, e-mailing or telephoning elected representatives (such as MPs, MEPs, MSPs, councillors); by boycotting or buying specific products for political reasons; by taking part in demonstrations and marches, and so forth. This chapter focuses specifically on the roles and functions of organised interests in British democracy and is predicated on the assumption that most citizens seeking to promote, defend or advance a cause look for a relevant group as an effective transmission belt.

(Interest) groups are seen as crucial to democracy for several reasons. Firstly, they facilitate citizen involvement beyond the periodic casting of votes. If involvement is limited to voting, citizens may not feel particularly satisfied that they have done enough, or been afforded sufficient opportunity, to affect outcomes in the areas of greatest concern to them. Involvement in non-party political organisations may provide a more nourishing and satisfying participatory diet. Secondly, some authors have portrayed groups as the democratic successors to political parties. Even leading party scholars have argued that interest groups have become increasingly important as citizens eschew involvement in parties in favour of groups: 'Fewer individuals now take on political roles as loyal party members, perhaps preferring to participate via non-partisan single-issue groups' (Farrell and Webb 2000, 123). Others have pointed to the explosion in the number of groups since the 1960s and the growth in membership levels. The evidence of greater group mobilisation is compelling. The 1998 *Directory of British Associations* listed over 7,000 organisations and associations – half of which had been formed since 1960. In 2005 membership of the UK Labour Party was estimated at below 200,000, whilst that for the Conservative Party was around 300,000 in 2002. In 2004 Eurobarometer reported that only 2 per cent of UK citizens (a mere 880,000) were members of a political party. Forty years earlier the combined membership of the two UK governing parties was around 3 million. Today group members far outnumber their party counterparts. The National Trust has some 2.7 million members and the Royal Society for the Protection of Birds (RSPB) and the Consumers' Association over 1 million; the Countryside Alliance claims over 100,000 ordinary members and a further 250,000 associate members.

Thirdly, groups are important participants in the policy-making process, acting as intermediaries between government and the citizenry, bargaining and negotiating over policy details. Such functions serve further to legitimate the policy-making process. Fourthly, there has been a revival of interest in the civic and democratic contribution of groups, stimulated by debates surrounding the concept of 'social capital' (see below). The current (or recurring) theme is that citizens' political engagement and involvement is on the wane (this is evidenced in declining voting turnout and diminishing levels of social and political trust). It has been argued that a revitalisation of patterns of political and civic engagement will compensate for the assumed deficiencies of modern democracies.

## Political participation and patterns of involvement

One of the key questions with regards to participation is: Who participates? The standard model of participation is that those with higher socioeconomic status (SES) participate more than those with low levels, i.e., citizens rich in specific resources – money, skills and education – predominate. In a recent UK population survey Pattie et al. (2004, 85, 103) reconfirmed this finding. Less affluent citizens, those in manual occupations and those with the least education were the most politically inactive. Wealthy citizens in professional or managerial occupations with high levels of educational attainment participated the most. Individuals with household incomes above £50,000 were found to be twice as likely to have engaged in five or more political actions and eleven times more likely to be a member of five or more groups than those with incomes below £10,000. Manual workers were twice as likely to take no political action compared to professionals or managers.

So, what proportion of the UK population are members of groups? And what types of groups do they join? Pattie et al. (2004) estimated that almost one third of the UK population are members of one group (excluding membership of motoring organisations). In 2004 Eurobarometer reported that 44 per cent of the UK population were not members of any group and that 29 per cent were members of one group, 16 per cent of two and 5 per cent of three. Figure 6.1 shows the types of organisations that UK citizens join. It is not surprising that non-political organisations are more popular (sports, outdoor activity groups, hobby clubs etc.). However, Pattie et al.'s (2004) data point to groups being the democratic successors to parties because citizens are also members of professional, environmental, human and animal rights groups. Of course, the proportion of the population who are members of overtly political groups is low (in 12 of the 23 categories it is 2 per cent or below). Nevertheless, as Pattie et al. (2004) highlight, a membership level of 1 per cent translates into over 440,000 members. The cumulative effect of individually low rates can be substantial.

Yet membership is only one aspect of involvement, and arguably not the most important. It is perfectly possible for individuals to join an organisation and to remain completely passive. What proportion of group members are active? Pattie et al. (2004) found that most political participation in Britain was of an individualistic rather than collective form. Typically, it involved donating money, signing a petition, boycotting products, ethical shopping and so forth rather than attending meetings, rallies or a demonstration. Thus, Pattie et al. (2004, 77–8, 98–9) found that donation was the most popular activity – 62 per cent of the respondents had donated money, 30 per cent had raised funds for a

**Figure 6.1** *Types of organisational membership in Britain*

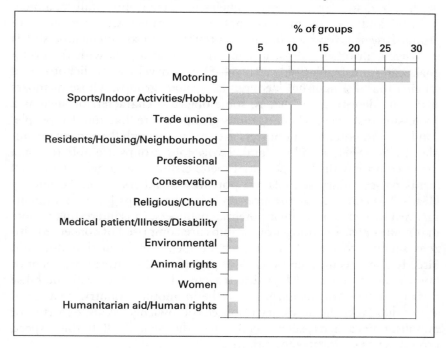

*Source*: Data from Pattie et al. (2004, 98)

group, 41 per cent had never attended meetings and 51 per cent never participated in decision making. In summary, the picture is mixed. A significant proportion of UK citizens are group members (about one third), but active involvement is a minority sport – passive (or 'cheque-book') participation is the norm.

## Groups and the policy-making process

### Categorising groups: the sectional/promotional and insider/outsider distinctions

#### *The sectional/promotional distinction*

Over the last 50 years or so scholars have categorised groups in various ways. For example, Stewart (1958, 25) distinguished between *sectional* and *cause* groups. Sectional groups seek to advance the common interests of their members; their membership is normally restricted to that particular section of society (for example, farmers, doctors, lawyers, trade unionists and so on). Cause groups represent some belief or principle (such as human rights, poverty, homelessness, environmentalism, animal welfare) and seek to advance that specific cause. Cause groups are primarily seen as representing non-economic interests and membership is inclusive – in other words, any individual that agrees with the group goals can join. Dunleavy (1991, 54–5) also developed a dichotomised schema that distinguished between *exogenous* groups, whose members share an 'identity set' – that is, some objective characteristic such as a professional status; and *endogenous* groups where 'like-minded people' combine and potential supporters are spread through the society (examples include Shelter and Oxfam). *Exogenous* groups are able to make direct contact with their potential membership in a targeted way – all heads of secondary schools are potential members of the Secondary Heads Association, for instance. Endogenous groups have no straightforward way to identify their potential members. (It is interesting to note that many cause or endogenous groups are comprised of concerned citizens seeking to remedy an important social problem that does not directly affect them, such as AIDS or poverty in the African continent or homelessness.) There are logistical reasons why groups may not mobilise their clientele – for instance, it may be in another country, or a social group that lacks the necessary resources (knowledge, skills, expertise or mobilisation capacity) such as children or the mentally ill. In this respect, groups act as surrogates for citizens.

It is clear that these dichotomous categorisations have much in common. Moreover, their parsimony and (rough) correspondence to the empirical world make them attractive. However, there is the problem of blurring boundaries. For example, Fathers 4 Justice and the Shared Parenting Information Group (SPIG) UK can be seen as promoting 'responsible shared parenting after separation and divorce'. But these bodies are also partly sectional interests representing separated and divorced individuals seeking greater access to their children. The British Medical Association (BMA) also blurs the distinction, campaigning for enhanced terms and conditions for members, whilst also promoting public health in general. In 2005, along with the British Heart Foundation and Action on Smoking and Health (ASH) – a cause group created by a sectional interest (the Royal College of Physicians) in 1972 – the BMA pressed government for a total ban on smoking in public bars in England and Wales. As this shows, groups can engage in both sectional and promotional activities.

### The insider/outsider distinction

Interest groups rely on two types of lobbying strategies – those of *insider* and *outsider* (Grant 1978). Groups that pursue an *insider* strategy are involved in a closed, behind-the-scenes non-confrontational relationship with politicians and civil servants. These groups must be prepared to 'behave responsibly' and keep the details of their negotiations confidential. They are viewed as legitimate interests by government and are engaged in a process of bargaining and exchange inside *policy communities*. Policy communities contain a limited number of groups and relevant civil servants. To become a member of a policy community groups need to possess (or be perceived to possess) a resource that government deems valuable – in other words detailed and authoritative information, implementation power, or the ability to ensure compliance by members with policy decisions. The benefits of insider status are great and may include advance notice of potential or actual policy changes, regular and routinised consultation on relevant issues, involvement in policy design and implementation and so forth. In short, groups that enjoy insider status have a greater impact on policy outcomes than those organisations 'outside the tent'.

*Outsider* group strategies are based on appeals to the public via media campaigns and other high-profile activities such as demonstrations, protests, petitions, boycotts, direct action, and in a very small minority of cases, violence. In 2005, Forest (Freedom Organisation for the Right to Enjoy Smoking Tobacco) placed a number of advertisements in national newspapers claiming that survey research demonstrates that a majority of British citizens opposed a total ban on smoking in pubs, bars and restaurants in England and Wales. The Make Poverty History (MPH) campaign asked supporters to register their support online and specifically stated that it didn't want supporters' money, but their names. Greenpeace and the pro-hunt lobby engaged in direct campaigns (Greenpeace occupied the cargo ship *MV Etoile* in the Bristol Channel claiming that it was carrying illegal genetically modified animal feed and pro-hunt campaigners infamously invaded the House of Commons). The Animal Liberation Front (ALF) reportedly engaged in a campaign of intimidation and attacks on individuals (and property) at Darley Oaks Farm in Staffordshire where guinea pigs are bred for medical research. (The ALF could be labelled an *ideological outsider*. Unlike most groups that attempt to influence policy outcomes it does not seek insider status, believing that such 'cosiness' would compromise its anti-system principles.) Clearly outsiders lack the privileged access enjoyed by insiders and have to increase pressures on policy makers through public and media-oriented activities. The aim is to politicise the relevant issue and remove it from the relatively 'closed' confines of the policy community to involve a wider range of participants.

Groups most closely associated – although not exclusively – with insider politics are professional and business groups (the Law Society, the Institute of Directors, the National Farmers' Union, Chemical Industries Association, and so on). While many insider groups articulate sectional interests this does not mean that all sectional groups are insiders. In addition to this, groups are not trapped into insider- or outsider-style politics. There are occasions when sectional or cause interests or 'insiders' and 'outsiders' will draw on a combination of tactics and strategies. Outsiders would not be averse to pursuing insider strategies (indeed many covet insider status) and outsiders do not baulk at more high-profile activities. In September 2005 the BMA publicly accused the government of speaking with contradictory voices. On the one hand the government said that its preferred option on smoking in public places was to ban smoking in establishments that served food. Simultaneously the Department of Health launched a £5 million advertising campaign warning of the dangers to adults of secondhand/passive smoking in their own homes. The Blair administration became embroiled in an unusually non-insider high-profile spat with the Criminal Bar Association over legal-aid fees. There are also many examples of cause groups being effective on the 'insider' track (the Snowdrop Campaign, the RSPB, the Howard League for Penal Reform).

## Pressure group resources and functions

Why do democratically elected governments listen to unelected pressure groups? Largely for two main reasons: (1) groups have useful resources (such as a large membership; policy expertise; economic and social power; and implementation power); and (2) groups carry out certain functions that can be seen as democratically beneficial. So what kind of resources are useful? Members, especially in large numbers, can be important. They provide some of the funds necessary to carry out professional campaigning. For organisations such as Greenpeace members are vital because they provide almost 90 per cent of the groups' total income. Big numbers also maintain government attention. After all, members are voters and the larger the membership the greater the organisational claims of legitimacy and representativeness. For example, groups such as the Consumers Association and the RSPB with 1 million members (and bodies such as the Earl Haig Fund, National Pensioners' Convention and National Society for the Prevention of Cruelty to Children with over 1 million supporters) will be seen as legitimate. (The distinction between *members* and *supporters* is largely based on the fact that members pay an annual subscription and enjoy certain membership privileges whereas supporters may simply donate money with no membership rights.) At interview, an RSPB representative said, 'Having a million members is a great lobbying and persuasive tool to dangle in front of the government ... that's why we put a lot of emphasis on keeping the million' (Jordan and Maloney 1997, 191). Numbers count!

Accurate and detailed information on particular policy problems is a significant resource. Policy makers do not know all the intricate details of every policy area and rely on groups to provide information that permits them to formulate good, workable (and implementable) policy. Thus car manufacturers, environmental, consumer and safety groups will provide policy makers with detailed *technical* information on the environmental impact and safety of motor vehicles. Many groups also possess *political* knowledge relating to the political system: i.e. how to mobilise and campaign effectively in Westminster and Whitehall. Technical or political knowledge can also be seen as substitute goods that can compensate for a lack of other resources.

Governments also heed groups that are socially or economically significant (professional associations, such as those of doctors, lawyers and teachers, peak associations and multinational companies). Business is influential because it has many advantages in the policy-making process, most notably its economic significance. Business success is crucial to the success of the British economy and employment levels. The oil and alcohol industries generate large sums for the Treasury in excise duty and corporate tax as well as being major employers. Business also possesses a great deal of technical and political knowledge. Finally, many groups in the policy-making process have the responsibility for implementing policy decisions and can be said to hold *implementation* power. Governments do not and cannot directly implement specific policy proposals. If specific types of tests are to be introduced in schools, it is teachers who have to make them work. Similarly, if new laws are introduced relating to policing then it is the police that hold the implementation power. If teachers or the police refuse to implement specific changes or do so in a selective manner then the policy aims may be subverted or undermined altogether. Thus policy makers realise that it is important to carry the implementers of policy with them when they are seeking to make reforms. There are few examples of organisations refusing to implement policy wholesale, but many of partial implementation – with the result that a policy has not achieved its intended aims. For example, the Scottish Health Campaigns Network (SHCN) highlighted the manipulation of waiting list figures in 2005 to reach government-set targets. Through the use of codes attached to patients by health boards in Scotland, some 36,000 people were removed from 'guaranteed waiting-time lists'. The SHCN also claimed that patients were being offered treatments at very short notice or when they were on holiday, forcing them to refuse the treatment at that point and subsequently being allocated codes that removed them from the lists.

It is clear from the above that resources are important in an organisation's attempt to affect policy outcomes. However, what types of functions do organisations carry out that could be seen as enhancing the democratic process? First, groups have a *representational* function. Groups represent people before government. Those with an interest in an issue can join a political organisation and advance their shared concerns. This perspective sees groups as a useful and necessary addition to representative democracy. However, not all scholars share this view. Defenders of the party system may argue that groups distort the democratic process, because governments become embroiled in a bargaining game with unelected (and unrepresentative) entities.

Pressure groups also have a *participatory* function, facilitating citizen involvement in the political system (beyond voting). Groups provide a linkage between the governed and government. Without such linkage citizens may become alienated and the stability of democratic systems would be undermined. Groups perform an *educative* function, informing the public about hazards or dangers, or the consequences of their consumption patterns. Citizens are aware of the environmental consequences of their consumption partly as a result of the educative activities of environmental groups. Groups are always highlighting new or emerging problems. In 2005 the Soil Association claimed that the fruit and vegetables provided free in schools had 25 per cent more pesticide residue than those sold in shops. Groups play a key role in setting the political agenda. They can generate public (and media) support for their aims and force issues onto or up the agenda. The Make Poverty History campaign is one of the most recent and notable examples. Finally, and related to agenda setting, groups monitor programmes and may uncover the partial or non-implementation of policies (as in the NHS waiting-list example above).

## 'New' and 'newer' types of political participation

Three types of involvement have become increasingly prevalent (and important) in recent years: political protest, chequebook participation and cyberactivism. The volume of protest activity appears to have grown and the issue areas that have witnessed such actions are increasingly diverse. Chequebook participation has become ubiquitous touching almost every area of political participation. Finally, cyberactivism and the growth of e-mail and internet usage have the potential to be an important participatory tool.

## Political protest

While political protest may have a contemporaneous feel, it actually has a very long history, dating from the Chartists in the mid-19th century via the suffragettes in the late 19th and early 20th century, to the Campaign for Nuclear Disarmament (CND) in the late 1950s and the anti-cruise missile protests at Greenham Common in the 1980s. Of course, recent years have witnessed a large number of high-profile protests – opposition to the community charge/poll tax (1990), Brent Spar (the successful Greenpeace direct-action campaign against the deep-sea disposal of this oil platform in 1995), the export of live animals (veal calves) from the UK (1995), Snowdrop Appeal (Dunblane massacre, 1996), second runway at Manchester airport (1997), proposal to ban fox hunting (1998, 2004–05), petrol protest (2000), the Iraq war (2003), Fathers 4 Justice (2004) and the G8 protests (2005).

Protest groups come in all shapes and sizes and pursue a variety of strategies and tactics to advance specific causes (such as petitions, sits-in, product boycotts, civil disobedience and direct action). In the animal rights/welfare field activities range from traditional lobbying and peaceful campaigning to direct action and sometimes illegal activities. For example, groups such as the Royal Society for the Prevention of Cruelty to Animals, Animal Aid and Compassion in World Farming engage in peaceful activities that oppose cruelty to animals. At the opposite end of the spectrum lie groups such as the ALF or Stop Huntingdon Animal Cruelty (Shac). Shac has targeted employees at the Huntingdon Life Science laboratories – even resorting to physical violence against staff and carrying out fire-bomb attacks.

Traditionally protest campaigns were undertaken by (left-leaning) 'new politics' groups (peace, environmentalism, human rights, and so on) perceived as engaging in 'unconventional participation' (as opposed to conventional involvements such as voting, joining groups or parties, contacting politicians). However, such modes of protest are no longer the preserve of the left. Indeed, they have become so commonplace that it is no longer meaningful to describe them as unconventional. The 'establishment' anti-fox-hunting campaigners who invaded the House of Commons in 2005, or the Rossport Five (three farmers and two retired teachers) who were imprisoned in June 2005 for their direct action protest against the construction of a gas pipeline in North Mayo in Ireland, do not quite fit the profile of left-leaning anti-system protesters.

It is also interesting to note that protest activities have an increasingly transnational remit and focus. For example, Greenpeace's Brent Spar campaign in 1995 was part of an internationally coordinated campaign throughout Europe. Greenpeace (Germany) orchestrated a boycott of

Shell petrol stations in Germany, while the British direct-action protestors occupied the oil platform. There were also anti-capitalist campaigns in London in 1999 and Edinburgh in 2005, and the Stop the War and the Make Poverty History coalitions involved campaigners from many countries.

It is clear that there is a great deal of protest politics taking place in the UK political system. However, it is important to ask ourselves the thorny question: What difference does it make? The Make Poverty History march in Edinburgh had an estimated 225,000 participants. The *Guardian* (13 July 2005) reported that 360,000 Make Poverty History supporters e-mailed Prime Minister Blair and that 9.3 million wristbands were sold. There were circa 3 million texts for 'free' tickets to the Live8 concerts in Hyde Park and Murrayfield. (It is, however, interesting to speculate how many e-mailers, texters and wristband wearers actually attended the Edinburgh rally.) The aim of this campaign was to press the G8 leaders to drop African debt and to establish a fairer trade system. However, while Bob Geldof proclaimed the G8 summit a success, post Live8 many charities did not share his enthusiasm:

> ... the World Development Movement described the agreement as 'a disaster for the world's poor'. Action Aid complained that 'the G8 have completely failed to deliver trade justice'. Christian Aid called July 8 'a sad day for poor people in Africa and all over the world'. Oxfam lamented that 'neither the necessary sense of urgency nor the historic potential of Gleneagles was grasped by the G8 ...' (George Monbiot, *Guardian* 6 September 2005)

It also emerged that Germany and Italy might not meet their commitments and the Chancellor, Gordon Brown conceded that the debt relief funds included in the aid package promised by the G8 was not all additional funds. It has been estimated that between $8 and $12 billion of the $25 billion promised at the Gleneagles summit was new money, the remainder having been announced prior to the meeting. It is worth juxtaposing the response of the US federal government in the immediate aftermath of Hurricane Katrina. The US Congress appropriated $62.3 billion and it is reported that the total federal contribution could easily exceed $200 billion (*San Francisco Chronicle* 14 September 2005) – completely dwarfing the funds allocated by the G8 for Africa. The Stop the (Iraq) War coalition actually mobilised greater numbers on the streets than the Make Poverty History campaign, but it had no effect on the US–British decision to remove Saddam Hussein.

There are, however, many examples of successful campaigns: the

Snowdrop Campaign led to the banning of handguns in the UK; the Anti-Poll Tax Federation was important in the replacement of the community charge/poll tax with the council tax; Greenpeace's Brent Spar protest; the petrol protests in 2000 also influenced the Chancellor's excise-duty deliberations – although the 2005 event was a damp squib. The Stop the (Iraq) War coalition and Make Poverty History campaigns may not be able to claim the same degree of success. Nevertheless, these mobilisations demonstrate the symbolic importance of protest and played a key role in terms of keeping the issues on the political agenda and raising public consciousness.

Finally, it is worth noting that groups do not measure success simply in policy-outcome terms. Fathers 4 Justice claims that its high-profile media-oriented campaigns since 2000 have been highly successful (stunts included one group member dressed as Batman scaling Buckingham Palace and another handcuffing themself to the then Children's Minister, Margaret Hodge). The group points to increased media coverage – grabbing more newspaper headlines than many other well-established campaign groups such as Amnesty International and Greenpeace. Fathers 4 Justice claimed that the number of media articles on theor chosen issue has increased by over 700 per cent and that this has '*engaged the political establishment* and encouraged opposition parties to take up their fight' (original emphasis) (www.fathers-4-justice.org).

## Chequebook participation

The 1960s ushered in a period of expansion in the number of (public-interest) groups in the UK. Many of these organisations were in the 'new politics' genre (Greenpeace, Friends of the Earth) and evolved into large-scale bureaucratised chequebook groups populated by full-time professionals. Chequebook groups seek mimimalistic participation for supporters. In other words signing a cheque or completing a direct-debit form is the beginning and the end of the involvement for the overwhelming majority of supporters. For these groups a mass membership is an important tool in the process of campaigning. As highlighted above, it provides the necessary financial resources (through subscriptions and donations) and enhances organisational claims to legitimacy and representativeness.

Many chequebook groups are unashamedly oligarchic. Accordingly, these organisations have been criticised for the absence of internal democratic procedures and social-capital-building capacities. Chequebook participation is seen as creating links between the individual member and the group, not between members. The membership ties that exist are to 'common symbols, common leaders, and perhaps common ideals, but not to one another' (Putnam 1995, 71) and citizens eschew democratic participation in favour of indirect political participation. There are several reasons why these bodies have opted for such an organisational structure. First, being a supporter- as opposed to a member-based organisation circumvents the problems of internal democracy and policy interference. Second, it is impracticable (and impossible) to involve directly tens or hundreds of thousands of members in a group's activities. Third, is the growth of patronage. Some organisations are heavily reliant on patronage and do not require a grassroots membership. Fourth, for many groups members have become a 'luxury' because they can exercise influence without them. As Crenson and Ginsberg (2002, 147) argue, 'The new politics of policymaking attempts to open itself "to all those who have ideas and expertise rather than to those who assert interest and preferences". Those admission requirements exclude the great mass of ordinary citizens.' Affecting outcomes appears to require less membership muscle and the ability to represent the members and rather more policy expertise and professionalism.

To provide a balanced assessment of the role of chequebook groups in democracies it should be noted that these organisations do not see it as part of their raison d'être to expand participatory democracy or to build social capital. The aim is to campaign for the relevant interest as effectively as possible. The organisational view is that contributions are given freely and if contributors disagree with policy positions or campaigning tactics then they are free to withdraw their support. This is a market-based perspective with a supplier–customer-type relationship. Many groups undertake sophisticated market research to gauge members' views on a variety of issues and it could be argued that group direction is steered by supporter/member attitudes. To a certain extent there is some (however tenuous) degree of responsiveness. There is also evidence that chequebook participators are content (and in many case actively seek) to *contract out* the participatory function. A survey of members of the campaign groups Friends of the Earth and Amnesty International (British section) found that an overwhelming majority of members said that they did not join these organisations to be 'active in political issues', and over 70 per cent believed that the groups offered the best means to advance human rights and environmental protection (Jordan and Maloney 1997). In fact, a Council for the Protection of Rural England representative claimed the group feared losing members by pressing for active involvement: '... people want to give money and they don't want to do anymore than that ...' (Jordan and Maloney, forthcoming 2006). In this light, chequebook participation can be seen as a purposive activity: contracting out protest to professional campaigners. Finally, Rosenblum (1998, 234–5) is critical of those who dismissively label chequebook involvement as synthetic, '... *it is churlish to deny that this is democratic participation on a massive scale* ... it brings day-to-day politics that are otherwise distant and physically remote ... home' (emphasis added).

## Cyberactivism

The political potential of the Internet is great given that some 30 million adults (around 70 per cent of the UK population) have access to it. Of course, much e-contact does not have a political component – Ward et al. (2003, 664) found that only 17 per cent of the respondents in their sample used the internet for political purposes. Nevertheless, electronic communication was an important tool in the organisation of anti-capitalism protests in Seattle (1999), London (2000) and Genoa (2001) and the Stop the (Iraq) War (2003) demonstrations. It also has the potential to create new forms of involvement (electronic voting, e-polling, e-consultation and e-petitions).

The contribution of the Internet to political involvement is hotly disputed. The gamut of views runs from the optimists who see it as having the potential to reinvigorate democracy by widening involvement and expanding participatory opportunities to those who see it as breeding uncritical, ill-informed, atomised citizens broadening social cleavages and hampering collective action. However, in which direction does the evidence point? Ward et al. (2003, 662) found that the Countryside Alliance's e-bulletin was important in generating participation. Some 31 per cent of members that used the Internet said that the Alliance's website '... was an important stimulus in their decision to take part in the march on London' in 2002. With regard to widening political involvement, Ward et al. (2003, 665) discovered the Internet reinforced some existing biases and simultaneously expanded the participation of other under-represented groups: almost one third of e-participators were 'educated upper-middle-class' citizens (the 'usual suspects'), while manual workers comprised only 16 per cent of those that participated via the Internet. Ward et al. (2003) also found that those aged between 15 to 24, while being a relatively small group in their sample, were amongst the heaviest e-participators – outsurfing those in the 45–54 age range. They concluded that the Internet makes:

> ... a modest contribution to participation and mobilisation. Whilst the internet does not universally lower the costs of participation, it may bring some new individuals and groups into the political process – notably younger people ... it seems most likely to assist the increasingly prominent development of protest networks, flash and single-issue campaigns. (Ward et al. 2003, 667)

In short, the Internet has acquired the potential to be an important mechanism for increasing political knowledge, interest and involvement, especially among the young. It has proven to be a useful tool in the mobilisation and coordination of protest activities on a national and transnational basis.

## Social capital

The concept of social capital is in vogue in political (and social) science. The (apparently) exponentially expanding literature has gathered momentum for two main reasons. First, the concept has transferred relatively easily across disciplinary and subdisciplinary divides. Second, it has promised so much for so many. It has been claimed that social capital has a significant impact on economic, social and political life. Associations are core to the social-capital model. The leading social-capital scholar – Robert Putnam – believes voluntary associations are so crucial that he not only correlates membership with civic and democratic well-being, but even human morbidity and mortality:

> ... social capital makes us smarter, healthier, safer, richer, and better able to govern a just and stable democracy ... The more integrated we are with our community, the less likely we are to experience colds, heart attacks, strokes, cancer, depression and premature deaths of all sorts ... As a rough rule of thumb, if you belong to no groups but decide to join one, you cut your risk of dying over the next year in *half*. If you smoke and belong to no groups, it's a toss-up statistically whether you should stop smoking or start joining. (Putnam 2000, 290, 326, 331, original emphasis)

In his highly influential volume – *Bowling Alone* – Putnam (2000, 18–19) argues that '... the core idea of social capital theory is that social networks have value ... social capital refers to connections among individuals – social networks and the norms of reciprocity and trustworthiness that arise from them.' These social networks have a political impact:

> ... civil associations contribute to the effectiveness and stability of democratic government ... both because of their 'internal' effects on individual members and because of their 'external' effects on the wider polity. Internally, associations instill in their members habits of cooperation, solidarity, and public spiritedness ... Externally ... a dense network of secondary associations ... contributes to effective social collaboration. (Putnam 1993, 89–90)

Warren (2000) subsumes these internal and external effects within three broad categories – *developmental, public-sphere* and *institutional* effects. First, developmental effects facilitate and bolster the development of the democratic capacities of citizens. Associations enhance individual political efficacy by helping citizens develop political skills (those of oral presentation, negotiation, bargaining and compromise for instance), civic virtues (such as tolerance, mutual respect, trust, reciprocity, respect for justice, the rule of law and the rights of others) and critical skills (Warren 2000, 71–6). Second, we can point to public-sphere effects. Associations perform a public communication and deliberation function. They act as a conduit for citizen concerns and play a key role in forcing issues onto the political (and public) agenda(s) (examples include environmental and health problems and human rights abuses) (Warren 2000, 77–82). Third, we can identify a range of institutional effects. Groups act as countervailing powers and are heavily involved in the development and implementation of policy. Involvement in policy-making processes 'underwrite(s) the legitimacy of the state' and the legitimacy of policy outcomes (Warren 2000, 82–93).

Thus groups are seen as generators of social capital, engendering civic and political skills and democratic values; as such they act as an important lubricant for the 'proper' functioning of democracies. In general, the social-capital argument is that the denser and more vibrant the associational life, the healthier the society and democracy. Putnam (1993, 2000) provides a largely positive perspective on the social-capital model. It is important to note, however, that social capital is not necessarily a universally beneficial resource – social capital has a dark side. While it can be used to foster democratic outcomes by, for instance, facilitating the mobilisation of disadvantaged minorities or charitable or humanitarian aid organisations, it can also be an important resource for neo-fascist or racist groups. High levels of social capital can facilitate the perpetuation of economic, social and political inequality and can be a sign of a highly fragmented society. For example, in Northern Ireland there may be high levels of social capital within the separate communities, but the riots and violence following the (100-metre) re-routing of an Orange Order march at Whiterock, North Belfast in September 2005 is clearly not a sign of a well-functioning, integrated society. In response to such criticisms Putnam (2000) emphasised that social capital can emerge in two forms: bonding and bridging. Bonding creates strong intragroup ties that can, although by no means always, have pernicious qualities. Bridging creates ties that reach across diverse social groups and engenders tolerance, trust, reciprocity and mutual understanding and accommodation.

Putnam (2000) further argued that there has been a process of civic

erosion over several decades in the US: a declining number of associations and memberships. He highlighted declining participation rates in
bowling leagues in the US as indicative of the erosion occurring throughout the associational universe. Putnam discovered that while the total
number of bowlers increased by 10 per cent between 1980 and 1993, the
number of bowling leagues fell by 40 per cent. Hence his argument that
Americans were 'Bowling Alone'.

Is there any evidence of civic erosion in the UK? Hall (2002, 25) found
that average association membership in the UK increased by 44 per cent
between 1959 and 1990 and that '... overall levels of associational
memberships in Britain seem to have been at least as high in the 1980s
and 1990s as they were in 1959, and perhaps somewhat higher.' Pattie et
al. (2004, 51–2) found that civic commitment (a key social-capital
measure) was high: 'Seven in ten stated that they were willing to give
blood; a similar number are willing to assist in a Neighbourhood Watch
scheme; one in two are willing to assist in renovating a local park or
amenity.' They also found that British citizens were far from politically
apathetic. Over 75 per cent of their respondents had engaged in one or
more political actions (in the previous twelve months) and the mean
number of individual actions was 3.6. When chequebook involvement
(simply donating more) was excluded from the analysis the mean
remained high at 2.7. Pattie et al. (2004, 80) concluded that '... contrary
to the claims of political apathy, people frequently participate in activities
designed to influence political outcomes.' While Hall (2002, 25–7)
argued that '... most recent studies of the voluntary sector in Britain
conclude that it is extensive and vibrant.' In short, the British appear not
to be Bowling Alone.

Another key component of the social-capital model is trust – both
social and political. The social capital thesis maintains that social trust is
crucial to the health of democracy because when citizens trust each other
they are more likely to join organisations and to be cooperative in their
everyday lives. Political trust is also important because if citizens have
high levels of trust in political and other state institutions then they will
feel politically integrated and are more likely to participate. Pattie et al.
(2004, 36) found that the mean social-trust score for people with whom
citizens have contact was 6.59 – which they argue is close to the more
positive end of their 11-point (0–10) measurement scale. They also cite
evidence from the British Social Attitudes survey which shows that social
trust in the UK in the last 20 years has remained relatively stable. What
about political trust? Pattie et al. (2004, 37–8) found differing levels of
trust in various institutions: highest in the police, courts, and civil service
and least in government, political parties and politicians. The differences
are large, ranging from an average of 6.29 for the police to 3.26 for

politicians (on the 11-point scale). As outlined in the introduction, such low regard for core political institutions has been advanced as one of the explanatory factors accounting for declining voter turnout.

However, these trust measures are among the general population. Are there any differences between these levels and those shown by associational members? The social-capital model predicts that group membership engenders higher levels of social and political trust among citizens. In a survey of organisational members in Aberdeen (and Mannheim, Germany) Maloney and van Deth (2005) found that levels of social and political trust were significantly higher. The average level of trust in friends, co-associational members and office holders, and colleagues in Aberdeen was over 9 (on the same 11-point scale used in Pattie et al.'s research). Trust among UK citizens generally was above 7. With regard to political trust the pattern was identical to that found by Pattie et al. (2004): highest in the police, courts and the civil service and least in parties and politicians. However, group members have higher average levels of trust in all institutions – running from 7.68 in the police to 4.75 in politicians. The organisational membership data from Aberdeen provide some support for the social-capital model's prediction about the 'positive' benefits of membership. However, several interesting questions emerge from these findings. First, are politically trusting citizens more likely to join organisations? Or do associations breed such trust? Second, what are the implications for democracy of relatively high or low levels of political trust? Low political trust can be seen as an indicator of political alienation that bodes ill for democracy. Alternatively, it could be viewed as democratically healthy, demonstrating that citizens are attentive and critical.

## Conclusion: groups, participation and democracy

Verba et al. (1995) argue that debates about the decline of civic vitality and civic participation have missed the most important issue. That, they suggest, is not simply '… the amount of civic activity but its distribution, not just how many people take part but who are they'. While Hall (2002, 21) reported that associational memberships in the UK had grown in the 1959–90 period and that levels of social capital in Britain have 'remained relatively robust', he nevertheless noted that '… disparities among social groups in the distribution of social capital have widened over the period …'. Clearly the persistent problem for democracies is that of equality: citizens with higher socioeconomic status (SES) are over-represented in all areas of political involvement. They are more likely to join political parties and groups (holding multiple memberships), sign petitions, contact elected representatives, and so on. Governments and politicians are liable to respond to the priorities of participators. This creates a 'democratic paradox': those who potentially have the most to gain from the system (disadvantaged groups) participate the least. In recent years the equality problem has been accentuated by the recruiting practices of many (large-scale) interest groups. These organisations target individuals with specific sociodemographic profiles (typically high SES) and lifestyles because with them there is a greater chance of converting predisposition into membership. Such activities have distorted participation even further.

Finally, there are competing views on the net democratic benefit of group activity. Scholars with *pluralist* sympathies see the group system as beneficial. Those who hold a more *elitist* view perceive it as favouring certain groups. Elitist scholars are not impressed by the large number of groups in the political system: proliferation proves absolutely nothing about the distribution of power and does not necessarily increase competition. For example, if one particular interest (such as business) is over-represented in the group universe then 'other' interests may simply be 'crowded out'. Elitists also point to the lesser or non-involvement of many disadvantaged social groups and argue that power is concentrated in the hands of a few key groups and institutions in society (corporate interests). Most famously, Schattschneider argued that:

> The flaw in the pluralist heaven is that the heavenly chorus sings with a strong upper-class accent ... Pressure politics is a selective process ill designed to serve diffuse interests. The system is skewed, loaded, and unbalanced in favor of a fraction of a minority. (Schattschneider 1960, 35)

The pluralist perspective sees groups as enhancing democracy. Group proliferation is perceived as beneficial and groups provide a key linkage between citizen and government. Groups compete and while some interests are resource-rich and more influential, pluralists argue that these groups do not dominate the policy-making process in the way that elitists suggest. Such interests do not 'win' all the time and those with fewer resources are not perpetual losers. Groups act as surrogates for individuals and the broader representation delivered by the group system is democratically advantageous. In short, groups are integral to and inseparable from democracy: without groups there would be no democracy.

## Chapter 7

# The Half-hearted Constitutional Revolution

MATTHEW FLINDERS

This chapter examines the Labour government's programme of constitutional reform since May 1997, with a particular emphasis on developments towards the end of the 2001–05 Parliament. As there is now an admirable body of work that describes how specific elements of the British constitution have been reformed under New Labour the aim of this chapter is not to describe but to analyse and evaluate the manner in which the constitution has been reformed. Moreover, this chapter seeks to examine the implications this has both for British democracy and for the manner in which students of politics interpret and understand British politics and government. The reforms enacted by the Labour government have undoubtedly been far-reaching, but they have not been radical. The 'constitutional revolution' has been designed, implemented and in many ways restrained by an increasingly questionable conception of the Westminster model (WM) that has sought to retain parliamentary sovereignty. However, important reforms have clearly been implemented, the full consequences of which may not become obvious for some time.

The first part of this chapter focuses on constitutional developments since May 1997. The second reviews the extent and breadth of the constitutional reform process by examining the House of Lords Bill and the Constitutional Reform Act 2005, measures which provided lightning rods for wider concerns and anxieties regarding its long-term trajectory. The third part examines the manner in which the Labour government's constitutional reforms have altered the nature of British democracy, and suggests that the British polity is best understood as a fledgling system of multilevel governance which is evolving *within* an increasingly fragile WM, and considers the long-term implications of this situation.

Before examining developments since 1997 it is worth briefly reflecting on the fact that a range of competing interpretations or understandings relate to the aims and priorities of a political system's constitutional arrangements. Understanding these varying positions (and the tensions

117

arising from them) helps explain why the British constitution has evolved in the manner it has, why certain elements have not been reformed, and why there is an oft-noted discrepancy between a commitment to radical reform in *principle* and actual reform in *practice*. In essence, constitutions form the mechanism through which a basic democratic tension is played out and reconciled: the tension between providing the government with the capacity to govern while also ensuring that certain procedures and processes are followed, basic limits exist and those wielding public power are held to account. Birch's *Representative and Responsible Government* of 1964 sought to clarify and illuminate this tension by highlighting what he called the 'Liberal' (emphasising open, transparent and accountable government) and 'Whitehall' (stressing strong, stable government) views of the constitution (see Table 7.1).

The history of the British constitution is really based around views and arguments regarding how best to balance these views. In the nineteenth century the participatory demands of reformers concerning the extension of the franchise demanded new, or at least revised, mechanisms through which the capacity of ministers (and their officials) to govern could be insulated and protected. It was in this context that the convention of ministerial responsibility to Parliament was enshrined as the constitutional tool or 'buckle' through which both the Liberal and Whitehall views of the constitution could be balanced (Flinders 2002b). However, the development of mass-based political parties and tight party management within the House of Commons shifted the balance of power in favour of the executive in ways that had not been anticipated in the middle of the nineteenth century. Throughout the twentieth century a large number of books – including Low (1904), Hewart (1929), Hollis (1949), and Butt (1969) – reported the existence of an

**Table 7.1**    *Comparing the Liberal and Whitehall views of the British constitution*

| Liberal | Whitehall |
|---------|-----------|
| Parliamentary government | Strong government |
| Representative | Responsible |
| Inclusion | Exclusion |
| Responsiveness | Distance |
| Participation | Stability |
| Accountability | Realism |
| Direction | Control |
| Exposure of ministers | Insulation of ministers |

over-mighty executive, lamented the diminishing role and power of parliament and put forward a range of reform proposals.

The ascendancy of the executive went beyond institutional relationships, also affecting the value basis or morality of the constitution. Governments are likely for obvious reasons to prioritise the implementation of their policies ahead of measures that may frustrate their capacity for governing. Judge (1993) suggested that a 'negative executive mentality' exists which supports and protects the Whitehall view of the constitution and seeks to reject or weaken, through the government's control of backbenchers, reforms designed to shift the balance back towards the Liberal view. This leads on to a second point: those who argue that constitutional reform is necessary are adopting an explicit normative (or value-laden) position. For much of the twentieth century those whose sympathies lie with the Whitehall view could convincingly have maintained that the constitution was working perfectly well and was in no need of reform – it was delivering stable government with the capacity to govern within a framework of parliamentary control between general elections and popular control at general elections.

In many ways, however, the day-to-day reality of modern politics is far more complex than the Liberal and Whitehall views represent. Moreover, factors such as history, tradition, political culture, and existing institutional design create an intricate web of constraints that militate, in many ways, against anything other than incremental reform. The two views outlined above, however, do provide a useful framework for understanding how different values underpin whether constitutional reform is necessary and to what degree. The two views could be understood as opposite poles with most political systems sitting somewhere in between. Britain, during the 1980s and 1990s, was perceived as drifting too far towards the Whitehall view end and a reform momentum developed that was intent on shifting the balance back towards the Liberal view (see Flinders 2005a). Finally, the Whitehall/Liberal distinction also helps, to some extent, to explain the frequent failure of new governments to make good their pre-election promises to institute far-reaching constitutional reform. The movement from opposition to government (and vice versa) generally produces a swing from one view to the other. New governments frequently renege upon their commitments to wholesale reform and embrace the strong-government Whitehall view while outgoing governments often develop a zeal for the Liberal view. The interesting feature of New Labour's transfer from opposition to government in May 1997 was that they were so heavily committed to a number of aspects of constitutional reform that reneging on these commitments was simply not feasible.

## New Labour and the constitution

Having swept into power on 1 May 1997 Labour unleashed an almost frantic programme of constitutional reform. No less than 20 bills relating to constitutional reform were steered through Parliament during the first three parliamentary sessions facilitating devolution to Scotland and Wales, incorporation of the European Convention on Human Rights in a Human Rights Act, freedom of information legislation, reform of the House of Lords, operational independence to the Bank of England, and a range of other measures (see Table 7.2).

This degree of constitutional (hyper)activity was driven by two factors. First, implementing a number of these reforms, notably devolution, was irresistible due to a combination of popular pressures and long-standing pre-election commitments. Second, the government's commitment to staying within the previous Conservative administration's spending limits restricted major social and economic policy initiatives, thereby allowing the parliamentary timetable to accommodate a large amount of constitutional legislation without intense pressure from other members of the Cabinet for legislative space.

Table 7.2    *New Labour's main constitutional measures 1997–2005*

Referendums (Scotland and Wales) Act 1997
Scotland Act 1998
Government of Wales Act 1998
European Communities Amendment Act 1998
Bank of England Act 1998
Human Rights Act 1998
Northern Ireland (Elections) Act 1998
Regional Development Agencies Act 1998
Greater London Authority Act 1998
Registration of Political Parties Act 1998
European Parliament Elections Act 1998
House of Lords Act 1999
Freedom of Information Act 2000
Local Government Act 2000
Political Parties, Elections and Referendums Act 2000
Regional Assemblies (Preparations) Act 2003
Constitutional Reform Act 2005

Towards the end of the 1997 Parliament, however, a degree of constitutional fatigue set in. A number of senior ministers felt that constitutional issues had taken up too much time, were of little interest to the general public, and might have created a range of constitutional hurdles that might later thwart the government in pushing forward with major social, economic and public-sector reforms (see Morrison 2001). It is also important to appreciate that Tony Blair has never been a fully fledged supporter of constitutional reform. Many of the policies implemented during the first term were the legacy of John Smith's period as leader of the Labour Party which Tony Blair felt he had a moral and political duty to see through, albeit in a more limited manner than John Smith may have envisaged.

'The calm after the storm' might usefully sum up the general feeling in relation to the constitution at the end of New Labour's first term in office. A great number of potentially far-reaching reforms had been enacted but there was a sense that the time had come to allow these changes to 'bed in'. Moreover, there was also a feeling that the reform process may have moved too quickly; that the programme was bereft of any underpinning rationale, principled foundations or an awareness of its long-term consequences. William Hague's (1998) comment that 'Labour has embarked on a journey of constitutional upheaval without a route map' was not simply a partisan point. It reflected a deeper concern that the constitutional project lacked clarity with regard to both principles and outcomes. Lord Irvine (1998), then Lord Chancellor, sought to counter this criticism by arguing:

> The strands do not spring from a single master plan, however much that concept might appeal to purists. We prefer the empirical genius of our nation: to go, pragmatically, step by step, for change through continuing consent. Principled steps, not absolutist master plans, are the winning route to constitutional renewal in unity and in peace.

And yet the principles upon which the government's steps had been taken were far from clear. New Labour's first term therefore ended with an awareness that a great deal had been achieved but that there were still a number of areas of 'unfinished business', notably in relation to reform of the House of Commons, House of Lords and regional devolution within England. There was also a growing recognition that the reform process needed to be supported by a reformed institutional structure within Whitehall.

In June 2001 New Labour was re-elected with a Commons majority of 166. However, it was clear that the party's priorities had changed and also that the wider political context had altered. This distinct contextual change has in many ways mitigated against the Liberal view and placed greater emphasis on the benefits of the strong-government-imbued elements of the Whitehall view (as discussed above). This can be attributed to two key factors:

- First, the government's commitment to public services and the New Labour mantra that it is 'delivery that matters' prioritises results over processes and rests on a belief that the public are less interested in participation and scrutiny but do want high-quality public services delivered at the lowest possible cost (Shaw 2004). Indeed, the pressure on the government to deliver on health, education and so on creates an environment that favours strong government.
- Second, the increased emphasis on security post 9/11, with the political climate both nationally and internationally now being heavily shaped by security and anti-terrorism measures. In Britain these concerns have legitimated the executive taking on new powers and limiting rights in prescribed situations, while there has been a more general acceptance of the limits of the Liberal view and the benefits of and need for strong government in certain situations.

During the first two sessions of Labour's second term the main constitutional developments included a limited package of parliamentary modernisation, further government papers and statements on the future of the Lords, and the publication of a White Paper on devolution to the English regions. Constitutional matters were not, therefore, a priority for the government. Paradoxically, the importance of this period lies not in any reforms but in the sustained criticism and pressure on the government. Attention focused on areas where the government was seen as failing to implement meaningful reform (for example, reform of the House of Commons) or was constantly putting off making decisions or firm announcements (for example, introducing a Civil Service Act or considering reform of the Westminster electoral system). The government's attempts via the whips to manipulate the composition of the Commons select committees in July 2001, combined with the subsequent tensions between Parliament and the executive over the deployment of troops to Iraq, created considerable anxiety (Byrne and Weir 2004; Tyrie 2004). Parliamentarians and constitutional observers began to detect a clear shift in the governing mentality of New Labour that could arguably be interpreted as a swing from the Liberal to the Whitehall view of the constitution.

In response to these concerns and more established criticisms of the reform programme the government attempted to seize the initiative in June 2003. The catalyst came in the form of a government reshuffle that included the removal of Lord Irvine and the announcement that the post of Lord Chancellor was to be abolished and most of the responsibilities of the Lord Chancellor's Department transferred to a new Department for Constitutional Affairs (DCA) headed by Lord Falconer. In the next Queen's Speech at the opening of the 2003/04 parliamentary session the DCA received the major share of the legislative timetable. Moreover, the government's future legislative programme included two major constitutional bills – the House of Lords Bill and Constitutional Reform Bill. Not only did these reforms attempt to tidy up Whitehall in the aftermath of devolution but they also represented an attempt, in the form of Lord Falconer, to situate the reform programme on the shoulders on an individual who would be willing to engage in debates concerning the values and principles behind the constitutional changes. The two major bills, on House of Lords reform and the creation of a Supreme Court, marked an unexpected attempt to push on with the reform programme and seize the initiative from critics.

## Principled progress and retrospective reasoning 2003–05

In contrast to his predecessor Lord Irvine, a distinct feature of Lord Falconer's tenure as Lord Chancellor and Secretary of State for Constitutional Affairs since June 2003 has been his willingness, even enthusiasm, to elaborate the values on which the constitutional reform programme is based. In a series of speeches Lord Falconer has sought to retrospectively provide the ideological and ethical foundations for the reform programme:

> [T]he constitutional issue at stake is one of the most important in a liberal democracy – the relationship between citizens and the state ... Since 1997 this Government has been involved in a sustained attempt to revive and redefine that relationship for the twenty-first century. Three progressive values have underpinned our approach:
>
> - The first has been to enhance the credibility and effectiveness of our public institutions.
> - The second has been to strengthen our democracy and public engagement with decision-making.
> - The third has been to increase trust and accountability in public bodies. (Falconer 2003; see also 2004a, 2004b)

The elaboration of values is difficult at the best of times, their intrinsic vagueness making them open to criticism. However, the benefit of the three 'progressive values' outlined by Lord Falconer is that they not only provide a number of benchmarks against which the success of the reform programme might be judged, but they also illustrate the innate complexity of constitutional reform. What terms such as 'effectiveness', 'credibility' and 'accountability' actually mean will depend not on agreed and neutral criteria but on political choices or views about the role of the constitution.

Parliament, for example, has two inherently contradictory roles. First, to sustain the executive and pass legislation, which it would appear to do well. Second, to hold the executive to account, which it does rather less well. For those committed to the Whitehall view, enhancing the 'credibility' and 'effectiveness' of Parliament could involve implementing reforms to facilitate the passage of more legislation through Parliament with fewer opportunities for scrutiny and delay. However, for those committed to the Liberal view, reforms would be preferred that strengthened Parliament's capacity to fulfil its scrutiny function.

Accountability is an equally complex concept that can be delivered through a range of mechanisms and processes (Flinders 2001). Whether a reform has actually increased accountability will depend on the priorities and values of an individual and the relative weights ascribed to different forms of accountability. Many of the public-sector reforms that were implemented during the 1980s and 1990s were constructed upon a belief amongst Conservative ministers that new forms of market or 'consumer' accountability would empower individuals and increase transparency (Waldegrave 1993). Critics, on the other hand, interpreted these reforms as reducing accountability and making the structure of the state more opaque rather than transparent (Stewart 1994). Declaring a commitment to increasing trust and accountability means little unless the specific manner in which this will be achieved and the values underpinning this process are elucidated. This becomes more pressing when other government reforms appear to confuse traditional lines of accountability, as in the case of the creation of the Department for Constitutional Affairs.

## The Department for Constitutional Affairs

When the creation of the Department for Constitutional Affairs (DCA) was announced in June 2003 confusion surrounded the initial statement that the territorial departments, the Scottish and Welsh Offices, were to be abolished. For a short time the situation was unclear. Facing an outcry from Scottish and Welsh interests (not to mention Welsh and Scottish Labour MPs) the nameplates outside the Scottish Office and Wales Office in Whitehall (which had been removed only hours earlier) were hastily restored and an announcement was made that the departments would continue to exist – but within the new DCA. The situation in relation to the territorial Secretaries of State was clearer but still represented a rather awkward fudge of constitutional boundaries. No longer would Scotland and Wales have their own representative and voice within the Cabinet but they would have to share a minister who represented their interests while holding another ministerial portfolio. Alistair Darling, the Secretary of State for Transport, took on responsibility for Scottish Affairs and Peter Hain, then Leader of the House, now Secretary of State for Northern Ireland, became responsible for Welsh Affairs. The creation of joint portfolios confuses the constitutional lines of accountability. Do the civil servants within the Wales Office, for example, owe their duty of loyalty to Lord Falconer, the Secretary of State for Constitutional Affairs, in whose overarching department they are located, or to Peter Hain, the Secretary of State for Wales as well as Northern Ireland?

Constitutional research centres such as the Constitution Unit, based at University College, London, and a number of parliamentary committees, notably the Lords' Constitution Committee, had for some time been advocating the merger of the territorial departments with one minister being made responsible for all devolution matters as well as intergovernmental relations. Such a reform would have dovetailed with the government's wider drive towards 'joined-up' government within Whitehall (see Flinders 2002a). Moreover, the DCA is not really a Department for Constitutional Affairs at all but is more akin to a Department of Justice. Responsibility for major aspects of constitutional policy, such as English regional devolution, remains spread across a number of departments. The reprieve granted to the territorial departments and their rather awkward constitutional position appears a classic example of British 'muddling through' rather than rational and transparent modernisation. The decision to create the DCA was clearly announced before the specific details of the structure and responsibilities of the new department had been clarified or agreed within the Cabinet (indeed, several ministers admitted to having been taken aback by the announcement). Another unexpected development came in the 2003 Queen's Speech with the inclusion of plans to proceed with reform of the Lords.

## Reform of the House of Lords

In line with the 1997 manifesto, Stage One of the House of Lords reform was implemented with the passage of the House of Lords Act on 11 November 1999 that removed all but 92 hereditary peers from the Lords. The rest of the first term and early stages of the second were marked by a well-documented series of commissions, White Papers and debates, all of which failed to arrive at even the barest sense of agreement over the future role, composition and powers of the second chamber (Flinders 2003). The Labour Party's 2001 general election manifesto committed the party to making the Lords 'more representative and democratic while maintaining the primacy of the House of Commons'. This led to the publication of a White Paper, *Completing the Reform*, in November 2001, which proposed that only 120 members (20 per cent) of the reformed second chamber should be elected.

The proposals received widespread criticism and in an effort to make progress on Stage Two of Lords reform, the Government supported the establishment of a Joint Committee of both Houses to review the issue. The Joint Committee published its report on 11 December 2002 in which it put forward no less than seven options for both Houses of Parliament to choose between in a free vote, which took place on 4 February 2003. Although the House of Lords voted for a fully appointed second chamber, the House of Commons rejected all the options for change. Not only did this leave the government's plans in disarray but the voting records of individual members of the Cabinet illustrated the lack of consensus within the government (Tony Blair and Lord Irvine supported a fully appointed second chamber while Robin Cook, Charles Clarke and Patricia Hewitt favoured a significant elected component).

In May 2003 the Joint Committee of both Houses of Parliament, which had been reconvened to try and find a way forward on Lords reform, issued a report in which it requested that the government provide the committee with an indication of its current thinking on the role and composition of a revised second chamber. The government published a rather blunt response in July 2003 in which it stated 'there is no consensus about introducing any elected element in the House of Lords,' thereby offering the committee no guidance on how it should proceed. However, on 18 September 2003 the DCA published another White Paper (the Labour government's third on the topic) on reform of the Lords without any advance consultation and the Queen's Speech on 26 November 2003 duly included a commitment to press ahead with reform.

The government's announcement of its intention to remove the remaining 92 hereditary peers from the Lords received a largely disparaging response. The House of Lords Act in 1999 had been passed due to an agreement between the Labour government and the Conservative Leader in the Lords, Viscount Cranborne, that the 92 hereditary peers would remain in the Lords until the government implemented Stage Two of the reform process (namely the full introduction of a newly constituted and reformed second chamber). The fact that the government was attempting to remove the hereditary peers without any real ideas or plans to move to Stage Two was seen by many as deceitful and treacherous, not least because Viscount Cranborne had been sacked by the then Leader of the Conservative Party, William Hague, for brokering that agreement. Moreover, for a government rhetorically committed to participation, consultation and openness the sudden and abrupt nature of the announcement did little to assuage concerns that it had become remote, even presidential in style. A debate ensued concerning whether the government had even had the common courtesy to inform members of the Joint Committee of both Houses about its plans. Irrespective of the specific accusations and counter-claims, it is sufficient to note that the whole affair was not well handled by a government with a reputation for 'spin'.

Indeed, the government appeared overly keen, even desperate, to move on with reform of the Lords and its proposals obviously created wider questions about the role, powers and composition of the future second chamber to which the government could offer no coherent answers. This fuelled criticism that the government lacked any coherent vision of the reformed constitution as a whole or appreciation of the possibly negative consequences of reform in one area for other aspects of the constitutional configuration. Finally, the government's plans to remove the remaining hereditary peers did not sit comfortably with its commitment to move towards a more Liberal conception of the constitution. If anything it represented a move that would centralise power and further dilute an important restriction or check on the power of the executive. This was because the 2003 House of Lords Bill signalled the government's intention to proceed on the basis of a wholly appointed second chamber, while the removal of 92 overwhelmingly Conservative peers would actually shift the balance of power within the second chamber towards the Labour Party. However, in March 2004 the Secretary of State for Constitutional Affairs announced that a decision had been taken not to proceed with the House of Lords Bill but that Labour would return to the issue in its manifesto for the next general election. The reason for this dramatic announcement was the intense opposition that the government was facing to its second constitutional bill of the 2003/04 parliamentary session, the Constitutional Reform Bill.

## The Constitutional Reform Bill

On 12 June 2003 the government made a surprise announcement that it intended to create a Supreme Court, establish an independent Judicial Appointments Commission for judicial appointments and abolish the post of Lord Chancellor. The role of the Lord Chancellor, who was simultaneously a member of the executive, the legislature and the judiciary, had for some time been a topic of disquiet. This had been exacerbated by passage of the Human Rights Act (HRA), incorporating into UK law the European Convention on Human Rights (ECHR), which stipulates that a fair trial must involve an impartial and independent judge (who is not a member of the government bringing the case). The HRA factor created a sense of urgency and reforms to the second chamber (in which the highest judicial court sat) provided the opportunity to instigate a clearer separation of powers.

The government's plans would remove the Law Lords from the House of Lords and locate them in a new Supreme Court building. A new independent Judicial Appointments Commission would select members of the new Supreme Court. However, the plans are not as radical as they might first appear. The Supreme Court would not have the power to strike down legislation; New Labour's plans for a Supreme Court are therefore weaker than the situation found in many other political systems due to the dominance of the concept of parliamentary sovereignty. Indeed the Lord Chief Justice as of 2004, Lord Woolf, described the government's plans as 'second-class' due to the fact that the proposals have been designed in such a way as to protect the supremacy of Parliament and therefore do not include the powers, commonly invested in a Supreme Court, to strike down legislation.

How then can the creation of a Supreme Court without the existence of a rigid constitution and the judicial capacity to veto legislation amount to a meaningful alteration of a political system? Without an agreed written constitution the courts have little to 'bite on' in terms of gauging the constitutionality of government action or legislation. The continuing relevance of the notion of parliamentary sovereignty has been clear in relation to the arrangements for incorporating the nearest thing that Britain has to 'higher-order' laws – the HRA. When the government enacted the HRA the procedures for judicial review were carefully designed to maintain parliamentary sovereignty. Consequently, the courts were not empowered to strike down legislation that they deemed to be irreconcilable with the HRA, but simply to issue a 'declaration of incompatibility'. This does not annul the legislation in any way, but commences a procedure in which Parliament is invited to review an Act and possibly revise it in light of the court's views. However, Parliament is under no obligation to alter the legislation and is therefore free to judge the constitutionality of its own laws.

Despite numerous calls for the Constitutional Reform Bill to be published in draft form to facilitate careful scrutiny, the government introduced the Bill into the House of Lords on 24 February 2004. Not surprisingly, the progress of this Bill was not smooth. On 8 March the government suffered a defeat on a vote on the Bill that saw it referred to a Lords committee for further scrutiny. However, after six months' scrutiny the 16 members of the committee on the Bill failed to come to any agreement on any major issues. In fact their final report of July 2004 preferred to make no recommendations on a range of major issues and the challenge of achieving consensus was starkly illustrated just days after the committee's report was published when the House of Lords voted by 240 votes to 208 to support a Conservative amendment that would retain the post of Lord Chancellor. Beyond the Palace of Westminster the government became embroiled in a major dispute with the Law Lords concerning not just the powers of the planned Supreme Court but where it would actually be located. In the end one of the final acts of the 2001–05 Parliament saw the Constitutional Reform Bill receive Royal Assent and thereby become law, but only after the government had been forced to accept that the office of Lord Chancellor should be retained and a new concordat had been signed between the Lord Chancellor and the Lord Chief Justice setting out the division of functions and responsibilities. The specific tensions and problems surrounding the Constitutional Reform Bill resonate with a number of common themes that encapsulate New Labour's approach to the constitution more broadly.

## Common themes 2001–05

A striking failure of Labour's second term in relation to the constitution was its relative failure to complete most of the unfinished business carried over from its first term. If anything, the overall situation was more confused, bordering on the chaotic, at the end of the second term. The future of the House of Lords remained unclear, the Constitutional Reform Act had been passed but only in an eviscerated manner; plans for elected regional government in England were in disarray (particularly after the resounding No vote in the North East regional referendum in November 2004); and the issue of electoral reform for Westminster remained firmly shelved. The government's attempts to proceed with reform of the constitution during the later stages of its second term in office do, however, exhibit a number of uniting themes.

First is a lack of consultation in relation to constitutional policy making. The announcement of the government's decision to create the DCA, abolish the post of Lord Chancellor, proceed with reform of the Lords and create a Supreme Court all came as major surprises to those not within Tony Blair's inner circle of friends and advisors. This fact sits uncomfortably with Lord Falconer's assertion that a core value underpinning the constitutional reform programme as a whole has been a commitment to increasing participation in decision making. Second is a lack of detailed preparation in advance of making official announcements. Indeed, 'too much vigour, not enough rigour' became something of an epithet for Labour's approach to the constitution. This was particularly stark in relation to the creation of the DCA and the confusion surrounding the future of the Scottish and Welsh Offices. At times the government appeared strangely steadfast in its determination to push on with reforms or experiments in the face of pleas for caution and more preparatory work. For instance, when the Electoral Commission, the House of Lords and a Commons committee all advised the government not to use all-postal voting in four regions for the June 2004 local and European elections, citing the need for more time to build the necessary implementation and support structures and develop processes to guard against fraud, the government pushed ahead with the experiment. This led to a number of problems involving the distribution of voting papers, confusion surrounding how to complete the papers, and accusations of intimidation and electoral fraud. The outcome of this was a critical report by the Electoral Commission and the government's decision not to proceed with regional referendums in Yorkshire, Humberside and the North West. What might have been interpreted as a move to counter public apathy and rebuild trust, in line with Lord Falconer's progressive values, was devalued by its hasty implementation.

Taken individually, while Labour's constitutional reform proposals may conceivably have been viewed as a good idea, a lack of consultation, inadequate preparatory work, and poor media management led to the government being perceived as floundering, ill-prepared, over-hasty and, at times, simply shoddy. It also provided critics of the reform programme with rich pickings in terms of highlighting obvious problems and issues that should have been picked up and addressed in the policy-making process that should precede any public announcement. A lack of consultation and detailed preparatory work only fuelled accusations that the government was acting in a high-handed manner and lacked any obvious appreciation of the implications that reform in one area may have for other aspects of the constitutional infrastructure.

Possibly the most substantive theme coming out of each of the above case studies is that they seem to verify that long-standing concern that Labour's reform programme lacks any grand vision or underpinning framework. David Marquand eloquently captured this anxiety when he wrote,

> It is very British, this [constitutional] revolution. It is a revolution without a theory. It is the messy, muddled work of practical men and women, unintellectual when not positively anti-intellectual, apparently oblivious of the long tradition of political and constitutional

reflection of which they are heirs, responding piecemeal and ad hoc to conflicting pressures – a revolution of sleepwalkers who don't quite know where they are going or why. (Marquand 1999)

There is, however, one central theme that does provide a degree of consistency that unites all aspects of Labour's constitutional reform programme – a commitment to the sanctity of the Westminster model. It is this commitment that explains many of the tensions and paradoxes that this programme reveals. It is also clear, however, that while being committed to this model the government has been willing to introduce reforms that weaken or hollow out several of its central tenets. The Labour government has, in fact, created a multilevel polity within an increasingly frail conception of the Westminster model. It is this fact that explains a number of the apparently intractable constitutional challenges faced by the Labour government.

## The Westminster model and multilevel governance

The idea of multilevel governance (MLG) is receiving increasing attention within the literature on British politics (Gamble 2000; Hay 2002). Pierre and Stoker (2000, 29) state that '[g]overning Britain – and indeed any other advanced western democratic state – has thus become a matter of multilevel governance'; Marsh et al. (2003, 314) observe that 'multilevel governance has become a new mantra.' Although MLG remains a contested concept its core tenets emphasise the growing distribution of power across and between different levels of government; the evolution and creation of new power centres; the importance of formal and informal networks; the existence of 'fuzzy' accountability, and a general increase in the fluidity and transfer of political power (Bache and Flinders 2004a). This stands in contrast to the central characteristics of the Westminster model with its emphasis on control, hierarchy and clear lines of accountability (see Table 7.3).

The two models provide useful heuristic tools, not only due to their capacity to understand institutional reform but also because they inculcate certain normative values that bear a direct relationship to the distinction between the Whitehall and Liberal views of the constitution. The Westminster model was deeply ingrained with the elitist and or 'realist' values of the Whitehall view (Johnson 2001), but Bache and Flinders note that proponents of multilevel governance frequently employ the concept of MLG not just as a descriptive or analytical term to describe change but also as a 'normatively superior mode of allocating authority' (2004a, 195–6). The dispersal of power, development of new governing

Table 7.3   *Contrasting organising perspectives: the Westminster model and a multilevel polity*

| Westminster model | Multilevel polity |
|---|---|
| Centralised state | Disaggregated state |
| *General principles* | |
| Hierarchy | Heterarchy |
| Control | Steering |
| Clear lines of accountability | Multiple lines of accountability |
| *External dimensions* | |
| Absolute sovereignty | Relative sovereignty |
| British foreign policy | Multiple foreign policies |
| *Internal dimensions* | |
| Unitary state | Quasi-federal state |
| Parliamentary sovereignty | Inter-institutional bargaining |
| Strong executive | Segmented executive |
| Direct governance | Delegated governance |
| Unified civil service | Fragmented civil service |
| Political constitution | Quasi-judicial constitution |

*Sources*: Adapted from Rhodes (1997) and Bache and Flinders (2004b)

arrangements and the emergence of new forms of accountability suggested by MLG are considered to be a realistic characterisation of recent political developments and also a 'good', 'superior' and 'beneficial' mode of governance. Moreover, the devolution of power and the creation of new democratic arenas above and below the nation state could be interpreted as limiting the power of the British government; creating new avenues for participation and popular control, which resonates with the Liberal view outlined above.

Comparing the two columns in Table 7.3 suggests that the constitutional reforms enacted since 1997 have transformed the British polity from the archetypal Westminster model to a form of multilevel governance. Devolution has replaced the unitary state with a quasi-federal version; ministers must now coordinate with their counterparts in Scotland and Wales rather than simply directing; the transfer of responsibility upwards to Europe and downward to the regions risks making accountability opaque as politicians attempt to avoid responsibility for errors or failures and partake in complex 'blame games'; and a unified civil service has been fragmented as a consequence of devolution. As the Secretary of State for Constitutional Affairs, Lord Falconer, acknowledged, 'Devolution has, undeniably, made some decision-making more complex ... Our new multilayered state requires new skills which Governments within federal or quasi-federal structures have long had to master' (2003).

This would, however, be just one interpretation of the reform process. It is equally valid to argue that the Westminster model remains a more reliable interpretation of both the institutions and the values of the British polity. Indeed, New Labour has taken great care to implement its constitutional reforms, however precariously, within the traditional Westminster model of British government (see Flinders 2000a, 2000b). Consequently, Lord Norton (quoted in Morrison 2001, 509–10) notes that 'The Westminster model has been modified, perhaps vandalised, but it has not been destroyed' and Tom Nairn (2000, 70) states that 'the mainframe has remained sacrosanct.' It is for this reason, much to the dismay of reform groups, that the potential radicalness of the reforms has been curbed or restricted by the twin conventions of parliamentary sovereignty and individual ministerial responsibility to Parliament. These two conventions, pillars of the Westminster model, dilute the very essence of many specific reforms while also ensuring that the constitutional reform programme as a whole does not provide explicit limits on executive power. The Freedom of Information Act retains a ministerial veto over the release of information; the reformed Lords must not threaten the supremacy of the Commons; the Human Rights Act does not allow the courts to strike down legislation or compel the government to amend it; the independent Judicial Appointments Commission will not actually appoint judges but make recommendations to the Secretary of State for Constitutional Affairs. In addition, because no Parliament may bind its successor, any future government could theoretically repeal or emasculate any aspect of the Labour government's reforms.

The question arises of why a government that has committed itself to far-reaching reform and has implemented such a wide range of constitutional changes should place such great weight on upholding the sanctity of the Westminster model. The official reason is that parliamentary sovereignty and ministerial responsibility to Parliament provide a clear line of accountability between the electorate and the government, while also ensuring that decisions are taken by elected and accountable ministers rather than unelected and unaccountable judges or officials. A more sophisticated answer might attempt to strip away this constitutional veneer and examine the underlying distribution of power that is created by the Westminster model. In reality, due to the near-complete fusion of the executive and legislature, Bagehot's 'efficient secret' of the British constitution, underpinned by the nature of the electoral system and tight party management, parliamentary sovereignty is a euphemism for executive domination. The convention of ministerial responsibility empowers ministers with the right to take the final decision on matters, while interpreting reform proposals that recommend transferring decision-making powers to other constitutional actors or arenas as 'unconstitutional'. It is this failure to dilute the central axis of political power, enshrined in the conventions of parliamentary sovereignty and ministerial responsibility, which led Morrison (2001, 501) to conclude about New Labour that '... despite all the reforms to the periphery, the core of the British political system of elective dictatorship has remained intact.'

The government's programme of constitutional reform is littered with ministerial opt-outs, possible exemptions and reserve powers. Gauging the extent of reform in Britain and the degree to which the nature of British democracy has altered since May 1997 is, therefore, difficult due to the fact that it demands a normative judgement on the willingness of the executive not to invoke its reserve powers but to rule according to an executive mentality that is willing to cede power. The government is, in essence, saying 'you can trust us not to use these reserve powers unless it is absolutely necessary.' And yet the momentum for constitutional reform in the 1980s and 1990s grew from the fact that the public had lost its trust in politicians. Moreover, although current ministers may act with constitutional restraint, there is no guarantee that a future government will act with such self-discipline. Reformers emphasise that the whole point of constitutional reform is to entrench certain limits on executive power. And yet it is possible to suggest that fundamental laws and entrenched constitutions are simply incompatible with the very notion of parliamentary sovereignty.

The current situation creates an argument between those who interpret Labour's constitutional reforms as de facto entrenched aspects of an increasingly codified constitution and those who interpret such an approach as politically naive. In the former group, for example, Maer and her colleagues state that 'constitutional law is growing into a more distinct body of fundamental law. Although technically these constitutional laws have no higher status, politically they are entrenched in a way that ordinary statute law is not' (2004, 254). Against this position a number of scholars suggest that there is little evidence that the constitutional legislation introduced by New Labour is any more secure than any other legislation. Byrne and Weir (2004) highlight the manner in which the British government used its parliamentary majority to push through Parliament the Anti-Terrorism, Crime and Security Act 2001, which involved derogating from Article 5 of the European Convention on Human Rights less than two years after its enactment in the Human

Rights Act. The idea that human rights are politically entrenched and cannot be easily taken away seems difficult to reconcile with the reality and experience of political power under New Labour. Even when the Law Lords ruled in December 2004 that Part Four of the Anti-Terrorism, Crime and Security Act of 2001 was unlawful (that is, they quashed the derogation order from the HRA) the government swiftly tabled a Prevention of Terrorism Bill giving the Home Secretary the power to impose stringent control orders on anyone irrespective of nationality or whether they had been charged with or convicted of an offence, which became law on 11 March 2005.

The Westminster model/MLG dichotomy identifies shifts in the nature of British governance and provides a counterpoint to the conceptual domination the Westminster model previously enjoyed. The distinction between them is not, however, sharp or simple: Britain has not moved from a Westminster model to an MLG. The reality is far more sophisticated and dynamic due to the fact that an embryonic MLG structure is evolving within and against the parameters of the Westminster model. It is the tensions and anomalies arising from this interaction between attempts to retain traditional aspects of the Westminster model, at least in theory, and the simultaneous instituting of reforms that undermine (or at least set in train dynamics that are likely to destabilise) core tenets of this model that explain and underpin many contemporary issues in British politics.

## Conclusion: the constitution and British democracy

So what then were we left with at the end of Labour's second term? What sort of political system have these reforms created? To what degree has New Labour altered the nature of British democracy? It is reasonable to suggest that the nature of British democracy has changed. There has been a shift towards a more pluralist Liberal-inspired form of democracy in which the executive has undoubtedly ceded some powers. However, it is in assessing *the degree of change* that debate reigns. As discussed above, although the Labour government has been willing to introduce reform they have done so within a constitutional infrastructure that arguably protects executive power at all costs. The degree of change has therefore been large, possibly significant, but it has certainly not been radical (Flinders 2005a).

The most important indicator of the 'success' or impact of Labour's constitutional reforms could possibly be the degree to which they have increased public trust and confidence in politicians and political institutions. 'Restoring trust, restoring faith, restoring confidence in politics' has been the core aim of the programme (Falconer 2003). Social surveys and research projects suggest, however, that public trust and confidence have fallen since 1997 and Bromley et al. conclude that the constitutional reforms have not only not restored citizens' trust and confidence in government but that few people believe they have made much difference to the way Britain is governed (2004). From this it could be suggested that New Labour has failed in relation to the core aim of its constitutional reform programme and it is possible to argue that the reason for this is not just its commitment to maintaining the Westminster model but also that its discourse of radical reform actually increased public expectations and then made the contrariety between rhetoric and reality more stark, leading to even greater disillusionment.

It is, however, possible to argue that the reforms have sown the seeds of what may one day flower into more deep-seated changes. There is no such thing as a constitutional settlement because constitutions are by definition dynamic, iterative and adaptive entities. It is for this reason that the government's attempts to retain the Westminster model may in time become unrealistic. Devolution, for example, has developed a momentum that is likely to create a 'snowball' or 'ratchet' effect as weaker regions demand more powers and stronger regions consolidate the powers they already have. Questions such as why proportional voting methods have been implemented for local, regional and European elections but are still deemed inappropriate for Westminster elections, and why a written constitution is appropriate for the European Union but not for Britain, are receiving increased attention and may in time lead to a more explicit and coherent review of Britain's constitutional arrangements.

It may well, therefore, be too soon to evaluate the impact and outcome of New Labour's constitutional reforms. Indeed, the dynamics and momentum of reform raise questions about the degree to which a government can control reform processes once certain cracks and wedges have been put in place. Devolution, as we have seen, has developed its own impetus. Members of the Cabinet have already conceded that the government's decision in March 2003 to hold a vote on the floor of the House of Commons on the deployment of troops to Iraq has effectively created a new constitutional convention that future prime ministers would find it difficult, if not impossible, to depart from. The Labour government, particularly in light of its reduced Commons majority, 66 seats but based on the vote of only 21.6 per cent of the electorate, the lowest share ever recorded by a winning party, is facing increasing pressure to honour its manifesto commitments in relation to holding a referendum on the electoral system for Westminster. In addition, the nettle of Stage Two reform of the House of Lords will have to be grasped at some stage. Other issues on the political agenda include: implementing a Civil Service Act; the government's review of the rules concerning the provision of 'papers, persons and records' to select committees; restarting the Northern Ireland devolution process; and reviewing the powers of the Greater London Authority and the Mayor of London. In terms of future developments, the politics of the British constitution is therefore likely to form a critical aspect of New Labour's third term. This will be particularly so as the anomalies and tensions arising from the evolution of a multilevel polity *within* a Westminster model framework become ever more apparent.

## Chapter 8

# Devolution and the Lopsided State

CHARLIE JEFFERY

Politics beyond Westminster is both very different in the UK after devolution and remarkably unchanged. It is different because of the devolved governments that now exist in Scotland, Northern Ireland and Wales. But politics in England – which makes up around 84 per cent of the UK's population – remains remarkably unchanged.

The exception is the Greater London Authority (GLA), which was established in 2000 on the basis – like the Scottish Parliament and the National Assembly for Wales – of a manifesto commitment of the incoming Labour government in 1997. That manifesto also set out a prospect of regional devolution in the rest of England where there was 'demand'. After much prevarication, the policy of 'devolution on demand' was finally tested in November 2004 when a referendum was held on the introduction of an elected regional assembly in the North East region of England. The result was an overwhelming 'No', a decision that means that regional devolution in England is now off the agenda. As a result, with the exception of the GLA, England will continue to be governed for the foreseeable future from the UK centre at Westminster, not by institutions with a mandate 'beyond Westminster'. This leaves the UK as a particularly lopsided state. Few other states have the same pattern in which the preponderant part is governed centrally while the peripheral parts are self-governing in most fields of domestic policy. Perhaps the closest contemporary examples are Finland and Portugal, where in each case the mainland is governed centrally, and remote islands – the Åland Islands, and Madeira and the Azores respectively – have extensive self-government.

Moreover, where devolution has transformed politics beyond Westminster, it has done so asymmetrically. The Scottish Parliament, Northern Ireland Assembly, National Assembly for Wales and the GLA are all very different (Table 8.1), and are exercised in quite different institutional settings.

The lopsided balance between England and the other nations and the

**Table 8.1**   *Lopsided devolution in the UK*

| Nation | % UK pop. | % UK GDP | Form of government |
| --- | --- | --- | --- |
| England | 83.6 | 85.7 | Direct rule by Westminster with growing regional administration of central government policies, but no elected regional government except in London |
| *London* | *12.2* | *19.1* | *Greater London Authority with responsibilities for strategic policy coordination in transport, economic development, policing, and fire services; elected executive Mayor held to account by separately elected Assembly* |
| Scotland | 8.6 | 8.1 | Scottish Parliament with primary legislative powers in matters not reserved to Westminster (most fields of domestic policy); limited fiscal autonomy; majoritarian government |
| Wales | 4.9 | 3.9 | National Assembly with secondary legislative powers dependent on Westminster legislation; majoritarian government displacing initial vision of 'corporate body' |
| Northern Ireland | 2.9 | 2.2 | Northern Ireland Assembly with primary legislative powers in matters not reserved to Westminster (or not temporarily held back by Westminster subject to the security situation); proportional government to secure cross-community balance; embedded in international relationships with Republic of Ireland |

asymmetry of arrangements for governing the different component parts of the UK are nothing new. They were reflected in the territorial arrangements of government that existed prior to devolution. The UK central government had (and in modified form still has) Scottish, Welsh and Northern Ireland Offices as cabinet-level departments with a remit of policy implementation in their respective nations; there was no equivalent department for England. The functions of these territorial departments were not uniform. Adapting the traditional terminology of 'union state' (Rokkan and Urwin 1982), James Mitchell (2006) has aptly called the UK a 'state of unions', in which different arrangements of union had been made (remade in the case of Ireland/Northern Ireland) between a dominant England and the other nations at different times and in different political contexts. What devolution did was to democratise this 'state of unions', transferring different sets of territorial competences formerly exercised from within central government to separate devolved governments established by new electoral processes. The only real historical break in the devolution reforms is the GLA, although the GLA's main responsibilities were also inherited from a range of London-wide authorities and agencies with policy functions in transport, policing and so on.

## Recent developments in the four nations

### Politics in Wales

The second election to the National Assembly for Wales took place in May 2003 (Table 8.2), with Labour emerging with 30 out of the 60 Assembly seats. This gave it an effective majority of 1, since the Presiding Officer (Speaker) of the Assembly by convention does not vote. Under First Minister Rhodri Morgan Labour formed a single-party government, abandoning their earlier coalition with the Liberal Democrats. Morgan's administration has been keener to establish a distinctive profile vis-à-vis Westminster than its Scottish counterpart, using the rhetoric of 'clear red water' to convey a sense that it is of a more traditional Labour hue than 'New Labour' in Westminster (Morgan 2004). It has resisted the agenda, increasingly seen in England since 1997, of providing 'choice' in citizens' access to public services and of performance monitoring by targets and league tables, preferring to restate 'traditional Labour' commitments to universalism. Significantly, Welsh Labour MPs at Westminster have been uneasy with this distinctive agenda, fearing that health and education in Wales – though devolved policies in theory accountable to Welsh voters in National Assembly elections – would be judged by targets for England set in Westminster. Indeed, both in Wales

**Table 8.2**   *The 2003 election in Wales, compared to 1999*

| Party | Constituency vote % | Regional-list vote % | Constituency seats | Regional seats | Total seats |
|---|---|---|---|---|---|
| Conservative | 19.9 (+4.1) | 19.2 (+2.7) | 1 (=) | 10 (+2) | 11 (+2) |
| Labour | 40.0 (+2.4) | 36.6 (+1.2) | 30 (+3) | 0 (−1) | 30 (+2) |
| Liberal Democrats | 14.1 (+0.7) | 12.7 (+0.2) | 3 (=) | 3 (=) | 6 (=) |
| Plaid Cymru | 21.2 (−7.2) | 19.7 (−10.8) | 5 (−4) | 7 (−1) | 12 (−5) |
| Others | 4.8 (+0.1) | 11.8 (+6.7) | 1 (+1) | 0 (=) | 1 (+1) |
| Total | 100 | 100 | 40 | 20 | 60 |

and in Scotland the devolved administrations came under some criticism in the 2005 Westminster election campaign for 'failing' to reach targets made for England that they had not set.

Though some of Morgan's 'clear red water' is no more than oppositional rhetorical – useful in conveying a sense of a government pursuing distinctive Welsh interests against a remote Westminster, even if Westminster is run by the same party – some clear policy differences have emerged. For example, the Assembly has pioneered new initiatives in early years/child-care policies and committed itself to the reduction and eventual abolition of prescription charges. It has also reorganised the National Health Service to work on local government boundaries in Wales, in part to enable joint working with local authorities to pursue a preventive public health agenda, in part because it inherited only a weak administrative infrastructure and policy capacity from the old Welsh Office and needed to draw on local government resources and expertise (Greer 2006).

Because of these capacity deficits there is a sense in health and in other fields that the Assembly government has been 'captured' by local public-sector interests (Jeffery 2006). That those local public-sector interests are traditionally dominated by Labour points to an emerging feature of devolution in Wales: despite the aspirations before 1997 for an inclusive 'new governance' (Chaney et al. 2001) Wales remains a Labour strong-hold, and Welsh Labour is not pluralist by instinct. One of the other major divergences in Wales from the wider English/UK pattern can be understood in that light: the 2004 decision to abolish most Assembly-sponsored quangos in Wales by bringing them under direct Assembly control. This decision raised concerns among commentators both about whether the Assembly government has the administrative capacity and skill to run major functions like economic development and further education in-house (cf. Cooke 2003) and about whether the Assembly as a legislature has the capacity to hold adequately to account an Assembly government beefed up by the quangos. More generally Morgan and Upton (2005, 79) argue the decision had the effect of rendering Wales 'more state-centric and less pluralist', bringing with it the danger that 'the embryonic devolution project morphs into big government rather than empowering civil society to manage itself'. Of course centralist, one-party domination is not unusual in comparative regional politics, and should hardly surprise in a nation traditionally dominated by Labour and with a form of electoral system less proportional than in Scotland and more likely to embed Labour dominance in the Assembly. But that does not make its emergence in Wales any less striking.

## Institutional developments in Wales

Wales has a curious arrangement for devolution. It is based on the National Assembly issuing secondary legislation within the framework of primary legislation made by the UK Parliament in Westminster. Unlike in Scotland, there is no neat split between powers reserved to Westminster and powers devolved to the National Assembly. Empowerments of the National Assembly to enact secondary legislation are contained in a patchwork of over 400 laws in the Westminster statute book (Lambert and Navarro 2005). Some of these 'transferred functions' are contemporary but some stretch back for well over a century. Many are couched in highly restrictive terms, though the post-devolution transfers generally leave more leeway to the Assembly in defining policy than those inherited from before. As a result, even insiders, let alone the general public, find it difficult to know just what it is the Assembly can or cannot do (cf. Cole and Storer 2002).

The complexity of the legislative process was one of the prompts for the Commission on the Powers and Electoral Arrangements of the National Assembly for Wales, set up in July 2002 under the Labour peer Lord Richard. There were two other prompts. The first was the dissatisfaction with the design of the Assembly as a 'corporate body' with a collective identity and responsibility which – unlike in Scotland – lacked a formal distinction between government and opposition. By 2002 the Assembly had agreed through internal review to move to a de facto separation of the 'Welsh Assembly government' and the 'Assembly Parliamentary Service' under the Presiding Officer (speaker) of the Assembly.

There was also dissatisfaction in some circles – mainly in the Labour Party – with the electoral system used for Assembly elections. This variant of the 'additional member system' (AMS) (see Farrell 2001) is semi-proportional. It combines 40 traditional single-member-plurality

**Box 8.1   Recommendations of the Richard Commission in Wales**

- Transformation of the National Assembly into a legislative assembly with primary legislative powers on all matters not reserved to Westminster
- Widening of the scope of the Assembly's discretion in secondary legislation as an interim measure pending award of primary legislative powers
- 'Corporate-body' model to be abandoned in favour of clear separation of executive and legislature
- Assembly to increase in size from 60 to 80 AMs to deal with extra legislative workload
- 'Additional-member' electoral system to be replaced by single transferable vote

constituency contests with 20 'top-up' seats drawn from regional lists and designed to introduce an element of proportional representation. But the Labour Party in Wales was never keen on any move away from first-past-the-post (Osmond 2005, 6–7) and has developed a particular dislike of regional-list AMs, especially those whom Labour candidates had 'defeated' in constituency contests (Bradbury and Russell 2005).

The Richard Commission reported in March 2004, and recommended changes on all three fronts (Box 8.1). Its report was well received, described by one observer as 'the most serious such analysis produced in the UK since the Royal Commission on the Constitution chaired by Lord Kilbrandon reported in 1972' (Trench 2005a, 35). But it was contentious among some of the Welsh Labour MPs who remain deeply ambivalent about devolution, and the White Paper on Welsh devolution published by the Wales Office in July 2005 was extremely cautious about giving the Assembly new powers, seeing the Richard recommendations on powers as something to be achieved only in stages and over the longer term. The White Paper did endorse the consensus on ending corporate status, but recommended no change in size or electoral system (beyond the ending of dual candidacies in both constituencies and regional lists) (Wales Office 2005).

## Politics in Scotland

Scotland has not had a similarly intense institutional debate to that in Wales since devolution. In a sense it had already had its debate about the shape of devolved politics in the Scottish Constitutional Convention – a cross-party and civil-society organisation which expressed a Scottish elite consensus on devolution – from 1989 to the mid 1990s (Scottish Constitutional Convention 1995). More generally, though, politics in Scotland has developed in a muted political atmosphere. This had something to do with the debilitating controversy over the cost of the new Parliament building, which dragged on until an enquiry reported in September 2004 (Scottish Parliament 2004). But it also had to do with what Mitchell (2004) has called the 'capability–expectations gap', a sense that the 1990s debate created unrealistic expectations about the changes devolution would bring in Scotland. This has been reflected in public assessments of the performance of the Parliament, which are sceptical about the difference the Parliament has made and the influence it has (Bromley and Curtice 2003, 13–16). Significantly, expectations of devolution's impact were much lower in Wales, where the post-devolution sobering-up process has therefore been less painful (Jeffery 2004, 305).

The atmosphere of frustrated expectation has helped subdue political debate in Scotland, where there has been no mainstream equivalent of Rhodri Morgan's rhetorical flourishes in defining distinctive Welsh interests. The 2003 election campaign was fought by all four major parties – Labour, the Scottish National Party, the Liberal Democrats and the Conservatives – as a technocratic competition about who could deliver public services best. The perceived absence of a real contest between the main parties led to both the main governing party (Labour) and the main opposition party (the SNP) losing support. Aided by a more proportional version of the additional-member system than in Wales, a number of smaller parties (the Greens, the Scottish Socialists and one representative of the Senior Citizens' Unity Party) were able to take advantage of the anti-establishment mood and enter or strengthen their place in the Parliament (Table 8.3).

The outcome of the election was a renewal of the Labour–Liberal Democrat coalition established in 1999, and led by First Minister Jack McConnell since 2001. In its first term that coalition introduced a range of distinctive policies in high-profile, high-spending fields such as health and education (including abolition of up-front tuition fees, free long-term care, and higher teachers' pay), at times amid some dispute with the UK government at Westminster (McLeish 2004, 141–4). More recently there has been a tendency to cleave a little more closely to the Westminster line on high-cost public services in the fields of health and welfare (Fawcett 2005), though differences are clear in other, less costly fields, such as immigration, where McConnell has pursued a more immigration-friendly line in light of falling Scottish population figures, or in the introduction of the proportional single transferable vote (STV) electoral system in local

Table 8.3   *The 2003 election in Scotland, compared to 1999*

| Party | Constituency vote % | Regional-list vote % | Constituency seats | Regional seats | Total seats |
|---|---|---|---|---|---|
| Conservative | 16.6 (+1.0) | 15.5 (+0.1) | 3 (+3) | 15 (–3) | 18 (=) |
| Labour | 34.6 (–4.2) | 29.3 (–4.3) | 46 (–7) | 4 (+1) | 50 (–6) |
| Liberal Democrats | 15.4 (+1.1) | 11.8 (–0.6) | 13 (+1) | 4 (–1) | 17 (=) |
| Scottish National Party | 23.8 (–4.9) | 20.9 (–6.4) | 9 (+2) | 18 (–10) | 27 (–8) |
| Greens | – | 6.9 (+3.3) | – | 7 (+6) | 7 (+6) |
| Scottish Socialist Party | 6.2 (+5.2) | 6.7 (+4.7) | 0 (=) | 6 (+5) | 6 (+5) |
| Others | 3.4 (+1.7) | 8.9 (+3.3) | 2 (+1) | 2 (+2) | 4 (+3) |
| Total | 100 | 100 | 73 | 56 | 129 |

government elections from 2007. Proportional representation in local elections was a condition of coalition with the Liberal Democrats, and has been introduced against fierce Labour opposition at the local level. Labour in the Scottish government has been less concerned, seeing it as a way of breaking up some of the 'old' Labour fiefdoms in the Central belt run, as Alan McConnell (2004, 115) put it 'in perpetuity ... by elitist, cronyist councillors who have the potential to bring the party into disrepute'.

## Institutional developments in Scotland

There may have been none of the intense institutional debate in Scotland that Wales has had, but there are two issues which show how the devolution settlement in Scotland is developing. The first is the surprisingly frequent usage of 'Sewel motions' by the Scottish Parliament. Sewel motions are named after the then UK government minister Lord Sewel who envisaged during the passage of the Scotland Bill 'instances where it would be more convenient for legislation on devolved matters to be passed by the UK Parliament'. This procedure was activated 41 times at the request of the Scottish Parliament during its first term 1999–2003 (Keating 2005, 113), and has continued to be used regularly since.

At first sight Sewel motions might seem like an abdication of responsibility to Westminster, but Michael Keating's analysis reveals a rather more nuanced picture, in which Sewel motions are used to save parliamentary

**Box 8.2   The funding of devolution**

- The funds made available to the devolved institution are allocated by the UK Treasury as a 'block'. These allocations are unconditional; the devolved institutions can spend the blocks as they wish within the framework of their powers.
- The baseline size of the territorial blocks was in principle fixed in the period 1979–82 (Mitchell 2003, 10) at levels which reflected a historical pattern of higher per-capita expenditures in Scotland, Wales and Northern Ireland as compared to England.
- Year-on-year changes in the size of the territorial blocks are made in relation to UK-level decisions on spending on 'comparable' policy programmes in England, and are made on a per-capita basis. This is the so-called 'Barnett formula', after the Chief Secretary to the Treasury in 1979, Joel, later Lord, Barnett.
- The effect of the Barnett formula is for Scottish (and Welsh and Northern Irish) per-capita funding to 'converge' on the lower English level. In other words, while the Scottish per-capita baseline was initially fixed at around 120 per cent of per-capita spending in England, subsequent per-capita additions are made at 100 per cent of per-capita spending in England. The long-term effect is to pull down per-capita spending below the initial 120 per cent figure and towards the same level as in England.

time on uncontentious matters, to close potential cross-border loopholes, especially in criminal law, or to assert a Scottish prerogative but reserve its use for a later time (Keating 2004). There are problems with the device, however, not least that it takes legislation for Scotland beyond the reach of the scrutiny of the Scottish Parliament (Page and Batey 2002). Moreover, whilst it works well now, when Labour is the leading party both in Scotland and at Westminster, it may not work so well if and when a different party is in power in either place.

A second institutional issue has concerned the way devolution is financed. The UK's territorial financial arrangements – which apply in much the same way to Scotland, Wales and Northern Ireland – have a number of key features, which are explained in Box 8.2. The financial arrangements for devolution are problematic in two main ways. First, they leave Scotland (and Wales and Northern Ireland) highly dependent on the UK Exchequer. Second, because block funding is raised from the UK tax payer and awarded unconditionally by the UK Treasury, the accountability of spending decisions by the devolved administrations is at best indirect. These issues sparked an animated if rather ill-informed debate in Scotland about greater 'fiscal autonomy' in the 2001 UK general election campaign (Heald and McLeod 2002). Although that debate quickly became consumed in party-political point scoring, its longer-term effect was to set in train fuller reflection on some of the oddities of the Barnett system which is now producing more concrete proposals (Hallward and MacDonald 2005). 'Westminster' has, however, so far shown little sign of thinking through the arrangements for financing devolution beyond simply projecting forward the pre-existing Barnett-era arrangements.

There is an advantage in this continuity of arrangements: it has allowed UK and devolved institutions to avoid the kinds of dispute over territorial finance which are commonplace in other decentralised states (Jeffery 2003a). But there are also disadvantages. The inherited system of territorial finance does not take into account 'need' – for example structural economic weakness, or the higher cost per capita of providing public services in thinly populated areas – in any systematic way. Also, the convergence effect of the Barnett formula should lead in time to a tightening of devolved budgets. The potential for conflict over funding is clear. It is amplified by the dependence of the devolved blocks on spending decisions made by Westminster for England. It is conceivable that a future Westminster government could rebalance the role of market and state in the provision of public services, significantly reducing public expenditures. Those reductions would feed through into the devolved blocks whether or not the devolved legislatures agreed with an enhanced role for markets. Once again there is a potential 'lopsidedness effect' on the devolved nations caused by an undevolved England.

## Northern Ireland

Devolution in Northern Ireland is a special, and increasingly rare, circumstance: special because it is bound up with the peace process which has unfolded since the mid 1990s; rare because the devolved institutions have been suspended since October 2002. Continued suspension reflects a failure of trust between Northern Ireland's unionist parties and Sinn Fein, the political party associated with the Irish Republican Army (IRA), and now the leading party of the Irish-nationalist tradition in Northern Ireland. The immediate cause of the 2002 suspension (which followed a number of earlier, shorter, suspensions between 1999 and 2002) was the revelation that the IRA was still collecting intelligence on the security services in Northern Ireland. There was a backdrop of wider unease that the process of disarmament ('decommissioning') by the IRA was proceeding too slowly and opaquely.

The 2002 suspension opened up a period of behind-the-scenes negotiations which produced periodic expectations that a commitment from the IRA to a permanent end to military activity was close. On two occasions – in October 2003 and December 2004 – a breakthrough was almost reached, though on each occasion it was dashed by arguments about the lack of transparency surrounding IRA decommissioning. The failure of trust revealed on these occasions was then hardened by a major bank raid in Northern Ireland in late December 2004, which was widely assumed to be the work of the IRA, and the murder of a Belfast man, allegedly by a group of IRA members, in a pub in January 2005.

These cycles of painstaking negotiation and carefully prepared breakthroughs dashed at the last minute have had a polarising effect on Northern Irish politics (Table 8.4). The pro-conciliation Ulster Unionist Party (UUP) has lost credibility among the unionist community, allowing the more intransigent Democratic Unionist Party (DUP) led by the veteran Protestant fundamentalist Ian Paisley to become the largest unionist party. At the same time the centrist nationalist party, the Social Democratic and Labour Party (SDLP), has lost ground to Sinn Fein (SF), whose association with the IRA even amid bank robberies and murder appears to be doing it no electoral harm. In 1997, the two more centrist parties (the UUP and the SDLP) outpolled the two more extreme parties (the DUP and SF) by almost two to one. Since 2003, the two extremist parties have been outpolling the centrists.

It is difficult to imagine how the institutional framework established in the 1998 Belfast Agreement which launched devolution can be made to work amid such polarisation. That Agreement set out a system of proportional government designed to involve all parties with significant electoral support in an 'involuntary coalition' under a joint First Ministership with a First Minister from one of the two communities,

**Table 8.4**   *Electoral polarisation in Northern Ireland 1997–2005*

| Election | Parties | | | | Groups | |
|---|---|---|---|---|---|---|
| | DUP | UUP | SDLP | SF | 'Centre' | 'Extreme' |
| | % | % | % | % | (UUP+SDLP) | (DUP+SF) |
| Westminster 1997 | 13.6 | 32.7 | 24.1 | 16.1 | 56.8 | 29.7 |
| NI Assembly 1998 | 18.0 | 21.3 | 21.9 | 17.6 | 43.2 | 35.6 |
| Westminster 2001 | 22.5 | 26.8 | 20.9 | 21.7 | 47.7 | 44.2 |
| NI Assembly 2003 | 25.7 | 22.7 | 16.9 | 23.5 | 39.6 | 49.2 |
| Westminster 2005 | 33.7 | 17.7 | 17.5 | 24.3 | 35.2 | 58.0 |

unionist or nationalist, and a Deputy First Minister from the other. A number of other mechanisms were introduced to enforce cross-community consensus on contentious issues, including 'super-majority' clauses in the Assembly and institutional frameworks for embedding the Assembly in 'north–south' engagement with the Irish Republic and 'east–west' engagement with UK institutions.

For this set of densely interlocked institutions to work there needs to be a willingness among political parties to cooperate across the community divide. But the results of the 2003 Northern Ireland election have made them close to unworkable. The DUP is now by some way the biggest party and would nominate the Northern Ireland First Minister. Sinn Fein as the leading party of the other community would nominate the Deputy First Minister. The two First Ministers would jointly lead government in Northern Ireland. However, the DUP refuses any overt contact with Sinn Fein, and has hardened that position since the outburst of criminality and violence at the turn of the year 2004/05. Continued 'direct rule' by Westminster – in other words the pre-devolution situation – is the necessary consequence until and unless the DUP is prepared to work openly with Sinn Fein.

## England

England remains what Robert Hazell (2000, 278) has called the 'gaping hole in the devolution settlement'. There have been no plans (and there is negligible popular support) for an English Parliament equivalent to the devolved institutions in the other UK nations. The only devolution reform implemented in England has been the GLA in London. The GLA was however seen as a special case, not part of the wider regional devolution process, even though in some respects it provided a template for regional devolution plans elsewhere in England.

The Labour government came to power in 1997 with a twin-track plan for the English regions. The first track was to build on earlier Conservative policies of establishing stronger mechanisms of central government in the regions in order to implement Westminster policy more effectively. The Government Offices for the Regions (GOs) introduced by the Conservatives have been steadily strengthened and their reach extended across more central-government departments. Regional Development Agencies (RDAs) with a remit for regional economic development were introduced in 1999. And Regional Chambers of 'stakeholders' were set up to provide a measure of regional accountability for the work of the RDAs, and have since taken on a wider range of functions.

The second track of policy, associated closely with Deputy Prime

Minister John Prescott, was to democratise this decentralised apparatus of central government by establishing elected regional assemblies (ERAs) which would take over the work of the RDAs and the Regional Chambers. That second track was announced in the 1997 Labour manifesto, only for nothing to happen in the 1997 Parliament, with the pledge being repeated in almost exactly the same form in the 2001 Labour manifesto: regions which demonstrated 'demand' for regional government through a positive referendum vote could have an ERA. It took until May 2002 for a White Paper to emerge setting out what ERAs would do (Cabinet Office/DTLR 2002). The powers planned for ERAs were very modest (Box 8.3), reflecting the success of central-government departments in resisting any transfers of their functions (Select Committee on the Office of the Deputy Prime Minister 2005, 21–2), and underlining John Prescott's isolation as the only Cabinet member in Westminster committed to elected assemblies.

There followed a cosmetic consultation exercise in the regions on 'levels of interest' in holding a referendum which led to the announcement that the three northern English regions (North East, North West and Yorkshire and the Humber) would be the first to have a referendum (Jeffery 2003b). But in July 2004 the North West and Yorkshire and the Humber were struck off the referendum list, ostensibly for technical electoral-process reasons, but in reality because the government knew they were unwinnable.

The referendum held in the North East in November 2004 emphatically rejected Prescott's ERAs, by 78 per cent to 22 per cent. Opposition was strikingly uniform. No significant group – whether demarcated by

---

### Box 8.3 Proposals for elected regional assemblies in England

- Twenty-five to 35 members, elected by the additional-member system, led by a small 'cabinet'
- 'Strategic' role in setting policy objectives and coordinating regional policy actors, but with policy implementation dependent on arm's-length assembly 'functional bodies', including RDAs, local authorities and other regional 'stakeholders'
- Strategic role in: economic development; planning; housing; transport; culture, tourism and sport; public health; rural policy; environment; crime reduction; and fire and rescue
- Funding by block grant from central government plus limited power to 'precept' (surcharge) local domestic property tax

age, gender, social class or political affiliation – voted in favour of an ERA in the North East. No local-authority area voted in favour (Rallings and Thrasher 2005). There were a number of reasons for this overwhelming rejection, not all of which had anything to do with ERAs. The referendum was held at the end of the second term of a government embroiled in an unpopular conflict in Iraq, and amid a general sense of disillusionment about politics and politicians, and to an extent the referendum was used as an anti-government protest.

But there was also a clear sense among North Easterners that the region was ignored by central government in London, did not get its fair share of the nation's resources, and was economically disadvantaged (Rallings and Thrasher 2005, 4). There was at least some fertile ground for establishing an institution to give voice to the North East and to pursue a vigorous economic-development agenda. Voters evidently felt, though, that the institution proposed would make no difference. The 'No' campaign in the referendum was highly effective in presenting the proposed Assembly as a toothless talking shop. Even the 'Yes' campaign admitted much the same point by presenting the ERA as a 'starting point' which would lead to further powers being granted at some unspecified point in the future (Tickell et al. 2005). Voters drew the conclusion that the ERA would make no discernible difference in addressing the needs of the North East (Rallings and Thrasher 2005, 5).

One reason for thinking that conclusion odd is the GLA. The GLA has a directly elected figurehead and a different mix of policy responsibilities, but essentially the same model of 'strategic' powers dependent on others for implementation. Yet it was approved by an overwhelming 72 to 28 per cent in the 1998 referendum, and is now well established. People think it has made a difference, especially in using congestion charging to boost public transport and on crime (Margetts 2005). Some of this may be down to having a mayor as an unequivocal leadership voice, especially one as vigorous as Ken Livingstone (who was re-elected in 2004). Rather more is due to the agreement among Londoners that 'London' is a coherent community with a general interest which needs to be addressed through its own institutions of government (cf. Margetts 2005), as it had been before the (unpopular) abolition of the Greater London Council in 1985. It is that sense of general interest that the English regions lack. No matter how much Northerners feel disadvantaged by Westminster centralism, regional government was not judged to be a credible alternative option (cf. Heath et al. 2002, 174–6). What that leaves us with – as the North East vote confirmed – is a non-devolved England and little prospect of ameliorating the lopsidedness that a non-devolved England brings to the post-devolution UK state.

## What the public thinks

Yet asymmetric devolution in a lopsided state appears to be close to public preferences. Majorities in both Scotland and Wales are in favour of devolution, and support in both nations for independence or a return to direct rule from Westminster are minority viewpoints. Even in Northern Ireland where a significant minority supports unification with the Irish Republic, devolution remains the most popular among the various constitutional options (MacGinty 2003). Perhaps most significantly the English support neither national nor regional devolution, but instead continued direct rule by the UK Parliament. But nor do they oppose devolution outside of England. Scottish devolution is supported by about the same proportion of the English as Scots. In other words, asymmetric devolution 'appears to be about as popular in England as it is in Scotland or Wales' (Curtice 2006).

There are still underlying concerns about some of the equity issues raised by asymmetric devolution, especially about the 'West Lothian Question' (where Scottish MPs at Westminster can vote, say, on health policy in non-devolved England, while English MPs cannot vote on health policy in devolved Scotland). But those concerns have remained largely abstract and immune to the periodic attempts by the Conservative Party (which is strong in England, but weak in Scotland and Wales) to mobilise resentment in England. That may not remain the case following the 2005 Westminster election which left Labour with a much smaller majority and will expose it to more frequent accusations that it has won votes on Westminster laws which apply to England only on the basis of votes cast by Scottish and Welsh Labour MPs, to whose constituents the laws in question do not apply. The West Lothian Question will certainly remain a potentially problematic issue now that regional devolution in England – which some saw as a way of evening out some of the UK's lopsidedness – is off the agenda.

The potential for territorial political mobilisation around the West Lothian Question or other issues may well depend on how strongly a sense of common identity linking the nations of the UK and underpinning a solidarity between them is maintained. As yet devolution has had little impact on 'Britishness', except for a sharpening of the distinction among the English between identities of Englishness and Britishness. But even so around three quarters of the English still see Britishness as one of their identities, about the same proportion of the Welsh, and around 60 per cent of the Scots (Curtice 2006). There is a different pattern in Northern Ireland, where Britishness is a sharply held identity among Protestants while the overwhelming majority of Catholics see themselves as Irish. But Northern Ireland excepted, there appears to be a facility to combine 'local' national identities with an overarching Britishness.

That ability to express plural identities also has some reflection in voting behaviour in Scotland and Wales. There have now been five elections in the devolution era (Table 8.5). The election results reveal a pattern which has been confirmed in both academic survey research and commercial opinion polls: Labour as a party of the 'Union' does better in Scotland and Wales in voting intentions and election results for Westminster elections; and nationalist parties (the Scottish National Party and Plaid Cymru) do better in voting intentions and election results for devolved elections. This is not simply an example of 'mid-term protest', as ideas on 'second-order elections' (Reif and Schmitt 1980) might suggest, but a systematic distinction in some voters' minds on a 'horses-for-courses' basis: while Labour at the moment is favoured as a party for managing the Union as a whole, it (and the two other 'Union' parties) are seen as less capable of pursuing Scottish or Welsh interests within the Union, and lose out to parties that are seen to 'stand up' for Scotland and Wales, namely the SNP and Plaid Cymru (Jeffery and Hough 2003, 259–60). Devolution in this sense is about Scottish voters giving 'Scottish answers to Scottish questions' when they think of voting in a Scottish Parliament context and 'UK answers to UK questions' when it comes to Westminster (cf. Paterson et al. 2001, 29).

## Devolution and policy variation

What this differentiation of voting behaviour does *not* mean is that the Scots or the Welsh have different policy priorities compared to the English. A growing collection of survey data shows that the Scots and Welsh – perhaps contrary to the popular myth – are not significantly more left-wing than the English; with a few exceptions they share much the same policy preferences, and are not enthusiastic about the possibility of policies in, say, health or education varying from one part of the UK to the next (Jeffery 2005a). Support for devolution is less about pursuing distinctive policy agendas in different places than about a sense of ownership of the policy process in more 'proximate' devolved settings.

But though there is no obvious popular basis for policy variation, both the dynamics of devolved democratic processes, and some of the institutional features of devolution, can lead to divergent policies (Greer 2006). The following four factors are especially important.

### 1  Differences in patterns of party competition tend to produce differences of politics

At Westminster the main competition is between left and right. In Scotland and Wales the nationalists pull the terms of party competition

**Table 8.5** *The Labour–Nationalist trade-off in UK and devolved elections 1997–2005*

| Party | 1997 UK % | | 1999 devolved % | | 2001 UK % | | 2003 devolved % | | 2005 UK % | |
|---|---|---|---|---|---|---|---|---|---|---|
| | Scotland | Wales | Scotland | Wales | Scotland | Wales | Scotland | Wales | Scotland | Wales |
| Labour | 45.6 | 54.7 | 33.6 | 35.5 | 43.9 | 48.6 | 34.6 | 40.0 | 39.5 | 42.7 |
| SNP | 22.1 | – | 27.3 | – | 20.1 | – | 23.8 | – | 17.7 | – |
| Plaid Cymru | – | 10.0 | – | 30.6 | – | 14.3 | – | 21.2 | – | 12.6 |

*Note:* Devolved election figures are for constituency vote.

to the left of centre. Different voting systems also produce different types of government: what is likely to be permanent coalition government in Scotland and a finely balanced situation in Wales, which has already produced minority government, coalition government and wafer-thin single-party majority government. Scottish and Welsh governments need in other words to be more inclusive, importing into government some of the left-leaning dynamic of party competition and opening up pressures for policy variation.

## 2  Policy communities have recalibrated since devolution

Some interest groups with a UK-wide organisational structure are now working in more territorially differentiated ways, with more emerging in Scotland-only (or Wales-only) guises (Loughlin and Sykes 2004). The emphasis in the devolution debates on civic participation and inclusion has also invigorated civil-society organisations and activities in the devolved territories. In these ways territorially bounded policy debates emerge which may, or may not, share the same concerns as those pursued in policy communities centred around the Westminster Parliament.

## 3  In Scotland and Northern Ireland, devolution is based on the separation of reserved and devolved powers

There are few equivalents of the mechanisms frequently used in other decentralised systems which allow the central state to set state-wide policy standards. In the Welsh case such possibilities do exist, but even there the tendency is for the National Assembly to use its powers with growing discretion and declining Westminster regulation.

## 4  The financial settlement underpinning devolution is unusually permissive

Within the block grant awarded by the UK Treasury, the devolved administrations are not tied to a particular spending pattern, can switch across budget headings at will, and are not bound to deliver UK-wide policy objectives. In other decentralised states it is normal for at least some substantial part of the funding for devolved or regional governments to be allocated conditionally by state-level governments in order to meet state-wide objectives. But the UK government has no mechanism within fields covered by the block to 'buy' its way into devolved autonomy to meet such objectives.

## Managing UK–devolved relations

Given that the institutions and processes of devolution seem to favour policy variation, it is surprising that intergovernmental coordination between central and devolved governments in the UK is, comparatively speaking, weakly institutionalised. By its very nature, asymmetrical devolution encourages bilateral rather than multilateral (that is, UK-wide) discussion of policy objectives, and there is little strategic policy discussion at senior official or ministerial levels to organise the balance of UK-wide and devolved objectives in, say, health policy or transport. The institutional mechanisms set up to coordinate the work of UK and devolved governments – concordats setting out the 'rules of the game' and a Joint Ministerial Committee (JMC) for developing coordinated policy initiatives and resolving disagreements – have barely been used.

Mostly, contacts between UK and devolved governments are conducted on an informal basis, both between officials in different administrations, and through the channels of the Labour Party, which has been the majority party in Westminster and the leading party of government in Scotland and Wales for the whole of the devolution era. The only areas in which there has been systematic coordination between UK and devolved governments have concerned EU matters which impinge on devolved competences. The UK government at the outset committed itself to including the devolved governments in UK policy formulation for the EU, recognising the overlap of devolved and EU competences, and over time a practice of intense coordination has emerged in which the JMC-Europe meets regularly, and the devolved administrations also contribute to weekly meetings to define the UK line in Brussels negotiations. Similarly, though outside the JMC system, UK and devolved agriculture ministers (and UK and Scottish fisheries ministers) also coordinate their work systematically in developing what are de facto joint UK–devolved policy positions (Jeffery 2005b).

In other words it takes an external impetus – the need to have a single UK position in EU negotiations – to prompt post-devolution UK into acting as a coordinated political system. In part that reflects the prehistory of devolution. Before 1999 Scottish, Welsh and Northern Irish concerns were coordinated with English and UK-level concerns in largely informal processes of discussion between departments of central government. That practice has been projected forward into the devolution era, facilitated at the outset by continuities among the civil servants involved, which has helped the smooth implementation of the devolution reforms.

But it arguably also encourages complacency and a failure to think through some of the likely medium-term dynamics of devolution. Unsurprisingly UK government departments are often poor at identifying when UK-level policies, applied to the largest part of a lopsided UK, England, have knock-on consequences for devolved competences. This has not yet produced overt conflicts because of the ability to finesse disputes within the Labour Party, but Labour will not always be in power everywhere, and such conflicts will then be more problematic. Similarly, another 'lubricant' for the avoidance of conflict has been the rapid growth of public expenditures since 1999 which, despite the convergence effect of the Barnett formula, means that UK government departments and devolved governments have had more cash to spend. That period of growth of public expenditures is exceptional, and will come to an end at some point, heralding a more difficult era of debate on territorial finance and territorial 'justice' (Adams et al. 2003).

## Conclusion

In other words, the smoothness with which devolution initially bedded down is not likely to endure. The prompt for change may well come from some mix of economic downturn (and downward pressure on public expenditures) coinciding with (and helping to cause) a change of government either at the UK level or in a devolved administration. It remains to be seen whether a system of coordination based on informal linkages rooted in pre-devolution *intra*governmental practice will be capable of running *inter*governmental relations between administrations run by different parties.

As well as the difficulty of trying to run aspects of the current system, like the 'piggy-backing' of Welsh concerns onto Westminster Bills or Sewel motions for Westminster legislation on Scotland, there could also be more fundamental problems. A UK government committed to policies which cut back on public expenditure in England would also reduce budgets in the devolved nations via the Barnett formula – even though the democratic mandate of the devolved governments might be for a different, higher-expenditure policy mix. More generally a UK government which lacked party channels for coordination with the devolved administrations could simply show (even) less consideration for the 'spill-over' effects of policies made for England on the rest of the UK, and would be much less likely to include the devolved administrations so fully in developing UK positions for EU negotiations. In those circumstances the relative equanimity with which citizens view asymmetric devolution may erode; subterranean tensions over equity of representation (the West Lothian Question) or public spending (the Barnett formula and relative 'needs') may come to the surface and create new territorial cleavages in public opinion.

For all these reasons a series of commentators (Hazell 2003, 300–1; Select Committee on the Constitution 2002, 5; Trench 2001, 173), largely reflecting on experience in other decentralised states, have recommended a formalisation of the UK's intergovernmental relations to establish a more overt practice of balancing UK/English and devolved concerns, thus building institutional shock absorbers for that future point when different parties run different governments. The UK Government's (2003, 3) response has been to dismiss such recommendations, amid a confidence that ministers and officials would continue to work together in the way they do now as a 'second nature irrespective of the political persuasion of the administration involved'. That sounds like a triumph of hope over any conventional understanding of party politics in the UK, where 'second nature' is that of adversariality, not cross-party cooperation.

The challenge of managing a lopsided state when electoral processes throw up divergent mandates is one which should not be underestimated. That it has been underestimated reflects the ease with which pre-devolution practices of intragovernmental accommodation of territorial interests could be transformed into intergovernmental practices. The continuities which have underpinned that transformation have been a tremendous short-term advantage for the implementation of the devolution reforms in a context of pan-British Labour dominance. But the complacency which those continuities have encouraged threatens to become a crippling disability over the longer timeframe in which partisan conflict will enter, complicate and disrupt the territorial equation.

## Chapter 9

# Britain, Europe and the World

MICHAEL SMITH

Traditionally, politics and policy making in Britain, as in other democracies, were based implicitly on a model that distinguished very clearly between 'domestic' and 'international' contexts. In the domestic context, global and economic factors notwithstanding, governments could in principle control the important resources and mechanisms, and thanks to the legitimacy with which they were endowed through popular election, they could claim to be carrying out the will of the people. That did not make things easy, but it certainly made them different from what happened in the international arena, where Britain was in competition (sometimes deadly competition) with other governments, and where the defence of the 'national interest' occupied a central place. In the international arena, the defence of the realm might demand secrecy and a set of very 'undemocratic' devices, by contrast with the popular control exercised however indirectly through Parliament. The saying 'politics stops at the water's edge' summed up some of the key assumptions built into this model. But involvement in the EU and a host of other European and international bodies has seriously eroded this implicit framework, enmeshing Britain in a host of international commitments and undertakings, and imposing a vast range of more or less formal rules on the making and conduct of policy.

As a result, politics and policy making in Britain centre increasingly on both European and international issues and they are more subject than ever before to international obligations and restrictions. These are most evident in the European Union (EU) context, where Britain has signed up to an extensive and often legally binding set of policy frameworks centred outside the country. The Labour governments since 1997 have been especially energetic at signing up to such commitments, but they have only continued trends established since the UK joined the EU in 1973 (Geddes 2004). These commitments have both benefits and costs for the British: on the one hand, they often add international resources and support to the British position, and help governments to further their aims; on the other hand, they can also inhibit governments from pursuing what might be seen as the more beneficial line for purely national advantage. To this general point can be added the more particular effects arising from the growth of what is often termed 'multilevel governance': it is often the case that once European or international commitments have been assumed by national governments, they lead to new patterns of policy making some of which by-pass the national government altogether (as for example in the allocation and use of regional assistance in the EU).

## Europe in British government and politics

It is widely noted in the literature on Britain's membership of the EU that whilst British government has been thoroughly Europeanised, British politics have not (Allen 2005). By this is meant that the administrative machinery and the formal structures of government, both at central and at regional and local level, have been permeated by the European influence channelled through membership of the EU. The EU is a major source of legislation which must be implemented at the national level; it is a major source of funds and other resources that enable policies in a number of sectors to be carried out; and it is a key source of legitimacy for government officials working in an increasingly Europeanised context. Although Britain has been characterised as an 'awkward partner' in the EU (George 1998), this has not always been because of the failure of its government structures to adapt to the demands of EU membership; rather it has been in some cases because the government has been all too aware of the extent to which British government is becoming Europeanised and has wished to use the same government structures as a channel for resistance to further encroachments from Brussels (Bogdanor 2005a; Young 1999).

The EU has been a major and continuing source of political cleavages in Britain and these cleavages have run both between and within political parties (Allen 2005, 127–31; George 1998; Young 1999). In broad terms the Liberal Democrats can be described as being more supportive of and the Conservatives more critical of the EU, whilst Labour, the governing party since 1997, has been critically supportive, yet displaying persistent tensions between being more and less European. Of course, these dividing lines are often much less clear and settled than they might appear. They are certainly more nuanced within parties. The emergence of a single-issue party focused on the issue of EU membership and little else, the UK Independence Party, has further underlined intra- and interparty tensions. The result is an odd mixture of claims and counter-claims. On the one hand, the claim is made that Britain is a 'good European', implementing EU legislation and actively working with and through EU institutions; on the other hand, there is the persistent suggestion that Britain cannot be dictated to by the EU and should both challenge and thwart the 'threat' posed by Brussels. These differences serve to generate highly contentious politics around the growing influence of the EU in the everyday life of the UK.

In terms of British government, some would claim that the very structure of the British state has assumed a more European aspect, especially since the late 1990s (Geddes 2004, Chapter 8). Devolution, the granting of a degree of domestic policy autonomy to Scotland, Wales and (in principle) Northern Ireland, has given Britain a more decentralised appearance, something which would not be out of place in a number of continental European countries. British governments might have spent a great deal of time denouncing the perils of federalism at the European level but Britain has begun to look quasi-federal in itself, with all of the consequent attention to the division of functions and resources between the national and the subnational levels of government.

One of the consequences of this set of developments, both in central and in devolved government, is that in significant respects Britain has become part of a system of 'multilevel governance' (Hooghe and Marks 2001). There is increasingly a sense that the UK national level is only one of several different and interconnected levels at which politics and policy making take place. It has even been argued that this trend might eventually lead to the fusion of national and European systems of governance, a situation in which it would be impossible (and also undesirable) to distinguish between what is 'British' and what is 'European' (Rometsch and Wessels 1996). There are, of course, many ways in which this is not yet the case in Britain and one would imagine there would be strong resistance to such a tendency given the degree of Euroscepticism found in Britain (and demonstrated by the fact that Britain has yet to join the European single currency, and is unlikely to do so any time soon, if ever) (Geddes 2004). It just might be, however, that there is a logic leading British government and many of its practitioners towards a more European focus for its activities. It is already the case that British domestic ministries spend a substantial proportion of their time and effort on European issues. The same is true for both the House of Commons and the House of Lords, and even for the judicial system insofar as it is concerned with matters of European law.

The European dimension in British government goes far beyond the rather technical issues of dealing with the EU and its real and symbolic centre, Brussels. It could be argued that EU membership has significantly reshaped the structure of British government itself and fundamentally affected the relationship between government and citizens. For instance, it is very clear that constitutional politics displays a European tendency, for whatever reasons. Even without the adoption of the proposed European Constitution, something rendered moot by its rejection in the French and Dutch referenda of May and June 2005, the British constitution cannot escape the influence of Europe. In terms of economic management, the increasing regionalisation and devolution of British government, combined with the availability of resources for key policy purposes from Brussels (for example through the European Regional Development Fund), the EU influences what the British government does and can do. Finally, it has to be noted that the activities of a wide range of British government departments have acquired a strong European dimension, and that officials have in many cases spent the whole of their careers dealing with European counterparts in a variety of European settings.

This process sits uneasily with the practices of politics in Britain. The Blair government has been highly sensitive to the Eurosceptic tendency in British politics and endlessly anxious not to be outflanked by the Conservatives in its EU policy. Labour emphasises the fact that its EU policy is pursued in the British interest. It proudly presents itself as pro-European, but also as Eurorealist. For instance, the Blair government was anxious not only to claim that the negotiation of the abortive European Constitution was a British victory reflecting its interests, but also to ensure that economic management remains at the national level by vigorously resisting all calls for taxation or social security expenditure to be handled at the EU level. A robust Eurorealism, working through Europe while putting British interests first, also explains why Britain has strongly opposed any suggestion that its budgetary rebate, obtained by the Thatcher government in 1984, should be diluted or ended without wider financial reform – particularly reform of the Common Agricultural Policy (CAP), which is adamantly opposed by the French.

## British policy making

It is suggested that thanks to the EU there is some form of 'authority leakage' in many parts of the British policy-making process, with the locus of certain decision making migrating from the national to the European level. This is most noticeable in areas such as agriculture and external trade where commitments made under the EU mean that there is relatively little left in the way of national policy-making autonomy, but it can also be observed across a wide spectrum of British policy making (Allen 2005; Geddes 2004). In certain policy areas British policies are not made in a vacuum. In addition, a good deal of policy making between Britain and the EU on matters where the EU is significant takes place between the devolved administrations in Edinburgh and Cardiff and Brussels rather than through Whitehall and Westminster. Thus, in certain areas where substantial responsibility is devolved to the Scottish Parliament and the Welsh Assembly – for example, on regional-development issues – policy making has been at least partly Europeanised, and carried out in both a European and a Scottish and Welsh national context.

Britain has consistently resisted the extension of EU competence to cover areas of economic policy such as taxation. The Chancellor of the Exchequer, Gordon Brown, has stoutly insisted on the relevance of his five 'economic tests' before Britain can even consider adopting the euro:

- convergence between the UK and eurozone economies;
- the capacity of the system to deal with economic shocks;
- its effect on investment in the UK;
- impact on the financial services industry in the UK; and
- impact on unemployment in the UK (Aspinwall 2003; Geddes 2004, Chapter 7).

The government has made plain that it will not recommend British entry into the euro, which will be decided by a national referendum, until it judges that it is in the British national interest to join. Nonetheless, it could be argued that economic management at the purely national level rather than the European level is under challenge and that certain decisions, say the level of excise taxes or value added taxes, cannot be taken in isolation from the existence of the Single European Market and the needs of cross-border intra-European trade. The substance of much policy, including the most fundamental aspects of government such as the setting and collection of taxes and the management of the currency, have therefore been somewhat Europeanised.

Another way in which British government has been reshaped by the EU involves the judicial applicability of EU law, but Europeanisation also goes beyond the EU. One of the most important judicial reforms undertaken by the Labour government has been the incorporation into British law of the European Convention on Human Rights, through the Human Rights Act of 1998. As a result, for a very wide range of concerns to do with the rights of citizens and of those living in Britain, there is now an inescapable European dimension to the activities of the judicial system, a dimension which has been significant in such areas as the rights of migrants, refugees and asylum seekers (Geddes 2005) and also affecting the adoption of new counter-terrorist legislation. On the one hand the Blair government has been able to use EU immigration and asylum policies as an additional dimension of their national policy, whilst accepting some intrusion into the national policy process (Geddes 2005), but on the other hand efforts to implement new measures against those suspected of terrorist activity are brought up short when the judiciary invokes the Human Rights Act. Finally, British diplomacy is impacted by the EU, particularly in the area of Common Foreign and Security Policy (CFSP) and European Security and Defence Policy (CESDP). As a result, the machinery of the Foreign and Commonwealth Office and increasingly that of the Ministry of Defence, as well as associated departments such as the Department of International Development, has been pragmatically adapted to the increasing salience of the European dimension in British diplomacy (Allen and Oliver 2006; Hocking and Spence 2003).

## Britain in the European Union

The impact of the EU on the structure and functioning of British government and its policy-making processes is only one side of the coin. The other side is the British impact on the structure and functioning of the EU and its policy competences. This is best explored by understanding the ways in which Britain has approached its EU entanglement. Britain, even under the leadership of Mrs Thatcher, has signed up to a number of the most important European initiatives, but has always been considered an 'awkward partner', a foremost Eurosceptic, together with Denmark, and a focus for resistance within the European project. Britain is seen as an 'insular polity', particularly given its imperial history and its close reciprocal links with the US, and these are said to cloud its European vision and qualify its Europeanism. Many have suggested that Britain is an insufficiently committed European, a common obstacle to continued European integration and a threat to the majority consensus within the EU (Bogdanor 2005a; Young 1999). There is some substance to these charges, since it has undoubtedly been a key aim of many British governments to stem the tide of integration and to defend the independence of the British state and its parliamentary sovereignty (Bogdanor 2005a). Since the mid 1990s, though, the position has been rather different. The Labour governments led by Tony Blair, despite retaining many of the 'red lines' (on such issues as taxation, employment and broader economic management) that previous Conservative governments had adopted, have pursued a much more positive European strategy and made a determined effort to play the European game. Naturally, they do so only when it is perceived to be to Britain's national advantage to do so (Smith 2005).

Britain's engagement with Europe has often revealed other fault lines within the EU, most notably within the so-called Franco–German axis, often the motor of European integration. It has become apparent that there are severe tensions both within and at times between France and

Germany, and their separate and connected crises have been a key focus of the problems in European integration since 2000. Combined with the changing nature of the EU itself, including such factors as the major enlargement of 2004 which saw the EU expand from 15 to 25 member states, this has created new challenges and opportunities for British policy making. The Blair government has been willing to exploit these opportunities, but in attempting to do so it has come up against a number of important constraints located both within and outside the EU itself (Allen 2005; Forster and Blair 2002; Smith 2005).

## The European Constitution

During the past five years the key focus of much of the EU's political activity has been the attempt to develop and then ratify a new Constitutional Treaty. Provision was made in the Nice Treaty of December 2000 for the development of a further stage in the constitutionalisation of the EU, which was confirmed in the Laeken Declaration of December 2001. A European Convention was established under the chairmanship of the former French president, Valéry Giscard d'Estaing, its participants nominated by national governments and parliaments and selected from among EU institutions; the aim was to draft a European Constitution which would subsume and expand the existing EU treaties and overhaul the EU's decision-making structures, institutions and procedures in light of the EU's expansion from twelve members in 1993 to 25 members in 2004 with the admission of new members from Central and Eastern Europe and the Mediterranean.

The British position on the Convention was one of full and active participation – but also of fierce defence of what the government defined as 'red-line' issues, those on which it would not yield, and of the prerogatives of the member states. The 'red-line' issues predictably included powers over taxation, social security and immigration policy, but also other issues, among them foreign and defence policy, on which the Blair government was only willing to proceed in specific ways. As a result, the Convention was used actively by the British to pursue a number of reforms in which they had been interested over the long term, in particular those aimed at strengthening the leadership of the European Council (which represents the 25 member states) and at improving foreign-policy coordination. On foreign and defence policy Britain and France successfully pushed for a European foreign minister and to bring together a number of existing powers and competences.

It is clear from this that the UK was as much as any other member state an active participant in the Convention – and in some areas, British individuals or groups took a key leadership role. For instance, the

Secretary-General to the Convention was the highly experienced British official, Sir John Kerr. As a result, when the draft European Constitution drawn up by the Convention was amended and finally agreed by the European Council in June 2004, Britain was able to claim that all of its 'red lines' had been defended, and that it had managed to achieve its preferred solutions in many areas of the text. There was an irony, however, given that one of the aims of the Convention had been the promotion of debate about the EU, when in Britain there had been hardly any public debate at all. The pro-European criticism, that the Blair government neglected the European message and did not properly take on Eurosceptic forces, was thereby reinforced by Britain's half-hearted attempts to build public support for the European Constitution.

Of course, in the EU agreeing a treaty is often the easy part; the hard part is the process of then ratifying the treaty, particularly where referenda have been used. While the British government was initially anxious to avoid holding a referendum, Blair changed his mind and bowed to mounting public pressure to do so in April 2004. From that point on, the government espoused the idea of a popular vote, but, given the very real possibility (some say likelihood) that the British electors would vote down the Constitution, wanted to delay it as long as possible, perhaps so that voters might feel pressure to vote in the affirmative if all other EU member states had accepted the treaty. In the event, although it does not appear this formed part of a British plan, Blair's acceptance of a referendum put pressure on other governments, notably the French, to also hold such a vote. The upshot of this was that the French and the Dutch electorates rejected the Constitutional Treaty by considerable margins in May and June 2005. Some commentators saw this as the ideal result for the Blair government. It had been prepared to seek popular support for the now defunct Constitution, something which was very much an uphill battle in Britain, but had now been excused the need to hold a referendum in the wake of French and Dutch rejection. The Treaty was dead, despite the many measures that Britain had wanted, was put in abeyance by the European Council in June 2005, and nobody could blame the British for its demise.

## Economic management

Britain has consistently sought to severely restrict the economic competence it is prepared to grant the EU level, particularly increased competences for the EU institutions. More generally, Gordon Brown has been persistent and blunt in his refusal to give up any national powers in respect of taxation and social security. At the same time, in the face of continued public opposition to abandoning the pound sterling, the government has delayed any decision on the euro and Brown's five economic tests, which are in many ways strongly political rather than purely technical, have been used as the rationale for not even considering the promised referendum on the issue (Allen 2005; Smith 2005). In effect there has been no active consideration of the euro as a practical policy option since 2003 even though the government is notionally in favour of it in principle.

Opposition to – or token support for – the euro does not mean that the Blair government has no interest in economic reform at the EU level. On the contrary, it has willingly challenged what it considers as the underproductive economic policies of its fellow member states, championing deregulation and competitiveness across the EU as the means of achieving economic growth and development as in the manner pursued by Britain under Thatcher, Major and Blair. This push for economic-reform measures found its most comprehensive expression in the adoption by the EU of the Lisbon Agenda, a series of ambitious linked measures that it was claimed would, by boosting research and innovation and improving education, focusing on growth and employment, make the EU the most dynamic and competitive knowledge-based economy in the world by 2010 (Smith 2005).

It is intended that the Lisbon Agenda, containing some 28 main objectives and 120 subobjectives, with 117 different indicators now reporting across 25 member states, will not be implemented by the classic EU method where the Commission makes proposals that are debated, amended and accepted by the European Council or the Council of Ministers. Instead, it will be pursued by a more decentralised method based on member states adopting agreed targets which would be actively monitored by the Commission and other EU bodies – the so-called 'open method of coordination'. In a way, this was the perfect solution for the British, with their well-known aversion to the Brussels bureaucracy. It was hailed by some as the triumph of the 'British model' in the EU. By 2005, however, results were not impressive, and the continued stagnation of a number of major economies in the EU means that the 2010 target will probably not be met.

Britain has also taken a key role in a number of other measures relating to economic management at the European level over the past five years. Gordon Brown has been instrumental in pushing forward the coordination of taxation regimes (but emphatically not the harmonisation of taxes) with the aim of reducing tax avoidance across the EU and beyond. The major British preoccupation as the second Blair government unfolded – and most certainly as the third Blair government started – was, however, the question of the EU budget. By comparison with major national budgets the EU budget, amounting to around €100 billion annually, is relatively puny. It calls for large contributions from a number of the older EU member states, whilst many of the newer members are net recipients (Parker 2005). Britain, always a major contributor, would make by far the biggest contribution if it were not for the rebate negotiated with considerable acrimony by Margaret Thatcher in 1984. Even with this rebate, which gave Britain back some £3 billion a year in the early 2000s, Tony Blair claimed that Britain still made a contribution to the EU budget two-and-a-half times as big as that of France in 1995–2005. Without the rebate Britain's contribution would have been 15 times that of the French. This is why Blair insisted that the rebate could only be negotiated if negotiations were also opened on the Common Agricultural Policy from which countries such as France benefit considerably. An ill-tempered European Council in June 2005 failed to open the negotiations, but as in other areas the issue persisted into the British Presidency in the later part of that year. After hard-fought negotiations in which the British showed a new willingness to concede on part of the rebate (perhaps because if they had not, it would have escalated to make the UK contribution disproportionately small over the budgetary period), an agreement was reached in December 2005. This agreement foresaw a reduction in the rate of growth of the rebate, ostensibly because the UK was to forego the part that would have been paid by the new member states, but only a review of CAP spending in 2008 rather than any concrete commitment to reform.

## European diplomacy

Since the early 1990s Britain has been an active participant in and often a leader of developments in the sphere of EU foreign and security policy. In 2001, along with the French, Britain had taken a leading role in the move from the Common Foreign and Security Policy to the Common European Security and Defence Policy. The British were fully engaged with the development of the European Rapid Reaction Force (ERRF), agreed to during the late 1990s, but subsequently modified by events and the fact that many member states were unable or unwilling to commit the necessary resources to its operations. By 2004 the ERRF had transmuted into the development of so-called 'battle groups', forces of 1,500 personnel drawn from national forces, and integrated cross-national military units, rapidly deployable in an emergency and to be used for a range of humanitarian and peace-keeping tasks. Britain has also played a leading role in the development of planning capabilities for operations under EU command, and in general the period saw the acceptance within the British defence establishment that they were becoming part of an EU defence structure. This was not, however, seen in exclusive terms, and priority was still given in many respects to NATO as the keystone of Britain's contribution to collective defence in such places as the former Yugoslavia; not only this, but the British pursued independent operations in conflicts such as those in Sierra Leone, Afghanistan and Iraq.

Britain also played a leading role in promoting EU diplomatic efforts in a range of important international disputes, particularly the Israeli–Palestinian conflict, and in the development of EU diplomacy towards Iran, especially in the context of the Teheran regime's quest for a nuclear-weapons capability. The Blair government has coordinated with the French and the Germans to constitute the 'EU3' of major member states that have pursued a diplomatic solution, albeit with uneven success and in the face of American scepticism. Britain has tended to see itself as part of a possible three-sided 'directorate' in key areas of EU diplomacy, collaborating with France and Germany; such an arrangement has often created suspicion among lesser EU member states (Parker 2004).

In light of this it was no surprise that Britain strongly supported the proposals contained in the abortive European Constitution to create a 'European foreign minister' and an 'external action service' (which would effectively be an EU diplomatic service). While the European Constitution has been sidelined by the French and Dutch referenda, such measures have not necessarily been completely lost since, with British support, many have already been under way and are likely to continue to evolve. Britain continues to pursue the 'politics of scale', collaborating at the EU level for the sake of greater effectiveness in pursuit of shared and common international goals. This type of solidarity has been apparent not only in traditional diplomacy, but also in new areas of international concern where the EU has developed significant policy stances such as on the Kyoto Protocol on climate change, a measure that was rejected by the Clinton and Bush administrations in the US, and the International Criminal Court, a means of administering justice to those accused of war crimes, again a measure opposed by the US. Thus, the diplomacy of international institutions and regimes, a key area of EU activity, has seen the British playing an active and often a leading role.

## Britain, Europe and the world

Britain has to be located not only in the European context but also in relation to the other global arenas in which both Britain and the EU play a role. Managing both in the pursuit of a foreign policy has often been a global and regional balancing act under the Blair government (Gamble 2003; Wallace and Oliver 2005). Tony Blair has consistently pursued two dominant themes. First, making a linkage between international rights and national responsibilities, especially for 'rogue regimes' such as those in Iraq or Zimbabwe. Second, emphasising Britain's role – and its unique capacity – as a pivotal power, holding the balance or building a bridge between the US and EU member states in a changing global system (Blair 1999, 2004). This is a challenging agenda for British foreign policy, particularly in light of the not inconsiderable tensions and differences that have divided the US from its European counterparts and allies in recent years. As such, Britain's foreign policy clearly reveals the interaction of the European and the international level.

Britain's Europeanism is called into question by some in light of its ongoing close relationship with the US. Post 9/11 the British–US relationship – and that of Tony Blair and George Bush – led to Britain playing a leading role in the US-led war on terror, embracing the October 2001 intervention in Afghanistan and the March 2003 invasion of Iraq (Kampfner 2003). It had long been clear that one of Tony Blair's central diplomatic aims was to stay close to the US (Riddell 2003; Wallace and Oliver 2005). This aim also chimed with the emphasis on rights and responsibilities in international politics: the UK had certain responsibilities as a pivotal power between the US and Europe, and these extended into the broader international system and issues of world order. When the Bush administration took office in 2001, Blair eagerly (and for some, surprisingly) renewed the close relationship he had enjoyed with the previous incumbent, Bill Clinton, and this close alignment was greatly intensified in the wake of the 9/11 attacks. Britain's post-9/11 support for the US was echoed by all other EU member states (*Le Monde* declared that 'We Are All Americans Now') and Britain played a key role in mapping out the unified EU response to the terror attacks. Militarily, this encompassed the actions carried out alongside the US by a large number of EU and NATO member states, and in the non-military field, it included promoting new pan-European security measures such as arrest warrants and the freezing on a global scale of funds controlled by pro-Islamist organisations.

In taking this position, the Blair government was thus operating well within the dominant consensus among EU member states (Hill 2004). But at a very early stage – and some have claimed as early as February 2002 – it became apparent that the Bush administration had other targets to deal with in mind, specifically Saddam Hussein and Iraq. Some suggest that Blair's increasing entanglement with the aims of the Bush administration in Iraq placed in jeopardy the very strength that he claimed for British diplomacy: how could Britain claim to act as a pivotal power if it had thrown in its lot with a US policy that was emphatically opposed by some key member states of the EU, notably France and Germany? Blair strongly supported the US policy and felt that in supporting the US he would also be able to both shape and restrain its policy in important areas, thus fulfilling at least part of the assumed role of a pivotal power. This was, however, a very risky enterprise. It also seems clear that Tony Blair's emphasis on rights and responsibilities – a consistent theme of his public statements from 1997 onwards – lent the Iraq expedition a distinctly moral tone, in which Saddam Hussein, the Iraqi dictator, had both jeopardised and forfeited his right to remain in power. Finally, it is also clear that Iraq was a test that the EU collectively could never pass. Britain's policy was opposed by France, Germany and others, but it was also supported by other EU member states including many of the states due to enter the EU in May 2004. The was therefore no settled European line on Iraq – and no EU position on the matter – on which Britain could be judged (Smith 2005).

British policy toward Iraq, one of the most debated and most controversial issues of the last ten years in British politics, was arrived at through the interaction of national, European and broader global responsibilities. The uneasy balance between Britain's European and wider international obligations has been especially delicate over the past four years. The war on terror and the invasion of Iraq have placed great strain on Britain's credentials as both a European and a global force, since Blair's strategy requires not just closeness to the USA but also a strong EU in which the Britain plays an active role (Stephens 2005). Conditions in the past five years have not made this an easy position to manage or to sustain.

## Global governance beyond Europe

In general terms, however, despite the transatlantic divisions that were exposed over Iraq, relatively harmonious forms of international diplomacy continue to operate at the highest levels. Although it might seem that there is little in the way of 'constitutional politics' at the global level – there is, after all, no world government – there has been a growing tendency among analysts and policy makers to focus on issues of global governance, in which a wide range of international institutions and negotiation processes have a role. Britain is located within a system of European multilevel governance, but in certain key areas this system extends beyond Europe to the global level and Britain has also been an energetic and active participant in several examples of global-governance processes and institutions. Perhaps most obviously, the Blair governments have taken a leading role in the attempts to advance sustainable development among poor countries, and in doing so have mobilised a number of institutions and groupings. On issues of international debt relief, Britain has sought to use the Commonwealth as an important sounding board and source of support. More importantly, its leading role in (and 2005 chairing of) the G8 grouping of leading industrial countries has enabled it to promote a comprehensive and orchestrated attempt to raise the profile of international development, particularly to advance wide-ranging measures of debt relief and economic assistance for sub-Saharan Africa. In this effort, the target was not only other major governments but extended to Tony Blair's active espousal of the aims of Live8, and the involvement of developmental NGOs and development activists such as Bono, Bob Geldof and others in the G8 discussions.

Britain under Blair has thus been a leading advocate of global governance and of action to rectify, when possible, global injustice and inequality. This has, however, led to some important tensions in British policy, which has to be pursued in several institutional contexts at once. On debt relief, the government has had to navigate British, EU and global institutions, not only within the G8 but also in a host of other institutional contexts such as that of the United Nations (UN). Another example of such interconnected, internationalised politics has been Britain's engagement in UN reform. The UN had a troubled time in the early 2000s and, as a result, there was a widespread feeling that it needed reform, a feeling expressed in important reform initiatives by the UN Secretary-General, Kofi Annan. Britain broadly supported many of these proposals, including the possible increase in the number of permanent members of the UN Security Council (of which Britain was a founding, permanent member). In order to pursue this set of issues, Britain had to manage their ramifications in the EU (where Germany was anxious to be recognised as a permanent Security Council member), in the Commonwealth (where the reforms had a different set of resonances especially for the poorer countries or those who supported India's claim for a Security Council seat) and also in its relations with the US. The global politics of constitutional reform was thus an area of active British interest and engagement, but it demanded a delicate balancing act and negotiating skills.

As indicated above, Britain's engagement at the global level also implies an active interest in economic management. The Chancellor, Gordon Brown, has actively led debates about debt relief, development and the international management of currencies through the International Monetary Fund (IMF) and other bodies. Britain's leadership of the G8 during 2005 provided an additional series of opportunities for the Blair government to shape the agenda for discussion of international economic management. Naturally, as in other areas, these initiatives came up against a series of linked pressures from within the EU and among other developed economies. By 2005, as the euro's role as an international currency grew, inevitably prompting some challenge to sterling's international role and influence, there were active discussions of a monetary G3 or a G4 where the US dollar and the euro would be joined for international management purposes by the Japanese yen and/or the Chinese currency, the renminbi. This is not to say that sterling's international role has been eclipsed, but that it has been surrounded by a new range of international monetary forces which threaten to further reshape its role. Thanks to the continued prominence of the City of London in international share dealing and financial transactions, Britain remains central to many processes of international economic management, but the early 2000s have certainly given strong evidence of important new trends.

## Conclusion: a complex imbalance?

Over the past five years the complex and shifting relationship between the national, the European and the global in British politics and policy making has been characterised by equally complex imbalance and occasional strain. The process of British government has become enmeshed in a wide-ranging process of multilevel governance, in which the British constitution has been reshaped and in which there is an interplay of national, European and global forces. At the same time, there are persistent cleavages in British politics between forces that emphasise the need for national independence and those that accept or promote Europeanisation and internationalisation. British policy making is increasingly infused with European and broader global forces, to such an extent that an increasing amount of British policy making takes place outside Britain and the institutions of policy making have been (unevenly) Europeanised and internationalised.

Britain has taken an active and mainly positive role in processes of European governance and policy making, but there have also been important areas of tension and contradictions, especially in areas where British politics remains strongly divided. As such, Britain's attempts to act as a pivotal power in the global arena, striking the balance between different levels of international governance and between the pressure of involvement with the EU and the US, have led to major tensions both in the international and European arenas and within Britain itself over the nature of Britain's international role. Someone once said, 'to govern is to choose'. It is clear that in examining the relationships between Britain, Europe and the world, the past five years have seen both a continued reshaping of the context for choice and some critical and very uncomfortable choices, the implications of which have still to be fully worked out.

## Chapter 10

# Security Policy in an Insecure World

MICHAEL COX and TIM OLIVER

The main aim of British security policy has been – and seems set to remain for the foreseeable future – the maintenance of its close tie with the United States. This is an aim driven by a desire in London to influence the way Washington acts as the pre-eminent power in a unipolar world – often referred to as 'pax Americana'. The British–US relationship has not been without its problems and difficulties. As the period after 2001 reveals only too graphically, the partnership with the US has carried with it an increasingly high price for Britain in general and Prime Minister Blair in particular. The result has generated political difficulties in Britain and more broadly produced something close to a crisis in relations with a number of Britain's major European and international partners. For some, the July 7 attacks in London suggest that it has turned Britain into a more prominent battleground of sorts with those waging *jihad* against the 'West'. The Atlantic dimension to British foreign policy remains as strong as ever; relations with the US are central to how Britain pursues its security interests around the world. However, this choice is to some extent balanced by the growing foreign-policy role of the EU and by the tensions created by Britain's other international allies, commitments to multilateralism and international law.

Many within the US State Department long believed that Britain's influence was on the wane and that its usefulness for the US would be measurably increased by Britain decisively throwing in its lot with Europe. Others recognised that pro-European Britain had established a role for itself with which it still felt entirely comfortable – in association with the US itself – and that it was not about to abandon its powerful patron across the Atlantic. Indeed, this 'special relationship' not only brought the British advantage in the shape of economic aid and privileged access to something that most other West European countries resented and envied in equal measure – American military and intelligence resources – but it also helped secure for it a place at the high table of international politics. As critics and supporters both pointed out,

London's close connection with Washington permitted Britain to exercise the kind of global role it could increasingly not have hoped to have on the basis of its own resources alone. Whenever confronted with a choice between Europe and the US, Britain – excepting Edward Heath's government – always privileged Washington over Brussels. The best choice open for Britain, it was felt by officials, was alongside its powerful (and English-speaking) imperial successor across the Atlantic, rather than with a grouping of European/Continental states.

From within the EU Britain has retained a close partnership with the US. The end of the Cold War, Britain's increasing economic association with the Continent of Europe, even the odd spat or two with Washington in the 1990s over Bosnia and Northern Ireland made no difference to the British–US relationship. If anything the partnership became more intimate: first, between Margaret Thatcher and Ronald Reagan, as they took on communism and espoused the virtues of capitalism during the 1980s. Second, between Tony Blair and Bill Clinton as they tried to carve a new international 'Third Way' between social democracy and neo-liberalism during the second half of the 1990s. Third, between Blair and George Bush in the wake of 9/11. If this was a relationship built more on sand than concrete, more on sentiment than shared interests – as some continued to believe – then it certainly did not look like it as one century gave way to another.

## Britain and 9/11

British, US and EU foreign policy were all transformed by the events of September 11 (Andrews 2005). In response Britain undertook a role that was militarily, diplomatically and politically substantial. While it was Jacques Chirac who was the first foreign leader to visit the US after the attacks it was Tony Blair who was the most eager to rush to America's aide, although to what extent he influenced the course of decision making in Washington has been doubted (Hill 2005). The attacks also provoked an unprecedented reaction from NATO, invoking Article V which states that an attack upon one member of the alliance was an attack upon all. However neither NATO (nor the EU) was represented in Afghanistan and the pursuit of al-Qaeda. Instead individual states such as Britain or Germany contributed military support. The US, in its desire to see swift and decisive action, brushed aside offers of other multilateral support, in doing so provoking feelings of frustration from those they did not invite to contribute.

Britain itself was not immune to taking such a unilateral approach, notoriously with Tony Blair organising an informal dinner in Downing

Street on 4 November 2001 with the leaders of Germany and France at which they were to discuss Europe's response to Afghanistan. Anger at this British-led approach, which excluded many others, led to the dinner being rapidly expanded to include the Dutch, Italian and Spanish Prime Ministers and the EU's High Representative for Common Foreign and Security Policy, Javier Solana. It only served to fuel feelings of British arrogance among some of its EU partners. Yet for Britain and Blair, it was a pragmatic means of reaching agreement on coherent action in an enlarged EU which would in turn guarantee smoother relations with Washington and swift international action (Kampfner 2003; Riddell 2003).

## The legacy of Kosovo

The Kosovo war of 1999 saw increased tensions between the US – who did most of the fighting – and the Europeans who insisted on the war being conducted through NATO in which every member, from Luxembourg upwards, commanded a veto over the targets US warplanes were to attack. The US approach to Afghanistan and Iraq, known as 'coalitions of the willing', was born of such experiences. The experience also reaffirmed the British attitude of opting to remain close to the US. While Blair had been disheartened by President Clinton's apparent weak leadership over Kosovo, he had not quite chosen to throw in Britain's lot with the Europeans despite signing the Anglo–French St Malo declaration to develop a European defence capability. For Britain keeping the US engaged in Europe remained central to plans to reform the EU's emerging foreign and defence capabilities with NATO playing a central role, not to use the EU as a counter-balance to the US.

At the height of the Kosovo war Blair set out his own approach to international affairs during a speech he gave in Chicago; a speech to which he was to return in understanding the post-9/11 world. The Chicago speech, known as the 'Doctrine of the International Community', set out several key themes:

> This is a just war, based not on any territorial ambitions but on values. We cannot let the evil of ethnic cleansing stand. We must not rest until it is reversed. We have learned twice before in this century that appeasement does not work. If we let an evil dictator range unchallenged, we will have to spill infinitely more blood and treasure to stop him later ...
>
> America's allies are always both relieved and gratified by its continuing readiness to shoulder burdens and responsibilities that come with its sole superpower status. We understand that this is something that

we have no right to take for granted, and must match with our own efforts. That is the basis for the recent initiative I took with President Chirac of France to improve Europe's own defense capabilities ...

Non-interference has long been considered an important principle of international order. And it is not one we would want to jettison too readily. One state should not feel it has the right to change the political system of another or foment subversion or seize pieces of territory to which it feels it should have some claim. But the principle of non-interference must be qualified in important respects. Acts of genocide can never be a purely internal matter. When oppression produces massive flows of refugees which unsettle neighbouring countries, then they can properly be described as 'threats to international peace and security'. When regimes are based on minority rule they lose legitimacy – look at South Africa. (Blair 1999)

This was one of the most theoretical speeches on foreign policy ever given by a British prime minister, previous speeches having tacked more towards the importance of pragmatism and realism in pursuing the UK national interest (Bogdanor 2005b; Hill 2005). More broadly the speech was a program that:

- encouraged and supported American military engagement in support of ambitions that were far beyond Britain's capability to achieve;
- expressed renewed confidence that the European and American sides of British foreign policy could be reconciled and that there was a continuing community of values across the Atlantic;
- reaffirmed that Britain could perform the role of a 'transatlantic bridge' holding the two sides of the Atlantic together to promote these shared values in an unstable world;
- finally, gave a definition of foreign policy framed in ethical terms and explicitly opposed to regimes such as Saddam Hussein's, provided several years before George W. Bush assumed office.

Of course, stating theoretical objectives is one thing, achieving them in practical terms something else; a fact Tony Blair was to discover in the subsequent unfolding of international events.

## Blair's wars

In the era following September 11 Tony Blair returned to and developed many of the themes he had outlined in Chicago, in particular the idea of 'liberal intervention' and the rejection of outdated Cold War-era concepts of sovereignty and national interests. In particular, the prime minister was drawing upon the work of Robert Cooper, a British diplomat, who argued that the world was composed of three types of state:

- lawless, pre-modern states too weak to enforce the rule of law, such as Afghanistan;
- modern states pursuing foreign policies and national interests very much in the style of the nineteenth century or the Cold War, such as China, Russia and perhaps the USA;
- postmodern states which have overcome the need for power politics in favour of multilateralism and integration, such as the members of the EU. (Cooper 2003)

Britain belonged firmly to the latter. However a challenge lay in whether such 'postmodern' states could employ the methods of an earlier era – force, sometimes pre-emptive, and acting beyond the rule of law – in order to safeguard and advance the world they had achieved. This seemed especially urgent when dealing with organisations and individuals such as al-Qaeda and Osama bin Laden who made use of failing pre-modern states to advance their cause, which, if combined with advanced weapons, could prove disastrous. Blair, it seemed, was prepared to undertake such a task, from intervention – militarily if necessary – in Afghanistan to providing assistance in Africa. There was, it seemed, no problem too big for Britain to set out to solve.

A powerful testament to Blair's commitment is to be found in the level of British military intervention since 1997 (Kampfner 2003), something in contrast to his pre-1997 stance when he said little on foreign or defence policy, something prompting Peter Mandelson to write 'won't TB fight wars?' on a draft Labour Party document that made no reference to defence (Dunne 2004, 893). Table 10.1 excludes mention of Britain's participation in many other military linked operations, most notably UN-led operations such as in the former Yugoslavia (SFOR), Cyprus (UNFICYP) or elsewhere.

## Britain and the Iraq war

Given the long involvement of British forces in Iraq and Blair's willingness to use military force the decision to commit Britain to the 2003 Iraq war should have been no surprise. Yet Britain's approach to the war in Iraq appeared to further fuel feelings that Britain's commitment was always to the US and not to Europe or other allies. Indeed, as the former German Chancellor Gerhard Schroeder once noted, the British transatlantic bridge often cited by Blair seemed to go in only one direction. Yet

**Table 10.1**    *British military interventions 1997–2005*

| Location | Date | Level of commitment |
|---|---|---|
| Iraq – Operation 'Desert Fox' | December 1998 | USAF with RAF bombing of Iraqi facilities to 'degrade' Iraq's WMD capability<br>Britain had been involved in enforcement of the UN 'no-fly' zones since 1991 |
| Kosovo – NATO operation 'Allied Force' | 1999 | 1,600 sorties by RAF, 10,500 ground troops, large Royal Navy deployment |
| East Timor – Australian-led UN intervention | 1999 | 300 personnel with logistical support |
| Sierra Leone – support for the democratically elected government and UN presence | 2000 | 4,500 personnel deployed with Royal Navy support |
| Afghanistan | 2001 | 2,000 troops deployed with Royal Navy ships, RAF support and reconnaissance |
| Democratic Republic of Congo – French-led EU operation ARTEMIS (with NATO assets) | 2003 | 100 troops |
| Iraq | 2003 onwards | Invasion force totalling 46,000 personnel. Large RAF and Royal Navy presence<br>As of 2005, 8,500 British troops remained deployed mainly in South Eastern Iraq |

*Source*:  Taken from various Ministry of Defence Reports, www.mod.gov.uk

the logic by which Britain went to war in Iraq was significantly different to that presented by the US, with Blair particularly placing an emphasis upon international law, for both domestic and European purposes. For Blair the decision to follow the Bush administration in attacking Iraq was very much a result of his own personal conviction that the action was morally correct and necessary and it also reflected the concern to ensure that Britain always sides with the US (Wallace and Oliver 2005).

## The road to war

September 11 provoked a fundamental change in the foreign policy of the Bush administration. Until that day British diplomats had worried that the US was becoming more isolationist than over-zealous in its use of power. This abrupt change provided an opportunity for US neo-conservatives (of whom more later) to advance their agenda involving transformation of the Middle East, with regime change in Iraq followed by Syria and Iran. Following the overthrow of the Taliban in Afghanistan, President Bush used his State of the Union message in January 2002 to identify Iraq along with Iran and North Korea as part of an 'axis of evil'. For his part, Tony Blair did not need convincing of the urgent need to tackle Iraq. In his 1999 Chicago speech he had stated that:

> Many of our problems have been caused by two dangerous and ruthless men – Saddam Hussein and Slobodan Milosevic. Both have been prepared to wage vicious campaigns against sections of their own community. As a result of these destructive policies both have brought calamity on their own peoples ... (Blair 1999)

As early as 1997 Paddy Ashdown, then leader of the Liberal Democrats, noted in his diary that all Blair could talk about during a meeting was Saddam Hussein and weapons of mass destruction. '[Blair has] seen some of the [intelligence] stuff on this. It really is pretty scary. [Saddam] is very close to some appalling weapons of mass destruction [WMD]. I don't understand why the French and other [sic] don't understand this. We cannot let him get away with it. The world thinks this is gamesmanship. But it's deadly serious' (Ashdown 2001, 138). While it is quite clear that Blair would not have considered an invasion of Iraq if the US had not intended to do the same, he was nevertheless keen to see action. But Parliament, his party and the public were much less convinced of the urgent need to tackle the issue of Iraq.

This is not to argue that everybody except Blair saw Iraq as posing no form of genuine threat. To many the intelligence provided about Iraq – and indeed Iraq's own actions – all seemed to point to the conclusion that Saddam was involved in some form of WMD-related activities. Blair can be criticised for poor judgment in the face of US pressure, but he cannot be condemned for doing what he felt was the correct thing when he faced insufficient counter-arguments. It seems in part this was the result of some form of 'groupthink' setting in amongst the key decision makers and advisors, with few questioning or having the courage to argue that the case was wrong. Combined with the absence of any possibility of justifying invasion on humanitarian grounds (because of its lack of basis in international law, but something which Blair also accepted) the issue of WMD became the central justification for war (Hill 2005).

That this was allowed to develop has been attributed to Blair's own style of government and of managing foreign policy. Blair has led something of a distant relationship with the Foreign and Commonwealth Office despite a large number of his advisors being former diplomats. Debate in Cabinet has similarly been sidelined, and although the Cabinet was consulted over Iraq, as Robin Cook observed, 'Tony gave cabinet plenty of time to discuss Iraq. But most in the cabinet had lost the habit of dissent' (quoted in Hennessy 2004, 10). At the source of this loss of the habit lay a preference for informality and discussions amongst a small group; often a requirement when dealing with a foreign-policy crisis. For the Blair government, however, informality became something of a working model with a small group of advisors meeting with the Prime Minister in his office, nicknamed 'the den'; something termed a 'denocracy' (Seldon 2005). As a result the government committed Britain to solidarity with the US over Iraq based upon information that could have been better scrutinised, while relying upon managing the media and overcoming Parliament which, although being the main source of pressure and danger to the government, failed to spot flawed arguments presented to it (Danchev 2005).

The US was to a large extent keen to see British participation. Yet the US and British agendas for war were different, Washington only appearing to modify its rationale for war in order to help Blair secure the support of the House of Commons. The most apparent differences lay with the divergent attitudes towards the United Nations and the Middle East peace process, with the Bush administration's indifference or contradictory messages contrasting with Blair's search for a form of internationally recognised legitimacy and visible progress in bringing about peace in Israel and Palestine.

Attempting to modify this American position became something of a raison d'être for Blair as he strove to make use of the close relations he had developed with Bush. Blair's strong response to September 11 provided him with a high level of prestige and respect in America but the effect of his influence was questioned by the argument that he appeared to have committed Britain to war before gaining concessions from the US (Hill 2005; Meyer 2005). Undeniably, however, Blair was a more eloquent ambassador for the US–British position and was able to articulate the key arguments more fluently than President Bush.

At the same time it appears that some within the Bush administration did little to make it easier for Blair to carry his own government or his country behind him. In the divided Bush administration the case that Colin Powell and the State Department could make to British listeners was repeatedly undermined by others in the Pentagon and elsewhere. The more Blair and British diplomacy engaged with the political dynamics of Washington the more they bound themselves to the eventual outcome while also alienating several heavyweight figures. Vice President Dick Cheney's relationship with Blair was best described as 'cool' and it remains unclear whether the March 2003 suggestion by the US Secretary of Defense, Donald Rumsfeld, that the US would be willing to intervene in Iraq without the British, was intended to be helpful.

Resolution 1441 was the best that could be achieved in building a UN Security Council consensus. The resolution – the result of protracted discussions and compromises – offered Iraq a final opportunity to comply with its disarmament obligations, threatening 'serious consequences' if it failed to do so. Problems emerged however over the need for a second resolution to authorise the use of force. The compromises of 1441 left plenty of room for US hawks on one side, and states who sought more time for the UN's weapons inspectors on the other, to interpret the document in contradictory fashion regarding whether or not it authorised the use of force. Britain was stuck in the middle. Blair, having initially sought a second resolution, eventually argued 1441 gave all the necessary authorisation.

Thus the British government slipped towards presenting a case for intervention in Iraq, based on evidence it should have known to be thin, to justify support for an American administration to which it had bound itself and which sought military action for different reasons. From this difficult position Blair found himself facing a series of repeated crises and dilemmas. The February 2003 'doctored dossier', 'Iraq: Its Infrastructure of Concealment, Deception and Intimidation', was plagiarised from various sources, most notably a Californian student's thesis. Blair's Cabinet, though having lost the habit of independence, showed signs of weariness while Labour MPs expressed uneasy at the relationship with the Bush administration, with a handful of rebels hoping for an opportunity to oust Blair. In the end the whole untidy process of going to war in Iraq led to the resignation of two Cabinet ministers (Robin Cook, former Foreign Secretary and then Leader of the House of Commons, and Clare Short, Secretary of State for International Development) and to the largest ever Commons backbench rebellion. The British government stood alongside the US, but it did so with a deeply divided country and amid poor relations with many of its European neighbours and international allies (Wallace and Oliver 2005). Estimates of the numbers of people who marched in London on 3 February 2003 to protest against war in Iraq range from 750,000 to two million – amongst the largest demonstrations London had ever seen.

## Post-war dilemmas

The post-Saddam situation has if anything intensified the pressure on Blair due to the failure to locate WMD and the catalogue of mistakes that have characterised post-war policy towards the rebuilding of Iraq. The failure to locate WMD – presented in Britain as the central reason for military action – has plagued Blair more than it has the Bush administration, which saw and presented the Iraq war as more than just about WMD. Inquiries conducted by Lord Hutton and then by Lord Butler cleared the Prime Minister and those around him of any misdemeanors, but left a negative impression of the style with which Blair and the government had approached the issue of WMD and the war in Iraq. Butler's conclusions made for uncomfortable insights into how intelligence, policy making and public relations had been brought together in a process that was suspected of having been subjected to strong and inappropriate political influence (Runciman 2004).

It has become something of a truism that there was no plan for dealing with Iraq after President Bush declared 'Mission Accomplished' on 1 May 2003. Such plans as did exist were undermined by political pressures and institutional rivalry, most notably in the US where the State Department's 'Future of Iraq Project' was undermined by the Pentagon which was put in charge of post-war reconstruction as the war began (Packer 2005; Phillips, D 2005). As a result the US and Britain went to war with inappropriate plans which reflected political and institutional bargaining rather than on-the-ground realities.

Painful questions have been raised about the waste of lives, especially British lives, and arguments continue to rage regarding what exactly the UK gained from involvement in the Iraq war (see Table 10.2). For some the conflict wrecked Britain's commitments to multilateralism, to the UN and international law, and damaged relations with her European partners. Relations with Germany and France reached a low point and any attention the Prime Minister hoped to give to European affairs, such as committing Britain to the euro, seemed dashed (Riddell 2005; Smith 2005).

Terrorist attacks in Madrid in March 2004 and London in July 2005 also sent a strong reminder that the wider war on terror was still very much a going concern. Many argued that Britain's close association with the US made it a more prominent Western target (Chatham House 2005). While progress had been made in Iraq, most notably the election of a Transitional Assembly in January 2005 and a parliamentary National

Table 10.2    *Casualty figures for Iraq to early November 2005*

| Period | US: fatalities | US: injured | UK: fatalities | UK: injured | Iraq: civilian deaths | Other coalition fatalities |
|---|---|---|---|---|---|---|
| Initial hostilities (21 March–1 May 2003) | 140 | 542 | 33 | 155 | 4,833 (min.) 5,980 (max.) | 0 |
| After 1 May 2003 | 1,918 | 14,678 | 64 | 2,548 | 22,082 (min.) 24,322 (max.) | 103 |
| Total | 2,058 | 15,220 | 97 | 2,703 | 26,915 (min.) 30,302 (max.) | 103 |

*Notes*:
(1) Military figures include all personnel killed by hostile action, illness or accidents. Injury figures are approximate. Civilian deaths are estimates with maximum and minimum figures. The table excludes the deaths of such individuals as journalists or aid workers.
(2) Figures largely taken from icasualties.org and iraqbodycount.net.

Assembly in December 2005, the situation of lawlessness verging on civil war could be seen as a more genuine threat to Western (as well as Iraqi) security. This was all the more so when it was suggested that the wider 'war on terror' was being left to drift due to the concentration on Iraq.

In the run-up to war Blair had sought two assurances from President Bush. First, that the reconstruction of Iraq would be handled in an effective way, with post-war Iraq involving the UN. Second, that Bush would address the Israel–Palestine problem (Stothard 2004, 218; Wallace and Oliver 2005, 173). Neither of these aims was met. The chaos that engulfed Iraq drove out the small UN presence and, while President Bush committed the US to the creation of a viable Palestinian state, his approval in April 2004 of the Israeli withdrawal from Gaza effectively discarded the Middle East peace roadmap to which Blair thought he had helped commit the US.

## Britain between the US and Europe

Like so many other British prime ministers since the Second World War, Tony Blair has become impaled on the horns of the Europe–US diplomatic dilemma that has caught so many of his predecessors. The historical relationship with the US has brought significant gains, but the experience of Iraq calls into question how much longer this is sustainable when little is seen to be given in return by the Americans. The Europeans, on the other hand, have been divided and frequently portrayed as weak, with Euroscepticism remaining a strong impulse in British domestic political debate (Forster 2002; Wallace 2005). Like many prime ministers before him Blair has tried to overcome these differences by playing the role of a bridge; but with the two sides appearing increasingly to grow apart in the way they view the post-Cold War world it seems likely that Blair's bridge may be a 'bridge too far' (Wallace and Oliver 2005).

## American Martians

For many Europeans there could be no bigger indicator of the widening of the Atlantic than the very figure of President Bush himself. With his Texan drawl, moral absolutes, religiosity and cowboy appearance he provokes deep feelings of unease and hostility amongst many Europeans, especially when compared to the previous presidency of Bill Clinton. Yet Clinton was not all Europeans hoped for either; his presidency saw tensions over issues which would come to characterise the rifts between Bush's America and Europe. For example, the Kyoto Protocol, signed in December 1997, was pre-emptively rejected by a unanimous 95–0 Senate vote in July 1997 and it was under Clinton that America discovered that European multilateralism in the form of the EU and then NATO could not deal with the Balkans.

That said, Bush's approach has been particularly assertive. His administration has fought against the International Criminal Court, refused to support the Ottawa Land Mine Convention, rejected parts of the Biological Weapons Convention, and withdrawn from the Anti-Ballistic Missile Treaty in order to develop a missile-defence system. Bush's 'war on terror' is not seen in Europe as a simple good vs evil dichotomy, as some in America might view it. Talk in the Bush White House of space-based warfare and the need to avoid a 'space Pearl Harbour' shows only too dramatically the differences in how the Europeans and Americans view the world.

The observation by Robert Kagan, an American neo-conservative, that 'Americans are from Mars, Europeans are from Venus', neatly summarised what for many is the essential difference in how Europe and America view the issue of power (Kagan 2003). While America – as Mars, the God of War – develops a missile-defence system to ward off a possible North Korean (or Chinese) nuclear attack, the Europeans – as Venus, the Goddess of Love – are barely able to transport troops to areas neighbouring the EU. The US currently has 40 per cent of the world's total military expenditure; Europe taken as a whole barely matches this. And while military power isn't everything, America's overwhelming fire-power means that for the foreseeable future she will be called upon to deal with failing states, organised terrorist networks, to guarantee peace deals and to handle the worst international humanitarian crises. From the perspective of the US the efforts of Europeans to use only economic and diplomatic incentives seem almost quaint when faced with interna-tional threats in the form of an al-Qaeda seeking WMD.

## European Venusians

Europe, it would seem, is considered by some as being a 'freeloader' on US power in a dangerous world. In recognition of this there have been moves by the EU to close the gap, or at least offer some form of alterna-tive capability to the US. In April 2003 the crisis over Iraq prompted a meeting between France, Germany, Belgium and Luxembourg to discuss defence cooperation in a way that to some threatened the future of NATO. However, the summit showed how hollow EU foreign, security and defence policy would be without the participation of Britain. It was therefore no surprise that throughout the Iraq crisis Britain, France and Germany continued to engage in a trilateral relationship over defence and foreign-policy issues.

In the same year the EU published its own security strategy entitled *A Secure Europe in a Better World* (European Council 2003), written in large part by the aforementioned Robert Cooper and based in large part upon British and French thinking. Its positive reception in Washington delighted London, again demonstrating the British desire for Britain and Europe to seek to support and not counter the US. The strategy was a response both to the changing international situation and a to the US National Security Strategy set out by President Bush in September 2002. In military terms the EU – and Britain – was attempting to create a European Security and Defence Policy which would be able to manage crises with a larger military capability. Indeed, by late 2003 the member states of the EU were able to rapidly deploy and sustain forces of up to 50,000–60,000 persons (Giegerich and Wallace 2004).

Questions remain as to how realistic these aspirations are and how the EU strategy document, which lays great importance on multilateralism, fails to explain how to deal with defective multilateral institutions. Nevertheless it constitutes part of the slow process started in the 1970s of building a European defence and foreign policy, something which has long commanded strong British support. From such developments we can discern a growing British reflex towards working more with

European allies, something we might term a Europeanisation of British foreign, security and defence policy. However, this is easily sidelined by London (Allen and Oliver 2006).

## British Earthlings?

If Europeans are from Venus and Americans from Mars then the idea of Britain as a 'transatlantic bridge' would seem to accord it the place of Earth. Indeed, the UK has long been subject to the strong but varying gravitational pulls of Washington and Brussels. It remains to be seen how Britain will deal with the momentum towards a stronger European capability in defence and foreign policy. As with Germany and France – the other key players in developing Europe's foreign, security and defence policies – Britain looks set to continue to work with Europe (in particular France and Germany) to mutual benefit while retaining the ability to work with other countries where either a European or a German–French–British relationship is not feasible (Smith 2005, 721). Britain (like France) has made it clear that she will retain a permanent seat in the UN Security Council irrespective of moves to create a European foreign minister. The replacement of Trident – Britain's nuclear deterrent – seems set to be developed with the Americans and not the Europeans (Clarke 2004), although new Royal Navy aircraft carriers are being developed with France and the Eurofighter is set to become the workhorse of the RAF. The British military and intelligence community continues to work closely with the US, but keeping up with the Americans is becoming increasingly expensive. British ambivalence over the future of the EU in the world is matched only by her unease at whether or not Washington will continue to listen to London's concerns.

Britain will also have to come to terms with the increased attention the US directs towards the role performed by the EU in international relations; President Bush's 2004 visit to the European Commission and Council buildings in Brussels reflected the important role the EU plays not only in economic terms but also in homeland security, intelligence, immigration and dealing with terrorist or criminal money laundering. With the transatlantic economy now more deeply integrated than any other areas of the world and relations touching upon domestic issues as much as on foreign policy and trade, differences will need to be overcome in a wider European–American context (Hamilton and Quinlan 2005). However, the wider US political elite remains largely indifferent to the power of Europe. For the US, as Micklethwait and Wooldridge point out (2004, 299), Brussels is generally somewhere you go to discuss trade, not foreign policy. This largely helps explain the US difficulty in understanding why Turkish membership of the EU is controversial and not likened to Mexico being admitted to the North American Free Trade Agreement (NAFTA).

## The Blair and Bush doctrines

The very particular approach Tony Blair has taken to foreign policy might be termed a 'Blair doctrine'. First set out in Blair's Chicago speech, re-emphasised after September 11 and endlessly during the run-up to the war in Iraq, this doctrine shares many similarities with the stance of President Bush. Both were a response to the changing nature of international relations, supporting the necessity of pre-emptive strikes in a world where failing states posed a serious threat to all nations. The two doctrines have also fared badly in light of developments in Iraq. Examining these two doctrines allows us to draw out some of the key developments in both British and international security over the past few years.

### Blair's world

On foreign affairs Tony Blair travelled light in 1997. He had never outlined or discussed a particular approach to foreign policy, or indeed shown much interest in the area save for discussions about Europe which were more of a domestic nature than foreign. Nonetheless, he did litter his speeches with references to globalisation, the interconnected world, the network economy, and the end of national sovereignty as understood in the Cold War era. He emphasised the importance of Britain cooperating with her international (particularly European) partners instead of being isolated as he accused the Conservative government of remaining. Once in power Blair developed a close interest in foreign affairs, seeing in it not only a chance to escape the confines of domestic government (and the power of his Chancellor Gordon Brown), but also a chance to engage more directly with the issues he had previously outlined (Seldon 2004). Here, particularly after 1997, Blair argued that humanitarian intervention was justified in the internal affairs of another country and he set out in the Chicago speech a series of criteria for such an intervention:

- Are we sure of our case?
- Have all diplomatic options been exhausted?
- Can the military option be prudently undertaken?
- Is there a will to see it through to the end?
- Are national interests involved? (Blair 1999)

Blair returned to these issues in his Labour Party conference speech following the attacks of September 11. Seeing in the disaster a chance to bring about real change he said, '... this is a moment to seize. The kaleidoscope has been shaken. The pieces are in flux. Soon they will settle again. Before they do, let us reorder the world around us' (Blair 2001). A similar approach had already paved the way for military intervention in Kosovo, Sierra Leone and East Timor and would now ease the way to intervention in Afghanistan and in turn the war in Iraq. It ingrained in Blair the idea that Britain must play the role of a bridge between the United States and Europe. This was essential if the Atlantic alliance was to remain the fundamental axis for the preservation and advancement of a liberal world order (Seldon 2004, 407).

## Bush's world

Born of the experiences of September 11, the 'Bush doctrine' – most clearly set out in the 2002 US National Security Strategy – asserted the right of the US to take pre-emptive action to assert American power in a more unilateral way, without the constraints of multilateralism, and in a way designed to reorder the world and spread liberal democracy. In setting out his doctrine to Congress on 20 September 2001 Bush made it clear that those who harboured terrorists would be targeted as well: 'Every nation, in every region, now has a decision to make. Either you are with us, or you are with the terrorists' (Bush 2001). In taking this stance the US attempted to reinterpret many of the ideas surrounding 'just war theory' – that the only acceptable war is one of a defensive nature – by arguing that a threat does not need to be imminent before self-defensive actions can be taken.

This approach was an exceptionally ambitious one, and one which drew heavily upon neo-conservative thinking (Mann 2004; Micklethwait and Wooldridge 2004). The 'neo-cons' were considered to be a politically active group, led by officials in the Bush administration such as Paul Wolfowitz, then Deputy Secretary of Defense, and strongly supported by the powerful Vice President, Dick Cheney. They had long expressed frustration with the Clinton administration's foreign policy and argued that the world was a dangerous place where America's security would depend on it asserting its interests to remain an unchallenged hegemon. Their agenda, most clearly encapsulated in their Project for the New American Century, saw regime change in places such as Iraq as being desirable in themselves but also in the long-term security interests of the US. In such an American, unipolar world competition in the international arena would be relegated to trade and lesser issues, in turn allowing the US to avoid playing by the rules or being bound by commitments to allies or multilateral institutions (Mann 2004).

## Worlds collide?

So, as one commentator asked, is Blair the original neo-con (Rawlence 2004)? Had Blair and Bush embraced essentially the same agenda in trying to advance democracy and liberal humanitarian intervention? If so, did choosing to be close to Bush, who could command more force than even Britain could muster at the height of her imperial power, offer Blair a chance to realise his doctrine of removing dictators, upholding human rights, confronting states with WMD, bringing international terrorists to justice and bringing peace to the Middle East? But, as we saw above, the Americans seemed to listen to Blair 'only when his suit matched what they wanted to wear anyway' (Seldon 2004, 624). The Blair–Bush doctrines were incompatible when they faced opposite experiences of power – the US as the global hegemon, Britain as a post-imperial power with a willingness to wage war, but bound by commitments to institutions and treaties the British people and Parliament were uneasy at breaking.

That said, Britain, the US and the EU have all developed an increasing interest in state intervention in the face of state failures, or what Cooper would call the pre-modern world (Cooper 2003). Britain's engagement in Sierra Leone matches similar French-led interventions in the Great Lakes region of Africa and Ivory Coast (Badie 2004) and similar American interventions in Central America. EU forces today operate in Bosnia, Macedonia and Central Africa. Increased intervention – especially humanitarian intervention – has become a norm of the post-Cold War era, although the European and British approaches lack the almost nationalistic approach to international affairs that the US seems to be driven by.

Experiences in post-war Iraq and Afghanistan have, however, taught both Washington and London that while America has more than enough military power to wipe away its enemies, rebuilding and policing countries liberated from such enemies are different matters entirely. Such work requires the assistance of foreign powers, NGOs and international organisations, many of whom are still smarting from the rows over Iraq. Indeed, America and Britain's failings in Iraq – to locate, or explain the lack of, WMD and to provide for a more stable post-war order – only serve to move mutual allies into distancing themselves from the policies. Progress in the form of Iraqi elections has been marred by bloody violence on a daily basis which shows no signs of ending anytime soon. Even the elections have led to reduced expectations with the realisation that a democratic Iraqi government will contain a strong Islamic tone and could well have a distinctly anti-American stance. In such a context the Bush administration's aims for Iraq have been continually downgraded.

The agreement of Libya to renounce its WMD programmes – something seen as a result of Iraq – was also set within a wider system of economic and political pressure from the EU. The belief that unilateralism could achieve American aims was dealt a further blow when the 'axis-of-evil' state of Syria was forced to withdraw from Lebanon by demonstrations by the local population combined with American and French pressure. On a wider level both the US and Britain have suffered losses to their 'soft power' (the ability to 'inspire' the peoples of the world) with surveys regularly showing both held in lower regard than ever before. As a result the Bush and Blair doctrines seem to be in tatters. Attempting to reorder the Middle East has proved exceptionally difficult, not to mention even starting on the rest of the world.

Given the difficulties in stabilising post-war Iraq some suggest that it will be some time before the US and Britain go to war in the same way. The approach of linking rogue states and terrorism, as happened with Iraq, was very much a strategy belonging to the Middle East, albeit one that also includes to a certain extent North Korea. The belief that there is a 'magic military formula' allowing the US to act unilaterally to transform failing states is considerably undermined without additional multilateral institutions or agreements. Of course, Iraq may be stabilised and could be converted into a flourishing democracy. In such a context the Bush and Blair doctrines would be seen as a success, but even optimists would probably now admit that this seems a long time away.

This is not, however, to argue that the US or Britain will avoid further conflict. America remains – and is set to remain – not only the greatest power in human history, but one driven by a strong belief that it is a benign hegemon. Britain, while not wielding such power or self-confidence or self-righteousness, remains – and is set to remain – a power committed to engagement around the world in support of its ideals and with a penchant for supporting the US.

## Conclusion

British security policy has long identified a close relationship with the US as a central guiding principle for Britain's place in the world and its relations with Europe. The experiences since September 11 have not radically changed this; they indeed appeared to have 'reaffirmed the vice-like grip of Atlanticism on Britain's identity' (Dunne 2004, 908). But this helps to highlight the following three sets of continuing tensions which have characterised British foreign, security and defence policy in the post-9/11 era.

First, in both the Cold War and the post-Cold War world Britain's security interests have been advanced through a close relationship with the US. This relationship is characterised by Britain offering private counsel and support in the hope that US power can be harnessed and steered. The former British Ambassador to the US, Christopher Meyer, reports that when he was appointed to the post Blair's senior advisor, Jonathan Powell, told him, 'We want you to get up the arse of the White House and stay there' (Meyer 2005, 1). Peter Riddell summed up this general approach more genteelly as being one of 'hug them close' (Riddell 2003). Blair's premiership seems set to be defined by his following such a policy, particularly with regard to Iraq.

Second, while hugging the Americans close has had its associated problems, Britain's also being close to Europe provokes serious domestic problems along with questions about the future of Britain's international position. In an EU of 25 member states Britain is perhaps no longer seen as quite the 'awkward partner' it once was (George 1998). It can, however, be argued that Britain's relations with the EU under Blair have been one of 'missed opportunities', ranging from staying outside the euro, to institutional reform, to garnering stronger public support for Europe (Smith 2005). As a leading international player Britain brings to the development of European foreign and security policy qualities it fails to bring to economic or social discussions. Yet here too there remain key tensions, most notably over the future of NATO. While determined to see a more developed role for Europe in the world, backed up by a genuine defence capability, the UK would be loth to be bound by the EU on issues where it feels a strong national interest. In this sense the UK's commitment to European foreign and defence policy remains 'Janus-faced'.

Third, the Blair and Bush doctrines have much in common. The US, Britain and the EU have all adapted to meet some of the new challenges of post-Cold War security threats. Profound differences exist, however, in how the three view the issue of power and its application, as demonstrated most potently in the works of Cooper (2003) and Kagan (2003) (Cox 2005). That these differences also extend to a whole array of issues ranging from the social to military spheres bodes ill for the idea that Britain can continue to provide a bridge across the Atlantic, or some might add, across the English Channel. Europe's inclinations towards softer power versus the Bush administration's preference for hard power and Blair's attempt to mix the two have placed serious strains on British foreign, security and defence policy.

# Chapter 11

# The Politics Of Multicultural Britain

GILLIAN PEELE

One much-noted feature of the July 2005 terrorist attacks in London was the extent to which the indiscriminate bombing affected individuals of many different races and creeds. The images of the dead, missing and injured encapsulated the cultural mosaic which is contemporary London. Not surprisingly – given that the bombers were born and brought up in Britain – the bombings also focused renewed attention both on Britain's cultural diversity and on how well that diversity was being managed. Although the overwhelming response of the population was to draw together across ethnic and religious lines and to condemn the violence, the bombings raised questions about why such extremism should have taken root in Britain's Islamic community and what, if anything, could be done about it. They also raised fears that the United Kingdom's ethnic minorities, in addition to feeling stigmatised by any strengthening of the country's anti-terrorist legislation, would become the target of revenge attacks and that there would be an increase in the 'Islamophobia' which had caused concern even before the September 2001 attacks on New York and Washington DC (Runnymede Trust 1997). Such a backlash was not long in coming, with reports of an increase in racially motivated attacks on individuals, on mosques and on Islamic centres across the country. The bombings also underscored the extent to which the ethnic diversity which is now central to the politics of the United Kingdom, as well as to the politics of many other European states, is shaped not just by domestic events but is tied to the wider dynamics of the international arena.

The changing contours of the debate about multiculturalism – what it means, its limits, its stresses and strains – are of vital importance not just for Britain's minority communities but for the society as a whole. It raises a host of issues about the character of the British state and its institutions and about the British government's evolving approach to the challenges of the country's demographic diversity. The events of the early twenty-first century have also created new political opportunities for far-right

193

groups such as the British National Party and a potential for radical and extreme politics within the minority communities themselves.

## A diverse society

The story of how Britain became a more diverse society has been well told before (see for example Hansen 2000), but four key points are worth noting in any discussion of the contemporary politics of ethnicity and immigration.

First, concern about immigration took on a new character in the post-1945 period. Although there had been opposition to immigration in the late nineteenth and early twentieth century (when hostility to Jewish immigrants from Eastern Europe in particular had led to the passage of the 1905 Aliens Act), immigration after the Second World War became increasingly controversial because so much of it was non-white. It is, however, worth remembering that there was little regulation of immigration in the nineteenth century and up to 1905, though this did not necessarily indicate widespread tolerance toward ethnic minorities. What did emerge was a split between the concerns of the policy-making elite and those of the wider society where the impact of immigration was directly felt. Thus as late as 1948 the United Kingdom passed legislation which granted British citizenship to a large slice of the world's population in the British Empire and Commonwealth (Joppke 1999). In the post-war period Britain encouraged immigration from Eastern Europe and continued to allow the free movement of peoples between the Republic of Ireland and the United Kingdom despite the Republic's exit from the Commonwealth in 1949 (Paul 1997). The New Commonwealth immigration which produced Britain's contemporary ethnic diversity occurred in a relatively short period when poor economic conditions in the migrants' countries of origin prompted them to seek work in Britain and acute labour shortages in key British industries – such as transport and the National Health Service – encouraged the recruitment of workers from the Caribbean and later from South Asia. It was only when this non-white immigration from the New Commonwealth became extensive that it was seen as a problem and the traditional liberalism in relation to rights of entry and abode was questioned.

Second, although Britain had long nurtured a myth of itself as an open and tolerant society, the arrival of these immigrants was met with hostility and in some cases violence (Winder 2004). Starting with the Commonwealth Immigrants Act of 1962, a series of increasingly restrictive laws were passed, with any new primary immigration from the Commonwealth being ended with the 1971 Immigration Act which effectively closed the door to unskilled immigrants. Subsequent changes to the immigration rules severely restricted secondary immigration – the ability of an immigrant to bring his or her family to the United Kingdom – which mainly affected Asian immigrants since the early Caribbean immigrants had tended to come as a family unit. Over the years the drive to restrict entry to what has been called 'zero immigration' (Joppke 1999) led to wholesale revision of the definition of British nationality, unilaterally removing the right of residence in the United Kingdom from members of Commonwealth and former British overseas territories.

Third, by the 1980s it was asylum rather than immigration in the strict sense which came to dominate the debate about rights of entry and the control of Britain's borders. Asylum had not been a high-profile issue before the 1970s but it moved to centre stage as the number of applicants for asylum rose dramatically, generating intense public concern. Part of the reason for the rise in asylum applications was the eruption of ethnic conflict in many parts of the world including Sri Lanka, Africa and Eastern Europe. Three pieces of legislation were passed by the Thatcher and Major governments to reduce the numbers of asylum seekers coming to the UK: the 1987 Carriers Liability Act, the 1993 Asylum and Immigration Appeals Act and the 1996 Asylum and Immigration Act. The number of people seeking asylum per annum peaked in 2002 at 84,130. Since then numbers have fallen, not least because of government initiatives to cope with illegal entrants and tighten border controls and to deter asylum seekers by such controversial measures as restricting the welfare benefits of failed asylum seekers (Home Affairs Select Committee 2005). Britain has generally been thought well placed to control its borders, not least because of its position as an island and because of the executive's relative freedom to develop policy without stringent parliamentary or judicial scrutiny (Layton-Henry 1994). Nevertheless, the administration of immigration and asylum controls has often occasioned controversy. The Home Office, especially its Immigration and Nationality Directorate, has been regularly criticised for its failure to process applications and deal with the backlog of asylum requests, its inability to remove failed asylum seekers and more general problems such as its botched computerisation (Moxon 2004). Despite ministerial efforts to improve the situation, a series of embarrassing incidents under Labour continued to fuel public concern about the efficiency of the administrative procedures for dealing with asylum; and in 2005 a National Audit Office report suggested that the removal of failed asylum seekers was slow – and that as of May 2004 as many as 283,000 failed asylum seekers were still in the country (National Audit Office 2005). Although this administrative failure would have caused concern at any time, the possibility that there might be a link between asylum seekers and terrorism further exacerbated the sensitivity of the issue.

From the 1980s onwards ministers of both parties found themselves in conflict with the judiciary over the fairness of procedures for resolving asylum applications. The extension of administrative-law remedies to ministerial decisions was always bound to be controversial but it was especially so in an area where ministers feared popular opinion. From the government's perspective the prospect of a seemingly endless queue of asylum seekers was politically dangerous. On the other hand the plight of people caught up in life-threatening situations inevitably placed ministers in a difficult situation. For example, the worsening political scene in Zimbabwe generated intense controversy and in October 2005 a failed asylum seeker won the right to remain in Britain despite Home Office opposition. What the asylum issue underlines is that the extent to which an individual state can control its boundaries is limited not just by globalisation and transnational linkages but by the vicissitudes of international events which can generate human rights dilemmas to derail the toughest of policy stances.

And fourth, the emphasis on restricting entry that permeates so much of government policy was until very recently not complemented by any positive conception of British citizenship (Hampshire 2005). This was in marked contrast to the French approach to citizenship or indeed to that of the United States. However, the last few years have seen a sustained effort to make becoming a citizen more of a milestone for the individual and to emphasise the benefits and the obligations of citizenship.

### Britain's ethnic mix

The 2001 census revealed that Britain's minority ethnic population was 4.6 million – 7.9 per cent of the mainland population. (Ethnic minority data were not collected for Northern Ireland.) This represented a rise of 53 per cent from 1991. The largest number of minority ethnic members were originally from South Asia, with Indians (1.8 per cent of the total) forming the largest single group. The next largest group were Pakistanis (1.3 per cent of the population). Black Caribbeans, whose migration to Britain after the Second World War is generally seen as a critical turning point, constitute 1 per cent of the population. People of mixed race (a new category introduced into the census in 2001) now represent 1.2 per cent of the population.

Britain's minority ethnic population is spatially concentrated. About 45 per cent of all ethnic minorities live in London which is home to 78 per cent of the black African community and 61 per cent of the black Caribbean community as well as to over half of the Bangladeshi community. Outside London significant portions of the minority ethnic population are resident in the West Midlands (13 per cent), the South East (8 per cent), the North West (8 per cent) and Yorkshire and the Humber (7 per cent). While the black African and Caribbean population is heavily concentrated in London, Britain's communities of Pakistani and Indian origin are more dispersed with a greater percentage of the population of Pakistani origin living in the West Midlands or in Humberside and Yorkshire than in London.

Within the minority ethnic population there are important cross-cutting divisions. Religion is an increasingly important cleavage, although it was not until 2001 that the census included a question about religious adherence. This showed that, while 71.6 per cent of the population described itself as Christian, there are now important non-Christian religious minorities within the United Kingdom (Table 11.1).

By far the largest non-Christian group is the Muslim minority, who constitute 2.7 per cent of the population. This is of course the religious/minority ethnic group which is now in danger of stigmatisation as a result of the apparently growing appeal of what one authority has called 'neo-fundamentalism' to second- and third-generation Muslims (Roy 2002) as well the one whose mores and values most often seem in conflict with the secular character of much of British society (Modood 2005). The five largest Muslim populations are in London (607,000), Birmingham (140,000), Greater Manchester (125,000), Bradford (75,000) and Kirklees (39,000) (Hussein 2004). Whereas the Hindu and Sikh communities are relatively homogenous in terms of ethnicity, Britain's Muslims are of varied ethnic backgrounds: two thirds are of South Asian origin but about 8 per cent are of African origin and about 12 per cent are white. These divisions were initially barriers to a common Islamic identity but a series of pivotal events, such as the *Satanic Verses* controversy of 1989 (where the author Salman Rushdie was accused of

**Table 11.1**  *Religious minorities in the UK at 2001 census*

| Religion | Percentage of UK population |
|----------|------------------------------|
| Muslim | 2.7 |
| Hindu | 1.0 |
| Sikh | 0.6 |
| Jewish | 0.5 |
| Buddhist | 0.3 |
| Other | 0.3 |

blaspheming Islam and had a death sentence pronounced against him in a *fatwa*), and more recently the war with Iraq, have contributed to a much greater sense of Islamic identity. Nevertheless there are important tensions and divisions among Britain's Muslim community. Although most British Muslims are Sunnis, this tradition itself contains different strands and is not monolithic. To that extent many observers would question whether Muslims in Britain constitute a single community.

The British Muslim population, although at 2.7 per cent somewhat smaller than that of several other European countries, is a fast-growing and young population (Hussein 2004). It is also a relatively disadvantaged community: a 2002 survey found that Bangladeshis and Pakistanis were two and a half times as likely to be unemployed as the white population and three times more likely to be on low pay. The same survey found substantial relative disadvantages in health and education as well as in housing. This is also a community which contains a substantial proportion of people who have become alienated to some extent from British society. A YouGov survey (2005) of British Muslims after the London bombings found a significant minority who had some sympathy with the bombers. Whilst only 6 per cent of respondents said that they thought the attacks were 'on balance justified' (and thought that further attacks would be similarly justified), a total of 24 per cent said that they had some sympathy – either 'a little' or 'a lot' – with 'the feelings and motives of those who carried out the attacks', and 32 per cent said that they believed Western society was 'decadent and immoral' and that Muslims 'should seek to bring it to an end' (although only 1 per cent said that this should be achieved by violent means).

In addition to the specific problems and concerns of communities such as the British Islamic community and how they relate to the majority community, there is of course the issue of how ethnic minorities relate to each other. Here there is some evidence of tensions from the wider international arena (for example, Hindu–Muslim or Muslim–Jewish antagonisms) being perpetuated in Britain, although there is also much evidence of cross-community cooperation in the activities of a range of specialist national and local bodies formed to combat racial discrimination (such as the Commission for Racial Equality, the Joint Council for the Welfare of Immigrants) as well as more generally in the routine operations and activities of trade unions and other pressure groups.

## The multiculturalism debate

The census figures indicate that the United Kingdom is now a society which contains a number of distinct minority ethnic and religious groups, although some commentators (such as Charles Moore and Melanie Phillips) would query whether ethnic minorities who together total less than 8 per cent of the population really make Britain a multicultural society. Those who discuss Britain in terms of multiculturalism are, however, usually engaged not so much in a debate about whether multicultural is an accurate description of the British population as about the normative and prescriptive aspects of multiculturalism. What are the implications of multiculturalism both for the way we view British society and for the framing of public policy?

One problem with providing an answer is that the word 'multiculturalism' is itself an ambiguous term (Watson 2000). Broadly speaking, multiculturalism emphasises the importance of culture for the individual member of society and for groups, and stresses the right of different cultures not merely to exist but to be recognised and acknowledged within a state or territory. Thus multiculturalism is not simply about tolerating the perpetuation of different cultures in the private sphere; it assumes that members of different cultures have the right to assert their different and distinctive cultures in private and in public, although as will be seen this claim that minority cultures have the right to public recognition raises a host of difficult questions, both for the state and for public institutions.

Multiculturalism therefore stands in marked contrast to doctrines of assimilation which would impose a single culture on minority groups whether by government coercion or by more discreet methods. Indeed multiculturalism in a democratic context draws a strong distinction between the different cultures which may coexist within a state and the state itself which in a sense should be neutral between these different cultural groups. Cultural identity and citizenship would thus be very different things and a single state could encompass many different cultures.

Although the idea that minority groups should assimilate to the majority culture has been heavily criticised in the last 30 years, the assimilationist model has shaped the approach to immigration in a number of countries. Indeed it remains dominant in many European countries including France where in 2004 the country's strong state tradition combined with its belief in state secularism led it to impose a highly controversial ban on the use of religious symbols in schools, including the wearing by Muslim girls of the headscarf or *hijab*. In the United States the traditional model of assimilation assumed that immigrants would gradually shed their distinctive cultures and adopt a new unifying American identity. This assumption, famously expressed in terms of the metaphor of a melting pot, was always flawed because it neglected both the extent to which some groups wished to retain own their cultural traditions and because it assumed a white, indeed Anglo-Saxon, American identity (King 2000). From the 1960s there has been much more emphasis on the rights of different groups to maintain their own cultures and identities as well as an increasingly explicit effort to celebrate the equal worth of America's different ethnic and religious traditions, including ones which were marginalised for much of American history. The image of the melting pot has been replaced by images in which component parts keep their distinctive identity in the larger composition, such as those of the salad bowl or the mosaic (Glazer 1997).

Within the United Kingdom the debate about multiculturalism has until recently been neither as explicit nor as pertinent as in France or the United States. Historically there have been episodes of attempts to eliminate distinct cultural identities – for example in the long (and unsuccessful) effort to eliminate the Welsh language. But from the 1960s and 1970s when right-wing critics of immigration, such as the then Conservative MP Enoch Powell, raised questions about how immigrants from different cultural backgrounds would fit into British society, there has been a tendency to avoid theoretical debate, concentrating on a series of practical measures to promote equality and eliminate discrimination and perhaps glossing over some of the more difficult issues posed by cultural diversity. More recently, however, beginning with the Rushdie affair, and continuing through the debate about the Parekh Report in 2000, to more recent concerns about alienated Islamic communities, the implications of multiculturalism in Britain have been probed more critically.

Multiculturalism usually entails a specific agenda of policies and programmes which focus on according equality and recognition to different traditions. In addition to taking a strong stand to eliminate discrimination, perhaps by measures of affirmative action to promote disadvantaged minorities, the state itself is expected to adapt to afford minorities explicit recognition. Usually there is an emphasis on education as a means for the preservation of language and tradition and as an instrument for promoting equality and mobility. In addition a multiculturalist agenda usually includes an insistence that members of minority groups have the right to affirm their identity by wearing distinctive dress, should have their holy days and religious practices accorded equal respect with those of the majority religion and should wherever possible be able to assert their different and distinct identity within society.

Yet these demands pose difficult dilemmas for policy makers in the United Kingdom, especially if they seek to promote equality and integration. To take just a handful of examples:

- Should separatist Islamic schools (which had started in 1981 but risen in number to about 300 in 2005) be regulated or given more public funding? This issue became especially controversial when David Bell, the head of the Office for Standards in Education (Ofsted), said in early 2005 that Muslim and other faith schools were failing to prepare pupils for life in a multicultural society and questioned whether they were sufficiently committed to communicating democratic values.

- What concessions should be made about school uniform to Muslim girls? How far should exemptions from the law be allowed on religious grounds even where they compromise the individual's safety as in the case of Sikhs who refused to wear crash helmets?
- Should the ritual slaughter of animals for *halal* or *schechita* meat (as demanded by Islamic and Jewish religious practice) be allowed?
- How far should the state tolerate attitudes and practices which assume the subservience of women, such as forced or arranged marriages?

In the case of the United Kingdom there is also the question of the extent to which the state itself, including as it does the institutions of the Church and the monarch, should be modified to accommodate different cultures.

Debate on these issues has been intense over recent years, creating unusual alliances and dividing normal political allies. For many conservatives the strong emphasis on national identity has often proved difficult to reconcile with the multicultural vision of society which accords equality to different cultures; the idea that immigrants had the right to demand that the host nation, rather than they themselves, should adapt was considered unacceptable (O'Sullivan 2003). For others on the right the whole idea of cultural assimilation was problematic in relation to non-European immigrants and the impossibility of genuine integration was a justification for excluding further immigration or even for advocating repatriation. The extensive argument about protecting the nation's culture (which marked the 1970s and 1980s and can be traced in the pages of such journals as the *Salisbury Review*) came to be labelled the 'new racism', because it focused so much on culture rather than ethnicity per se (Gordon and Klug 1986). For many conservatives the idea of multiculturalism was also suspect because of its association with political correctness, affirmative action and what they termed the race-relations 'industry'. Some on the right also had sympathy with the conservative moral values and family structures supported by some religious minorities, although this attitude also found sharp critics on the right (Hiskett 1992).

Increasingly, however, conservatives have emphasised the need to strengthen the ties that bind members of British society together rather than stressing the cultural values that divide them. In part these arguments are echoes of the 'cricket test', advocated by the former Conservative Cabinet minister Norman Tebbit, suggesting that the national cricket team which a minority ethnic person supported indicated their true loyalties. Implicit in Tebbit's test was a rejection of the idea that a citizen could be loyal to two countries. More recently a series of Conservative politicians have stressed the importance of reciprocal obligations and the need to strengthen the shared national identity and common values of all British citizens, with party leader David Cameron arguing that official bodies and councils should reduce the use made of minority languages and insist on the use of English. 'We should', he said, 'not allow our respect for other cultures to undermine our shared national culture'. Thus the conservative suspicion of multiculturalism because of its perceived dilution of the national identity seems to be finding an explicit focus in the need to reassert values which will integrate minorities.

Conservatives have not been the only sceptics about multiculturalism, however. To the extent that multiculturalism has often seemed difficult to reconcile with an overarching commitment to individualism and human rights, it has also incurred opposition from liberals. For many liberals multiculturalism is theoretically suspect if it privileges group rights and community values over individual reason. Feminists, for example, have often been highly critical of theories which appear to privilege culturally conservative ethnic groups which traditionally disadvantage women. To some degree this conflict has been resolved by insisting that multiculturalism must be conducted in the context of a wider framework of liberal values and human rights (Kymlicka 2001). Certainly multiculturalism raises difficult questions about the rights of dissenting minorities *within* communities and poses problems for the traditional liberal value of freedom of speech, as witnessed by such episodes as the Rushdie affair or the 2004 effort of Sikhs forcibly to prevent the putting-on of Gurpreet Bhatti's play *Dishonour (Behzti)* because it depicted murder and rape in a Sikh temple. Similarly, the extensive opposition (from comedians and writers as much as from politicians and the Archbishop of Canterbury) to the 2005 bill designed to outlaw religious hatred reflected concern that such legislation would inhibit freedom of speech on religious issues as well as satire. Indeed as some members of minority ethnic communities such as Monica Ali pointed out, such legislation could have been used to impede or even silence critics of faith communities.

Perhaps the most interesting recent criticisms of multiculturalism have come from within the minority ethnic communities themselves. A useful starting point to this debate is the reaction to the major report published by the Commission on the Future of Multi-Ethnic Britain chaired by Lord Parekh in 2000. Its recommendations (Parekh 2000a) represented the high-water mark of multiculturalism in the United Kingdom. It identified six tasks that needed to be done to turn Britain into a truly multiracial community – what they called a 'community of communities':

- rethinking of both 'the national story and national identity';
- understanding the transitional nature of all identities;
- achieving a balance between cohesion, difference and equality;
- addressing and eliminating all kinds of racism;
- reducing the inequalities in material benefits;
- building a 'human rights culture'.

In Parekh's view genuine multiculturalism required substantial adjustment by the majority culture and a robust process of dialogue between cultures (Parekh 2000b), but the largely hostile media response to the report framed the subsequent debate about multiculturalism in a way many found distorting. There was much opposition in particular to suggestions that British history should be rethought to make it more inclusive of cultures other than the majority one – a recommendation which echoed American curriculum debates. While Labour had implicitly accepted many of the assumptions of multiculturalism up to that point, the reaction caused Jack Straw, then Home Secretary, to beat a hasty retreat from its prescriptions. Thereafter the 9/11 bombings, the 2001 riots and general concern about the extent to which British society had become fractured prompted the Labour government to redirect its emphasis onto strengthening social cohesion and civic values.

Among the ethnic minorities themselves the promotion of multiculturalism has often seemed irrelevant to the real issues facing members of their communities. Thus one authority has pointed to surveys of minority ethnic youth which underline their lack of interest in the debate (Alibhai-Brown 2001). Controversially the idea of multiculturalism has also come under attack more recently from Trevor Phillips, the chair of the Commission for Racial Equality. He declared multiculturalism dead and argued that the United Kingdom was in danger of making a 'fetish of difference' which interfered with substantive equality (Phillips 2004). Phillips renewed his attack on multiculturalism following the London bombings by pointing to worsening ethnic divides especially in education, arguing that 'as a country we are not talking across the ethnic, religious and colour lines.' There was, he said, 'more residential segregation' and we are not making friends across the colour line: 'when we leave work we leave multi-ethnic Britain behind.' Britain, he argued, was creating a 'fertile breeding ground for extremists' (Phillips, T 2005). Phillips' views received a mixed reception. Whilst some on the right welcomed the retreat from multiculturalism, others found them offensive and inflammatory; yet others pointed out that the empirical evidence for the degree of residential segregation in Britain countered Phillips' claims. 'For all ethnic minority groups identified by the census, the indices of segregation fell between 1991 and 2001,' wrote the geographer Danny Dorling, noting that they fell fastest for people of black and 'other Asian' origin (Dorling 2005).

## New Labour and multiculturalism

Traditionally, Labour has generally been seen as more sympathetic than the other parties to minority ethnic concerns – and Labour's advent to power in 1997 was generally welcomed in minority ethnic circles, not least because ethnic minorities have traditionally been overwhelmingly Labour voters. In every general election from 1974 through to 2001, roughly four in five of all black and Asian voters who have turned out have backed Labour at the polls.

On the other hand, despite its support for stronger equality initiatives, Labour knew that it could not afford to be seen as soft on immigration or asylum, and contradictions soon emerged in Labour's approach to the agenda of multiculturalism. Some of the contradictions can be explained by what one set of authors have described as 'New Labour's talent for populist appeal' (Back et al. 2002), but there were substantial shifts of emphasis over the period from 1997. These reflected not just conflicting pressures but also changes of personality and policy emphasis in relation to immigration, with the government trying to combine a greater open-ness to migration which would enhance Britain's economic competitive-ness in the global economy with tight control of the asylum laws and illegal immigration (Duvell and Jordan 2003). Some initiatives, such as the dropping of the primary-purpose rule (the immigration rule which required a British national who married a spouse from overseas to prove that the primary purpose of the marriage was not to enable the spouse to settle in the United Kingdom), were generally welcomed by Britain's ethnic minorities; and the passage of the Human Rights Act 1998 and the Race Relations (Amendment) Act 2000 reinforced Labour's already strong record as a party willing to use the power of government to combat discrimination.

The Race Relations (Amendment) Act of 2000 reflected Labour's acceptance of much of the analysis in the Macpherson Inquiry into the death of the black teenager Stephen Lawrence (Home Office 1999). The report argued that many areas of British society exhibited 'institutional racism' – 'the collective failure of an organisation to provide an appro-priate and professional service to people because of their colour, culture, or ethnic origin' – and went on to recommend a more proactive approach to eliminating discrimination. The 2000 Act accordingly gave all public authorities a general duty to promote race equality and attempted to tackle indirect as well as direct discrimination. This general duty means that every public authority must eliminate unlawful racial discrimination and must promote equality of opportunity between people of different racial groups. The Home Secretary was also given power to impose specific duties on some public bodies such as schools, and the Commission for Racial Equality was given an extended role and powers in relation to enforcement. This legislation is noteworthy for two reasons:

- It indicates an intention to inject concern for racial equality much more systematically into British public policy at every level.
- The duty to monitor and assess the promotion of racial equality, through such devices as monitoring the proportions of ethnic minorities in different employment sectors, schools and universities by comparison with their total in the population, moves Britain much closer in many respects to the affirmative-action strategies familiar in the United States.

Labour's first White Paper (1998) on the subject of asylum, *Fairer, Firmer, Faster* (which ultimately provided the basis of the Asylum and Immigration Act 1999), promised a more streamlined approach to immigration control as well as to the way settlement and citizenship issues were handled. In theory what the government wanted to do was to clear the backlog in the process of handling asylum applications, bring a new openness to its administration and introduce a new covenant on hearing appeals against adverse decisions. In practice the White Paper was seen by many as a method of further tightening controls and reassuring the public that Britain was not a 'soft touch' for asylum seekers.

More generally, the government wanted to refocus much of the debate about immigration into a discussion of how policy could be linked to the country's economic needs; but this was difficult to do in a climate where there was such fear of the immigration issue's capacity to damage the government. The answer was to emphasise *managed* migration, a policy which culminated in February 2005 with the announcement of a five-year strategy for immigration and asylum, *Controlling Our Borders: Making Migration Work for Britain* (Home Office 2005).

David Blunkett, Home Secretary 2001–04, was also increasingly concerned about the lack of integration in many of Britain's cities which had significant minority ethnic populations. The severe urban disturbances which had occurred in Bradford, Oldham, Burnley, Leeds and Stoke in mid-2001 were in Blunkett's view indicative that these communities were fractured and divided societies. A series of local and national reports into the causes of the riots highlighted a depressing pattern of segregation and separation in these towns. In addition they blamed the unrest on a lack of leadership, irresponsible local media and extremist groups.

Most importantly, however, the riots triggered concern that the root problem was the lack of a strong identity and shared values that could unite the diverse communities in the troubled areas. Blunkett himself was deeply committed to the idea of strengthening citizenship education as part of his wider campaign for civic renewal. Accordingly when Labour's second White Paper on immigration, *Secure Borders, Safe Haven: Integration with Diversity in Modern Britain*, was published in February 2002 it placed a heavy emphasis on preparing people for citizenship, with a new language test for prospective immigrants and their descendants as well as a more formalised civil naturalisation ceremony along with a loyalty oath. The initiative received a mixed reception, with the Joint Council for the Welfare of Immigrants (JCWI), for example, deeply regretting the negative tone of the document and being sceptical about the new citizenship initiatives which it saw as raising further barriers for would-be immigrants.

Since 1997, therefore, the government has developed something of a 'new road map' for the contentious and linked issues of immigration, asylum, and integration (Flynn 2003). Tightly managed immigration linked to economic need has been balanced by a new emphasis on ways of strengthening the bonds that link ethnic minorities to the wider society. This goal, which would have existed even without the terrorist attacks of July 2005, became more important as it became apparent that 9/11 and the war in Iraq were having an impact on Britain's Islamic community.

In addition, since 1997 the British government has strengthened its efforts to tackle discrimination and promote substantive equality for minority communities. With the passage of the Human Rights Act of 1998, a step was taken which should make government decision making more sensitive to individual rights, although there remains room for disagreement between the executive and the judiciary in the contentious area of asylum decisions. There are thus now three broad sources of regulation and initiatives designed to prevent discrimination against minorities within the political system:

- the long-standing machinery of the Race Relations Acts and the Commission for Racial Equality which since 1965 have extended the definition of discrimination;
- the newer jurisprudence of the Human Rights Act of 1998 which incorporates much of the European Convention on Human Rights into British law;

- the law of the European Union which contains important directly applicable provisions especially with regard to employment and freedom of movement.

The government is still nevertheless acutely aware that racial discrimination remains a problem in many areas of British life. In the sensitive area of policing (where the Macpherson Inquiry identified institutional racism as a continuing problem in the police forces) there have been a number of subsequent efforts to monitor progress, both by the Metropolitan Police themselves and by the Commission for Racial Equality (Commission for Racial Equality 2004; Metropolitan Police Service 2004). Not surprisingly the House of Commons Home Affairs Committee has been especially concerned about the impact which efforts to detect terrorist activity could have on attempts to improve relations between the police and ethnic minorities who may find themselves subject to additional surveillance.

Labour's 2005 manifesto promised a new Equality Act which would restructure the machinery for dealing with discrimination, although following protests from the Commission for Racial Equality the merger of the various bodies handling discrimination will not be completed until 2009.

## Minority groups and the political process

From at least the 1980s efforts to mobilise ethnic minorities have shaped the dynamics of British local politics and party competition in the larger cities. Although fragmented on ethnic, sectarian and ideological lines, representative organisations of minority groups, such as the Muslim Council, are also increasingly organised and able to put forward their own agenda. At the national level political parties have to weave an awkward path between appealing to these groups for support and looking beyond them to the communities which they or may not accurately represent. At the same time issues related to ethnic minorities are sensitive ones for the population as a whole and governments are very aware of the danger of creating a backlash against minority communities.

The 2005 general election saw a step change in the political mobilisation of minority groups. Following the 2001 election where low turnout was found to be particularly marked among the young and the black minority population, sustained efforts were made to engage the minority ethnic population in the political process. Operation Black Vote (OBV) was established and formulated a black manifesto, listing a series of specific demands, including a commitment to Islamic schools and reconsideration of anti-terrorism legislation. Something similar had occurred at previous elections but the launch of the black manifesto and the general organisation of OBV was much more sophisticated than in previous elections, with OBV identifying 70 target constituencies where it was thought the combined minority ethnic vote could make a difference.

The major political parties also stepped up their efforts to recruit minority candidates and the 2005 election saw a record 113 minority ethnic candidates, a figure markedly up from the 65 who had competed in the 2001 election. The election returned 15 minority ethnic candidates including two Conservatives – the highest number of minority ethnic MPs ever elected to the House of Commons.

Yet the 2005 election was also notable for the extent to which asylum and immigration emerged as issues. This high-profile debate was widely regretted in many quarters because it was seen as an irresponsible playing of the 'race card'. Certainly for much of the post-1960 period politicians of the major parties (though not far-right groups such as the National Front and the British National Party) generally attempted to keep race off the agenda for fear of exacerbating social divisions (Copsey 2004). The United Kingdom Independence Party (UKIP) also carved out a hardline position on immigration and asylum, motivated not so much by racial antagonism as by a belief that the United Kingdom cannot cope with further population growth – that it is 'full up'. Think tanks such as Migration Watch (which has regularly challenged Home Office figures) also helped keep the issue on the agenda. That immigration was recognised as one of the few issues in 2005 on which the public perceived a major gulf between the parties also fuelled the debate. Conservative leader Michael Howard, himself the son of an immigrant, as he frequently reminded the public, made the issue central despite the opposition of some of his Conservative colleagues. In a well-publicised speech at Telford on 10 April 2005 Howard promised to 'get a grip' on immigration and to reduce substantially the numbers of immigrants. Howard also wanted enhanced border security, strict health checks on would-be immigrants and, in a radical move, committed the party to withdrawing from the international framework (the Geneva Convention) governing the treatment of refugees. Yet most senior Conservatives are also keenly aware that they cannot afford to write off the growing number of minority ethnic voters and that they cannot risk looking, in the words of one black Conservative peer, 'mean and xenophobic' (Taylor 2001).

Labour's 2005 vote fell sharply in constituencies with large Muslim populations, as a direct result of the government's stance on the Iraq war. Most spectacularly George Galloway, running as a representative of the

Respect Party in Bethnal Green and Bow, defeated Oona King, a minority ethnic MP with a good constituency reputation.

## The politics of extremism

Despite the efforts of the major parties to maintain a cross-party consensus on race, its power to shatter conventional politics has always been apparent. Indeed it was precisely because politicians were so fearful about the social and electoral consequences of debating immigration that there was frequently an understanding that it should be kept off the agenda (Messina 1989). The riots of 1958 in both Nottingham and Notting Hill were powerful factors in the decision to bring forward restrictive legislation. The speech made by Enoch Powell in 1968 in which he warned of 'rivers of blood' was notable because it gained support from trade unionists even as it incurred condemnation from the then party leader, Edward Heath. More recently just before the 2001 election the Conservative MP, John Townend (who was standing down at the election) caused intense controversy by claiming that Britons were becoming a 'mongrel race'.

For the extreme right, immigration and race are central to their agenda. The British National Party (BNP) is the latest in a series of far-right parties for whom race and immigration are major issues. These parties have frequently used tactics and language which have put them outside the mainstream of political debate. The BNP, which was formed in 1982, has recently appeared to change its tactics, sensing that a series of issues including asylum and the impact of 9/11 have created new opportunities for the party. Under Nick Griffin (who replaced John Tyndall as leader in 1999) the BNP has developed its party organisation, honed its electoral strategy and attempted to present itself as a credible right-of-centre mainstream party. Especially since 2001 its propaganda has focused increasingly not on all ethnic minorities but on Muslims, whom it deems to be alien as a result of religion and political loyalty. Concentrating especially on the North West of England and towns with established patterns of racial antagonism, the BNP has made modest electoral gains. In 2002 it won three council seats in Burnley and had further success in the area in 2003 so that by the end of 2004 it had 17 council seats altogether.

In the general election of 2005 the BNP put up 119 candidates, and saved its deposit – that is, gained 5 per cent or more of the vote – in 34 seats. Although this achievement was no seismic electoral breakthrough, the BNP improved its vote, gaining almost 200,000 votes compared to the fewer than 50,000 it had gained in the 2001 general election; and it raised its profile and gained media attention. The BNP is unlikely to see a major electoral advance in the near future but it retains the potential to inflict damage at council level, especially in by-elections. Where the BNP is dangerous, however, is in its ability to inflame racial tensions – as has been evidenced in a number of the disturbances in the UK – and to spread offensive propaganda, which has led some representatives of ethnic communities to call for it to be banned. In September 2005 a shipload of its newspaper was seized because of its racially offensive content.

Extremism is not however the exclusive preserve of the BNP. As moderate Islamic leaders have pondered how best to reduce the appeal of terrorist organisations within their community, they have had to acknowledge that British foreign policy especially in Iraq has encouraged support for extremists. Thus Islamic leaders such as Sir Iqbal Sacranie, the Secretary General of the Muslim Council, suggested that foreign policy was a contributory factor in radicalising Islamic youth. Some Islamic extremists such as Anjem Choudary, the leader of the militant Islamic group al-Muhajiroun have gone further. Not only have they pointed to the British role in Iraq as a powerful factor in the terrorist incidents but they have suggested that British Muslim leaders should not meet with the prime minister. Choudary refused to condemn the London bombings and indeed predicted that they might be repeated in a 'cycle of blood'. Similarly the radical Muslim Sheikh Omar Bakri Mohammed blamed voters for the London attacks, arguing that greater efforts should have been made to change British foreign policy.

The British government for its part has stepped up its efforts to counter Islamic terrorism and extremism by consulting as widely as possible with the Muslim community. Part of the problem for the British government as it seeks to isolate extremist elements among British Muslims is that it does not know how far the representative organisations with which it deals (such as the Muslim Council) can reach out to, let alone influence, the sections of the Islamic community who are susceptible to appeals to neo-fundamentalism or mobilisation behind extremist causes. Nor is it easy to know what initiatives might help win over those Muslims who now appear alienated from British society. To that extent the London bombings may have the salutary effect of requiring the government to acquire a much better and more detailed understanding of the fissures and fault lines within British Islam.

## Conclusion

The debate about multiculturalism in the context of the United Kingdom has recently entered a new phase, with politicians wrestling with questions about how to create a greater sense of identification with Britain among the country's ethnic minorities. Although this task has been given a new urgency by the threat of terrorism, much of the concern about the success of existing approaches to integration was already surfacing given that existing strategies of integration had been called into question by what seemed like a continuing segregation of minority communities from the mainstream of British life. How far the new stage in the multiculturalism debate will produce more effective policies for securing social equality or the integration of Britain's diverse minorities remains to be seen. What is clear is that the agendas of those minority communities – whether filtered through mainstream parties or sectional groups – are likely to remain a continuing and challenging element in the British political system.

## Chapter 12

# The State and Civil Liberties in the Post-9/11 World

## MICHAEL SAWARD

On 7 July 2005 four suicide bombers killed 52 people and injured many more on public transport in central London. There had been many warnings since the attacks on the United States on 11 September 2001 that Britain was also a prime terrorist target. The heavy involvement of the UK in the US-led invasion and occupation of Iraq in 2003 was perceived by many as increasing the chances that Britain would be targeted, though the government has maintained that the invasion of Iraq had not in itself increased this threat.

After '7/7', Prime Minister Tony Blair declared that 'the rules of the game have changed.' The 'war on terror' had arrived, at great human cost, on home soil. And as the rules of international conflict and security had changed, he argued, so must the government's approach to individual liberties in Britain; the government would need to change certain rules too, taking new measures in order to protect British citizens from terrorist threats. Blair often repeated his view that the most basic liberty of all was the right to life; to protect British lives, some other civil liberties may need to be curtailed.

The Government's key response to 7/7 was the Terrorism Bill 2005, the fourth major piece of anti-terrorism legislation since 2000. This legislation proposed to extend from 14 to 90 days the length of time that suspects could be held without charge, and created new offences of glorifying or inciting terrorism, attending a terrorist training camp or making preparations for acts of terrorism. These proposals extended and deepened challenges to traditional civil liberties in Britain, but in the context of 'changed rules'. The prime minister lost the vote in the House of Commons on the 90-days detention proposal in November 2005, though he fought for it vehemently in the face of likely defeat, arguing that 'We are not living in a police state but we are living in a country that faces a real and serious threat of terrorism' (BBC News 9 November 2005, http://news.bbc.co.uk/1/hi/uk_politics/4422086.stm). After the vote, he claimed that 'the country will think parliament has behaved in a deeply irresponsible way'; quoting a senior police officer, he said 'We are not looking for legislation to hold people for up to three months simply because it is an easy option. It is absolutely vital. To prevent further attacks we must have it' (*Sunday Times* 13 November 2005). In short: the people want and need protection from proven, immediate threat; the measures needed may be extraordinary, but they are also necessary.

The Blair government's anti-terrorism laws have been at the core of heated debate about security, civil liberties, and the proper understanding of (and relationships between) the two. Challenging traditional civil liberties in the face of external threats is not new in Britain, as I shall describe briefly in a moment. But varied voices accusing the Blair government of chipping away at time-honoured citizen rights and liberties have invoked more than the government's approach to the war on terror. Policies concerning, for example, the regulation of asylum seekers, the planned introduction of identity cards, action on anti-social behaviour and the challenge to the right to trial by jury have been framed by critics as evidence of a government that places too little value on basic citizen liberties. There is even speculative talk about the emergence of a new type of state, one whose regulation of the behaviour of citizens runs deeper than before in a democracy, giving rise to concerns about the 'security state', or even the emergence of a 'post-democracy'.

In democratic systems such as Britain 'democracy' is never static; it is a label as well as a thing, and there is much dispute about what institutions and attitudes that label should be applied to. Both the substance and the symbolism of British democracy shift and change in the context of these debates about civil liberties. Competing conceptions of democracy run underneath many of the debates about civil liberties and the protection of citizens. The trade-off between security and civil liberties is very much of the moment. But this is far from being the first era in which critical observers have perceived governments encroaching on basic rights and liberties. Equally, is it the first time that governments have perceived the need to take steps to curtail the liberties of those they see as posing dangers to the polity or the society? Taking the 'long view' serves to remind us that such disputes are centuries old. Momentous questions of the liberty of the subject go back to Magna Carta in 1215 at least. Habeas corpus, the right of the individual not to be subject to arbitrary arrest, has been part of English law since the late seventeenth century. These principles are part of a broad and complex historical trajectory of rendering the executive accountable to Parliament and through the latter to the people. There are many historical examples of these rights and liberties being challenged by governments. In the late eighteenth century, Prime Minister William Pitt's government arrested and charged with treason several people suspected of dangerous sympathies with the anti-republican ideals of the French

Revolution. The unsuccessful trials that followed were conducted in the name of national security. The fear of France under Napoleon, and over Irish rebellion in 1871, saw suspensions of habeas corpus and the use of detention without trial respectively.

More recently, the Defence of the Realm Act of 1914 imposed wide powers of internment and of restrictions of liberty. Shortly prior to the outbreak of World War II, the Emergency Powers (Defence) Act authorised the Home Secretary to lock people up on the basis of his belief that a person was 'of hostile origin or associations'. Those identified as sympathising with fascism, most notably Oswald Mosley, were interned during the war. The so-called 'troubles' in Northern Ireland from the 1960s to the 1990s saw the abandonment of trial by jury, the authorisation of detention without trial, the introduction of internment and the passage of the Prevention of Terrorism Act 1974, which was renewed annually. The perception that recent anti-terrorism legislation undermines civil liberties has its own reasons and style (and there are new and distinct characteristics to the threats that the government has based its justification for legislation upon), but there is a rich historical context into which all of the current debates fit (Bindman 2005).

## Policies in question

Fears about the undermining of civil liberties under the Blair government have centred mostly upon anti-terrorism legislation. But those fears, and accusations, are often expressed with respect to other policies of the government, notably around asylum seekers and identity cards. Asylum seeking and immigration (legal and illegal) have become hot political issues around the world, not least across the European Union (EU), in recent years. In the past 20 years, asylum applications to EU states have grown enormously. The peak was in 1992, where the number of applications was over 684,000 (up from 50,000 in 1983). The number in 2002 was 381,600 (Loescher 2005). Over this period, Germany was the largest recipient of asylum applications in Europe, though Britain took that mantle from 2000. In each of the years from 1998 to 2001, Britain received over 90,000 asylum applications and over 110,000 in 2002.

Under the Blair government, there have been a range of measures, legislative and administrative, designed to limit the number of asylum applications. Border-control measures at points of entry into the country have been increased. Detention of those whose claims have been refused has risen in prominence. Detention, in centres such as the UK's largest, Yarls Wood in Bedforshire, has been controversial. Accusations of racist abuse by staff, the lack of educational provision for children in detention, and a lack of safety for women and children in detention have been prominent (*Guardian* 27 July 2005). Benefits have also been an issue; the 1999 Immigration and Asylum Act took asylum seekers out of the UK benefits system and introduced shopping vouchers for refugees. This was seen as a way to make asylum seeking a less attractive option to those considering entering the country. Under the Asylum and Immigration Act 2004, benefits in some parts of Britain could be withdrawn from asylum seekers whose applications had failed, giving rise to fears that families could become homeless and face the prospect that their children might be taken into care (*Guardian* 10 August 2005). From the government's point of view, controlling the numbers of asylum seekers was a question of the integrity of borders and internal security. Its actions were variously heckled and supported by often sensationalist tabloid newspaper headlines likening the numbers of refugees coming (or potentially coming) to the UK as a 'flood', and linking asylum seekers to criminal activity and terrorist threats (Huysmans 2005).

Concerns about the treatment of asylum seekers centred upon the withdrawal of benefit rights and the undesirable conditions in which they were detained or maintained. These were matters of civil rights, along with concerns about the deportation of failed asylum seekers to countries where they may face danger. A very different issue that nevertheless sometimes became linked to asylum seeking (and indeed anti-terrorism legislation) was the government's proposal to introduce identity cards for UK citizens. The Identity Cards Bill of 2005 was seen by the government as a means to combat illegal immigration, fraud, terrorism, organized crime and theft of identity. Critics raised concerns about what the information on the identity cards (which would include biometric data on individuals) could be used for, and worried that their introduction could lead to the criminalisation of many who refused to carry them. Many critics have viewed identity cards as potentially undermining the liberties of UK citizens.

Issues of asylum and identity cards have in recent years increasingly been linked to anti-terrorism measures. Often ill-informed commentary linked refugees to the import of the terrorist threat into Britain; and debates around identity cards have regularly included disputes about whether their introduction would or would not assist authorities in protecting citizens against terrorist threats on UK soil. But it is on anti-terrorism legislation itself that the most prominent debates about civil liberties have taken place.

There are four pieces of legislation which have defined the Blair government's response to what it perceives as an immediate threat from terrorism.

First, the *Terrorism Act 2000* built on prior laws arising from the long-standing situation in Ireland, offered broad definitions of terrorism and associated offences, and gave power to proscribe organisations deemed to pose terrorist threats to the UK. It also enhanced powers to seize terrorist property and disrupt terrorist financial activity; granted police powers with regard to terrorist investigations (such as stop-and-search powers); created several offences specific to terrorism, such as fund raising, dealing with proscribed groups in various ways, and training terrorists; and required an annual report on the operation of the Act to Parliament.

Second, the *Anti-Terrorism Crime and Security Act (ATCSA) 2001* was passed in the wake of September 11 and amounted to the first major response by the British government to those attacks. The main provision of ATCSA concerned detention without trial of foreign nationals suspected of involvement in terrorism. The government saw extended detention as necessary, partly because international law prohibited the deportation of suspects where their lives may be in danger. At the same time, the government maintained that although law enforcement agencies may have strong grounds for suspecting involvement in terrorism, little of the evidence would be admissible in a criminal court or would be impossible to reveal in Court without exposing sensitive capabilities or endangering sources of information. Further powers under the Act involved the creation of offences related to hoaxes involving dangerous substances and further tools to combat the financing of suspected terrorist activities. The Act also gave the police more powers to hold and question suspects. ATCSA was targeted by many for its overturning of long-standing British judicial principles, particularly in its legitimising of indefinite imprisonment of suspects without charge or trial. Detainees could not see the evidence against them or have it tested before a court in the usual way. There was a special secure court without a jury, the Special Immigration Appeals Commission (SIAC), to which a limited number of lawyers were allowed access, which could hear appeals by detainees. Eleven men were detained under the Act and held in Belmarsh prison in South London, without charge. Nine appealed to the highest court in the country, the House of Lords, in the latter half of 2004. The detainees' lawyers argued that the relevant measures in the ATCSA 'were an affront to democracy and the internationally accepted notion of justice' (*Independent* 5 October 2004).

The Law Lords, the highest court in the UK, ruled, in December 2004, that detention without trial as expressed under the Act contravened the European Convention on Human Rights as it allowed detentions 'in a way that discriminates on the ground of nationality or immigration status' by justifying detention without trial for foreign suspects, but not Britons. Britain has 'derogated' (opted out) from the European

Convention with respect to detention without trial. The Convention allows such derogation under circumstances amounting to an emergency situation in face of imminent threat to the country. But the Law Lords were scathing in declaring this unlawful. Lord Hoffmann argued that 'The real threat to the life of the nation ... comes not from terrorism but from laws such as these' (quoted in *Observer* 19 December 2004).

Third, the *Prevention of Terrorism Act 2005*, passed by Parliament after heated debate in April 2005, was effectively the government's response to the House of Lords ruling on ATCSA. The Lords declared the sections of ATCSA which dealt with detention of foreign terrorist suspects incompatible with European human rights law on two basic grounds: it was discriminatory in that it singled out non-British citizens, and that it was a disproportionate response that did not justify Britain opting out of the relevant European human rights laws. The Prevention of Terrorism Act essentially replaces detention of suspects by a process of 'control orders'. These control orders could take a variety of forms, the most stringent and controversial of which was 'house arrest' – a phrase commonly used in debates on the Bill but avoided by the Home Secretary, Charles Clarke, and his government colleagues. Unlike the detention provisions in the ATCSA, these control orders could be applied equally to British nationals and foreign suspects. As under ATCSA, there would be limited and restricted types of judicial involvement, but at the end of the day the Prevention of Terrorism Act grants power to the Secretary of State, acting under advice from the security services, to impose various restrictions on the liberty of individuals who could not be deported and who, if their cases were brought before the courts in the conventional manner, would be unlikely to receive sentences commensurate with the Home Secretary's view of the extent of the threat that their activities posed. With regard to the latter, the sensitive nature of the intelligence upon which these judgments would be made in the first place, and the inadmissibility of phone-tap evidence in the courts, also in the government's view made use of the conventional court procedures inappropriate. After the Lords ruling on ATSCA, the Belmarsh detainees were released, but the majority of these men became subject to control orders under the new legislation.

Fourth, the *Terrorism Bill 2005*, the most recent anti-terrorism measure, was put together in the wake of the attacks in London in July and was working its way through Parliament at the time of writing. Its central elements were heightened government powers to deport people from the UK who are considered to be promoting terrorism; the extension of powers to detain suspects for up to 90 days without charges being laid before a court; and a new offence of 'glorifying, exalting or celebrating' terrorism. The proposed legislation also targeted incitement of terrorism and the dissemination of material perceived to promote terrorism.

Political opponents of the government, and civil-liberties groups, expressed concern in particular about the increased detention provisions – a further challenge to basic principles of not being detained without due legal process, from their point of view – and about the ambiguity of 'glorifying' terrorism, which they feared might result in much wider restrictions on freedom of speech. Some critics asked whether open support for Nelson Mandela prior to the dismantling of apartheid in South Africa would have amounted to an offence under the proposed laws. The Blair government was defeated on one key proposal in the Terrorism Bill in November 2005 when the House of Commons rejected detention without trial for 90 days in favour of a lower period of 28 days. Initial media coverage focused on the whether this defeat, the first time the Labour government had lost a Commons vote, represented the beginning of the end of Blair's prime ministership.

## Political rhetoric and underlying ideals

How do present debates surrounding such controversial measures as the effective policing of terrorism invoke different visions or conceptions of democracy? For example, political actors, in making principled and practical objections to government actions, offer their own implicit or explicit criteria against which to judge the government's or system's performance. Particular political actors tend to be the 'carriers' or 'purveyors' of competing models of democracy as can be glimpsed when we trace some key threads in the debates surrounding the 2001 and 2005 anti-terrorism legislation in particular.

Debates around anti-terror legislation are replete with key words and signifiers which carry powerful but ambiguous resonances. 'Freedom' is deployed on the side of those proposing restrictions on certain classes of people in the name of 'security'. The idea of the state as a provider of 'protection' for citizens in a democracy has played a key part too. The very survival of democratic systems and practices in the face of the 'threat' posed by international terrorism is invoked by the UK government. The value, renewal and survival of democracy, the role of the state in protecting basic democratic rights and freedoms, are precisely the sorts of issues that go to the heart of what democracy is, and what it ought to be. A range of principles have been invoked and expounded in the debates around anti-terrorism legislation. In addition to concerned and interested citizens, a range of actors were involved:

- the government;
- opposition parties and their parliamentary spokespersons;

- opponents outside Parliament such as civil-liberties groups;
- the judiciary; and, not least
- media figures.

A range of factors were also in play in these tussles:

- the manner and speed with which legislation was passed;
- the public debate as played out in the news media;
- concern for the proper role of the judiciary within a democracy;
- the deep historical character of the liberties of the individual which some perceived to be under threat (either by terrorism, or by the legislation designed to protect against it);
- the proper nature of the relative power of the executive in a democracy; and
- how one might judge the extent of a 'threat' and therefore what might be a proportionate response.

For the Blair government, the 'threat' of terrorism to Britain was immediate, it constituted an emergency, and it justified the taking of whatever steps were deemed necessary to combat it. The words 'threat', 'security' and 'protection' have permeated ministerial speeches and those documents introducing or defending the measures represented in the ATCSA 2001, the Prevention of Terrorism Act 2005 and the Terrorism Bill 2005. This has not simply been one thread amongst others in the Blair government's approach to its governing tasks in recent years, but very much at the centre of its rhetoric and specific proposals. Consider the Queen's Speech of November 2004, which was described as follows:

> The government's programme is overwhelmingly dominated by issues relating to crime, anti-social behaviour and, most obviously, security. It is littered with references to the threat from global terrorism and the fact that we all live in a 'changing and uncertain world'. And its tone is set by a series of measures including proposals for ID cards, an organized crime bill and a counter terrorism bill, all designed to address what Tony Blair believes is the greatest challenge of the modern world. (BBC News November 2004, http://news.bbc.co.uk/1/hi/uk_politics/4034903.stm)

The world is changing, the country faces grave threats, and has to act in a way adequate to these threats. The nature of the challenge is unprecedented: in Blair's own words, 'Here in this country and in other nations round the world, laws will be changed, not to deny basic liberties but to prevent their abuse and protect the most basic liberty of all: freedom from terror' (quoted in Huysmans 2004, 325). Note too that this is very much a *national* agenda. Although civil liberties campaigners and others applauded the Blair government's passing of the Human Rights Act 1998, which incorporated into British law the European Convention on Human Rights (discussed below), derogation or opting out of provisions of the Act under certain specified circumstances has been a core part of the government's measures against terrorist threats (as we saw, the Law Lords' important ruling of late 2004 contradicted key grounds of such derogation). The government has been keen to see that European law does not undercut, as it sees it, efforts to protect British citizens. For example, proposed new EU rules announced in September 2005 regarding rights of appeal for failed asylum seekers and illegal immigrants, how long they can be held, and safeguards with respect to returning deportees to countries where they may face torture, raised concerns within the government that their plans to deport terrorist suspects would not be able to go ahead. Home Secretary Charles Clarke has made it clear, in such cases, that he would act where possible to circumvent European restrictions, notably by signing bilateral memorandums of understanding against torture with the governments of nations to which deportees may be sent. The general point is that the British government has assumed its right to act as it sees fit in the face of new threats in a changed world; democracy and protection are a national matter before they are questions of European or other international standards or charters.

Clearly, this is democracy in 'protective' mode. The job of government is to protect the people, and to regard as important, but secondary, qualms about marginal restrictions on people's liberties where such restrictions bolster protection. New times and new uncertainties demand protective democratic action by government. Now, of course, protective measures beyond the normal remit of the law can only be acceptable if the character and immediacy of the new threats are such that they justify such measures. The Prime Minister's (and Home Secretary Charles Clarke's) view that the rules of the game had changed after 7/7 meant (presumably) that further restrictions on certain civil liberties in the name of a wider security may be needed, and that the government would not hesitate to introduce them. Government underlining and reinforcing of the sense of immediate and highly dangerous threat to the British people is ubiquitous. The Home Office's own briefing paper, *International Terrorism*, provides a flavour of this case. It outlines 'the nature of the terrorist threat we face and how it differs from previous threats of this kind', noting that to 'protect' is a key part of the necessary response. Throughout, though, the aim is 'reconciling liberty and security', acting 'without compromising the openness of our society or the freedoms we value'. 'Liberty with security' is the goal. But it must be realised that the threat amounts to an 'emergency', and 'democratic governments have long accepted that such emergencies may justify some temporary and limited curtailment of individual rights where this is essential to preserve wider freedoms and security'. The government has found such actions 'necessary', because it is dealing with 'an unprecedented challenge' (Home Office 2002a). So altering the laws so that for example forms of detention without the normal legal processes, control orders, limited judicial involvement, and new restrictions on freedom of speech, could be legal is a response to a threat that is both grave and new.

Although measures to deal with the terrorist threat are not permanent, no one should expect that they would not be needed for some time: 'we need to recognize the resilience of the terrorists. This is not a threat which can be overcome quickly or where negotiation is possible' (Home Office 2002a, 1). That fact is reinforced by ministers conveying their sense of the character of the enemy – it is not one thing, in one place, or even readily seeable or identifiable. As David Blunkett, the then Home Secretary, stated in the House of Commons in October 2002, 'al-Qaeda and its offshoots' have 'a network of cells and the loose confederation of those who are not parts of its central core but who are prepared to support and help it' (House of Commons debates 10 October 2002). In formulating laws and other measures to combat this amorphous, highly dangerous and immediate threat, Mr. Blunkett (a controversial figure, seen as a realistic progressive by supporters and an illiberal reactionary by his critics) wanted answers, not arguments which failed to recognise the threat's nature: 'All I want is that people come up with solutions, not with objections, because in the end the primary duty of Government is to protect our citizens from the undermining of their freedoms and democracy by those who know no bounds and have no understanding of the issues of punishment or prosecution when they take the lives of others through suicide bombing' (House of Commons debates 23 February 2004).

One can also see in the government's approach the effort to instill a sense of common purpose in the face of the 'threat'. As Charles Clarke, Blunkett's successor as Home Secretary, said in the House of Commons in 2005 in the debate about the Prevention of Terrorism Act: '[a]l-Qaeda and its associates have a strategy to destroy the central themes of our democratic society, and this House must decide how best we can address that threat. In so doing, we must seek to analyse and understand the threat that we face, which we have done – we have laid the results before this House and are trying directly to assess the threat … [W]e must acknowledge that British citizens as well as non-British citizens are focused on the target of seeking to destroy through terrorist activity the society that we seek to represent' (House of Commons debates 28 February 2005).

There are four threads in the government's style and rhetoric that are worth noting at this point:

Firstly, its approach implies that it is acting as the defender of basic rights and liberties. Most often, the government expresses this view in terms of its defence of the most basic liberty, that of freedom from terror, or of the most basic right, that to life. In the words of Tony Blair, the government has sought to 'protect the most basic civil liberty of all, which is the right to life on behalf of our citizens' (*Guardian* 16 September 2005).

Secondly, it asserts strongly its right as a national government to protect its citizens as it sees fit, within its European and international obligations where essential but by taking a separate legal or administrative path where it perceives that as necessary and feasible.

Thirdly, the government is fond in these debates of the discourse of 'balance'. The relationship between civil liberties and security in the changed world carries key questions of striking the 'right balance' between the two. It is careful not to deny the importance of fundamental civil liberties, but talk of balance is quite explicit in its aim to revisit, and if necessary to curb with reluctance and limitations, some cherished civil liberties.

Fourthly, it sees the balance between the executive and the judiciary in the UK shifting somewhat in this context. It is careful not to speak of undermining the traditional role of the courts in the UK system, least of all the judiciary's right to review the legality of legislation. But its anti-terrorism measures have been seen by many in the judiciary (as we shall see briefly below) as challenging age-old patterns of balance between the executive and judicial branches of government in the UK. The government's interpretation of 'balance' does not, on the whole, sit comfortably with other notions of constitutional balance between these separate arms of the British state.

The rhetorical justifications built around the terms 'protection' and 'security' carry particular interpretations of what and who needs protection and security. It is very much the British people, and its way of life, that needs protection and security. That sounds perfectly uncontroversial, and in one sense it is. But, as we shall see, it is not the only interpretation. Interestingly, talk of striking a new 'balance' between protecting Britons from terrorism and civil liberties also received support from other sections of the executive branch of the UK government. The head of Britain's internal security service, MI5, Dame Eliza Manningham-Buller, spoke in September 2005 of the difficulties of protecting citizens within the law when unclear intelligence leads authorities to believe that a terrorist attack is being planned, but where there is insufficient evidence to lead to charges being laid successfully. She defended the importance of civil liberties and 'hard-fought-for' rights, but noted that 'the world has changed and there needs to be a debate on whether some erosion of what we all value may be necessary to improve the chances of our citizens not being blown apart as they go about their daily lives' (BBC News 10 September 2005, http://news.bbc.co.uk/1/hi/uk/4232012.stm).

Other actors saw this 'balance' differently. Opinion in the judiciary was not uniform by any means, but there were many strong judicial criticisms of the key features of the legislation discussed here. The importance of the rule of law in a democracy was an important theme in judicial criticism. One of the Law Lords who ruled that the ATCSA provisions on detention without trial were unlawful, Lord Nicholls, said in his ruling that 'Indefinite imprisonment without charge or trial is anathema in any country which observes the rule of law' (BBC News 16 December 2004, http://news.bbc.co.uk/1/hi/uk/4100481.stm). One High or Appeal Court judge, speaking anonymously, expressed great concern about the Prevention of Terrorism Act's 'control orders' in a similar concern for the basic rule of law in a democracy: 'It has to be pointed out to the public that these quite draconian measures apply to them – not just to bad people but to everybody. They may think that the government will only apply them to bad people but there is a risk that they will be applied to cases where they're not justified' (*Guardian* 26 April 2005). Another High Court judge added: 'I think the executive takes too much power in relation to terrorism and in relation to shutting people up without trial' (ibid.).

Tony Blair warned in 2005 that he would have 'a lot of battles' with the courts if they acted to block the deportation of extremists, talking of renouncing part of the European Convention on Human Rights (*Independent* 11 August 2005). In return, senior judges have told the government that they would fight 'root and branch' any moves to undermine the independence of the judiciary. High-level invocation of democracy has been a key part of judicial warning shots aimed at the government's rhetoric over its anti-terrorism measures. A deputy High Court judge, Lord Carlile, said that 'If the Government undermines the judiciary, then the judiciary might be tempted to undermine the Government ... If we get into that state of affairs we undermine democracy. That is something the judiciary won't do, and the Government would be foolish to do it' (*Independent* 11 August 2005). A former Law Lord, Lord Clyde, said that 'The importance of the independence of the judiciary ... is beyond question. The function of the judiciary is to uphold the constitution. If a judge ... considers the constitution and the Human Rights Convention is in peril, he must act accordingly. This is vital for democracy' (ibid.). Here we can see that questions of 'balance' from the government's point of view are interpreted as an imbalance, a challenge or potential challenge to the basic principle of judicial independence.

The lawyers for the nine foreign terror suspects detained in Belmarsh prison were, not surprisingly perhaps, more fulsome in speaking of what they saw as the larger constitutional significance of the laws they sought to oppose. They told the panel of nine Law Lords that the relevant measures in the ATCSA 'were an affront to democracy and the internationally accepted notion of justice'. Ben Emmerson QC, representing seven of the detainees, was reported as claiming that the detention provisions 'threatened the values they were designed to protect', and was quoted thus: 'We say in a democracy it us unacceptable to lock up potentially innocent people without trial or without any indication when, if ever, they are going to be released' (*Independent* 5 October 2004).

The government's most recent proposals such as targeting the justification or glorification of terrorism have met with judicial criticism, along with criticism from civil-liberties group Liberty, an organisation that has been prominent in these debates. Addressing earlier concerns over the government's anti-terrorism legislation, Liberty expressed its belief that 'in a democracy, the values of public protection and the rule of law are not mutually exclusive.' It defended the presumption of innocence, which the detention and control-order provisions of anti-terror legislation were seen to have undermined: 'we appreciate that the presumption of innocence is never the most fashionable idea at times of heightened fear. It is, however, a key distinguishing feature of a healthy democracy' (Liberty August 2004).

With respect to the 2005 proposals to outlaw justification or glorification, Shami Chakrabarti, director of Liberty, asks, 'What is meant by "terrorism"? What kind of behaviour constitutes "justification"? Could this cover political debate about the circumstances in which it is acceptable to take up arms against non-democratic regimes across the world?' (*Guardian* 24 August 2005). Elsewhere, she said that 'glorification' was so broad that it would 'make loose talk a serious political offence' (*Independent* 16 September 2005). Critics from the judiciary, pressure groups and the press argued that the government already had at its disposal sufficient powers to prosecute those who incite violence; further legislation was unnecessary and, it has sometimes been suggested, involves a disturbing accretion of further powers to the executive.

There are other critics of course, too numerous to mention fully here. Geoffrey Bindman reinforced basic values of a liberal democracy, stressing the damage (as he saw it) to time-honoured individual rights and freedoms in the provisions of ATCSA: 'For the first time since 1945 the executive was given power to detain indefinitely without a charge being laid, and, crucially, without the detainee having the opportunity of answering the evidence by which the detention is justified.' He went on to argue, making the larger connection to the character of democracy, 'it is a disturbing feature of current British and American governments … that in the guise of protecting the public they are ready to abandon principles which are the hallmark of democracy' (Bindman 2005). Journalist George Monbiot was even more forthright. Criticising provisions such as the Terrorism Act 2000 for placing restrictions on legitimate protest, he wrote: 'Democracies such as ours will come to an end not with the stamping of boots and the hoisting of flags, but through the slow accretion of a thousand dusty codicils' (*Guardian* 3 August 2004). Blick and Weir, writing in the context of the 2005 proposals, argue for an urgent answer to the question of how effective the government's anti-terrorism proposals might be, considering that the government's strategy and laws 'will have a profound effect on British democracy, the rule of law, criminal justice, the conduct of police and security forces, civil and political rights and the shape of community relations perhaps for generations to come' (Blick and Weir 2005).

A Labour dissenter from the government's proposals in the Prevention of Terrorism Act, former Foreign Secretary, the late Robin Cook, articulated one key plank of a liberal conception of democracy in these debates when he addressed ministers' arguments that 'the safety of the public must come before the liberty of the individual': this is fine when it is your safety and somebody else's civil liberty. But liberty is indivisible. A measure that curtails the liberty of one citizen necessarily curtails the liberty of every citizen' (*Guardian* 4 March 2005). Leader of the Liberal Democrats, Charles Kennedy, offered a similar appraisal in his comments on the same proposals.

Of course, critics aim at different targets, argue in diverse ways, and seek to defend a diversity of institutions and values. Nevertheless, it is not stretching things too far to suggest that there are some central threads that bring together judicial, civil liberties and other critics:

- Government opponents point out that a range of rights and liberties need to be protected at all times. To quote Chakrabarti: 'We need to focus on what unites us in the struggle against terrorism – our fundamental values. These values are human rights; the bedrock of our beliefs, not a convenience, a luxury or a pick and mix' (*Refugee Council News* 26 August 2005).
- Critics tend to support strongly the independence of the judiciary and the fundamental and unshifting character of the rights and liberties that the judiciary exists to defend.
- The European and international rights obligations on the government are declared to be non-negotiable, not optional according to circumstances.

- The idea of 'balance' between security and liberty is regarded as suspect; instead, especially from the point of view of judicial critics, the 'balance' within the constitutional structure of British government between the powers of the executive and the judiciary is the most crucial balance to be sustained.

A good deal of these debates revolve around what actions, moral imperatives and laws are most 'basic' or 'fundamental'. In this context it is instructive to consider briefly the life and times of the Human Rights Act (HRA). After many years of debate in the UK, the HRA incorporated into UK law the European Convention on Human Rights, effectively making the Convention a codified and vital part of the British constitution. It contains provisions regarding the right to life, prohibition of torture, the right to a fair trial, rights to privacy, freedom of thought and conscience and religion, freedom of expression and assembly, and the prohibition of discrimination. The courts cannot strike down legislation on the basis of the HRA, but they can rule that legislation is incompatible with its provisions, and leave the response to that ruling to government and Parliament. The HRA has been subject to controversy and sections of the media – and the Conservative Party – have highlighted how, in their view, it has benefited unworthy groups such as travellers, prisoners, illegal immigrants and terrorist suspects. With regard to anti-terrorism laws, David Blunkett, when Home Secretary, warned judges that curtailing civil liberties in the fight against terrorism was a matter for Parliament, not the courts (*Guardian* 25 September 2001); Tony Blair has argued that 'Should legal obstacles arise, we will legislate further, if necessary, amending the Human Rights Act in respect of the interpretation of the European Convention on Human Rights' (quoted in *Guardian* 31 October 2005). Opponents of this view espoused the HRA's 'fundamental' character, arguing that the government and Parliament must operate within it rather than seek to challenge or modify its provisions; defenders of the government's view stressed the 'basic' role of the government in providing 'security'. Labour's willingness to amend the Act has been surpassed by the Conservative Party's action in setting up a commission to explore the 'reform, replacement or repeal' of the legislation. The Conservative spokesperson, Shadow Home Secretary, David Davis, said that 'Once we had inherited English liberties; now we have incorporated European rights ... once, the law limited the state and enlarged the sphere in which the citizen could be free; now, it imposes obligations on the state and limits the freedom of the citizen' (quoted in *Guardian* 23 August 2004).

## Security and protection: two competing ideas of democracy

Different actors, then, have prioritised different principles and (as they see it) necessities in the post-9/11 political context. There is widespread agreement that contemporary democracies face huge challenges. Government and critics both would recognise that they seek a 'protective' democracy. But the focus and style of the protection concerned differs markedly. Drawing partly upon models of democracy outlined by authors such as Lijphart (1999) and Held (1996) the Government's position can be called a *majoritarian protective model of democracy*.

This majoritarian protective model of democracy displays a number of key features, which will be familiar from the above account in varying degrees. Although proponents of this model would agree that certain civil rights and liberties are fundamental, there is a view that the ranking of such rights can shift and change according to political and other circumstances. So, for example, in the face of a new style of terrorist threat, the right to life or the right to basic security assumes a greater relative importance than the right to free speech, the right to free movement, or the right to legal due process. Implicit within this view is an idea that rights and liberties are, albeit to some limited degree that is difficult to specify, the gift of the state and not necessarily the inviolable prior possession of the free citizen. This model respects the constitutional role of the judiciary in democracies, but nonetheless reserves the right of the democratically accountable executive to respond to the perceived fears of citizens by encroaching on established judicial principles or routines, in extraordinary circumstances. The elected executive, in other words, is first among equals when it comes to fundamental issues of protection of (assumed) *most* fundamental citizen rights and liberties. Its proper concern lies with the shorter-term impact of protective measures on a minority who pose dangers.

This model is unapologetically *national*, regarding the nation state as the primary location for the enunciation of political interest and the interpretation of the appropriate scope and application of rights and liberties. It assumes that 'protection' (and security) should be interpreted in terms of threats to citizens posed by individuals and groups who target the society – enemies, internal and external ones, are what we need protection against. It also recognises that 'balances' are important in questions about rights and liberties, and it interprets balance as being between liberty, on the one hand, and security or protection from enemies on the other. The majoritarian protective model sees within this need for 'balance' the possibility of limited but legitimate trade-offs of some measure of liberty in the name of security and protection. It sees the state as a set of institutions which must change and adapt, often in drastic ways, to new threats and circumstances; sometimes it is necessary to change the rules. Finally, these changes are carried through in the name of most people, or all citizens, or the 'vast majority'. It is a model of democracy with a populist, majoritarian character.

In contrast, the model of the critics is best referred to as a *constitutional protective model of democracy*. According to this model fundamental rights and liberties are not the gift of the state but exist prior to the state and they are the inalienable possession of free citizens. It defends the strong judicial function of protecting those rights and liberties, and sees this function as fundamentally democratic even if judges are not themselves elected political actors (for theoretical accounts of the 'self-binding' character of democracy, see Elster and Slagstad 1988; Saward 1998). The primary concern of its advocates is the potential longer-term impact of measures on the rights and freedoms of all, not a minority. The constitutional protective model is more internationalist than the majoritarian protective model. It takes especially seriously international obligations and EU law, and denies that there can be a legitimate set of opt-outs from such obligations. The question of 'balance' is differently conceived; here, it is a question of constitutional balance between the executive and the judiciary. It is also highly sceptical that, in any fundamental way, the rules have changed. Constitutional protections in democracy are sacrosanct, they remain the bedrock of the rules of the system and even new and virulent threats are best combatted by deepening and defending those rules, rather than seeking to modify them. It is not the rules that change; the context changes, but the rules remain. Crucially, the constitutional protective approach highlights the need for the protection of citizens' rights and liberties *against the state itself*. Constitutionalists are wary of states grabbing powers, aware that powers adopted or created are rarely, if ever, given up. They are also suspicious that the targets of new, restrictive laws will not be the only targets in future – for example, restrictions on the freedom of speech and movement of a suspect minority today may in time become restrictions on a larger set of citizens, possibly even a majority, in the further future. One can see the suspicion of the over-mighty state in the efforts by some critics to promote time limits on the application of some new laws.

Some prominent theorists of democracy, including MacPherson (1977), have embraced this 'protective model'. The most important classical theorist of this 'model' is arguably the great English utilitarian theorist Jeremy Bentham. In general terms, it is no doubt a core responsibility of a democratic government to protect its citizens' lives and freedoms from external threat. But the central thread of the so-called protective model has pointed in a quite different direction. Consider the words of Bentham:

A democracy, then, has for its characteristic object and effect, the securing its members against oppression and depredation at the hands of those functionaries which it employs for its defence ... Every other species of government has necessarily, for its characteristic and primary object and effect, the keeping the people and non-functionaries in a perfectly defenceless state, against the functionaries their rulers ... (quoted in MacPherson 1977, 36)

Or, as the legal philosopher Jeremy Waldron has put it recently:

True, the events of September 11 have heightened our fear of the worst that can be done to us by individuals and groups other than the state. And an increase in the power of the state may be necessary to prevent or diminish the prospect of that horror. *But the existence of a threat from terrorist attack does not diminish the threat that liberals have traditionally apprehended from the state.* The former complements the latter; it doe not diminish it, and it may enhance it. (Waldron 2003, 205, original emphasis)

## Conclusion

Tony Blair has argued at different points in his premiership that his government is interested in what works, not in ideologically driven policy. But even if leaders and governments do not profess ideologies, invariably there are discernible threads in their thought and actions. One such thread in a series of policies and initiatives under Blair, especially in the broad area of criminal justice policy, has been to challenge an emphasis on individual rights and liberties and to seek a rebalancing in favour of community, obligation, and the rights of victims. At times this has become explicit, as for example in Blair's 'respect agenda', around which the government created a key position of 'coordinator for respect', sometimes called a 'czar', occupied by Louise Casey. After outlining a series of policy proposals designed to tackle 'anti-social behaviour' and putting victim rights and redress at the heart of criminal justice, the prime minister stressed the broader moral agenda:

a modern civic society, underpinned by reformed public services and an active welfare state, won't emerge simply through better laws, tougher enforcement of obligations, sanctions and more police. As well as modernising the criminal justice system and tackling anti-social behaviour we also need to revive the spirit of community and social cohesion. As Martin Luther King argued in the 1960s' struggle for civil rights, laws 'restrain the heartless; they cannot change the heart' ... Only by rebuilding cohesive communities and reforming our criminal justice system can we achieve our vision of a strong and fair society. It means abandoning the rhetoric and false choices of the past. Since 1945 our politics has too often failed to articulate a coherent response to crime and anti-social behaviour. Restoring civic responsibility is not a betrayal of social justice, but essential for its realisation. (quoted in *Observer* 10 November 2002)

Among the most prominent government policies within the broad range of this agenda are anti-social behaviour orders (ASBOs) which were first introduced in 1999. ASBOs can apply to anyone found to harass or alarm neighbours or neighbourhoods. A series of related measures have been enacted by the government to address the rights of victims. Blair has long made plain his belief that Britain's criminal justice system is balanced far too much in favour of the rights of the criminal at the expense of the rights of the victim (Blair 2002). In 2005 he signalled his intention to intensify this programme, through tackling binge drinking and other low-level anti-social behaviour by on-the-spot fines, seizing the property of offending families, appointing local anti-social behaviour 'sheriffs', introducing 'baby ASBOs' for under-10s. This vision of community, respect, and obligation permeates these developments accompanied by criticisms from other parties, community workers and parts of Whitehall. The anti-social behaviour and respect programmes form part of a populist vision of instilling a sense of obligation and community into citizens, indeed to mould citizens in a particular way. Protecting victims and the vulnerable is a key part of the rhetoric at least.

It is not stretching things too far to see close links between the government's anti-terrorism legislation and its broader agenda, as expressed through its respect and related programmes. Both display what I have called a majoritarian protective outlook on how democracy should be shaped and function. Likewise, critics of this agenda point to the dangers that civil rights and liberties are being placed under threat by the broader thrust of the government's criminal-justice reforms: the essence of the position of the constitutional protective vision of democracy. The fascinating connection between these two visions, as played out in anti-terrorism debates and beyond, lies in the internal tensions in the idea of states 'protecting' citizens. Amid the bluster and argument of day-to-day politics, basic conceptions of what democracy is, whom it protects from what and why, face off against each other. For some, the rules of the game have changed. For others, changed circumstances make the old rules more relevant than ever.

Chapter 13

# The News Media and the Public Relations State

## DOMINIC WRING

The central role the news media plays in generating political news, together with the recognition that television continues to be the most trusted source of voter information, has provided fertile territory for the spin doctor, a particular kind of public relations operative who has become increasingly commonplace in politics. The public relations state incorporates a behind-the-scenes, often largely secretive, network of spin doctors, communications directors, and political aides who communicate with print and broadcast journalists on behalf of the government they serve (Deacon and Golding 1994). Past prime ministers had employed such public relations operatives, but Margaret Thatcher first championed modern news-management techniques, so providing the institutional legacy that Tony Blair would considerably consolidate and extend. The contemporary public relations state, one in which strategic political communications are given the highest possible priority, therefore discharges three primary functions:

- advertising, whereby the government as communicator retains control over the content of the message, ordinarily by paying for its dissemination and promotion in various formats;
- opinion research, the investigation of public attitudes and values through the use of quantitative (surveys) and qualitative (especially focus group) methods;
- public relations, where the government as communicator attempts to promote a message by attracting and managing the attention of news organisations with a view to gaining favourable media coverage.

These three functions play a cumulative role within the modern political process, although advertising and opinion research have attracted nothing like the attention afforded the government's public relations operation, something reflecting both the growth as well as immediacy of public relations, which is itself a recognition of the power and significance of the news media (Curran and Seaton 2003).

231

The relationship between journalism and politics has long been the focus of a debate that intensified during the 1960s and 1970s with the growth of serious current-affairs broadcasting. Initially, politicians sought to ignore their media detractors, but by the 1980s, it had become essential for major politicians to employ public relations expertise to help them with news management. By the time of the 1992 general election the practice of news management was more routinely referred to as 'spin', a term which was to become synonymous with Labour under Tony Blair (Kuhn 2003). As prime minister, Blair expanded the public relations state he inherited from Margaret Thatcher and John Major, adding more staff and greater resources, as well as providing media managers with an enhanced status within government (Deacon and Golding 1994; Jones 1999). This formidable media-management apparatus has two objectives:

- to ensure that the vast and varied agencies of government remained 'on message', to bring greater coherence to the public presentation of government policy;
- to make effective communication and news management integral to the policy-making process rather than being an afterthought.

## Advertising and opinion research

The Blair government's use of advertising is supported by an extensive programme of ongoing and ad hoc market-research projects designed to refine and better target messages for key audiences. The government now vies with major companies such as Proctor and Gamble to be the largest advertiser in Britain, spending the record amount of £203 million in the financial year 2004/05 (Tiltman 2005). Much of this material relates to awareness raising and initiatives such as the recruitment of public servants and encouraging the take-up of public services. Under both Labour and Conservative governments the increased scale of spending on government advertising has been a persistent theme of critics, including Tony Blair himself, who made a concerted attack on it in an earlier incarnation as Labour's trade spokesman in opposition in the late 1980s. Blair was then concerned with the content of Tory government campaigns in support of privatisation and his government has in turn been accused of using advertising to extol rather than merely promote awareness of the New Deal and other contentious policies. There has also been criticism that some advertising has been timed to coincide with the run-up to elections, as well as debate over the ideological message being promoted (for example, anti-benefit-fraud campaigns reinforce the moralistic concerns of certain newspapers about 'sponging' amongst the poor, but deflect attention from more costly deviant behaviours such as tax avoidance by the rich (Golding and Middleton 1982)).

Advertising is public by its very nature and it inevitably attracts comments and reactions. It is however notoriously difficult to determine its effectiveness and this is a reason why there has been comparatively less debate over it than over the role of market research. Governments have long monitored public attitudes but the difference is that the modern operation is both more wide-ranging and costly. The Strategic Communications and Marketing section within the Cabinet Office coordinates an extensive programme devoted to performing this function. This work has been augmented by that of other Whitehall departments as well as by Blair advisors such as Philip Gould. Although nominally concerned with lay attitudes, opinion research has attracted much attention because of its perceived influence on elite thinking. Publication of a secret memo in 2000 from Gould to the Prime Minister proposing several government initiatives to boost Blair and win over voters offered a rare, candid insight into Gould's short-term preoccupation with voter concerns (Wring 2005c, 153–4). The leaked document was based on qualitative data drawn from focus-group participants rather than findings from larger-scale quantitative surveys. The former are more open to interpretation because the evidence consists of transcripts of discussions rather than statistics detailing large numbers of responses to specified questions. Critics have long questioned the validity and influence of this material but because of the secrecy surrounding the process (Gould's memo aside) Blair has been able to deflect such criticisms. More recently, however, Jon Cruddas, a former Downing Street aide turned MP, argued that the attention devoted to the 'dead hand of Middle England' through opinion research has prevented the emergence of a 'different form of Labour government' because policy had been forged: 'on the basis of the preferences and prejudices of focus groups or key swing voters in marginal seats to the detriment of more traditional bodies of ideas or traditions of thought within Labour' (Richards, S 2005).

## Public relations: spin and its discontents

Criticism of government advertising and polling has been muted when compared with the almost unending criticism of governmental public relations, Downing Street's principal form of strategic communication. This is perhaps inevitable when Westminster correspondents are personally familiar with those charged with representing and defending various ministers. This has meant many previously private and behind-the-scenes actors have become better known than many of the politicians they serve (Price 2005). Reporting the doings of government news managers has become a mainstay of the news media's coverage of politics. The first really powerful prime ministerial press secretary was Margaret Thatcher's close confidant Bernard Ingham, but his power was easily outstripped by that of Tony Blair's principal media advisor, Alastair Campbell, press secretary 1997–2001 and director of communications and strategy 2001–03. Campbell has been the subject of constant media attention (and endless criticism) and even commentators broadly sympathetic to Labour have characterised the Blair leadership as being preoccupied or even obsessed with 'spin'. Labour's opponents have been more scathing. John Major has described Labour spin as being the 'pornography of politics. It perverts. It is deceit licensed by the government. Statistics massaged. Expenditure announced and reannounced. The record reassessed. Blame attributed. Innocence proclaimed. Black declared white: all in a day's work' (Major and Heathcoat-Amory 2003).

Spin is a particular variant of news management which, by its nature, is a practice largely hidden from public view because it involves discreet lines of communication between politicians or, more precisely their 'gatekeeping' spokespeople (the 'spin doctors'), and selected media contacts (Jones 1999). It differs from more obvious and visible public relations work such as press conferences, keynote speeches and staged events because it tends to involve secretive contacts between powerful politicians (or their trusted proxies) and well-connected journalists working for reputable news-media outlets. This practice is nothing new. Westminster-based politicians and journalists have long adhered to an informal so-called 'lobby arrangement', named after the main antechamber leading to the floor of the House of Commons, where MPs traditionally met with journalists and held discreet, 'off-the-record' discussions. Over time these liaisons became institutionalised and a more semiformal, exclusive club was established in which a number of accredited parliamentary correspondents working for the most prestigious news organisations would enjoy routine access to politicians and their spokespeople. The influence of such spokespersons, increasingly defined as 'spin doctors', has been furthered by the growth of a 24-hour news cycle which has created a voracious appetite among a highly competitive group of journalists for stories with fresh angles.

Few media managers positively embrace the label of 'spin doctor', at least not whilst they are in post. They are more commonly known as 'communications directors', 'special advisors' or simply as 'ministerial aides'. They derive their authority and influence from being senior members of a major politician's entourage and by providing journalists with information beyond that offered by more junior press officers who normally only clarify, confirm, correct or deny factual information in a given story (Gaber 2000). Spin doctors either promote or demean a policy or a minister, most usually by privately briefing a journalist – or else a trusted correspondent or columnist – so spinning a story, all the while trying to avoid public exposure and the ostracism that might follow (Price 2005). For instance, at the height of the government–BBC fight over the BBC's reportage of the government's argument that Iraq had weapons of mass destruction (see below), Alastair Campbell's deputy Tom Kelly was named by the *Independent* as the source who had dismissed government scientist David Kelly as a 'Walter Mitty' figure lacking credibility. Making such comment – which was meant to be wholly unattributable – after Kelly's death was widely criticised and Tom Kelly was obliged to issue a fulsome apology at a time when numerous people were calling for his head. Yet while the source of unattributable comment is the subject of endless speculation, journalists usually keep such sources close to their chests. Much of the discreet interaction between politicians and journalists remains hidden from contemporaneous public view, something which helps intensify speculation about who has been briefing on what, against whom, and why. Of course, once the messenger becomes the message, as happened to Alastair Campbell during his time in Downing Street, the viability of the messenger is called into question. Spin identified is often spin neutralised.

Several Labour politicians have found themselves destabilised by having critical stories spun against them, most notably popular ex-Cabinet figures such as Mo Mowlam and less-well-known former members like David Clark. This can often erode a party's trust in the communications process itself (and the party's communicators), something that can well limit the effectiveness of spin in the long term, if not in the short term. More significantly, however, spin has encouraged an intensely speculative news culture. This can create a very hostile environment for a government encountering choppy political waters or for a government minister in trouble. For instance, Beverley Hughes was forced to resign as Immigration Minister in 2004 when she admitted to inadvertently misleading Parliament. Similarly, the publication of lurid details of Home Secretary David Blunkett's involvement with a married woman, amid media claims that he had abused his position in order to help his lover's nanny obtain a visa, eventually led to the minister's resignation. Blunkett's rapid return to office following the 2005 election ended abruptly, probably for good, with his second resignation within a year following new media stories about his private life and procedural issues in relation to his financial and business affairs. It is, however, the rivalry between Tony Blair and his Chancellor, Gordon Brown, or, more precisely, their respective 'camps', which has provided the longest-running government saga as played out in the news media. Tensions between the two, ever-present since 1997, rose considerably in summer 2004 when, following considerable speculation over Blair's future, he was eventually obliged to make an unprecedented announcement that, should he win the forthcoming election, his third term would be his last. The ensuing drama, which revolves around personal rather than policy differences, has provided a multiplicity of opportunities for the spin doctors and their media contacts:

- Blair spin doctors supposedly helped to instigate the resignation of Brown ally Andrew Smith from Cabinet in autumn 2004 by briefing the media against him and promoting the likely return of Alan Milburn, a staunch ally of the Prime Minister and a perceived enemy of the Chancellor.
- Brown was showcased in a highly sympathetic biography of him by Robert Peston of the *Daily Telegraph* in what was seen as a bid to portray the Chancellor as an alternative leader ready to take over from Blair.
- If Brown can rely on Peston, Jackie Ashley of the *Guardian* and William Keegan of the *Observer* for a sympathetic write-up, journalists like Trevor Kavanagh of the *Sun*, Andrew Rawnsley of the *Observer*, Tom Baldwin of *The Times*, and Patrick Wintour and Martin Kettle also of the *Guardian* have demonstrated a willingness to use Blair-friendly sources
- The second term of the Labour government saw various ministers proposed and then 'spun' as possible Blair-friendly alternatives to a Brown premiership, including David Blunkett, Charles Clarke, Alan Milburn, John Reid and, more recently, Alan Johnson.

The debate over the US–British intervention in Iraq and, to a far lesser extent, the Blair–Brown rivalry contributed to a slump in public confidence in the Prime Minister, which he sought to counter during the run-up to the 2005 election by engaging voters in discussions on television programmes like Channel Five's *The Wright Stuff* and BBC1's *Question Time*. Strategists hoped that this 'masochism strategy' would paint the Prime Minister as 'straight' and 'honest', eager to explain himself and to listen to voter concerns over contentious issues such as Iraq and student top-up fees. This approach was risky, but putting Blair at the forefront in the weeks and months preceding the launch of the formal election campaign, a crucial period in which millions are supposedly making up their minds how to vote (Miller et al. 1990), was considered a means in which an 'unspun' Blair could perhaps re-establish his rapport with the British electorate. Of course, given the chance, voters were more than capable of being confrontational and rude when allowed a rare chance to confront a party leader under studio conditions, something which produced animated and lively debates between Tony Blair and some vociferous detractors. Blair's principal election opponents, the then Conservative leader, Michael Howard, and the then Liberal Democrat leader, Charles Kennedy, sought similar coverage but their encounters with voters provided nothing like the drama of those involving the Prime Minister.

Blair further exploited his incumbency with other high-profile media events, among them inviting celebrity chef Jamie Oliver to Downing Street to discuss the latter's high-profile campaign to improve the quality of school meals, and making appearances on programmes like *GMTV* and *Richard and Judy*. This enabled Blair to reach out to large audiences of the target voters characterised as 'hard-working families' and 'school-gate mums' (Wring 2005b). More fundamentally they were the latest stages of a long-running strategy designed to restore public trust in the Prime Minister since the beginning of his second term, a period in which it had become increasingly clear that spin had become part of the problem rather than a possible means of repairing the government's reputation.

## Reforming the public relations state: the Phillis Report 2004

The controversy over government spin, and its possible contribution to the collapse in voter turnout at the 2001 general election, prompted Tony Blair to appoint *Guardian* newspaper chief executive Bob Phillis to head an inquiry into the role and organisation of government information management in early 2003. The work of the Phillis Review was made easier by the resignation of Alastair Campbell, Tony Blair's director of communications and strategy. During his near-decade-long service at Blair's side, Campbell became one of the most influential unelected figures in British politics. He was afforded the rare privilege of being able to instruct civil servants, a greater power than that enjoyed by most ministers, and in effect he wielded more influence across government than many ministers (Wring 2005a). Campbell's 2001 move from Prime Ministerial Press Secretary to the newly created post of Director of Communication and Strategy had been designed to take him out of the front line of media relations and give him a more strategic role. This proved a futile effort to damp down the intense and critical media speculation that had made him such a highly visible and controversial spin doctor. In June 2003 Campbell's intemperate public conduct in defending the government over Iraq guaranteed him an even higher public profile. The messenger had unquestionably become the message and it was arguably no coincidence that he left Downing Street at the end of August 2003. Campbell claimed he had long planned his departure to spend more time with his family and pursue other interests, but it is likely that this decision coincided with the desire of the Prime Minister to restore his reputation and 'move on' from Iraq. Where Blair had previously been eager to retain Campbell's services, he now accepted he had no alternative but to let him go. Campbell did not disappear, however. Such was his closeness to Blair – and such is the centrality of political communications to this government's mode of governance – that Campbell was retained as an outriding, unofficial, advisor and went back to work for the Labour campaign at the 2005 election.

The Phillis Review finally reported in January 2004, the same time as the Hutton Inquiry, an investigation into the government's management of the David Kelly controversy, which is discussed below. Indeed, Hutton was such a major event that it forestalled sustained analysis of Phillis and its proposed reforms. However, like Hutton, the report was enthusiastically received by Blair because he evidently concurred with its central argument: 'Communications should be an equal and respected third in the trinity of government policy making, public service delivery and communications. A culture within Whitehall that accepts and values communication both departmentally and across government is imperative' (Phillis 2004, 31). Phillis' key observations and recommendations were:

- Communication is about more than media relations.
- A senior civil servant should be appointed as Permanent Secretary for Government Communications.
- The Prime Minister's Director of Communications should have a clearer role and objectives.
- Government Information and Communications (GIC) should be replaced by a Government Communications Network (GCN), to be headed by the new Permanent Secretary.
- GCN would oversee public relations work as well as the marketing operations of the Central Office of Information.
- GCN would place more emphasis on local and regional communications.
- Greater public access should be encouraged through the Freedom of Information Act and by making government statistics and other data more accessible online.
- Media briefings should be televised.

Howell James, John Major's former Political Secretary, was brought back into the civil service and appointed to the post of Permanent Secretary for Government Communications, based in the Cabinet Office, in 2004. He supervised a team of spokespeople headed by Alastair Campbell's successor, the veteran Labour insider David Hill, who had been acting as Blair's Director of Communications since 2003. The Downing Street team was completed by Tom Kelly, one of Campbell's key lieutenants, and a newer arrival, Darren Murphy. While James and Hill have had nothing like the same public profile as had Alastair Campbell, the Phillis Review confirmed the importance of media communication to government by controversially asserting it was as important a function as policy formation and delivery (Gaber 2004). Even with Campbell officially gone, then, it seemed that his preoccupation with ensuring the government was 'on message' would live on; the principal difference perhaps being that the messenger would hopefully no longer be as prominent as the message.

It was hoped, not least by Bob Phillis himself, that the Phillis Review would curtail some of Downing Street's more excessive publicity-seeking tendencies as well as demonstrate that the government was changing its ways. This hope was somewhat dashed soon after the implementation of Phillis' key recommendations when embarrassing details were leaked of a private meeting involving senior civil servants charged with promoting the various departments of state. Sian Jarvis, Head of Communications at the Department of Health, reportedly complained that Downing Street asked for 'announcements before we have a policy ... Trust in government is so low we really need to exclude ministers from the presentation if we are going to build trust in delivery.' Even more damagingly Siobhan Kelly, Jarvis' counterpart at the Department of Culture, Media and Sport, suggested that ministers still sought to 'bury bad news', echoing the now infamous attempt by spin doctor Jo Moore to persuade civil servants to make most of the media preoccupation with reporting the September 11 attacks to release news that could otherwise have damaged the government (Cracknell 2004). Furthermore, if judged by its actions rather than its words, the government's ongoing commitment to its spin operation was amply demonstrated by its decision to increase spending on its 72 special advisors who were now costing the taxpayer a total of £5.5 million by the end of the financial year 2004/05 (Moss 2005). Like their disgraced former colleague Jo Moore, many of these aides continue to take considerable interest in news management in addition to their other day-to-day duties. In doing so they inevitably court more controversy and never more so than when special advisors such as Alastair Campbell were so centrally involved in the Blair government's defining moment, the decision to support the US-led invasion of Iraq in 2003.

## The propaganda war: selling the invasion of Iraq

If Labour's dependence on its media advisors was a marked feature of its first, relatively calm spell in office, then it became an ever more defining characteristic of a turbulent second term. A major aspect of the Iraq invasion, by far the most serious crisis to have confronted the government, was the way in which the case for supporting the US-led action against the country's dictatorial regime was spun by Blair, Campbell and others from the summer of 2002 until full-scale military operations began in March 2003. Two documents, the so-called dossiers published in September 2002 and February 2003, were used to justify the government's preparedness to support President Bush's controversial mission to depose Saddam Hussein on the grounds that Iraq possessed and could use weapons of mass destruction (WMD) and was therefore a 'clear and present danger' to the security of both the Middle East and the West.

The credibility of the government case was undermined somewhat when it quickly emerged that some of the evidence in the second so-called 'dodgy' dossier, published shortly before MPs voted on whether to go to war, had been plagiarised by Campbell's aides from a student's doctoral thesis posted on the internet (Oborne and Walters 2004, 325–6). Indeed, the government's efforts to make a reasoned public case for intervening in Iraq, to sell the war, as it were, to both the public and to Parliament through the news media, were often insufficient to convince a formidable body of opinion ranging from UN member states, notably France and Germany, to an increasingly vocal section of the Parliamentary Labour Party who refused to accept that Iraq posed an imminent threat to international security. The government sought to 'sell' the case for war by rigorous deployment of all the techniques available to the public relations state. Despite Blair's endless efforts to take to the airwaves to make his case for intervention, a majority of the British public appeared to disagree with his stance or, more particularly, the absence of a clear UN mandate for the US-led effort to overthrow Saddam, something which worried a government that had long prided itself on cultivating and maintaining public support. Opinion on the matter did, however, remain volatile, which is why the national newspapers that endorsed the proposed invasion – the *Telegraph, The Times, Mail, Sun* and *Express* – were considered valued allies of the government. Their total circulation of 9.4 million reached many more readers than did the anti-war *Independent, Guardian* and *Mirror* whose combined sales were 2.7 million. This is not insignificant given that, according to MORI polling, only 26 per cent of the British public supported the proposed invasion prior to its commencement in March 2003, yet once military action had begun this figure increased to 56 percent (Stanyer 2004). Furthermore, although the mainstream news broadcasters remained more detached observers than their print rivals, they nonetheless gave greater access to pro- rather than anti-war sources (Lewis and Brookes 2004). This is not to suggest it was the media that changed public opinion; rather it appears this shift came about from an often-stated desire to sustain the troops' morale whatever the political disagreements prior to the outbreak of hostilities. That said, the largely sympathetic representation of Downing Street's case was a factor in sustaining the momentum in favour of going to war.

Throughout the Iraq crisis the *Sun,* the best-selling daily, strongly supported the invasion by denouncing those it accused of wanting to appease the Ba'athist dictator Saddam Hussein. The paper dutifully repeated, as did others, the claims in the first government dossier published in September 2002 which stated Iraq was ready and able to use WMD against British military installations within 45 minutes. The assertion, purportedly based on MI6 intelligence gathering, proved to be one of the most controversial aspects of the case for the invasion. Following the subsequent routing of the Ba'athist leadership and the eventual revelation that Iraq had actually not possessed any WMD capability, the 45-minute claim returned to plague Blair as it was endlessly cited by critics to exemplify the government's duplicitous and mendacious spin operation (Miller 2003). Despite the best efforts of government media managers – and of Blair himself – the government found it almost impossible to, in the Prime Minister's words, 'move on' from the WMD controversy. The issue came to a head in late May 2003 when BBC Radio 4's flagship *Today* programme broadcast a claim by its defence correspondent, Andrew Gilligan, that the government had 'sexed up' its September dossier making the case for war. Gilligan followed this up with a *Mail on Sunday* article in which he identified Alastair Campbell as the responsible party. Campbell inevitably and fiercely rebutted the claim. Ministers and their advisors interpreted Gilligan's report as further evidence of the BBC's hostility towards the government over Iraq. Ironically, particularly in light of the furore sparked off by the Gilligan broadcast, the BBC's coverage of the invasion had, on reflection, been widely considered to be more receptive to Downing Street sources than rival television news outlets (Lewis and Brookes 2003). Yet the perception that the BBC's journalists were seeking to undermine the government remained strong within official circles and fuelled Alastair Campbell's demand for an apology from Gilligan, the editors of *Today* and from their superiors in the BBC's Department of News and Current Affairs, headed by Richard Sambrook.

Alastair Campbell continued with his criticism of BBC journalism at a meeting of the House of Commons Foreign Affairs Committee, a body then engaged in investigating the circumstances leading up to the Iraq invasion. Campbell vehemently attacked the BBC for broadcasting the 'lie' that he and others in the government had 'connived' to mislead MPs and the public by 'sexing up' the threat from the Iraqi regime (Oborne and Walters 2004, 332–3). He then followed up earlier correspondence with more letters denouncing Gilligan to Sambrook and Greg Dyke, the then BBC Director General (Dyke 2004, 265). A stream of communications between the government and BBC failed to resolve the dispute and, two days after appearing before the Commons committee, Campbell went public again as an uninvited guest on *Channel 4 News*. More remarkable than his decision to lay himself open to question on such a programme was the fact that Campbell apparently appeared without the prior consent of the Prime Minister (Oborne and Walters 2004, 334–5). *Channel 4 News* presenter Jon Snow opened the interview by suggesting Campbell's attacks on the BBC were 'a diversionary tactic' to, as others had argued, deflect attention from the substantive issues raised by Gilligan and others regarding the reasons given for waging war (Coates and Krieger 2004, 88). Campbell dismissed Snow's question with another robust defence of the government's integrity in an appearance that did nothing to resolve a stand-off between Downing Street and the BBC that was about to produce even greater drama and an unexpected casualty.

## The Hutton Inquiry

The row between the BBC and a Downing Street determined to defend its position over Iraq led to considerable speculation as to the basis of Gilligan's allegations. The subsequent identification by the government of Ministry of Defence advisor Dr David Kelly as Gilligan's source prolonged the argument and prompted a subsequent media-driven public firestorm that may have led the now publicly exposed and hitherto largely unknown scientist to take his own life in July 2003. This tragic turn of events obliged Blair, while en route to Tokyo from Washington DC, to launch an official inquiry into the events that had led up to Kelly's death. Lord Hutton, a veteran judge from Northern Ireland, was appointed to oversee the investigation and subsequent report. Far from marking the beginning of the end of this dramatic episode as some in government might have hoped, the ensuing process actually succeeded in intensifying the public debate over the evidence used to justify the case for military action.

The government hoped that the Hutton Inquiry would place the BBC at the centre of the investigation. Elected politicians have always felt more confident in dealing with the BBC and other public-service broadcasters compared with the privately owned print media. Like the BBC, the latter have not been strangers to controversy, but have found that the governments they have sought to challenge have appeared less willing and able to retaliate against them. This is largely because the so-called 'free press' are under no obligation to offer impartial coverage of elections or other political events. They are 'free to comment', while broadcasters are 'obliged to inform'. Consequently most politicians have sought to appease rather than confront editors and proprietors, especially those responsible for producing the often provocative agenda-setting national newspapers. Blair's various entreaties to Rupert Murdoch over the years demonstrate the attention he pays to trying to get key newspapers on his side. The revelation by former *Daily Mirror* editor, Piers Morgan, that he and Blair variously shared 'twenty two lunches, six dinners, six interviews, twenty four further one-to-one chats over tea and biscuits, and numerous phone calls' (Morgan 2005) only serves to underline this. In sharp contrast, however, British broadcasters have always been subjected to a formidable regulatory regime that has compelled them to remain non-partisan, but which has also afforded them more public trust and goodwill (Curran and Seaton 2003). The BBC has often felt particularly vulnerable to government pressure, not least because the government is responsible for appointing members of the BBC board of governors, setting increases in the level of the television licence fee and, crucially, periodically approving renewal of the BBC Charter.

The proceedings of the Hutton Inquiry, conducted amid considerable media scrutiny, effectively served as a post mortem on the Iraq invasion and enabled journalists to review the case for the Iraq intervention and comment further on the revelations that had emerged since the beginning of US-led occupation. The Hutton Inquiry dominated the news, not only because of media and public interest in Dr Kelly's death, but also because the unusually open nature of the hearings allowed a great deal of previously secret material to be brought into the public domain. Specialist correspondents such as Richard Norton-Taylor of the *Guardian* were thus given ample opportunity to develop their own understanding and analysis of the evidence. As a result, it was increasingly apparent that one of Blair's stated reasons for supporting the military engagement, the existence of WMD, had failed to materialise because Iraq had either never possessed or else had abandoned this fearsome capability.

The Hutton Report was finally published in January 2004 when it wholly absolved the government of having played any role in 'sexing up' the original dossier and totally castigated the BBC's reporting in the strongest terms, something which led to the resignations of Chairman of the BBC Governors, Gavyn Davies, the Director General, Greg Dyke, and the *Today* reporter, Andrew Gilligan. Both Davies and Dyke had been one-time Labour supporters. It is noteworthy that newspapers owned by proprietor Rupert Murdoch, like the *Sun*, *News of the World*, *The Times* and *Sunday Times* were to the fore in criticising the BBC, but their lauding of the Hutton Report was not widely shared by media rivals of whatever ideological disposition (Wring 2005a). The Murdoch papers' response to Hutton was perhaps conditioned by their owner's long-acknowledged hostility towards the BBC, which stems from a combination of business rivalry and political antipathy (Page 2003). Although other newspapers, notably the *Telegraph*, articulated a similar viewpoint, the more common media reaction to Hutton was forthright and damning. The front page of the *Independent* was, for instance, left totally blank other than for the word 'Whitewash'. The paper, a staunch opponent of the military intervention in Iraq, accordingly found itself on the same side of the argument as supporters of the invasion such as the *Express*, which ran with the same headline. Like-minded sentiments expressed by a formidable coalition of newspapers amounted to a comprehensive rejection of Hutton and, by extension, a robust defence of the BBC and its independence. Hutton variously found himself accused of being a government stooge and public sympathy drained away from the government as Labour spokespersons, led by the freelancing Campbell, were seen to be vindictively attacking the BBC and when the departure of the popular Greg Dyke met with universal condemnation by BBC staff.

Tony Blair understandably welcomed the Hutton Report as a confirmation of his integrity while Alistair Campbell, now departed from his Downing Street but still a confidant of the Prime Minister, claimed that his original complaints against the BBC had all been vindicated. But the swift reaction of Davies and Dyke ensured the pressure and media focus remained on Blair, the intelligence services and the wider government's conduct, particularly in the absence of any ministerial resignations over any aspect of the formulation or implementation of the controversial policy leading up to the invasion of Iraq (Dyke 2004). Ultimately the one-sidedness of the report actually proved counter-productive to Downing Street's case. Even though the government received an unreserved apology from Davies' acting replacement, BBC Deputy Chairman Richard Ryder, this also backfired because it emboldened the many journalists in the organisation and beyond who believed that Andrew Gilligan had broken a major if poorly presented story.

Blair must have hoped that Hutton would have helped restore faith in his government, but although there were sizeable if not devastating electoral consequences for Labour in the 2005 election, the death of David Kelly appeared to crystallise the doubts across various media about Blair's judgement and actions over Iraq. The findings of the Hutton

Report, when it was published, had less of an impact on elite and public opinion. This owed much to the fact that the public evidence presented in the Hutton Inquiry (and largely published on the Inquiry's website) enabled a varied range of commentators to offer a viewpoint and an informed opinion about the events leading up to Dr Kelly's death which in many cases were diametrically opposed to the actual findings reported by Hutton himself.

Iraq, arguably the defining moment of the Blair premiership, has prompted important questions dealing with how and why the government supported the US-led invasion of Iraq and how Tony Blair and Downing Street promoted and implemented that policy. The Hutton Inquiry garnered a massive, unprecedented amount of information, which included sensitive e-mails, memoranda and various drafts of documents circulated among Downing Street officials. Most notably, Alastair Campbell was seen to be at the centre of all of the important networks deciding British policy on Iraq. His role as one of the handful of people advising Blair throughout the crisis both demonstrated his personal influence and underlined Downing Street's preoccupation with putting news management considerations at the very heart of its policy-making processes. This had been apparent in the way the second 'dodgy dossier' supporting the proposed invasion of Iraq had been produced, shoddily as it turned out, for media consumption by Campbell's aides. Similarly implicit criticism of Campbell's influence can even be detected in the staunchly pro-government Hutton Report which stated that John Scarlett, the intelligence officer responsible for the September dossier, may have been 'subconsciously influenced' (assumedly by Downing Street and possibly by Campbell) to make the case 'somewhat stronger' (Coates 2003).

The importance of advisors like Campbell was later confirmed by a separate governmental inquiry, this time headed by the former Cabinet Secretary, Robin Butler, which culminated in a report published in July 2004. This again absolved ministers and aides of impropriety but did, however, offer a more critical assessment than Hutton and blamed the Prime Minister for fostering a 'sofa-style' approach to decision-making other critics suggested was more suited to the interests of the news agenda than those of good governance or of the wider public. Butler went further in an interview with the *Spectator* in December that year in which he said: 'I think that what happens now is that the government reaches conclusions in rather small groups of people who are not necessarily representative of all the groups of interests in government, and there is insufficient opportunity for people to debate, dissent and modify … The cabinet now – and I don't think there is any secret about this – does not make decisions' (*Spectator* 10 December 2004). Although

Butler was not specific, such 'small groups of people' invariably had special advisors – and public relations experts – counted among their number.

## Power without responsibility?

In 2004 John Lloyd published *What the Media Are Doing to Our Politics*, a riposte to those who blamed the government for spin and all its discontents, which damned the news media for having 'claimed the right to judge and to condemn; more, they have decided – without being clear about the decision – that politics is a dirty game, played by devious people who tell an essentially false narrative about the world and thus deceive the British people' (Lloyd 2004, 20). Andrew Gilligan's report and the BBC management's defence of him were prominent targets in a wide-ranging critique of the media's role in contemporary politics that focused on several interrelated themes:

- Politicians are now dependent on, and therefore are obliged to collaborate with, the media to ensure they have access to the public.
- Media access to politicians is being granted on increasingly harsh terms by skilled and influential journalists who are helping to foster a culture of public cynicism.
- Freedom of the press is being interpreted by journalists as their unrestricted right to reveal, interpret and describe with little regard to the consequences of their activities.
- The language of journalism has become more polemical and accusatory in tone over the last two decades, offering less nuanced analysis of complex problems whose causes are often attributed to scandal, incompetence or an impending crisis: 'Foreigners ... see a (British) media which is polemically extreme, rhetorically bitter and savagely dismissive' (Lloyd 2004, 102).
- Media, particularly the news variant, consciously avoid any recognition of their own power. Politicians are loth to raise this issue for fear of provoking ridicule and criticism.
- Media commentary has become far more commonplace, so much so that the distinction between fact and comment has been eroded, enabling journalists, especially broadcasters, to be more judgemental whether explicitly or implicitly.
- Politicians have been increasingly on the defensive since losing their dominance over the media during the 1960s due to the growth of critical investigative reporting, more questioning interviewers and the satire boom. Allied to this, one of the most powerful currents of our

times, popularised by journalists like John Humphrys and Jeremy Paxman, is that 'today's politics and politicians are a travesty of those who were with us in the good old days' (Lloyd 2004, 133).

Lloyd's argument rests on the contention that 'the threat the media now pose to democratic institutions ... is ironically at its greatest when the media are apparently at their most fearless.' In his view this owes much to the fact that many journalists too zealously adhere to former *Sunday Times* editor Harold Evans' famous advice 'always ask yourself, when you interview a politician – why is this bastard lying to me?' (Lloyd 2004, 13–17). John Lloyd's case is not particularly original. It resembles Stanley Baldwin's contention that the media had 'power without responsibility' (Curran and Seaton 2003) made in response to a concerted campaign waged against his leadership of the Conservative Party by the Beaverbrook press. It has been echoed more recently by philosopher Onora O'Neill and by Archbishop Rowan Williams. Lloyd's influence derives, however, from his prominence as a practitioner and it owes much to his standing in the eyes of government.

Lloyd's book features supportive interviews with Alastair Campbell and Philip Gould, Blair's key strategists. It is unsurprising that others associated with Downing Street, most notably Geoff Mulgan and Tim Allan, have sought to develop Lloyd's thesis. Allan, Campbell's former deputy who worked for Rupert Murdoch before becoming a lobbyist, decried the 'cavalier, untouchable attitude' of the BBC when 'mistakes are made' (Allan 2005; see also Mulgan 2004). Allan's disdain for the BBC was apparent when he leaked to the Murdoch-owned *Times* details of a private, after-dinner speech delivered in September 2005 by John Humphrys in which the BBC Radio 4 presenter heaped ridicule on certain ministers and suggested Labour politicians lied and 'couldn't give a bugger' about it. Publication of the story led to Humphrys' reprimand by a nervous new BBC management team. Humphrys had been the interviewer who had questioned Andrew Gilligan when he reported the charges that the government had overstated the case for the Iraq war in May 2003. Some saw it as fitting that he emerged as one of Lloyd's most vocal critics when he used part of his keynote MacTaggart lecture to the 2004 Edinburgh Television Festival Humphreys to refute the notion that journalism was a major cause of democratic malaise. Nick Robinson, before being appointed BBC political editor in succession to Andrew Marr, took up the theme when he argued that it was 'absurd to worry about public cynicism without at least mentioning those missing weapons of mass destruction, those unexpected tuition fees or "that good day to bury bad news"' (Robinson 2005). The broadcaster articulated a view common amongst journalists, one noticeably underplayed in

Lloyd's account, that it was spin, government-centric news management, which was the central problem in most political reportage.

The Lloyd critique did not dampen the enthusiasm of correspondents like Robinson, the then ITN political editor, and BBC2 *Newsnight's* Michael Crick for pursuing a confrontational style of journalism during the 2005 general election. Although the presence of the 24-hour rolling news channels run by Sky, ITN and the BBC made it easier to monitor every leader's utterances, even the most experienced reporters were frustrated by the aides and security that accompanied the politicians at each of their carefully planned and controlled public appearances. The arrival of the US-inspired phenomenon of 'astroturfing' (that is, assembling fake grassroots sympathisers), where party officials and vetted supporters representing 'real people' surrounded senior politicians at photo opportunities, formed another obstacle for the inquiring correspondent (Deacon and Wring 2005). Furthermore it is important to note that the principal targets of Lloyd's attack, political journalists working for the national news media, were also marginalised by spin doctors who were increasingly keen to cultivate local reporters because they were perceived to be more earnest and engaged in the issues of interest to their viewers and readers.

Lloyd's forensic questioning as to the motives of political journalists was not matched by any systematic analysis of the impact of media ownership on news coverage. Yet many observers have pointed to the power and influence of proprietors over what their reporters publish (see, for instance, Curran and Seaton 2003). In Britain most attention has focused on Rupert Murdoch whose News International corporation runs the largest group of daily and weekly national titles: *The Times, Sunday Times, Sun* and *News of the World*. There was no greater demonstration of the influence of Murdoch's power than when these and every one of his other 171 newspapers around the world supported the invasion of Iraq regardless of the strength of local not to mention editorial opinion (Greenslade 2003). The proprietor's influence in Britain was underlined when in September 2005, shortly after Hurricane Katrina had devastated the southern United States, Rupert Murdoch revealed details of a private talk with the Prime Minister: 'Tony Blair – perhaps I shouldn't repeat this conversation – told me yesterday that he was in Delhi last week and he turned on the BBC World Service to see what was happening in New Orleans. And he said it was full of hate for America and gloating about our troubles' (BBC Online News 18 September 2005). Besides confirming Blair's apparent and Murdoch's own, very real contempt for the BBC, the indiscretion highlighted the businessman's privileged access to Downing Street as well as his somewhat cavalier attitude towards a leader he now risked publicly embarrassing. It is difficult to envisage

Blair responding in kind, out of fear of an adverse response from a Murdoch press he has become dependent on for support. Consequently it is arguably media economics and not the culture of journalism emphasised by Lloyd which is the key issue in analysing the relationship between the media and politics in contemporary Britain.

## Conclusion

When elected Prime Minister in 1997 Tony Blair promised a new style of politics and made a point of saying he would expect the highest standards of conduct from his ministers whilst in office. But the very means by which the Blair government sought to promote its dynamism and abilities meant that its politicians became dependent on spin and (all too often) subterfuge. This was nowhere more apparent than during the Iraq crisis where the limitations of the public relations state were exposed in the same way as embarrassing and candid revelations about the subsequent occupation of that country. The weapons of mass destruction which had been central to the government's case prior to the conflict failed to materialise; no amount of spin could explain this away, even as Blair valiantly made the case for the need to 'move on'. Aside from the dramatic events surrounding Iraq it is arguably the case that the government's reliance on – and boasting about the effectiveness of – news management has helped gradually undermine citizens' belief in the government and its methods of governing. Greater public awareness of the concept and practice of spin has emboldened more journalists to confront a once seemingly omnipotent government with challenging and searching questions on health, education and other developing policy reforms.

Spin is not going to go away as some politicians proclaim. All remain heavily dependent upon it and, like propaganda, most assume it is something only associated with their opponents. Ironically, in his attack on political journalism, the author John Lloyd's description offers an arguably more fitting description of spin when he writes '(it) is not necessarily healthy, because it diminishes, rather than aerates or increases, freedom, and it increases the anomie and distrust within civil society' (Lloyd 2004, 12). Despite the controversies, bad faith and arguments the use of spin has generated it will continue to be used by senior politicians because they believe that it helps gain them favourable coverage and can tarnish the reputations of their opponents. This pragmatic consideration is a largely unspoken reality of modern politics and, despite what elected representatives say, it will always outweigh their sometimes professed mission that they are somehow seeking to enrich the democratic process.

More often than not their primary motivation in deploying public relations strategies is to win elections against another party or to undermine rivalrous colleagues belonging to their own. It would however be wrong to focus solely on politicians and their spin doctors as those largely responsible for fostering public cynicism about contemporary politics. Journalists, some more than others, are also worthy of criticism. This is not principally because of their supposed opposition to politicians – the 'them' of John Lloyd's book – but because of their complicity, and that of media proprietors, in dealing with and reporting discussions with politicians for a mutual benefit that can often run counter to the public interest.

## Chapter 14

# Managing Economic Interdependence: The Political Economy of New Labour

COLIN HAY

The economic performance of New Labour in office is, by any comparative historical standard, enviable. Assessed in conventional terms, with respect to levels of unemployment, inflation, the cost of borrowing and the rate of growth of the economy as a whole, the record far exceeds that of any previous Labour administration. What explains the seemingly good performance of the British economy since 1997? What are its prospects over the next five years? Can the impressive performance achieved thus far be sustained? To answer such questions the context, both domestic and international, in which it has been achieved must first be assessed. It is important, too, to consider the distinctiveness and, indeed, consistency, of New Labour's political economy. How can this political economy be characterised? How consistent has it proved? Does its very success provide the potential seeds of its own downfall?

New Labour's political economy is both distinctive and consistent – unusually so. What characterises it, in particular, is the extent to which it appeals to the language of external economic constraint, justifying both significant institutional change (such as central-bank independence) and its central preoccupation with reform of the labour market as necessary accommodations to the imperatives, in a global economy, of credibility and competitiveness respectively. Yet the consistency with which such perceived imperatives have been expressed and acted upon does not completely hide a series of underlying tensions and contradictions. Moreover, these may well serve to derail New Labour's political economy in an increasingly more difficult phase of the global business cycle.

Rightly or wrongly, New Labour's political economy is synonymous with Gordon Brown. His extended tenure as Chancellor has, at least in comparative terms, proved remarkably untroubled and the performance of the UK economy over which he has presided since 1997 is indeed impressive. Unsurprisingly, then, especially given the central role of the Treasury in almost all aspects of domestic policy, Brown has taken much

**Figure 14.1**　*Headline UK economic performance 1986–2004*

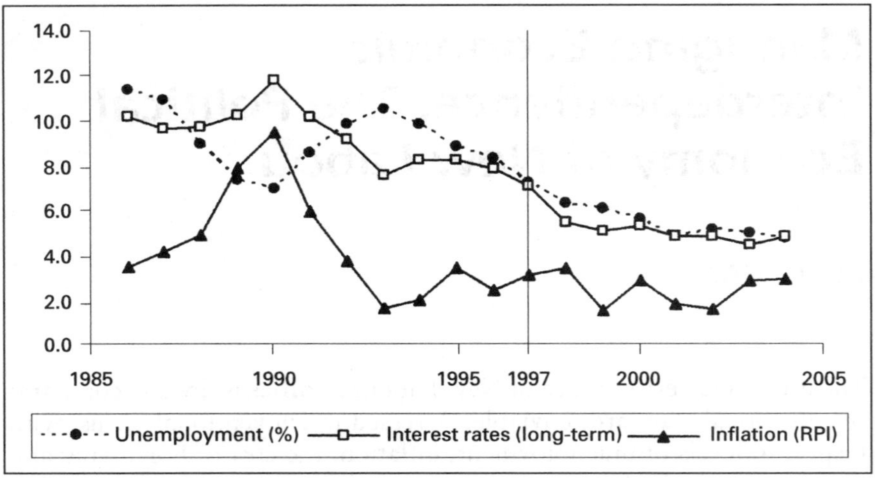

*Source*:　Data from HM Treasury, *Pocket Book Data Bank*

of the credit for New Labour's success. Yet whilst this is certainly under-standable – the Treasury has, indeed, reaffirmed its position as the primary department of government and the growth rates it is ostensibly responsible for have facilitated significant public investment and even some redistribution by stealth – there is something slightly paradoxical about this. For, arguably, the core characteristic of Brown's tenure at the Treasury has been the internalisation of the disciplines that globalisation is seen to entail and, more notably still, the displacement of responsibility for monetary-policy decision making from the Treasury to the Bank of England. In this respect, Brown has proved a remarkably orthodox Chancellor, his radicalism largely confined to insulating monetary policy from (party) political influence and constraining the policy autonomy the government might otherwise have enjoyed. This arguably bought him a certain degree of fiscal latitude, especially during Labour's first term in office. Yet it would be wrong to see that as evidence of macroeconomic radicalism on the part of the Treasury. Moreover, with successive growth targets in the third term having to be revised downwards, the Chancellor's room for manoeuvre has now all but disappeared.

## The economic record

A consideration of the personalities involved can tell us only so much about the nature, character and success of economic policy since 1997.

**Figure 14.2**   *Growth of real UK GDP 1985–2004, % annual increase*

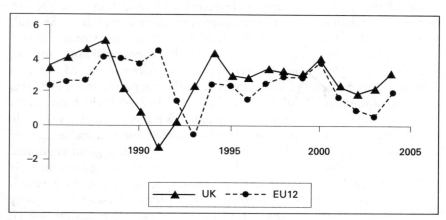

*Source*: Data from HM Treasury, *Pocket Book Data Bank*

An assessment of the extent of New Labour's achievement, and the extent of the Treasury's contribution to that achievement under Gordon Brown, needs first to interrogate the record of economic performance. Consider first the macroeconomy.

Figure 14.1 shows the picture with respect to unemployment, interest rates and inflation, situating that in its most immediate historical context; Figure 14.2 presents similar data for the growth of the UK economy, situating that in both a historical and comparative context. Both paint a very positive portrait – of stable growth, modest inflation, declining levels of unemployment and comparatively low interest rates (certainly by recent British standards). Since 1997, Britain has enjoyed a period of prosperity, consumer and business confidence and, above all, stability. And for this New Labour must certainly take some credit. Yet what both graphs also show is the relatively benign context in which New Labour has thus far been fortunate enough to govern. Governments cannot choose the phase of the global business cycle in which they come to power, but it is difficult to see how choice could have delivered a more propitious context for an opposition party anxious about its economic credibility to be returned to office.

As Figure 14.2 shows, Britain's recent period of stable and non-inflationary economic growth dates not from 1997 but from 1992 – indeed, from September 1992 and the debacle of 'Black Wednesday'. In a sense, Black Wednesday – in which sterling was forcibly ejected from the European Exchange Rate Mechanism (ERM) – was doubly beneficial for

Labour. First, the revaluation of the currency that it imposed served to project Britain onto its current trajectory of stable economic growth rather earlier than many of its immediate European competitors. Second, however, it also destroyed completely and at a stroke the Conservatives' reputation for economic competence, such that they could not – and did not – benefit in 1997 from the very impressive economic record they had achieved since September 1992. Indeed, whilst the period from 1997 has been one of impressive stability, it is the period 1992–97 which saw a real turnaround in Britain's economic trajectory. What is particularly notable about this period is the threefold combination of low and stable rates of inflation, low and steadily declining interest rates and good economic growth. Whilst this has continued since 1997, the initial achievement is one for which New Labour can of course take no credit. As Kenneth Clarke argued forcefully in his pitch for the Tory leadership at the party conference in October 2005, 'remember the strong economy which Labour inherited ... in 1997: low inflation; steady growth; falling debt ... We worked for it. We achieved it. Labour has benefited from it.'

Once set in its immediate historical context, then, New Labour's achievement, though still impressive, is less exceptional than it might at first appear. The same is true if we set the record in a broader comparative context. Britain has not been alone, since the early 1990s, in enjoying stable economic growth. True, growth rates dipped in the eurozone briefly in the mid 1990s, and throughout the world in the first years of the new century, whilst they remained somewhat more stable in Britain. From the British perspective, this is undoubtedly impressive.

Yet, as Table 14.1 shows, for the world economy as a whole such fluctuations as there have been have been modest and have not interfered significantly with a relatively stable and benign economic context. As this perhaps suggests, the real tests of New Labour's political economy have yet to come.

**Table 14.1**    *Economic growth 1985–2004, % average annual rate of growth of GDP*

| Area | 1985–89 | 1990–94 | 1995–99 | 2000–04 |
|------|---------|---------|---------|---------|
| UK | 3.86 | 1.26 | 3.00 | 2.66 |
| EU12 | 3.10 | 2.20 | 2.34 | 1.68 |
| G7 | 3.66 | 2.06 | 2.82 | 2.20 |
| World | 4.00 | 2.62 | 3.68 | 3.84 |

*Source*: Calculated from HM Treasury, *Pocket Book Data Bank*

**Figure 14.3**   *Britain's trade balance 1982–2004, £ billion*

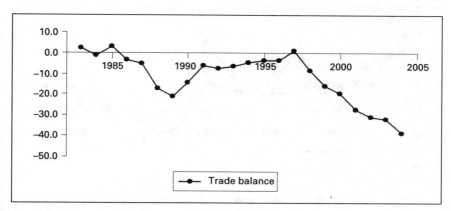

*Source*: Data from HM Treasury, *Pocket Book Data Bank*

That this is so is in part a consequence of other indicators of economic performance which do not present quite such a favourable picture as the headline rates of growth, unemployment, inflation and interest rates discussed thus far. Arguably, these aggregate figures mask a few more disturbing trends, particularly with respect to the performance of the productive economy.

Since 1997 and, indeed, some time before, the performance of the manufacturing economy has been weak. Moreover, as Figure 14.3 shows all too clearly, the period since 1997 marks not so much a continuation of an established trajectory as a distinct acceleration of a worrying trend. The graph displays Britain's trade balance since the early 1980s. Having recovered, to a balance position, by 1997 it shows a clear downward turn and continued precipitous decline to the present day. Britain is now consistently exporting less than it imports. Given that an ever greater share of these imports, as we shall see presently, comes from within the eurozone, this exposes Britain to inflationary shocks arising from any significant appreciation in the value of the euro against sterling. Moreover, whilst this has not resulted in a significant rise in unemployment, the shift from a manufacturing to a service economy has certainly resulted in far shorter employment tenure whilst extending significantly the average working day (Coates 2005).

It is not difficult to see why Britain's trade balance is so poor. For, as Figure 14.4 shows, since the mid 1990s and certainly since 2000, Britain's performance with respect to industrial production has been amongst the worst in the developed world. As David Coates has calculated, whereas in

**Figure 14.4**   *Britain's growth in industrial production 1994–2004, %*

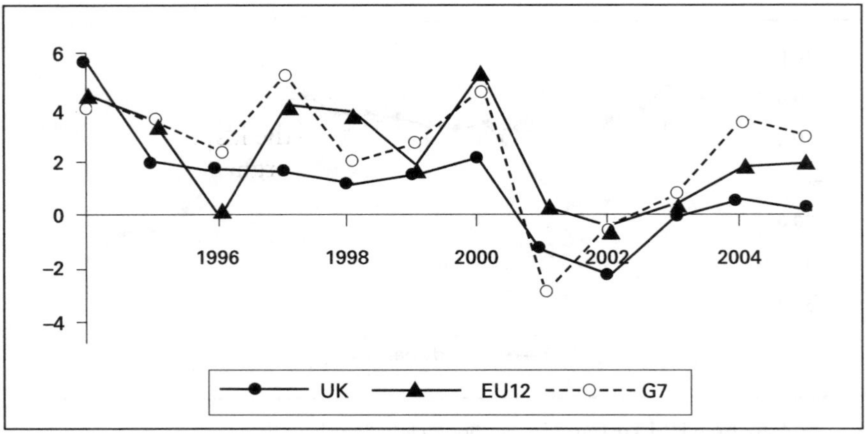

*Source*:  Data from HM Treasury, *Pocket Book Data Bank*.

1961 some 44 per cent of British workers were employed in manufacturing, by 1997 that figure had fallen to 22 per cent and it now stands at around 14 per cent (Coates 2005, 6, 8). This is not necessarily a bad thing; but it does have a series of consequences – notably the exposure of the British economy to inflationary shocks arising from any depreciation of sterling against the euro.

Whilst the competitiveness of the British economy has, as we shall see, been a near-constant and defining feature of New Labour's political economy, an ever diminishing proportion of Britain's workforce actually depends for its employment on success in export markets.

## The distinctiveness of New Labour's political economy

Headline indices of economic performance, however, do not provide the basis for an adequate assessment of New Labour's political economy. Indeed, without a consideration of its own claims about the distinctiveness, purpose and content of its political economy, it is difficult to know what precisely we are assessing – far less how that political economy is likely to cope with a different phase in the business cycle (a period of slower or negative growth). As is often the case when political scientists and political economists venture into the jealously guarded terrain of professional economics, terminological confusion abounds. New Labour's political economy has been characterised in a whole host of different (and often incompatible) ways (Arestis and Sawyer 2001; Balls

1998; Clift and Tomlinson 2006; Dolowitz 2004; Hay 2004; Hutton 1999). The ensuing debate has, unremarkably, generated rather more heat than light. For what it is worth, those closest to the economic policy-making process since 1997, notably Gordon Brown's former chief economic advisor Ed Balls, have tended to refer to their thinking as 'new Keynesian' (Balls 1998). Yet, as Greg Mankiw – the inspiration for much of this and, indeed, Balls' economic tutor – has argued, 'new Keynesian macroeconomics could just as easily be labelled new monetarist economics' (cited in Kirchner 1999, 611; see also Greenwald and Stiglitz 1993). As this perhaps serves to indicate, there is in fact precious little to choose between these contending terms.

Oddly, the dispute over the appropriate characterisation of New Labour's political economy in fact masks a fair degree of consensus about its content. For most commentators that political economy is both consistent and distinctive. It is characterised, in fact, by the assumptions which new Keynesian and new monetarist economics share (though for a different characterisation, see Clift and Tomlinson 2006). Amongst the most important of these are the following:

- an acceptance that an economy has, at any given point in time, an 'equilibrium rate of unemployment' and that the use of macroeconomic policy (concerned with the operation of the economy in aggregate terms) further to suppress unemployment is detrimental to economic performance;
- a rejection of the notion of any long-term trade-off between inflation and unemployment – this allows the control of inflation to be elevated to the status of macroeconomic policy objective number one without having to present unemployment as a price worth paying for price stability;
- a rejection of (Keynesian) demand management as an effective or appropriate means of macroeconomic policy;
- a consequent emphasis upon supply-side reforms, especially the removal of impediments to the efficient operation of the labour market, if the equilibrium rate of unemployment is to fall over time.

In addition to the policies which flow directly from such assumptions, New Labour's political economy tends also to embrace what is termed the new 'endogenous growth theory'. This emphasises investment in the skills or 'human capital' of the workforce.

Equally characteristic of New Labour's political economy is the extent to which its economic policies are conceived of, and justified in terms of, the appeal to a series of externally generated economic imperatives. Put simply, far more so than any previous British government, New Labour's political economy is presented as a necessary accommodation to the harsh economic realities of globalisation. This is clearly seen in its central preoccupation with the twin economic imperatives of (macroeconomic) credibility and (microeconomic) competitiveness. From the former follows, almost logically, New Labour's so-called 'open-economy macro-economics' (in other words, macroeconomics for a global economy) and from the latter follows, again almost by a process of logical deduction, its agenda of labour-market flexibilisation, supply-side reform and human-capital formation. Consider each in turn.

## Credibility

In the textbook economic theory from which New Labour's 'open-economy macroeconomics' is drawn, politicians (somewhat ironically) are opportunistic and instrumental. Market actors (particularly, here, financial-market actors) are blessed with 'rational expectations' and a fair degree of information. And international financial markets are assumed to be perfectly integrated and to be frictionless (the market is held to allocate resources smoothly, efficiently and instantaneously). Seen through the lens of these assumptions, the institutional architecture for the conduct of monetary policy in Britain in 1997 – namely, a non-independent central bank – was seriously in need of modernisation. The rationale for this was as follows:

- In the absence of an independent central bank, politicians – cynical and opportunistic as they are – will seek to exploit the short-term trade-off between unemployment and inflation which they perceive to exist in order to orchestrate a political business cycle from which they might benefit electorally.
- They will, in other words, trade inflation in the immediate aftermath of their anticipated re-election for higher rates of growth and employment in the run-up to that election – they will invest, rationally, in the electorate's 'feel-good factor' regardless of the longer-term economic cost.
- This is not good for long-term anti-inflationary performance nor, it is argued, for aggregate rates of employment across the business cycle.

If we assume, however, that market actors have rational expectations (in other words, that they are aware of the capacity of politicians for cynicism and duplicity), then the latter will anticipate the cycling of the former's preferences for the rate of inflation. And they will adapt their investment behaviour accordingly. In particular, they will anticipate inflation in the run-up to an election, behaving rationally in response to that expectation. In this elaborate textbook scenario, the consequences of *anticipated* inflation for the investment behaviour of market actors are just as severe as if that inflation were real. Accordingly, so long as control of monetary policy rests in the hands of public officials, unemployment, the aggregate rate of inflation and interest rates will all be higher than they need otherwise be.

In such a scenario what politicians face is a credibility deficit with the markets. If anti-inflationary credibility is to be restored, public authorities need to be able to make a credible commitment to a given inflation target. This can only be achieved by giving operational independence to the central bank – in other words, removing monetary policy from the grubby hands of elected politicians. In such a scenario (rational) inflationary expectations are diminished with consequent beneficial effects both upon the cost of borrowing and the equilibrium rate of unemployment.

There is, of course, something strangely perverse about all of this. Whilst it is increasingly common to see politicians seeking to demonstrate themselves to be credible and competent custodians of the economy, rather less familiar is witnessing them premise their public justification for institutional reform on the assumption of their own cynicism and opportunism. 'We, the politicians' – they seem to be saying – 'cannot be trusted to do the right thing when it comes to inflation, so we will mandate constitutionally someone to do this for us.' What makes this even more paradoxical is that although there is plenty of evidence of the existence of a political business cycle (see, for instance, Sanders 2005), there is rather less evidence that central-bank independence in fact improves anti-inflationary performance (Posen 1993, 1998). Recall that what is being suggested is that the ability to control inflation is, and must be, the principal objective of macroeconomic policy, that this rests on anti-inflationary credibility, and that such credibility can only be maintained through operational independence. The absence of compelling evidence that independence improves anti-inflationary performance is surely damaging. It suggests, at the very least, that the granting of operational independence to the Bank of England was rather less of a necessity than its public presentation assumed and that it was more a question of political choice than economic commonsense. This, as we shall see, is not an unfamiliar theme.

The absence of compelling evidence that central-bank independence improves anti-inflationary performance also raises the question of New Labour's genuine motivation for such a significant institutional reform. Two points might here briefly be made. First, that confirming evidence is hard to come by has not led most professional economists to reassess their conviction (supported by algebraic modelling) that central-bank independence *should* improve anti-inflationary credibility and hence performance. This is undoubtedly the message New Labour has been getting from its economic policy advisors. Whether warranted or not, then, the *belief* that central-bank independence is good for anti-inflationary performance is a crucial factor. Second, New Labour was always likely to prove itself hawkish in pursuit of price stability, even if at times this translated into rising unemployment. Consequently, insulating monetary policy from direct political influence and control was always likely to have some appeal for a party newly wedded to the need for monetary discipline.

### Competitiveness

It is not just New Labour's distinctive macroeconomics that has been legitimated by an appeal to the harsh economic realities of a new global economy. Indeed, rather more obviously derivative of a particular account of globalisation is its equally distinctive 'supply-side microeconomics'. As is widely noted, much of the novelty of New Labour's political economy rests on the sustained and systematic appeal to globalisation as an external economic constraint. Invariably, in such accounts, it is microeconomic and not macroeconomic policy that is the focus of attention (the former is concerned principally with incentives to motivate individual or firm-level behaviour, the latter with the management of the economy as a whole). Here, again, economic imperatives claim precedence over political discretion as, it is argued, heightened capital mobility serves to tilt the balance of power from immobile government and comparatively immobile labour to fluid capital. In such an inauspicious context for economic policy autonomy, the state (as fiscal authority) must adapt and accommodate itself to the perceived interest of capital (for labour market flexibility, a 'competitive' taxation regime and so forth) if it is not to precipitate a haemorrhaging of invested funds. The judgement of mobile asset holders (whether they hold invested or still liquid funds) is assumed to be both harsh and immediate. On the macroeconomic side, this is held to select for fiscal responsibility, prudence, and a rules-bounded economic policy (as a token of credibility and competence). On the microeconomic side, it is seen to necessitate flexible labour markets, low levels of corporate and personal taxation and, more positively, a good supply of appropriately skilled workers. The appeal to globalisation thus conjures a logic of economic necessity and, indeed, compulsion, driving a non-negotiable agenda for welfare and labour-market reform – whilst further shoring up the need for open-economy macroeconomics.

Once again, the justification for policy is presented not in its own terms, but as a necessary accommodation to the 'harsh realities' of new economic times in a (superficially) dispassionate, almost technocratic, manner. Appeal is again made to processes beyond the control of political actors which must simply be accommodated – and hence to a dull logic of economic compulsion which is non-negotiable.

## The context reassessed: negotiating globalisation

The appropriateness of New Labour's distinctive political economy thus depends crucially on its judgement of the external economic environment in which the British economy is now situated and has been situated since at least 1997. If it has discerned the imperatives of competitiveness and credibility in the global economy correctly, then there is every reason for thinking that its political economy is the best mix (indeed, possibly, the only mix) that can be delivered in an age of (appropriately) diminished expectations. If, on the other hand, its assumptions about globalisation or, indeed, its translation of those assumptions into appropriate policy-making imperatives, are inaccurate or ill-informed, then there is more cause for concern. For if New Labour has got its account of globalisation and/or the imperatives engendered by globalisation wrong, then it is also likely to have got its economic policy wrong and almost certain to have presented as necessary a range of policy choices that were far from necessary.

Consequently, an evaluation of New Labour's economic record requires an assessment of Britain's exposure to the international or global economy, not merely a description of performance over time. If the characterisation of New Labour's political economy takes us into a terminologically contested terrain, then the same is certainly no less true when it comes to characterising the context in which the British economy is currently situated. For whilst it is true that the degree of globalisation of the British economy is in essence an empirical question, it is also one whose answer is likely to be determined as much as by anything else by what one takes globalisation to mean. Whether the British economy has experienced globalisation or not depends, perhaps unremarkably, on what that claim is taken to imply. And there is no widely accepted definitional standard.

As Table 14.2 shows, definitions can be arrayed along a continuum. At one end of the spectrum we find those with the least exacting definitional standard. For such authors, economic globalisation is merely a synonym for openness – the greater the volume of trade, FDI and financial flows (expressed as a share of GDP) the greater the degree of globalisation. At the other end of the spectrum are those with the most exacting of definitional standards. For such authors openness is not in itself an indication of globalisation. In order to be seen as globalised, economies

Table 14.2   *Alternative definitions of globalisation*

| Conception of economic globalisation | Economic openness per se | Degree of integration with the global economy |
|---|---|---|
| Indices of globalisation | Volume of trade, FDI and financial flows as a share of GDP | Degree to which trade, FDI and financial flows are genuinely global in scope; diminishing influence of geography on economic flows |
| Definitional standard | Less exacting – globalisation and regionalisation indistinguishable | More exacting – globalisation and regionalisation counterposed |

must not only be open but the economic flows (of trade, FDI and finance) in which they are engaged must genuinely span the globe.

The crucial point for current purposes is that it is only by appeal to the most inexacting of definitional standards that Britain can be held to have experienced a process of globalisation since the 1960s. And such an inexacting definitional standard is incompatible with the assumptions about globalisation on which New Labour's political economy would seem at least publicly to be predicated. In short, there is a significant disparity between the assumptions about globalisation which ostensibly inform New Labour's political economy and the empirical evidence. Those assumptions, as we saw in the previous section, are that world markets are perfectly integrated and that in order to prove competitive, Britain needs to demonstrate a genuinely global comparative and competitive advantage. Just to be clear, it is not so much that New Labour believes international markets to be integrated perfectly, as that the political economy which informs its policies is predicated on such an assumption – an assumption chosen for its convenience in the production of algebraic models of the economy's operation. A growing body of empirical evidence does not bear out this claim.

## Financial market integration

The evidence most easily reconciled with the globalisation thesis relates to the operation of, and exposure of the British economy to, globally integrated financial markets.

**Figure 14.5**   *Daily average foreign exchange turnover 1988–2004,*
*$US billion*

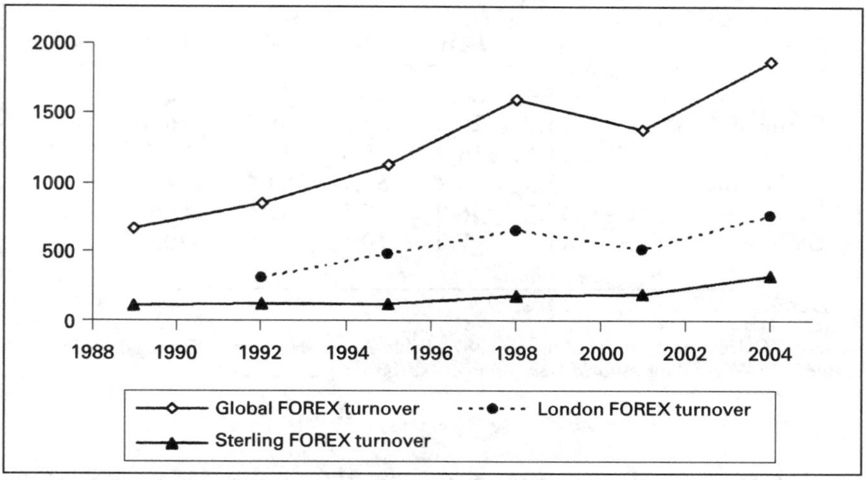

*Note*: Turnover expressed at April 2004 exchange rates
*Source*: Calculated from BIS (2004)

As Figure 14.5 shows, whilst the trading of sterling on foreign
exchange (FOREX) markets accounts for a smaller proportion of overall
turnover on such markets today than it did throughout the 1990s, the
proportion of world FOREX trading taking place in the City of London
has remained relatively constant and has followed the global trend. As
the volume of world financial-market turnover has increased, so too has
turnover in the Square Mile. Data like this would seem consistent with
the notion of the British economy as embedded within an ever more
tightly integrated world economy.

## International trade

A rather different picture emerges if we consider the openness of the
British economy with respect to trade. It is conventional to date globalisation from the 1960s and to cite as evidence exponential increases in
trade volumes (expressed as shares of GDP) since that decade. The so-
called 'sceptics' of the globalisation thesis point out, however, that the
inference one draws from such data is rather heavily dependent on the
choice of start date. Choose the 1870s rather than the 1960s as the start
point and a somewhat different picture emerges in which levels of trade
integration have only recently returned to the levels they achieved in the

**Table 14.3**   *Ratio of merchandise trade (exports plus imports) to GDP
at current prices 1913–2003*

| Country | 1913 | 1950 | 1973 | 1995 | 2000 | 2003 |
|---------|------|------|------|------|------|------|
| France | 35.4 | 21.2 | 29.0 | 36.6 | 46.6 | 44.2 |
| Germany | 35.1 | 20.2 | 35.2 | 38.7 | 56.3 | 56.2 |
| Japan | 31.4 | 16.9 | 18.3 | 14.1 | 17.7 | 19.9 |
| Netherlands | 103.6 | 70.2 | 80.1 | 83.4 | 112.5 | 108.9 |
| **UK** | **44.7** | **36.0** | **39.3** | **42.6** | **43.9**[*] | **38.7** |
| US | 11.2 | 7.0 | 10.5 | 19.0 | 20.7 | 18.5 |

*Note:* [*] data for 1994
*Sources:* Calculated from Maddison (1987, Table A-23); Hirst and Thompson (1999, 27, Table 2.3); World Bank, *World Development Indicators*, various years

final decades of the nineteenth century (Hirst and Thompson 1999, 27–32). How much damage this does to the globalisation thesis is an interesting question – though not one that can concern us here (see Hay 2006). Suffice it to note that the evidence for the British case conforms, if anything, even less well to the globalisation theory's predictions. For, as Table 14.3 shows, the ratio of merchandise trade to GDP (and hence the openness of the British economy) is in fact lower today than at any point since 1950. The fact that British trade to GDP ratios have fluctuated since 1913 between a peak of nearly 45 per cent (in 1913) and a trough of 36 per cent (in 1950) and that the average over this period of time (of around 41 per cent) is somewhat higher than current levels is surely an important counter to exaggerated talk of *inexorable* pressures leading to *unparalleled* degrees of economic integration (see also Hay 2006). In the light of this, it seems somewhat disingenuous to present British exporters as more fundamentally challenged than at any previous point by the imperatives of global competitiveness.

## Foreign direct investment

The aggregate picture with respect to foreign direct investment is perhaps rather more easily reconciled with the globalisation thesis. As Figure 14.6 shows, at least until the early years of the current century, inward foreign direct investment to the developed economies exhibits a trajectory of exponential growth. Moreover, the significant downturn since 2000 is largely attributable to a decline in (essentially unproductive) mergers-and-acquisitions (M&A) activity following a readjustment in world

**Figure 14.6**   *Foreign direct investment inflows (1998 = 100)*

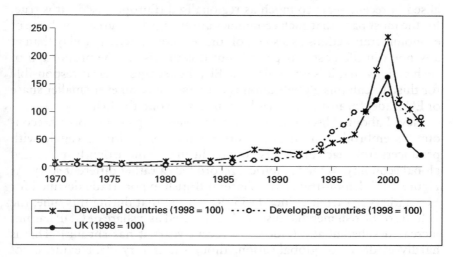

*Source*: Calculated from IMF *Balance of Payments Statistics Yearbook*, various years; UN *World Investment Report 2004*

equity markets (for instance, IMF 2004). It is not in itself an indication of any reversal of the globalisation process.

The British case follows, for the most part, the trend for the developed economies as a whole. Yet, since 2000, levels of inward direct investment to the British economy have fallen off rather more markedly than in almost any other developed economy. And whilst Britain's distinctly stock-market-based variant of capitalism has always attracted higher-than-average levels of unproductive FDI, a more detailed examination of the evidence reveals that there is more to this recent decline than the falling off of M&A activity. Here, too, it would seem, the recent trend has been for a deglobalisation of the British economy – associated, in particular, with the shrinking size of the manufacturing base.

## Europeanisation, not globalisation

Such aggregate data, however, do not tell the whole story. If the sceptics' case rested solely on Table 14.3 and Figures 14.5 and 14.6 it would not be very strong. What the data considered thus far fail to show is the extent to which the international trade, investment and financial transactions in which the British economy is involved are regional or genuinely global in character; this is where the sceptics' case is arguably strongest. For here the empirical evidence is far from equivocal and extremely damaging to the conventional globalisation thesis.

The sceptics' argument is that economies like Britain's have not glob-alised in recent years so much as regionalised (Europeanised). It is true, for the most part, that such economies are engaged in a greater volume of economic transactions as a share of total economic activity today than at any point in the post-war period. But it is the rise in the proportion of such activity that it is internal to the EU, they suggest, that is responsible for this. To call this globalisation is perverse; since an ever smaller share of EU trade, for instance, is with countries beyond the EU.

New Labour's discourse of competitiveness depicts the British econ-omy as embroiled in an ever more intense competitive struggle with producers from each and every country in an ever more tightly integrated global economy. Yet the empirical record tells a rather different story. As Figure 14.7 demonstrates, the share of British export trade destined for EU markets has tripled since 1955. Recall too that during this time, the volume of British merchandise trade expressed as a share of GDP has not increased substantially (indeed, in recent years it has shrunk). This is hardly evidence of globalisation, though it is very clear evidence of regionalisation. Indeed, both the proportion and volume of Britain's trade with the world *excluding the EU* have diminished significantly since the 1950s.

The British economy is, therefore, less and less dependent for success

**Figure 14.7**   *UK exports to the EU as a percentage of total exports 1960–2004*

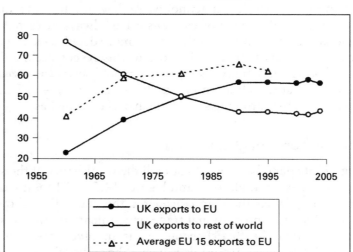

*Source:* Calculated from European Commission, *European Economy* (1996); *UK Trade Information Dataset* (www.ukintrastat.com)

on its comparative and competitive advantage in global markets, and ever more dependent on comparative and competitive advantage in EU/European markets. An undifferentiated model of the determinants of competitiveness in a fully integrated global economy is likely, then, to be an ever less useful guide to discerning labour-market and other economic-policy priorities.

Similar observations can be made about the competitive struggle to attract foreign direct investment. Britain's share of world inward foreign direct investment has fallen quite steeply in recent years. Yet perhaps the more important point is that the character of that investment, like the character of Britain's trading relations, is far from undifferentiated globally. Indeed, in 2004, no less than 98 per cent of inward foreign direct investment flows to the British economy came from North America, Japan or EU member states (the so-called 'triad' economies). Moreover, mirroring the trends in the trade data described above, an ever growing proportion of Britain's inbound foreign direct investment is from within the European Union. Finally, when it is considered that the vast majority of inward foreign direct investment from outside the EU is attracted by Britain's proximity and privileged access to the EU market, the notion that Britain is engaged in a genuinely global competition for foreign direct investment is rendered at best somewhat problematic.

## Tensions, contradictions and future prospects

As the above paragraphs suggest, there is a clear and growing disparity between the claims made by New Labour about the broader economic context in which the British economy is situated and the empirical record of trade, investment and financial flows to which it is exposed and in which it is engaged. If globalisation is to mean anything more precise than economic openness, such that it is meaningful to differentiate between regionalisation and globalisation, the British economy has been regionalising rather than globalising in recent decades. That trend continues. And however one chooses to label this consistent trajectory, one thing is clear – Britain's economic fortunes are determined to an ever greater extent by its competitiveness with respect to its nearest not its most distant trading partners.

This in turn suggests both that New Labour's political economy is far less obviously necessitated by globalisation's logic of economic compulsion than is often assumed and that a mischaracterisation of Britain's external economic relations in terms of globalisation may well lead (or may already have led) to poor economic-policy choices. It is to this second point that we now turn.

Given New Labour's impressive record of economic performance in office since 1997, it may seem odd to suggest that its distinctive political economy is based on a mischaracterisation of Britain's external economic relations. Indeed, it might well be suggested, if such a mischaracterisation is capable of sustaining such a prolonged period of good economic performance then either it cannot be that bad a mischaracterisation or it is one that should be actively encouraged. Yet, as hinted at already, Labour's good economic record to date may have had as much to do with its inheritance as to the policies it has pursued in office. Furthermore, the real test of its political economy may be yet to come, with the advent of a more difficult phase of the global business cycle.

New Labour's political economy is not without its contradictions; nor, seemingly, is it well placed to cope with a more recessionary economic climate. A number of prospective points here suggest themselves:

- The use of interest-rate variations as the sole policy instrument to control inflation is potentially damaging to British competitiveness.

The exclusive use of monetary policy (interest-rate variations) to control inflation tends to reinforce the historical tendency for Britain to suffer an interest-rate premium over its competitors whenever significant sources of inflationary pressures exist. This serves to suppress levels of productive investment, thereby contributing to capacity constraints (the inability of the economy to respond to increases in demand with increases in supply). At the same time, it tends to drive up the value of sterling, further penalising British exporters. Moreover, interest-rate variations are a blunt instrument of anti-inflationary policy – penalising, for instance, a manufacturing sector already in recession whenever significant inflationary pressures arise in more buoyant sectors of the economy.

- Much of New Labour's political economy is pro-cyclical in character.

New Labour's political economy tends to boost rates of economic growth on the 'up' phase of the cycle and suppress them on the 'down' phase. In other words, it reinforces rather than counteracts the business cycle, contributing to a greater variation in economic growth rates between peak and trough. This is especially true of its agenda of labour-market reform. The government is proud to boast and to defend a labour market more flexible than that of any of its European competitors. This undoubtedly has its benefits, but these are unevenly distributed across the business cycle, occurring principally when demand is high – and by all recent accounts demand is now falling consistently. Flexible labour markets are characterised by the absence of 'labour-market rigidities' –

such as works councils, compulsory consultation processes and generous compensation where labour shedding occurs. Each makes it easier to hire and to fire labour in Britain than in most European economies. In a relatively integrated European market, then, Britain can expect a high proportion of European labour shedding in response to excess capacity to occur on its shores. The magnitude of this effect is tempered somewhat by the declining significance of manufacturing to the British economy. Yet this is nonetheless a significant concern with the prospect of the advent of a more difficult phase in the European and global business cycle.

- New Labour's emphasis upon 'human-capital formation' (investment in skills) sits uneasily alongside, and in some tension with, its agenda of labour-market flexibilisation.

Highly flexible labour markets, like the British, tend to be characterised by high rates of labour turnover and short employment tenure. This presents a significant disincentive for employers to invest in the human capital of their employees. For why invest in the skills of your workforce when you can poach those trained by others? Similarly, why invest in the skills of your workforce when, by so doing, you merely improve their mobility in the labour market? New Labour's political economy identifies, as an endemic market failure, the tendency of private employers to undersupply skills and human capital. Yet its programme of labour-market reform provides yet further incentives for the market to fail to provide that investment.

- New Labour's ostensible commitment to labour-market flexibility has been compromised, more so than by anything else, by its failure to control house-price inflation (and, indeed, on occasion by policies that have further stoked house-price inflation).

The result is that house-price differentials are a very considerable and growing structural impediment to labour-market flexibility in the UK economy today. This has contributed to a significant social-housing crisis in many parts of Britain – notably London and the South East of England. Here high housing prices and relatively undifferentiated regional rates of pay have conspired to price core public-sector workers – like nurses and teachers – out of the housing market. The result is significant shortages in the supply of skilled public-sector labour.

- Since 1992 Britain's good headline economic performance has been driven by consumer demand. This, in turn, has been funded out of unprecedented levels of personal debt and the release of equity from house-price inflation.

The long and, until now, stable consumption boom that Britain has enjoyed for over a decade was fuelled first by rising stock-market prices and, more recently, by rising house prices (see also Hay et al. 2006; Watson 2003). Both have served to drip consumption potential in the form of released equity into the market place, but with the effect of driving up, to historically unprecedented levels, personal debt. The sustainability of this is now threatened as never before. House-price inflation has slowed significantly, inflationary pressures are beginning to build within the economy and consumer spending is now falling. What is more, the anxiety engendered by this sense of fragility is, arguably, now beginning to interfere with the Bank of England's ability to control inflation. Its Monetary Policy Committee seems today increasingly nervous about using interest-rate hikes to bring down inflation, for fear of puncturing an unstable house-price bubble and, with it, the consumer boom it has sustained almost uninterrupted since 1992. Though inflationary pressures are building it is the falling away of consumption potential that the Bank seems most concerned about at present.

This has a significant bearing on one further aspect of New Labour's political economy – its seemingly indefinite postponement of the question of membership of the Single European Currency (to which it remains ostensibly committed). Space does not permit a detailed treatment of this issue (though see Hay et al. 2006 for a recent assessment; see also Grant 2003). Should control of monetary policy pass from the Monetary Policy Committee of the Bank of England to its equivalent in Frankfurt, the ability to soften the burden on mortgage holders in this way would be eliminated at a stroke. In all likelihood, further instability and uncertainly would be injected into the housing market – to say nothing of the potential impact on macroeconomic-policy coordination. For the time being, it seems, membership of the Single European Currency is unthinkable, given the balance of public opinion. Indeed, it is almost certainly an issue the government is very pleased to have seen effectively taken off the political agenda by the French and Dutch 'No' votes in referenda on ratification of the European Constitution.

It is, of course, exceptionally dangerous to speculate about future economic performance and the above analysis is no more than an attempt to anticipate potential sources of tension and contradiction. It raises a number of causes for concern and reminds us that an economic-policy mix that works well during periods of high and stable demand may nonetheless be undermined by a downturn in the world economy. If New Labour (in combination with the Bank of England) can continue to deliver modest and stable economic growth, low inflation, low interest rates and low unemployment for the next five years it will have done exceptionally well.

## Conclusion

New Labour's third consecutive electoral victory is a major, and historically unprecedented, achievement. Though it has been accompanied by an appropriate dose of humility rather than a sense of euphoria, it nonetheless presents a significant opportunity to establish and consolidate a sizeable policy legacy for the 'Third Way'. Yet, if the above analysis is correct, as in 1974 and 1992, this may not be a terribly good election to have won. By 1974 the writing was on the wall for Britain's relatively brief flirtation with corporatism in the wake of the Yom Kippur war and the global escalation in oil prices. In 1992 the ERM debacle was just around the corner, an episode it seems unlikely that a Labour government would have handled very differently from that of John Major. Today, the economic prospects look, for the first time in a long time, far from benign. Domestic demand is falling and the consumption potential that steadily rising house prices have dripped into the economy since 1992 seems to be drying up. The Treasury's growth targets now look wildly over-optimistic and a significant shortfall in government accounts is opening up. What is more, there are good reasons for thinking that New Labour's political economy is rather better equipped to deal with phases of the business cycle that may well now have past. In short, its economic-policy record, however good this has been, is flattered by the phase in the business cycle in which it has thus far been achieved. The real test is yet to come.

## Chapter 15

# Modernising the Public Services

STEPHEN DRIVER

The reform of public services dominated the domestic agenda of the Labour government in its second term. The state of the country's hospitals and schools was a key election battleground as Labour looked for an historic third term – and the Conservative Party a route back to government. New Labour 'modernisers' presented the government's policies as a pragmatic and necessary response to the needs of supplying collective public goods in a changing society. Critics saw New Labour's political economy as yielding to the discourse of globalisation and the 'logic of no alternative' (Watson and Hay 2003). Certainly the government's reforms to the public sector are politically charged with Labour's links to trade unions and the party's commitment to social-democratic political economy in question. Since 1997, in return for extra resources, schools, hospitals and other public service providers have had to 'modernise'. For 'modernise' read 'work differently' – but how differently?

This chapter will examine how the structure and organisation of public services has changed under the Labour government, focusing on health and education. Obviously, public service provision stretches far beyond these two key services, but health and education are here used as the means to assess the rationale and coherence of Labour's 'modernisation' agenda and to examine the implications of its changes for social-democratic governance and political economy.

## Labour, social democracy and public services

The provision of public services is an integral part of the social-democratic state. Labour's post-war social democrats believed that once they got into power and the economy was running at full tilt, buoyant tax revenues would provide the resources to pay for a range of public services to alleviate poverty, establish social rights and bring greater equality to society in terms of both outcomes and opportunities. For these social democrats, the provision and organisation of public services was important. Left to private enterprise and the market, access to education, health care, housing and other social services would be rationed by ability to pay. To prevent this, such services should be removed from the market, funded collectively through taxation and provided 'free' by the state on the basis of need. Labour's social democrats also believed that both Westminster *and* Whitehall (and indeed, local town halls) should deliver collective services. Traditional forms of public administration could be rolled out to provide the public services that social-democratic thinking demanded.

In the 1980s and 1990s, the New Right had no time for social-democratic governance or political economy. Markets, not the state, should determine the allocation of rewards and resources across society. Individual freedom, not social justice, should provide the political compass for policy makers. Public spending was a drain on wealth creation – and should therefore be cut. Whenever possible or practicable the public sector should be replaced by private enterprise or be made subject to market-like forces and private-sector governance – a new public management was required.

In Thatcherism's prime, Labour politicians fought tooth and nail to defend the social-democratic state. But as the years of opposition wore on, it became increasingly apparent that any New Labour government would revise and modify Tory reforms to the public sector, not turn the clock back to the 1970s. The question of public-sector governance, to some extent, came to transcend traditional political divides. Left as much as right was drawn to new thinking on how to manage and administer public and private affairs (see Miliband 1994). New Labour modernisers urged the left to rethink the relationship between the individual and the state and to abandon its commitment to centralised collective public services. The state should be the guarantor of public goods, but not necessarily the direct provider. This rethinking of collective provision led Labour modernisers to take a less doctrinal approach to the balance between the state and the market in social-democratic governance. Decisions about the delivery of public services should be pragmatically taken on the basis of what worked, not what was ideologically correct (Le Grand 1998; Mulgan 1993).

## New Labour in power: 'modernising' public services

The Labour Party had two basic messages on public services when it won the 1997 election. First, a New Labour administration would not govern like Labour governments had done in the past by just taxing and spending. Public services could be improved in other ways. Second, a New Labour government would move Britain on from the market-based reforms of the Thatcher/Major years. Public services would be 'modernised' not privatised and the setting of 'targets' would provide the key benchmarks by which progress would be judged. The government would offer a 'Third Way' between traditional forms of public and social administration *and* the reliance on markets as mechanisms to reform the delivery of public services (Bevir and O'Brien 2001). The Conservative legacy – one based on the primacy of private interests and the private sector – would be challenged by reinstating the importance of the public sector and the value of social justice in guiding public policy making. But finding policies to match such ambitions has not proved straightforward.

## A question of funding?

Improving standards in public services for the incoming Labour government meant walking a tightrope between the Conservatives' market-based structural reform and Labour's traditional support for increased public funding for collectivist institutions. In education, grant-maintained schools were abolished and replaced with a new category of 'foundation schools', back in the local-education-authority fold, but with more autonomy than traditionally maintained schools. In health, the internal market was 'abolished' but the central element of that market, the split between the purchasers of health care (the GPs and local health authorities) and the providers (largely NHS hospitals) was retained.

At the same time, the Treasury found extra money (£2.2 billion) for health and education from the contingency fund in 1999. If the government was to reach its own targets to reduce primary-school class sizes and hospital waiting lists, extra resources were clearly needed. This was public-sector reform at its most confusing or, at least, politically expedient: a new government making good on policy promises accumulated over a long period in opposition. Indeed, some commentators went on to argue that there was very little of coherence or consistency in the government's programme of public sector reform (Savage and Atkinson 2001).

The 2000 Comprehensive Spending Review (CSR) changed all this. The three-year review, replacing the annual autumn statement from the Chancellor, set out the government's spending plans for the rest of the parliament and beyond. The CSR also aligned public spending with government policy objectives through public service agreements between the Treasury and spending departments. The review stands as one of the defining features of Labour in power over two terms. Public spending and the public services were back on the political agenda and they would stay there until the 2005 election.

By 1999 the share of government spending as a proportion of gross domestic product (GDP) had fallen to 37.4 per cent – a 30-year low. Gordon Brown's famed prudence was causing jitters on Labour's backbenches. But the 2000 spending review set government on course to grow again. The share of national income being spent by the government increased to 41.5 per cent by 2004 (Chote et al. 2004). However, this remains substantially below the average for European Union member states prior to enlargement in 2004. Defenders of the government nonetheless emphasised the radical character of Labour's public-spending increases in core social programmes from 2000 on. Their argument was that – in a buoyant economy and with a buoyant public-spending total – the percentage increases in education and health amounted to huge absolute increases. For them, on health, Labour had made Britain unique: it was the only leading industrial nation where the policy priority was to spend significantly more, rather than practise 'cost containment'.

For the public services, then, the big winners after 2000 were health, transport, education and the criminal justice system (Emmerson and Frayne 2005). Since 2001, health has seen its budget rise on average by 7 per cent a year – a rate that looked likely to continue following the 2004 spending review. The rate of increase in government spending on the NHS increased significantly under Labour compared with the rate under the Conservatives. Transport also did well: despite cuts during Labour's first term, spending increased by an average of 16 per cent after 2001. Public spending on education also rose substantially after 2001 with an annual average increase of 6.7 per cent. At constant prices, spending on health since 1997 will have increased by around £50 billion by 2008 and education by £25 billion. But it is worth noting that despite the Prime Minister's oft-quoted commitment to 'education, education, education', the growth in spending on education has over the course of two terms of a Labour government fallen behind transport; is only just ahead of policing and public order; and is less than one percentage point above the long-term growth rate in education spending (Emmerson and Frayne 2005; Kalestsky 2005). See Figure 15.1.

The renewed commitment to public spending on collective services took place as the Labour government embarked on a policy of redistribution by stealth. Dealing with the Conservative legacy meant changing government priorities to target resources on the poor via reforms to the tax and benefit system. The extra resources to the public sector have played their part. Increases in spending on health, education as well as housing subsidies were twice as valuable to those on the lowest incomes as to top earners in 2000/01 (Hills 2004).

**Figure 15.1**    *UK public spending 1996/97–2004/05*

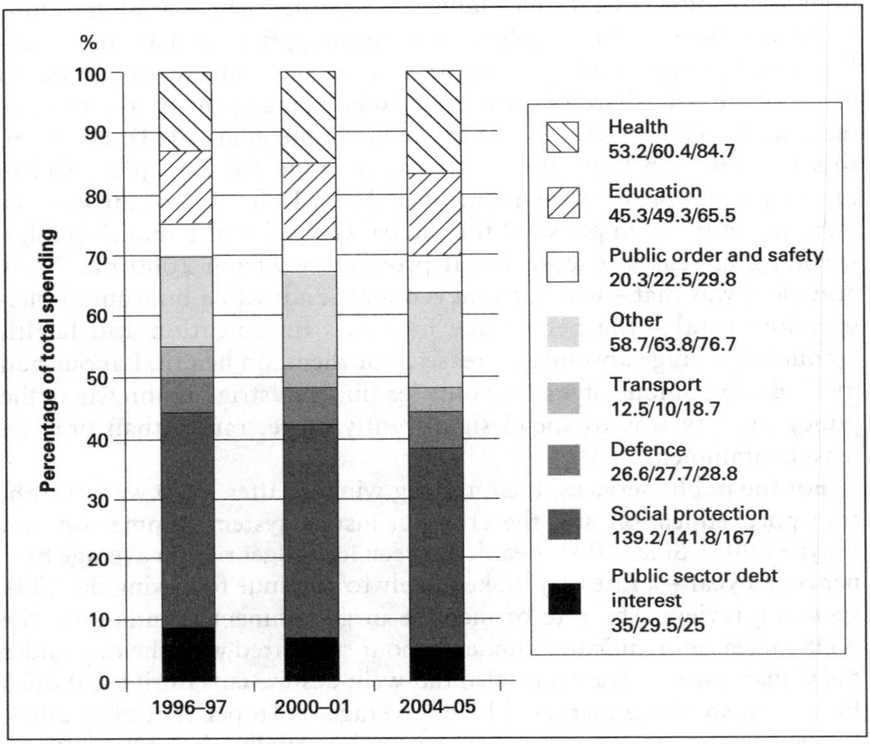

*Note*:  Figures in £bn, 2005/06 constant prices
*Source*:  Adapted from Emmerson and Frayne (2005)

## Money and 'modernisation': the delivery agenda

The funding increases for public services came with strings attached. The public sector would have to 'modernise' in return for extra resources. Key to modernisation is the idea of delivery. Behind the rather innocuous message that services should be delivered well – who could object? – was New Labour's signal to voters and to public-sector trade unions that this government would be different. The interests of consumers would come before the producers of services; and governments would be pragmatic about appropriate modes of service delivery to the consumer. Both messages challenged Labour's traditional attachment to public-sector institutions, those who work in those institutions and the trade unions that represent those workers. Modernisation would mean the public sector working differently. Working practices would have to change.

Terms and conditions of employment could be different, especially as services switched to the private sector. The social-democratic state was under threat once again – and it was a Labour government making the threats. It is little surprise then that the reform of the public sector has proved Labour's greatest domestic political challenge over two terms in power. For the Labour Party, it presses all the wrong buttons.

Labour's reform agenda was outlined in *Modernising Government* (Cabinet Office 1999) and in *Reforming our Public Services* (Office of Public Services Reform 2002); championed by the Prime Minister and the Chancellor (Blair 2001, 2005; Brown 2001); and driven forward across government by Downing Street, the Cabinet Office, including a new Delivery Unit and Office of Public Sector Reform set up after the 2001 election, and the Treasury. The public services, the government argued, should become more 'customer-focused' and 'user-led' – and that within a national framework of minimum standards, the delivery of services should be devolved and delegated to better meet the needs of local people. The decentralisation of public policy making, it was argued, would lead to innovations in public policy, as individuals were encouraged to behave more entrepreneurially and to take risks. Furthermore, decentralisation would underpin strategies that sought to break the culture of turf war between government departments and develop 'joined-up' policies and multi-agency partnership working. Major publicly funded programmes such as Sure Start aimed at families with young children in deprived communities were the result.

What the government left unsaid was that much of the new public management was here to stay. New Labour had no intention of turning the tide on managerialism (Massey 2001). Like the Conservatives before them, Labour believed that the public sector could learn lessons from the private sector. Business planning and performance management were necessary to deliver a public sector that was efficient, effective and economic and which met the needs of users. The public sector could not be left to the professional groups that traditionally ran it. In health and education, while the new government promised to 'save' public services, it soon became clear that New Labour had little interest in the status quo ante – before, that is, Thatcherism got to the public sector. Inevitably this set the government on a collision course with public-sector trade unions. The war of words between government and unions (even modernisers like the former TUC leader John Monks) escalated. To New Labour, unions were part of the 'forces of conservatism', getting in the way of the government's attempt to reform the public sector. To trade unionists, New Labour had given in to business and the New Right neo-liberal agenda on markets and the private sector (Ludlam 2004).

## Dealing with the Conservative legacy: health

Conservative policy makers sought to raise standards and efficiency in the health service through an internal market between the gate keepers of the NHS – the GPs and health authorities – and the main providers of health care, the hospitals. This internal or quasi-market left the NHS in public ownership. In practice the internal market had its limits: it proved almost impossible to let individual hospitals close as a result of market forces. But it did give greater managerial and financial freedom to the newly established trust hospitals, as well as to the GPs who became 'fund holders'. Unlike ordinary GPs, these fund holders could buy health treatments from competing local hospitals. Given that not all GPs were fund holders, the concern arose that a two-tier system was emerging between those patients that had access to better services because their GP was a fund holder and those whose GP was not.

Labour came to power promising to abolish the internal market. In practice, the new government reformed it. These reforms were set out in the 1997 White Paper *The New NHS: Modern, Dependable*. The central feature of these reforms was getting rid of GP fund holding and turning health authorities into primary care trusts (PCTs). Primary care budgets were given to the new PCTs (finally established in 2001 under the 1997 National Health Service Act) that brought together GPs and other local health professionals. PCTs have responsibility for the sourcing of health care and local health promotion. The idea is that a more collaborative network of local health professionals working with hospitals and other providers to source health care would replace the competitive internal market. PCTs would still source health care by contract, but these agreements would be longer (three- not one-year) and provide the basis for more stable *partnerships* between primary and secondary health care. In practice GPs still had a degree of choice where to send patients for secondary treatment, but the options open to GPs would be established by PCTs and providers contracted in advance to provide health-care services for the well being of the local population. The government's reforms to the commissioning of health and social care more broadly were extended with the establishment of care trusts under the 2001 Health and Social Care Act.

These attempts at tempering competition across the purchaser/provider divide were overshadowed by the record sums promised to the NHS in the 2000 and 2002 spending reviews (and the increases to National Insurance to help pay for these increases). The Prime Minister pledged that Labour would match average EU spending on health by 2006 following the review of NHS funding by banker Derek Wanless – who suggested that health spending should account for 12.5 per cent of GDP by 2022 (Wanless 2002).

The year 2000 also saw the government publish its *NHS Plan: A Plan for Investment, a Plan for Reform*. The plan listed a set of government targets that filled in the detail of where the Chancellor expected all the extra money he was handing out to be spent. Targets included waiting times for Accident and Emergency departments, for a range of operations and to see a GP. It set targets for beds, doctors, nurses and other health workers. Extra resources would depend on targets being met – and on old professional demarcations breaking down. Alongside the national plan were two new national health bodies. The National Institute for Clinical Excellence (NICE) was set up to determine what new treatments the NHS should cover ('evidence-based medicine') – a key to a new rationing system. The Commission for Health Improvement would act as an inspector, monitoring standards across the NHS and handing out quality marks. The government also established NHS Direct, a clinical-advice telephone service. All these measures were aimed at addressing the age-old problem of health provision: the different levels and standards of service from place to place and the ambition of policy makers to bring greater uniformity to the national service.

In many respects, these first-term reforms to the NHS were taking public policy beyond Thatcherism. Certain aspects of the devolved governance of the Conservative's health reforms were being retained – local purchasing, trust hospitals – but the quasi-market features of these devolved forms were being replaced by a more collaborative network or partnership approach. In theory, Labour's health reforms were shifting from markets to networks, from competition to collaboration. But the powers of central government remained much in evidence. *The NHS Plan* and its associated policy of target setting reinforced one view that far from decentralising public administration – and 'governing at a distance' – the Labour government was extending the powers of the central state (Newman 2001). While the Conservatives had taken on the medical professions with markets, Labour was going at them with a big stick. And it is this big stick, health experts point out, that can not only distort clinical priorities but can inhibit the local partnerships between health professions that Labour's plans for health reform in part rest on; and lead to government overload as Whitehall bureaucracies struggle with knowing what's going on locally (Dixon 2001).

## Dealing with the Conservative legacy: education

As in health, Conservative policies for education saw the introduction of an internal market whereby schools were encouraged to compete for pupils, whose parents were given far greater freedom to choose the school they wanted for their child. Resources were allocated to these choices and schools were given devolved powers (local management of schools or LMS) to manage these resources. Schools were also encouraged to opt out of local-education-authority control (and be funded directly by central government) and to specialise in particular areas of the curriculum. These policies inevitably undermined the role of local government in schooling. But the Conservatives were not content with letting markets raise standards in schools. The 1988 Education Act saw the introduction of a National Curriculum and the start of a regime of national testing.

The Labour government's first step in government was to abolish the assisted-places scheme – a Conservative policy designed to support bright pupils from poorer backgrounds in attending independent schools. Labour also pleased its supporters in the Schools Standards and Framework Act 1998 by bringing back into the local-government fold (as 'foundation schools') grant-maintained schools – though LMS (local management of schools) meant that this was not as significant as it might once have been. Indeed, subsequent Labour legislation reinforced local school governance, for example through the policy of 'earned autonomy' in the Education Act 2002.

Otherwise, Labour retained the basic architecture of Conservative reforms to schooling. Parents could choose the school for their child, if that choice was available. Frequently, due to intense competition for limited places, it was not. Schools continued to compete for pupils and be funded on a largely per-capita basis. Local management of schools was kept, as was the National Curriculum, national testing and the revamped schools inspectorate, the Office for Standards in Education (Ofsted), as well as its controversial chief Chris Woodhead. To many, this did not feel much like a Labour government taking education policy beyond Thatcherism.

But this picture of continuity and little change belies the shift in policy making under Labour. Certainly David Blunkett, Secretary of State for Education during Labour's first term, had little faith in the capacity of market forces to improve standards in schools. To be fair, the Conservatives could never quite make their minds up whether to trust the invisible hand of the market or the visible hand of government to raise education standards. And in the end, they tried both. During Labour's first term in power, the government grabbed whatever powers were available to the Secretary of State for Education (and invented some new ones, such as a new Schools Standards Unit) to intervene locally in schools and in local education authorities to deliver government policy. Indeed, the desire to 'get things done' across government departments saw Labour go quango-crazy as it thrashed around to find new means to intervene in public policy, increasing considerably the sphere of 'distributed public governance' (Flinders 2001).

In schooling these interventions largely concerned teaching, assessment, the curriculum and class sizes in primary schools, and in particular the introduction of national literacy and numeracy hours and their associated targets. The government made it abundantly clear that it thought not all teachers and not all schools were reaching the standards it expected of them. The early 'Fresh Start' policy gave ministers the powers to close down 'failing schools' and reopen them with a new head and senior management. Ofsted was given greater powers of inspection.

The Labour government also attempted to reform the balance between academic and vocational qualifications in schools and colleges. Following the 1996 review of qualifications for 16–19-year-olds by Lord Dearing, Labour moved to consolidate vocational programmes and to provide a currency for comparing these vocational and academic qualifications. Dearing supported retaining the 'A' Level examination. During Labour's second term, the government looked like overhauling the curriculum for 16–19-year-olds more radically. Under Estelle Morris, the renamed Department for Education and Skills published a Green Paper in early 2002 which repeated the long-held view that vocational programmes were 'undervalued'. With Charles Clarke as Secretary of State the following year, a commission was set up under Sir Mike Tomlinson that looked likely to endorse the department's view that there should be a 'unified framework of qualifications'. By the time the Tomlinson commission reported, in October 2004, the government's view had changed. Tomlinson's central recommendation, the unified framework of qualifications, was rejected by the new Secretary of State, Ruth Kelly, despite the widespread support for the proposals from across the teaching profession. The 'A' Level would remain – and the parallel systems of academic and vocational education.

Labour's education policies do not end with what is taught in schools. Teachers, governors and local education authorities would have to accept a far greater role for the private sector in the building and running of schools, as well as measures such as the introduction of performance-related pay. During Labour's first term, the government established 'education action zones' in which parents, local businesses and voluntary groups could experiment with schooling free from national regulations (under the School Standards and Framework Act 1998). In health too, the pressure was on the government to raise standards, as well as to increase the supply capacity of the NHS to meet the ever growing health demands of the population. Going private – and letting public-sector agencies behave more like private-sector ones – was the way forward for New Labour as it approached its second term in power.

## Going private

Going private has proved one of the most controversial aspects of Labour's reforms to the public sector. Across both health and education policy, the Labour government has looked to the private sector to increase the capacity of the public sector. When Labour took office in 1997 it was in no mood to roll back the managerial reforms started by the Conservatives. The new public management has no hostility to the private sector in the provision of public goods. But such involvement rings alarm bells for Labour supporters.

These alarm bells were set ringing when Labour's modernisation plans embraced the Conservatives' Private Finance Initiative (PFI). The initiative sees the private sector invest in public-sector capital projects, such as new schools and hospitals; and then in effect the government rents the new facility from the private sector for a given period of time. Today's private-sector investment is tomorrow's public spending. Under PFI, or public–private partnerships, as Labour called them, the private sector brings money, management and, very often, new ways of working to the table. The private sector also bears some of the risks of a project. By 2003, 563 PFI contracts had been signed. Since 1997, nearly all major hospital schemes – either complete hospitals or major extensions – have been financed and built under PFI. In 2000, the government set a target of delivering over 100 hospital schemes by 2010. By 2004, 68 had been completed or were under way, with PFI accounting for 64 of those projects. In education, 86 PFI schools projects worth over £2.4 billion and covering over 500 primary and secondary schools were in various stages by 2003. These projects ranged from building small new primary schools to the refurbishment of a whole school estate.

Labour modernisers argue that public–private partnerships bring much needed investment, skills and expertise to public-sector provision, as well as introducing a welcome diversity to Britain's monopoly provision of public services (Commission on Public–Private Partnerships 2001). According to the government, such partnerships do not amount to privatisation because the services themselves remain freely available on the basis of need. Moreover, PFI projects are seen as a way not just of building public-sector infrastructure off the government's balance sheet, but of improving in the longer term the efficient and effective use of resources once the infrastructure is built.

Critics, however, have damned public–private partnerships as an element of the creeping privatisation of public services under Labour. Such contracts, they argue, undermine the unity and universality of the public sector; create worse working conditions for public-sector employees; lock public bodies in to private-sector suppliers; distort clinical priorities; and divert resources away from front-line services. Critics also argue that the contracts offer poor value for money and that the evidence in favour of the transfer of risk from the public to the private sector has not been established by the government (see Pollock 2004 on the NHS).

There continues to be a robust debate about the value to taxpayers of private-finance deals to build new hospitals, schools and other public services. Studies of early hospital PFI deals by the National Audit Office show savings compared to publicly funded projects – although concerns were raised over the longer-term inflexibility that such deals could bring to responding to changing health needs (Economist 2004). But while the debate on the value for money of PFI procurement is important, it does not go to the heart of the *political* controversy over private-sector involvement in the delivery of public services. Privately financed public services not only bring in private-sector management and private-sector ways of doing things; PFI also breaches the great political divide for social democrats between public collective services and private markets – and may represent, as Matthew Flinders puts it, a 'Faustian bargain' between the economic gains of efficiency and political and democratic costs of private-sector governance (Flinders 2005b). Indeed, the debate on PFI procurement reflects a broader one on changing forms of account-ability under the new public management.

The logical extension of the Private Finance Initiative was to bring in more private-sector businesses to deliver public services – most contro-versially in the health service. 'For decades there has been a stand-off between the NHS and the private sector providers of healthcare. This has to end,' said *The NHS Plan* in 2000. Under Labour, it has. In fact, the private sector had been informally working with the public sector for many years. But this relationship was formalised in October 2000 when a concordat between the government and the Independent Health Care Association was signed by the then health minister Alan Milburn. This agreement sanctions and regulates the use of private health providers for more routine clinical procedures – and blurs the distinction between public and private in the health economy.

For the government, the concordat with the private sector is essential if the NHS is to increase its capacity and cut hospital waiting lists. In 2001, the government signed a deal with private health insurer BUPA to lease a number of its hospitals for NHS work. Both in Britain and over-seas, contracts were signed to allow NHS patients to receive private treat-ment (the first patients going abroad in January 2002). By May 2003, the Independent Health Care Association reported that the private sector had performed nearly 200,000 operations since the concordat was signed, helping the government bring in-patient waiting lists below one million for the first time in more than a decade. By 2004, private-sector providers performed 4 per cent of elective treatments – and the government set a target of 15 per cent by 2008. In a further bid to expand the capacity of the NHS, the government established in April 2002 a treatment-centre programme to create new specialist health units. By January 2005, 29 centres were open and many more planned (Department of Health 2005).

As with PFI, value-for-money concerns have been raised about the costs of these treatments, as well as the long-term implications of increasing the dependency on the private sector to solve Britain's health-care problems (Pollock 2004). Private-sector costs have often proved higher than comparable costs in the public sector, usually because 'spot purchasing' of treatments by the NHS has increased private-sector prices. The treatment-centre programme aims to drive down prices by bulk-buying health procedures from the private sector. This may reinforce the view that rather than privatising the NHS, the government is 'nationalising' private-sector health provision.

### The return of the market: foundation hospitals and health commissioning

Foundation hospitals were at the heart of the government's second-term reforms to the NHS – as was the principle of 'earned autonomy'. In important respects, creating foundation hospitals is a logical extension of trust-hospital status, key to the Conservative policy of giving greater freedom and responsibilities to local health managers in the internal market. Labour's plans, like the Tories', had the aim of getting Whitehall off the back of the local NHS decision makers and allowing more local, decentralised and, the government hopes, innovative decision making. With Labour's *The NHS Plan* in 2000, those hospitals seen to be doing well were given the green light (and those not doing so well, the red light) – and handed greater freedom in terms of monitoring and inspection. Traffic lights became star ratings – and the idea of good performance (three stars) earning autonomy became embedded in the policy of foundation hospitals announced by Alan Milburn in January 2002.

In basic terms, NHS hospitals would be given more independence under the policy and be allowed to be more like private-sector bodies, while remaining not-for-profit (see Box 15.1). The extent of these freedoms was at the heart of the disagreements between the Department of Health (and Downing Street) and the Treasury. The freedoms the new foundation trusts have to make decisions include powers to raise money on the open market (subject to a limit set by a regulator) and to retain surpluses and proceeds from the sale of assets and land. Foundation trusts are expected to use these financial freedoms to improve patient care by recruiting staff, building new facilities and funding treatments in the private sector.

Just as going private set alarm bells off among government backbenchers, so has allowing public-service providers to behave like private-sector businesses caused headaches for New Labour. The creation of foundation hospitals has revealed tensions between the government and its backbench supporters, as well cracks in the New Labour coalition – between Gordon Brown and Tony Blair. The Health and Social Care Act 2003, paving the way for foundation hospitals, was passed with the government's massive majority cut to 17 amid fears that the new-style trusts would lead to a two-tier health service, would destabilise local health provision and were a cloak for the further privatisation of the NHS (Pollock 2003). The government's commitment to 'modernisation' was leading to growing rebelliousness on Labour's backbenches in its second term.

Despite some of the powers of the new hospitals being cut, the first wave of ten foundation hospitals was launched in England in April 2004, followed by another wave of ten hospitals in June 2004 and more in January 2005. Tony Blair, who has staked much of his domestic reputation on public-sector reform, promised that all hospitals in England could be granted foundation status by 2008. Health policy, otherwise, is a devolved policy. In Scotland and Wales, the devolved governments have attempted, not altogether successfully, to stake out distinct policies, not just on the NHS but on schooling, the funding of higher education and personal care for the elderly as well.

The policy of creating foundation hospitals is part of a broader shift back to market forms of governance during Labour's second term, raising concerns that more diversity and choice in health provision would lead to widening inequalities in health provision. While welcoming the introduction of foundation hospitals as an opportunity for more innovative, accountable and responsive health provision to meet local needs, the chief executive of the health think tank the King's Fund challenged the government during the passage of the Bill through parliament to make innovations in health practice available to non-foundation hospitals and to the wider local health economy (King's Fund 2003). Foundation hospitals and a new health-commissioning system of 'payment by results' (whereby hospital budgets are tied to clinical activity, priced against a national tariff based on average hospital costs, not a block settlement from the local PCT) are seeing the return of the internal market between purchasers and providers. Today, most of the purchasing is done by PCTs rather than GPs, though this is likely to shift back to surgery level with 'practice-based commissioning'. Moreover, the government is set to extend these policies by guaranteeing that all NHS patients should be offered a choice of secondary-care providers, one of which will be from

---

**Box 15.1   What's so different about foundation trust hospitals?**

The Secretary of State can direct an NHS hospital to do anything the Secretary of State wants . . . now you have got to remove all that . . . (Alan Milburn, Secretary of State for Health, speaking to reporters during the passage of the Health and Social Care Bill 2003 that created foundation trust hospitals)

Foundation hospitals:

- are part of the National Health Service like other hospitals;
- are however legally independent of the Department of Health (and the Secretary of State);
- are run by a board of governors chosen by local people, hospital staff and patients;
- are not-for-profit 'public-benefit corporations';
- have greater powers to use the private sector;
- compared with other NHS hospitals, have more freedom to set their priorities and spend their money (including on staffing);
- can also take out loans from banks, subject to limits set by a regulator, and keep the proceeds from assets and land;
- must use these resources to improve patient care and are subject to national standards;
- from April 2005, are subject to 'payment by results' instead of lump-sum funding from primary care trusts to all hospitals.

---

the private sector (paid for at NHS cost). By April 2006, the range of potential providers to patients will be expanded to around 50.

One health expert called the new payment system 'the internal market with whistles' (*Economist* 2005), but the whistles are important in terms of the political economy of health care and the regulation of competition to ensure equity in health treatment. Labour's 'diversity-and-choice' agenda in health policy since 2001 has seen a shift to market forms of governance but within a mixed economy alongside networks and hierarchies (Dixon et al. 2003; Ham 2005). The setting up of a new Healthcare Commission in April 2004, replacing the Commission for Health Improvement, was in part a move by the government to reduce the regulatory burden on the NHS. But still the governance of health-care provision at the end of its second term remained caught between command-and-control management and a more 'pluralistic, quasi-market model' (Klein 2005).

## 'Bog-standard comprehensives' and city academies

The government's policy of creating city academies has generated similar controversy. Since 2001, Labour has turned its attention in education from primary to secondary schools. With characteristic directness (the phrase was used by the Prime Minister's press secretary Alistair Campbell in 2001), the problem with standards in the classroom was thought to lie with the 'bog-standard comprehensive'.

The comprehensive school was an integral part of Labour policies in the 1960s and 1970s. It marked a break with selective schooling and what many regarded as a bias toward middle-class children in the post-war education system. But the debate on standards in education, sparked in part by the Labour government in 1976, has seen Labour follow the Conservatives towards greater diversity in schooling. Those grammar schools (around 150) that escaped the comprehensive tide in the 1970s remain grammar schools. Labour, like the Conservatives, has moved to promote school specialisation in subject areas (with a target that all schools should specialise in one subject by 2008). The government has encouraged the setting up of 'faith-based' schools. And those former grant-maintained schools have retained important freedoms to own and manage their own land, assets and admissions under Labour's new foundation status – powers that the government would like all schools to have.

Where Labour has tested the patience of its supporters has been with its plans for independent state schools – city academies – where existing school provision is seen to be failing. The policy, driven forward by Andrew Adonis in the Downing Street policy unit, was enacted in the 2000 Learning and Skills Act and expanded in the Education Act 2002. Teacher unions and others attacked the new schools as a 'form of privatisation of public schooling' that benefited middle class parents and their children. The government responded by arguing that as in health, giving all parents, not just middle-class ones, greater choice over their children's schooling put pressure on the education system to raise its game. See Box 15.2.

City academies have many of the features of the Conservative policy to develop city technology colleges. Both involve the private sector in establishing new schools – something opposed by Deputy Prime Minister John Prescott. Under Labour's plans, academies remain state-funded and are free to students. But they have much more independence than most secondary schools. The sponsors of city academies – typically a business, faith or voluntary group – put £2m towards the cost of starting up the new school. Tax payers provide the remaining £20m or more start-up costs. The new schools have greater powers over the curriculum and

---

## Box 15.2   City academies vs 'bog-standard' schools

### City academies

- Private sponsor raises £2m towards start-up costs
- Department for Education funds rest of start-up and recurrent costs
- Private sponsor – business, charity, church – controls governing body
- Academy trust owns land and buildings
- Can opt out of national pay and working agreements
- But must follow National Curriculum

### 'Bog-standard' schools

- Maintained by local education authority
- School governors: mix of teachers, parents and local-education-authority (LEA) members
- LEA owns land and buildings
- Subject to national pay and working agreements
- But local management of schools and other measures already devolved much of day-to-day running of schools to governing bodies
- And specialist schools programme increasing diversity of schools at secondary level

---

staffing. By the 2005 election, 17 new academies were open – and the Prime Minister promised many more (despite a report in March 2005 from the House of Commons Education and Skills Select Committee that damned the new schools for failing to deliver better results; supporters of city academies said more time was needed).

### Paying for higher education

Paying for higher education has proved a further test of New Labour's commitment to the social-democratic state. Lord Dearing again had a hand in shaping the policy debate. Dearing's report on the funding of university education, published soon after the 1997 election, recommended the ending of 50 years of free tuition by the introduction of fees amounting to 25 per cent of course costs. The then Education Secretary David Blunkett agreed, arguing that those who benefited from a university education in terms of higher lifetime earnings could reasonably be expected to make an additional contribution to its costs. Critics argued that having a well-educated population would benefit the whole of society – and should, therefore, be paid for out of general taxation. Access to higher education was also an issue. Would tuition fees, amounting to £1,150 a year in 2005, deter those from poorer backgrounds, especially those from families with no history of higher education, from applying to study at university? Would mature students, who were being encouraged back into education under the policy of 'lifelong learning', be put off by the extra costs of university fees?

Blunkett argued in July 1997 that the government was 'determined to ensure that there is access to higher education for all those who can benefit from it'. The Teacher and Higher Education Act 1998 brought in tuition fees and included measures to support students from low-income families. By 2003/04, 43 per cent of students paid the full tuition fee, 43 per cent were exempt and the remainder paid part fees. For those students deemed independent, mostly the over 25s, more than 80 per cent paid no tuition fee.

Labour's 2001 manifesto promised, or at least appeared to promise, that the government would not allow universities to cover the full costs of courses through 'top-up fees' – in other words, to top up the existing flat-rate tuition fee. University Vice Chancellors argued that higher education needed more money if the sector wasn't to fall behind in the global education market. Labour agreed. In January 2004, the government's Higher Education Bill, which allowed universities to increase tuition fees, scraped through its first big test in the House of Commons with a majority of just five (the government majority at the time was 161). But concerns about access to higher education – what is known as 'widening participation' – became a central feature of the often difficult passage of the legislation through both Houses of Parliament. See Box 15.3.

A 2004 report into access to higher education further confirmed what most people knew: that a class divide marks going to university (Admissions to Higher Education Steering Group 2004; see also Halpin 2005). The final legislation saw a series of measures designed to temper the market in higher education. First, the new fees would not be paid in advance but out of graduate earnings (so are a form of graduate tax). Second, students from poorer backgrounds (in 2005, from homes having a household income of less than £21,185) would get a fee remission and a maintenance grant worth around £2,700 – and universities would be required to top this up by a further £300 if they were allowed to charge the maximum fee of £3,000 which, despite the variable nature of the new regime, it looked like most universities would do. Indeed, for a university to be able to charge the full variable fee, it must satisfy a new access regulator that it is doing enough to 'widen participation' by supporting students from non-traditional backgrounds. The government was also forced to accept in the bill's passage through Parliament an amendment that required a vote on raising the £3,000 fee ceiling after 2010.

## Box 15.3    Funding higher education

### Before 1997

- 'Free' tuition
- University fees for home students paid by local education authority (LEA)
- Student loans to fund maintenance

### 1997–2005

- University fees paid by LEA plus flat-rate tuition fee paid by student
- Tuition fee to be paid in advance of studies
- Exceptions to support students from low-income families
- Student loans to fund maintenance

### 2005 onwards

- University fees paid by LEA plus flat-rate tuition fee paid by student
- Universities allowed to charge 'top-up' fee up to maximum of £3,000
- 'Top up' to be paid from graduate earnings
- Fee remission for students from low-income families
- Students loans plus maintenance grants for students from low-income families

## Diversity, choice and public sector provision

At the heart of the argument over foundation hospitals, city academies and higher-education funding is a difference of view within New Labour on how to reform the public sector. On the one hand, there are those who see public-sector reform as a process whereby extra resources (including resources from the private sector) must be made more accountable against targets set by central government in public service agreements. This is the view of Gordon Brown (and the Treasury). On the other hand, there are those who see the need for far greater diversity – and autonomy – in the supply of public goods and greater choice available to the consumers of public services. This is the view of Tony Blair (and Downing Street).

There are important overlaps between the two views. Both see the need for substantial changes to the working practices of public service providers, including the breaking down of traditional job demarcations, as well as the involvement of the private and voluntary sectors to increase the supply capacity of the public sector (including supporting the extension of private home ownership in housing policy and private financing in transport and the criminal justice system). But there are significant differences of perspective on the future of collective public services under a Labour government. While the Brown/Treasury view has been open to private finance, the idea of giving greater autonomy to public agencies, whether foundation hospitals, city academies or foundation schools is viewed with suspicion. This is partly a Treasury worry about the ability of these agencies to bear risk – and about who will pick up the tab if things go wrong. But it also reflects the unresolved tensions within New Labour about how best to reform the public services – and how, and to what extent, these reforms are underpinned by social-democratic values.

The problem Gordon Brown has with greater diversity and autonomy in public service provision – what he sees as 'marketisation' – is that they will undermine the unity, ethos and political economy of that provision – and that they won't work (Brown 2003). Brown's fear that markets undermine the public service ethos of organisations such as the NHS follows long-standing concerns about the impact of new public management, from Margaret Thatcher's Efficiency Unit onwards, on the culture of the civil service and public service more broadly – concerns that stretch across the political spectrum.

In Brown's view, choice in the public sector must be limited to areas such as the booking of hospital appointments (where initiatives have been introduced for elective surgery), and managed by collective agencies such as PCTs. Too much diversity and choice in health and education lead to a 'two-tier' system that undermines the unity and equity of the system. This half of the New Labour coalition remains committed to the provision of certain public goods – health and education in particular – by largely nationalised monopoly providers. While Gordon Brown is open to making these providers more accountable to local patients, parents and communities – or put another way, giving these groups more voice – the Chancellor cannot deny the very visible hand of central government (however much he pleads his innocence). Governing from the centre has proved a key feature of Brown's Britain.

The view from Number 10 is somewhat different. Blairites such as Alan Milburn (whose views on the NHS shifted markedly between his time at the Treasury and at the Department of Health), former Trade Secretary Stephen Byers, and former Health Secretary John Reid do not see it this way (Milburn 2004; Reid 2005). Their perspective gives far greater weight to increasing the diversity of public-sector provision – a diversity that embraces the private sector – and to a more radical notion of 'personalised' public services: certainly one that encompasses notions of consumer choice and implies competition between service providers and a return to market forms of governance. For the Blairites, more voice in the provision of public services requires more choice. Drawing on the arguments of Julian Le Grand, Professor of Social Policy at the London School of Economics, who was seconded to the Prime Minister's Policy Unit in October 2003, the belief among the Prime Minister's supporters is that choice and diversity will challenge public service providers to improve standards for all (and therefore, bring a measure of social justice to that provision) whether or not choice leads to exit; the potential for such an exit – 'contestability' – might be just as significant as whether public-sector consumers actually switch suppliers (Le Grand 2003). Giving individuals more choice, and linking choice with the distribution of resources through a quasi-market system, empowers all citizens, rich or poor. It is in a bureaucratic system, the Blairites argue, that the middle classes are able to use their capital, cultural and material, to play the public sector to their advantage.

## Conclusion: 'modernisation' and the social-democratic state

Can the Labour government combine commitments to greater choice and diversity in public service provision – and the inevitable role of markets in making that choice and diversity possible – with traditional social-democratic commitments to collective public provision available to all on the basis of need? Seen from the funding end, the government is supporting collective public service provision through public funds – supplemented by some private finance (the value of PFI deals in 2001 was 9 per cent of total public-sector investment). These funds come with strings attached in terms of central-government objectives and targets and the accounting frameworks that are part of the new public management.

From this end of the welfare state, then, the question is whether tax payers are getting value for money from the extra funds being spent. This is not easy to judge. A leaked Downing Street Strategy Unit report in April 2004 suggested that public-sector productivity in schools and hospitals was falling. According to official figures, public-sector employment rose 10 per cent between 1998 and 2004 – up from 4.95 million to 5.45 million. The numbers of nurses, doctors and teachers have all increased – 12,300 more teachers, for example, between 2001 and 2004 – but so has the number of managers. Public-sector pay has also risen. Academic achievement in primary schools increased significantly during Labour's first term, but then stopped rising. Education performance among the country's poorest social groups remains low. In the NHS, some but not all health targets are being met and concerns remain that target setting continues to distort clinical priorities. In terms of value for money, inputs have increased faster than outputs. According to figures from the Office of National Statistics, in 2003 for every extra 10 per cent increase in public health spending, output increased by only 4 per cent. To the government's critics on the right, 'modest improvements' have come at 'immoderate cost' (Lea 2005). The problem the NHS faces is that its supply problems are largely long-term: it takes time to train more nurses and doctors and build new hospitals. For this reason, the government has looked to short-term measures, such as buying in services and staff from the private sector and overseas, to meet its own targets on waiting times for certain clinical procedures.

In the longer term, the public policy strategy of New Labour is to raise the productivity of the public sector. To do this the government is looking to market mechanisms and public-sector management. This is where the political problems for the government, both internally and with its supporters on the back benches and beyond, really hot up. The government's modernisation programme threatens established systems and cultures of working – managerial, professional and employee. The challenge to public-sector trade unionism, professional or non-professional, will no doubt intensify as private-sector management spreads further across the public sector. Unions will continue to claim that public-sector workers, often already on low wages, are paying the price for greater efficiency by cuts in wages and poorer working conditions. Labour modernisers insist that the opposition of the unions to public-sector reform is misplaced: it confuses the interests of those working in the public sector with those the public sector serves. A future Brown premiership is unlikely to mark a shift in this aspect of the modernisation drive, whatever the Chancellor's supporters in the unions might wish.

So does public-sector reform – certainly in its more radical Blairite guise – undermine social-democratic political economy? The social-democratic state redistributes resources on the basis of need, not property rights. The New Right challenge to this conception of the state was that individuals should become more privately responsible for their own and their family's welfare. This meant that the market and private enterprise should have a much greater role in serving welfare needs. In the end, Thatcherism's incursions into the social-democratic state were limited – largely to housing and pensions. In health and education, quasi-markets, not private enterprise, were as far as the Tories got.

Introducing choice and diversity challenges social-democratic political economy where those choices are attached to property rights. But there is a question mark where choices remain attached to public money and those choices reflect needs not private resources. Even policy suggestions by ultra-Blairites such as Alan Milburn (one of the New Labour modernisers) of handing money to buy services to individuals to spend where they want (in effect, creating vouchers) does not breach this funda-mental principle of social-democratic political economy. The debate on university funding is worrying for traditional social democrats because the issue here is not simply about the diversity of provision and competi-tion between providers (this already exists), but the private funding of higher education and the impact this has on the opportunities for students from poorer families to attend university. The concern is that 'marketisation' will give rise to (or reinforce) a two-tier higher-education system that is already marked by social inequalities.

Important questions remain about how far greater choice and diver-sity exacerbate the local and regional variations in the quantity and qual-ity of public services that have always existed. In certain respects, these questions are similar to the debate about how far devolution, or even local accountability, gives rise to unacceptable regional variations in public policy across the United Kingdom. For the Blairites pushing choice and diversity, the challenge is to show that markets deliver public goods. The evidence for gains from greater choice in consumer satisfaction, effi-ciency, responsiveness and experimentation is often patchy across the public sector and by no means clear-cut. If Labour is to combine commit-ments to social justice, social inclusion and 'personalised public services', the costs of putting into place systems that offer choice in the public sector but which prevent inequalities in outcome are likely to be great (Perri 6, 2003).

For the third-term Labour government looking to leave the founda-tions of a new progressive consensus in British politics, public-sector reform is a war still to be won: there are battles still to be fought in health, particularly education, but also across the public sector more broadly. Just as internal markets were 'politically managed' under the Conservatives, so the Labour government will need to oversee the distri-bution of public goods in a welfare state that is increasingly pluralistic and subject to greater individual choice in quasi-market systems. Unless the government can do this in ways that are seen to be fair, critics inside the party and out will continue to harbour doubts about New Labour's social-democratic credentials, however much public money it spends. And if the government's policy of 'money and modernisation' fails to deliver higher standards of education and better health care, then the next election will be the Conservative Party's opportunity to prove that it has something to offer British government and politics again.

# Chapter 16

# British Politics after Blair

ANDREW GAMBLE

British politics in the last 30 years has experienced two very successful and very dominant prime ministers, Margaret Thatcher and Tony Blair, the two longest continuously serving prime ministers in the last hundred years, and the only two to win three consecutive elections. But there is considerable dispute about their impact and their significance. Both transformed and some argue in the process did lasting damage to their parties, but did they both transform the country through their policies? Opinion is divided on this, particularly in the case of Blair (Seldon and Kavanagh 2005). A common argument is that while the 1979 election was a watershed election comparable to 1945, each producing radical governments which reshaped the institutions and policies of British government, the 1997 election was primarily important for ending the long reign of the Conservatives and returning Labour to government. New Labour, it is argued, governed within the new commonsense established by Thatcherism, accepting the constraints which that imposed. In thinking about politics after Blair it is first important to decide how true this account is. Is Blair the natural successor to Thatcher, the leader who has consolidated the new settlement which Thatcher inaugurated? Or has New Labour initiated or presided over a further change in the direction of British politics?

Some historical perspective is needed, too. The Attlee government looks very different now than it did in 1951, and the Blair government will no doubt also look very different in 50 years' time. Many of the judgements made today will not last (Bevir and Rhodes 2003). The Attlee government is now widely regarded as the high-water mark of British social democracy, as a bold and effective government that delivered lasting reforms (Morgan 2001). But at the time there was considerable disillusion among socialists and quiet satisfaction among conservatives that more had not been achieved, that so many of the expectations the party had aroused in 1945 had not been fulfilled, and that the government was unable to hold office for more than six years. The degree of disillusion with New Labour and Blair personally during the 2005 election makes it hard to imagine that the Blair government will ever come to be regarded nostalgically in the way that the Attlee government now is. But stranger things have happened.

One reason why so many of its supporters find it hard to feel warm towards the most electorally successful Labour government in British history is because of the comparison not just with the Attlee golden age of social democracy, but also with Britain's most recent radical government – the Thatcher government. Many think the Attlee and Thatcher governments changed the landscape of British politics, even if rather less than their supporters hoped at the time. The Blair government has not. It stands in relation to the governments of Thatcher and Major as the governments of Churchill, Eden and Macmillan stood in relation to the Attlee government. To assess the Blair government and what might come after it we therefore first need to understand what it inherited. This chapter starts by examining the Thatcher legacy in British politics, and how far the Blair government has accepted or modified it. Thatcherism and Blair's 'Third Way' will then be analysed to see whether these doctrines now exhaust the ideological universe, eclipsing all other ideological and practical alternatives, or whether those alternatives continue to exist. The chapter concludes by sketching out four scenarios as to how British politics might develop after Blair.

## The Thatcher legacy in British politics

The Thatcher government was radical in two main ways. It broke a number of political taboos, instituting reforms which reshaped British politics and rebalanced the power of major interests (Heffernan 2001). It also transformed the way in which the public sector was managed. These changes were consolidated and extended under John Major, and handed on to Labour (Marsh et al. 1999). By 1997 they were the new common-sense of British government. Labour had to prove that it could manage this new political economy as successfully as the Conservatives, and this constrained the kind of policies Labour could pursue. But other parts of the Thatcher legacy gave Labour more scope for reforms of its own. One of these was the increasingly centralised character of British government (Barnett 1997). The Conservatives had blocked constitutional changes which might have alleviated this, such as devolution to Scotland and Wales. A second legacy was the state of the public services, which by 1997 were widely perceived as seriously under-funded and deteriorating in quality (Hutton 1996).

### Economic reform

The Thatcher and Major governments were responsible for four key economic reforms – privatisation, industrial relations, tax and deregulation.

A series of privatisation measures returned most of the industries nation-alised in the twentieth century to the private sector, transforming the 'mixed' economy of the post-war years into an economy in which the state no longer directly controlled significant industrial assets. Telecommunications, gas, electricity, coal, water, steel, buses, railways, cars, shipbuilding and aerospace were all denationalised by 1997 (Moran 2003).

In industrial relations a series of laws helped break union power. The unions lost their legal protection in a number of key areas; the closed shop was outlawed, as was secondary picketing, and attempts were even made to dictate unions' internal governance arrangements (Marsh 1992). The effect of these measures combined with the rise in unemploy-ment to over three million decisively altered the relative strength of labour and capital, allowing management in many sectors a free hand to reshape and restructure their companies to maximise profitability. Rigidities in the labour market were removed, and labour markets became flexible again. Strikes fell sharply, as did union membership. The reforms helped create a low-wage, low-skill economy in many sectors, and there was a significant increase in poverty.

On fiscal policy, although the Conservatives did not succeed in bring-ing down the ratio of public spending to GDP, and therefore the general tax burden, they did effect some important changes in the distribution of taxes and in spending (Mullard and Swaray 2006). In particular they raised indirect taxes, principally by doubling VAT, while cutting direct taxes. They reduced the basic rate of income tax substantially from 33p in the £ to 23p, brought down the higher rate to 40p, ended the link between pensions and earnings, and allowed the value of many state benefits to erode, while reducing taxes on capital gains, inheritance, and companies. The progressive nature of the British tax system was substan-tially reduced, and unsurprisingly the Thatcher years saw a dramatic widening of inequality, a reversal of the trends of the previous three decades (Pearce and Paxton 2005).

The Thatcher government also opened up the economy to global competition, removing restrictions and controls. The most significant changes, apart from those to labour markets, included the abolition of exchange controls in 1979 and the 'Big Bang' in the City (Moran 1991). British industry was given the signal that it had to compete to survive and that the government would not prop up or subsidise any company that got into difficulty. Although there were exceptions to this, in general the policy was followed, leading to the collapse of large parts of traditional manufacturing in the face of the global slump triggered by the second oil crisis at the beginning of the 1980s. Britain as a result made the transition to an open economy dominated by services rather than manufacturing more abruptly and earlier than most other leading economies (Owen 1999).

The breaking of these taboos was accompanied by the emergence of new language and narratives to explain and justify the changes. The shift in language was most marked in economic policy, supplanting older discourses around incomes policy, industrial strategies, corporatism and the mixed economy. The framework of the discussion had been the national economy, how it might be managed and protected. After 1979 there was a sea change in the way the economy was discussed. The new framework became the global economy and how British economic institutions could be adapted to respond to its constraints and opportunities (Krieger 1999). There was a substantial weakening of the idea of a public sphere and public interest (Marquand 2004). Protection and security were replaced by ideas of openness and flexibility, and collectivist ideas of the public interest gave way to the pervasive language of individualism, consumerism, competition and choice (Crouch 2004).

## New public management

The Conservative governments of Thatcher and Major failed to extend their radical free-market ideas to reforming public services. The one major exception was council housing, where the right-to-buy policy proved popular and effective in shrinking the stock of housing in the public sector and increasing owner occupation. In other areas such as education and health, radical free-market proposals such as education vouchers and private medical insurance were much discussed but not implemented. Instead the Thatcher government sought to contain rising spending by squeezing budgets and taking radical steps such as delinking state pensions from inflation. These policies, pursued for over 18 years, eventually produced a public sector which was severely under-funded and public services which were plainly inferior to those in the rest of the European Union (Lowe 2005; Timmins 1995). The government remained committed to the principle of funding public services through the tax system, and became a convert to new ways of managing the public sector to raise its efficiency and make it more accountable.

In their 18 years of government the Conservatives became enthusiastic advocates of the new public management, with its emphasis on performance indicators, targets, and audit (Moran 2002; Peters and Pierre 2000; Power 1997). The new public management produced many conflicts with professionals in the public sector, such as doctors and teachers, because it involved weakening all forms of self-government by the professions, instead handing over power to a new breed of public-sector managers, who were expected to adopt many of the methods of the private sector. By this means the public sector was gradually transformed, much of the ethos of the old public sector was destroyed, and efforts were made to involve the private sector in the delivery of public services through a variety of new organisational methods, such as public–private partnerships and internal markets, and new financial means, such as the Private Finance Initiative (PFI) (IPPR 2001).

## Constitutional inertia

The radicalism of the Thatcher government was most felt in the economic sphere, but it also had wider consequences, some of them unintended. By centralising, in the hands of the state, powers to push through its radical market agenda the Conservatives unintentionally fuelled the campaign for constitutional reform (Evans 2003). Similarly the hostility of the Thatcher government to the European Union speeded the conversion of the labour movement and the trade unions from being advocates of withdrawal to supporters of further integration (Young 1999). Another important change which was hardly intended by the government was that the new culture of individualism, consumerism and flexibility was associated not only with Yuppie excess but also with the spread of multiculturalism and new forms of media and culture.

## The Blair government

How does the Blair government relate to this legacy? Three views are considered here, each of them with a certain plausibility.

## Thatcherism

The first is that the Blair government is the continuation of Thatcherism by other means, or at times the same means (Hay 1999; Heffernan 2001). The transformation of the Labour Party, which began under the leadership of Neil Kinnock and was consummated under Tony Blair, is said to have shifted the party away from social democracy towards neo-liberalism. Labour adopted a neo-liberal policy agenda, choosing to work within the constraints it inherited rather than challenge them. It also adopted an authoritarian, centralist style in the way it governed, repressing internal dissent, and running the Labour Party and subsequently the government through a small circle around the leader. This personal style of government was highly reminiscent of Margaret Thatcher, but Blair has taken it even further than she managed to do, sidelining the Cabinet,

Parliament and the party, and giving enormous prominence instead to media management (Hennessy 2005a, b).

In support of this argument there is the evidence that the Labour government since 1997 has not challenged the four key radical changes associated with the Thatcher government – privatisation, union power, taxation and deregulation. Labour has not brought any of the major industries denationalised by the Conservatives back into public ownership; it has made few changes to Conservative trade union laws; it has cut the level of basic-rate and retained higher-rate income tax; and it has maintained much of the deregulated, flexible economy bequeathed by the Conservatives; in particular it has not made any moves to reintroduce protectionism or to limit the openness of the British economy, and it has made financial stability the key goal of its macroeconomic policy (Coates 2005). Critics also point to the fact that inequality has continued to widen under Labour, although more slowly than under the Conservatives (Toynbee and Walker 2005).

### The 'Third Way'

The second view is that New Labour is a genuinely new political phenomenon, a 'Third Way' between free-market conservatism on the one hand, and national protectionist socialism on the other (Driver and Martell 2002; Giddens 1998, 2000). New Labour, by embracing both economic efficiency and social justice, has transcended the old ideological debates and created a new electoral base and policy programme for the left (Mandelson and Liddle 2002). From this standpoint Thatcherism is part of the old politics along with the social democracy of Wilson and Callaghan. It demolished a great deal, but was less successful in building the kind of social and economic order that commanded broad legitimacy. By combining an acceptance of markets with the idea of an active, enabling state, New Labour created a sense of purpose and direction which the Conservatives under John Major no longer seemed to possess, and in this way has become the true ideological architect of the post-industrial era in British politics.

In support of this argument there is the evidence of the constitutional-reform programme on which Labour embarked, which introduced some long-term permanent changes in the way Britain is governed, in particular the measures on devolution and the incorporation of the European Convention on Human Rights into British law, together with the new voting systems for elections outside Westminster; steps towards freedom of information and reform of the House of Lords, and the proposed setting up of a Supreme Court, amongst other measures (Bogdanor 2001; Evans 2003; Hazell 2001). The government also adopted a social justice agenda (White 2002), different in scope and character from anything previously attempted in British politics, centred around the establishment of a minimum wage; tax credits and other measures to tackle pensioner poverty and child poverty; new commitments on global poverty; as well as renewed emphasis on universalism, including the introduction of the first new universal benefit for 50 years, the child trust fund (Kelly and Lissauer 2000; Paxton 2003). This social justice agenda was combined with an emphasis on a vigorous supply-side economic strategy, involving competition, economic efficiency, promotion of the knowledge economy, and entrepreneurship.

## New Labour as Old Labour

A third view is that the Blair government in practice has been neither neo-liberal nor ideologically innovative, but bears more than a passing resemblance to Old Labour (Fielding 2003). Despite its rhetoric and its commitments not to raise taxes and to govern prudently, it has in fact been a classic tax-and-spend government, indeed the most successful tax-and-spend government Labour has ever produced, since in its first eight years there was continuous economic growth, no fiscal crisis, and after the first two years of spending restraint, continuous growth in spending on core public-sector programmes, with the result that spending on the NHS in real terms was planned to double under Labour by 2008 (Alcock 2003). This programme was not funded by any increase in income tax or VAT, but instead through a variety of taxes, including National Insurance, windfall levies on the privatised utilities, stamp duties on house purchase, and levies on pension funds, which the Conservatives called stealth taxes. Under Labour the proportion of taxation to GDP rose by five points to 42 per cent, a remarkable achievement in a period of growth, and one that was accomplished without any adverse reaction from the financial markets. The central thrust of the economic policy of the government, and the redistributive aims of its anti-poverty policy, appeared to underline its continuity with past Labour governments. Similarly its economic policy, despite the rhetoric which has often accompanied it, has been described as essentially Keynesian in its handling of the business cycle and its adoption of counter-cyclical measures to smooth out the cycle (Clift and Tomlinson 2006).

## Neo-liberalism

In assessing these different views it is important to remember that in the present era of the global economy all governments are 'neo-liberal' governments in the sense that the constraints within which they operate are set by economic and political forces outside the control of any one of them (Krieger 1999; Robison 2006). Attempts by governments to challenge or disregard those constraints have not been successful, and have led to policy adjustments. Within those constraints, however, governments have often found that they have the freedom to pursue a wide range of policies, just as they did under previous international regimes. It is the constraints and the way they impinge on national governments that have altered, brought about through the changes in the world economy in the 1970s and 1980s, particularly the huge changes in occupation, production and consumption associated with the decline of manufacturing and the rise of services (Castells 2000).

From this perspective, during the transformation of the Labour Party between 1983 and 1997 the party was forced to come to terms with these external changes as well as with the task of responding to Thatcherism and finding a viable electoral strategy. These pressures gradually pushed the party away from unilateralism in defence and from national protectionism in economic policy, and towards the rediscovery of some older traditions in the party, emphasising social justice and decentralisation. What did not occur was any simple embrace by the party leadership of neo-liberal ideas. Many in Labour's ranks were on the contrary attempting to provide a new version of social democracy (Lawson and Sherlock 2001), hence the flirtation with a number of different ideas, including stakeholding, the 'Third Way', the social-investment state, new social democracy, and the progressive consensus.

Specific neo-liberal ideas were important components of the ideological mix which produced some of the ideas of the 1990s. In particular they were decisive in the critique of national protectionism and state planning which brought about a more positive evaluation of markets, and of the role of markets and competition in generating prosperity, than in most previous social-democratic thought. This was a big shift, although already prefigured in some of the currents in the short-lived Social Democratic Party (SDP), particularly those associated with David Owen, former Labour Foreign Secretary and leader of the SDP between 1983 and 1990 (Owen 1981, 1984). What disappeared from Labour Party thinking about the economy were the old notions that social democracy was fundamentally opposed to market capitalism, and that the task of social-democratic governments was to moderate and constrain the effect of market forces. Similarly although New Labour remained committed to public funding of public services it was less committed to the interests of producers, and increasingly pressed the case for private providers, quasi-markets, accountability and choice.

New Labour thinking also drew on older socialist traditions to make state action legitimate again. The Thatcher government had started from the position that public spending was at the heart of Britain's difficulties, and that in principle state action should be a last resort, only after every possible solution using the private sector had been explored first. Labour tried to find ways to reinstate the importance of the public sector. To do this it drew heavily on ideas of social justice, redistribution, and the creation of an active state which could reassert a public interest (Commission on Social Justice 1994). The party also drew upon the decentralist tradition of pluralism and suspicion of the state which had been eclipsed by the rise of a collectivism emphasising centralisation and state planning (Hirst 1994).

It was not only the tradition of state planning and state collectivism which came to be repudiated in the 1990s. Still more crucial was the Labourist tradition and the corporatism which was associated with it. The original Labour coalition was formed between various kinds of socialists and trade unions who guarded their independence from the state jealously. The inability of the Labour coalition to resolve these deep differences was ultimately to lead to the failure of Labour governments in the 1960s and 1970s to acquire a reputation for economic competence (Coates 1980) and to forge lasting corporatist institutions on the Scandinavian model. The weakening of the unions during the 1980s made possible the emergence of a different type of social democracy in Britain, one familiar from experience elsewhere in Europe, but which had never been very successful in Britain because of the dependence of the Labour Party on the trade unions.

## Ideological alternatives

The emergence of first Thatcherism and then New Labour has for many commentators made the British ideological landscape very flat. History for them ended when the Berlin Wall came down, and neo-liberalism became the universally accepted and unchallenged ideology. There is some evidence for this. The similarity of the platforms of the three main parties fighting the UK elections in 2005 was much remarked. When the car company, MG Rover, went into receivership during the campaign, all three parties quickly ruled out any kind of state intervention to help it. This was a matter best left to the market. Commentators remarked on the absence of big ideas or big visions, and on the managerial character of many of the issues that were discussed. The choice appeared to have narrowed to who was trusted the most to deliver and improve public services (Crouch 2004).

None of this is particularly new. Complaints about the similarity of the parties were being regularly voiced in the 1950s. The 1970s and 1980s were a period of much greater ideological polarisation, but they look atypical now. Yet the consensus after 1945 was a coincidence of policies rather than a coincidence of underlying beliefs and values, and the very term 'consensus' to describe it has been challenged (Kerr 2001). Although differences remain, the consensus on such fundamentals as the market economy, the size of the public sector, and the role of the state appears much stronger now than it did in the 1950s.

Is the current ideological convergence likely to persist, or will ideological polarisation arise again in the future? One problem in deciding this question is that some part of the ideological polarisation arises from the nature of the electoral system and party competition, which obliges all parties to compete on ever narrower ground. This does not mean, however, that ideological traditions are exhausted. The ideological map is as varied as ever, which holds the possibility of renewal for any of the major traditions. This is apparent just from reading through all the manifestos for the 2005 general election – many of the minor parties, such as the Green Party, Respect, UKIP, Veritas, Plaid Cymru and the SNP display a range of ideological argument which is missing from the documents of the main parties. The wealth of ideas from the various think tanks like IPPR, Demos, the Fabians, the Social Market Foundation, the IEA, Civitas, and the Centre for Policy Studies, as well as the highly varied population of pressure groups and single-issue campaign groups also indicates that there is still an ideological ferment going on beneath the rather bland technocratic surface of British politics.

### Left of centre

On the left, the advent of New Labour completed the transformation of British social democracy into something closer to European social democracy, following the weakening and marginalising of the Labourist tradition. Both Labourist and old-left traditions have remained, however. The Respect party, which originated in protest against the Iraq war, developed as a coalition between the Socialist Workers Party (SWP) and radical Islamists, with George Galloway as its charismatic figurehead. It offered a heady mix of old Bennite policies on the economy, ultra-leftism, and anti-liberal communalism. Its manifesto promised renationalisation of all the industries denationalised since 1979 and major redistribution of income and wealth through much higher taxes on individuals and companies, as well as the disbanding of the British armed forces, the dismantling of British arms industries, and the repeal of all anti-terrorism legislation. The SWP seeks to use Respect as a vehicle for winning disaffected young Muslims to revolutionary politics through a platform of opposition to Western intervention in the Middle East, attacks on the police and anti-terrorism legislation, and support for the Sunni insurgency in Iraq. Many radical Muslim groups, however, such as Hizb-ut-Tahrir (considered for banning by the British government after the London bombings), have attacked Respect as a diversion for Muslims, and denounce any participation in electoral politics.

On the mainstream left, opposition to New Labour has likewise been fuelled by the Iraq war and also by those who sought a much bolder politics of reform to transform Britain into a European social democracy (Coates and Krieger 2004; Kampfner 2003). New organisations like Compass advocated the scrapping of the targets culture, new respect for public-sector professionals, the protection of the public sector from the encroachment of the private sector, combined with more radical measures to redistribute wealth and income, restore trade union rights, tackle poverty and complete constitutional reform. In this way it was argued New Labour could be replaced by real Labour, and a politics of principled social democracy be reborn. The key dilemma of social-democratic politics remained, however – how to drive up standards in the public services to persuade middle-income earners to continue to use them and be prepared to be taxed highly enough to fund them. Many social democrats rejected competition and the market, but they rejected the managerial controls of the new public management, too. There was also an unresolved tension between local autonomy and universal provision.

Many of the radical ideas on the left in recent times have come from the Green movement and the anti-globalisation movement. These are the inheritors of radical grassroots politics, from which Labour has become increasingly distant. At the heart of this politics is a strong suspicion of the state, and a desire to find solutions outside the state rather than through the state. There is support for local associations and local communities, and the principles of cooperation, solidarity and voluntarism, which were so important in the early history of the Labour movement (Wright 1996). As a result these movements tend to be anti-market, anti-corporate power, and anti-bureaucracy. In the case of the Greens they are also strongly anti-economic growth, and campaign against genetically modified (GM) crops, pollution and climate change, arguing that strong regulation should be imposed to change economic behaviour that is destroying the planet (Monbiot 2004). Accompanying this are arguments for redistribution, for fair trade, and for citizens' income, to provide everyone with a basic living standard. The Greens are strongly opposed to the present consensus on economic policy, since they believe in the idea of a local, sustainable economy which can provide economic security for its citizens. This would require a revolution in current economic arrangements, since the Greens are strongly opposed to free trade, multinational companies, financial markets, and the way the global economy is organised (Lucas and Woodin 2004). Few of these ideas were discussed in the 2005 general election campaign, but they certainly provide a radical alternative to the present consensus between the main parties.

This consensus currently extends to the Liberal Democrat Party, which since the 1960s has moved strongly towards social democracy, abandoning its old free-trade and laissez-faire tradition. Alongside its support for universal welfare the party also favoured radical decentralisation, communitarianism and economic democracy. Reconciling some of these ideas was never easy, but the party was at least a constant source of alternative thinking about the economy, and the only party that took seriously the radical thinking of economists like James Meade on how to combine social justice and economic efficiency (Meade 1964). The current direction of the party has been away from such radicalism, and towards the embracing of current orthodoxies, particularly on the management of the economy. At the 2005 election the party retained a distinctive position on fair taxation, expressed through its commitment to a 50-per-cent rate of income tax for higher earners, and a local income tax. This was combined, however, with spending commitments, such as abolishing university tuition fees, whose main effect would be to restore subsidies to upper- and middle-income groups. The party appeared likely after 2005 to move away from its fair-taxation commitments, however, moving on to the same ground as that held by Labour and the Conservatives. There were few signs of the radical economic thinking the party had once been famed for – it even proposed to scrap the child trust funds established by New Labour, a policy which the old Liberal Party would have championed. Where the Liberal Democrats did remain distinctive from the two other parties was in their strong support for civil liberties and their (qualified) opposition to overseas military interventions.

## Right of centre

On the right of the political spectrum the ascendancy of New Labour has been disorienting, and all parts of the right have struggled. The Conservatives as the umbrella catch-all party of the right have been plunged into turmoil over their identity and purpose, and have been constantly on the back foot against Labour since 1992. The agenda has been reshaped by Labour so that by the 2001 election, and repeated in 2005, the Conservatives fought the election endorsing the higher spending, and implicitly higher taxation plans, of the Labour government. The party kept proclaiming itself a low-tax party but could not find a convincing way of reconciling that aspiration with the evident desire of the electorate for increased investment in public services. Since the party was not prepared to advocate a big increase in private provision of health and education it was limited in what it could propose by way of tax cuts. It therefore became imprisoned on ground Labour had staked out, and tried to differentiate itself by promising a more effective war on waste, and better management of public services.

The most important developments on the right, however, were not on the traditional battlegrounds of tax and spend, and economic management, but on the more nebulous but increasingly powerful terrain of identity politics. The battles between modernisers and traditionalists in the Conservative Party over issues such as gay rights and the treatment of immigrants and asylum seekers were one sign of this. Another was the rapid growth of new organisations and campaigns on the right. These included the fuel-tax protests, the Countryside Alliance, the Christian Alliance and many more. New right-wing parties, like UKIP, and its shortlived breakaway, Veritas, appeared to signal the potential for a populist politics of the right aimed at targets like the European Union, crime and immigration. New right-wing pressure groups such as Migration Watch emerged.

Conservative strategy kept shifting between stressing the need to attract younger, urban voters, by repositioning the party on the centre ground, and reassuring its core vote, through messages which were anti-Europe, anti-crime, and anti-immigration. It was often caught in inconsistencies as a result. Its proposals in the 2005 general election for sharply reducing the entry of economic migrants conflicted sharply with its policy of supporting flexible labour markets, as the CBI rather brutally pointed out. Similarly its policy of voting against the government's scheme to charge university tuition fees was roundly condemned in several Conservative papers as a betrayal of the Conservative aim of giving the universities more autonomy and setting them free from dependence on the public purse. The Conservative political dilemma lies in modernising its appeal while at the same time retaining its core vote. David Cameron, elected Conservative leader in December 2005, has, however, made it clear that he intends to change policy to radically modernise the party in the hope of dramatically expanding its political base. To this end, copying the style of firm, authoritative leadership coined by Tony Blair (and designed by Margaret Thatcher) Cameron has set in train a far-reaching policy review, one in which he intends unpopular policy commitments to be abandoned, which he hopes will firmly situate the Conservatives on the political centre ground and help secure a significant advance at the next general election.

## Blairism without Blair

Labour's success in securing its first ever third full term of government was overshadowed by its declining share of the popular vote and its reduced majority, and also by the announcement by Tony Blair that he would step down before the next election. The Labour Party and the rest of the political class entered the new Parliament knowing that by the end of it there would be a different Labour prime minister. This being so it is possible to speculate on whether Blairism and the Labour ascendancy will end with Blair. There are at least four possibilities.

### Scenario 1: Business as usual

The first is that the Blair government proves to be a unique but also a transient phenomenon; unique because of its three consecutive election victories, and for the ascendancy which Labour established over the Conservatives in this period, but transient because the condition for its existence is Tony Blair himself, or perhaps more accurately the partnership between Tony Blair and Gordon Brown. At the 2004 Labour Party conference Bono, lead singer of U2 and prominent in the Make Poverty History campaign, likened Blair and Brown rather improbably to Lennon and McCartney (he did not reveal who he thought was who). However difficult and destructive at times, this partnership will undoubtedly be seen as one of the most important factors in the government's success (Naughtie 2002; Rawnsley 2001; Rentoul 2001; Seldon 2005), combined with the propitious economic circumstances which allowed Labour to achieve and sustain a reputation for economic competence. Blair's extraordinary ability to occupy a centre-right position while leading a centre-left government, and constantly to be governing against his party rather than with it or through it, was an essential part of New Labour's success in colonising so much of the ground which the Conservatives had always taken for granted was theirs. It was a strategy, however, which came badly unstuck over Iraq, partly because Blair became detached not just from opinion in his own party and on the centre left but from a large body of opinion on the centre right as well (Kampfner 2004).

It follows that Blair's disappearance from the scene removes the one politician capable of performing this particular high-wire act. With Blair gone, a Gordon Brown premiership will signal the return to a more normal two-party politics, in which the differences between the neo-liberal views of the right and the social-democratic views of the left will become more marked again, and the old economic battleground will acquire more salience. Labour will be under strong pressure from many of its members, MPs and trade unions to become real Labour, and reassure its core vote by a mixture of symbolic gestures and practical measures that signal that the Blair era is definitely over. This may re-energise the Labour movement, and reconnect the party to many of its disaffected members. But in doing so the particular magic of the Blair government will be lost, and a major opening will be provided for the Conservatives to move back onto the ground which Labour is vacating (such as the agenda of choice and efficiency in the public services) and to renew its appeal to those parts of middle England which have deserted it since 1992. Once the Conservative vote begins to revive the Liberal Democrats may see a large drop in their share of the vote unless they are prepared to move quite sharply to the right. Conservative electoral victories would still not be assured by this, but they would become more likely. Some supporters of Gordon Brown think that any losses in support for the Conservatives would be more than made up by the return of lost Labour voters to the party. The problem for Brown, however, will be finding a way to avoid disappointing that part of the electorate and Labour Party membership which is traditionally Labour, whose expectations about a Brown premiership are already very high, and at the same time still being reassuring to the much larger part of the electorate that does not identify with the Labour Party or its values. Brown has the skills to make the party feel better about itself, but his challenge will be demonstrating that under him Labour can still appeal to non-Labour Britain.

## Scenario 2: Progressive consensus

A second scenario is that the Blair government leaves behind it the foundations for a progressive consensus (Diamond and Giddens 2005), what some on the right call disparagingly the Canadianisation of British politics. This scenario suggests that as in Canada the British electorate may now have a permanent progressive majority, which long predates the Blair government, but which the Blair government has reinforced. At the 2005 election, 64 per cent of votes went to left-of-centre parties. The right fears that ways will be found to translate this advantage into a permanent left-of-centre control of government, since the alternative is the return of a Conservative government which might once more be tempted to enact radical right policies which the majority of the electorate rejects. Such institutionalisation of the progressive consensus would require the introduction of some form of proportional representation (PR) at Westminster. PR would draw the Liberal Democrats into coalition with Labour as has already happened in Scotland. This progressive coalition, which might be in office for a very considerable time, would re-engage with the European Union, and gradually transform Britain in every respect into a more normal European country, with the kind of enhanced welfare regime, reduced defence capability, non-interventionist foreign policy, and protected civil liberties characteristic of the European core.

The chances of this happening do not seem high, however, because so much of the Labour Party is firmly opposed to any change that would oblige the party to work with the Liberal Democrats. There is a stronger possibility that a Gordon Brown government might introduce electoral reform in the form of the Alternative Vote or some variant of it. This would not make seats proportional to votes, but it would ensure that in every constituency the winning candidate was elected by a majority of the votes cast through the redistribution of second preferences. The likeliest condition for this scenario to be realised remains the election of a hung Parliament, in which no party commands an overall majority. In this situation Labour and the Liberal Democrats might agree to form a coalition. Otherwise the strong resistance in the Labour Party to cooperation with the Liberal Democrats seems likely to scupper any attempts to move to PR. Despite the 2005 election result being once again grossly disproportional, allowing Labour to win a 66-seat majority with only 35 per cent of the vote, there was little evidence that many voters were concerned about it, or felt outraged. Only the *Independent* newspaper launched a campaign over the issue. The traditional unwillingness of the Conservatives to consider PR, because of their fear that it would entrench permanent Labour–Liberal Democrat coalition government, presently blunts the pressure for reform. If PR does come about therefore, and with it the institutionalisation of a progressive consensus, it will probably be as a result of a particular set of contingencies, and the ability of the Liberal Democrats to exact it as the price for keeping a minority Labour government in office.

## Scenario 3: Implosion

The third scenario is that the Blair government will run out of luck and out of money. Whether this happens before or after Blair leaves office is not of great significance, since the main casualty whenever it happens will be the reputation of Gordon Brown for economic competence. The main assumption of this scenario is that a fiscal crisis of a very familiar kind is brewing. The warnings from the International Monetary Fund (IMF) and the Institute for Fiscal Studies (IFS) in the 2005 general election campaign, and the kind of analyses of the coming global meltdown in sections of the financial press, point to serious internal problems in funding Labour's ambitious programme of rising public spending without substantial tax increases. The position may well be exacerbated by negative external changes in the global economy which some analysts foresee – a major US recession, and a continuing rise in the oil price, leading to much slower or even negative growth in Europe. In these circumstances Labour might lose its precious reputation for economic competence, being forced to choose, like all Labour governments before it, between increasing taxation or cutting spending, and losing popular support and credibility as a result.

In such circumstances of economic crisis and the discrediting of the government the Conservatives might not need the modernisers' strategy of making themselves attractive once again to the voters won over by Tony Blair to enter Labour's Big Tent. Instead a new aggressive tax-cutting, anti-immigration, anti-Europe agenda might do the trick. Some of the techniques pioneered in the 2005 election by Lynton Crosby, the Australian strategist recruited by Conservative Central Office, might return with extra force, and the Conservatives could once again push their vote towards 40 per cent, and win a parliamentary majority under the disproportional electoral system.

Cracking Labour's reputation for economic competence is certainly a prerequisite for a Conservative revival, but many Conservatives warn that it will not be enough on its own. They think the party must change its image in a much more profound way before it will be trusted again by the electorate. The efforts of the modernising wing are devoted to getting the Conservative Party to embrace modern Britain and identify with its diversity and pluralism, rather than appearing to condemn it. But despite these differences all wings of the party are tending to converge on a political programme which emphasises the end of centralised public services, new experiments to encourage greater diversity of provision through competition, while reassuring the electorate that the party will maintain the universal and state-funded character of certain services, particularly health and education (Carswell et al. 2005).

While the Conservatives fear Canadianisation of British politics, some on the left fear Australianisation – the return of a Conservative Party to government which then faces a demoralised and hollowed-out Labour Party, which has no basis of principle on which to oppose the development of the choice agenda in the public services, and lacks the means to recover as a coherent political force after the loss of morale and members under Blair. Much depends here on the kind of leadership Gordon Brown provides to Labour, and whether he is able to chart a new direction and find a convincing narrative for the party. If the government were to be overwhelmed by an economic storm, however, it might take a very long time for its credibility to be rebuilt, as the Conservatives themselves have painfully discovered.

## Scenario 4: Continuity

A fourth scenario is more pessimistic than any of the above for the health of British democracy. It regards British politics, in common with politics in many other established democracies, as having moved into a phase of anti-politics (Crouch 2004). In this scenario the negative aspects of Tony Blair's style of politics would be perpetuated. Politics would continue to be ideology-lite, technocratic and managerial whoever was in office. Media politics would become ever more dominant, and the corrosive effect of modern media upon the political process, and upon the character and behaviour of politicians, would intensify. The trivialisation of politics, and the rise of the political as spectacle, would make elections revolve around personal qualities of politicians, and lead to an endless succession of leaders able to project themselves as celebrities. The disaffection of increasing numbers of voters from this process, their cynicism encouraged by the media's own attitude towards politics and politicians, would lead to the elevation of lobby politics and court politics, and the effective disenfranchisement of most of the electorate, particularly the urban poor. If this is indeed the direction in which British politics is headed, the Blair years may come to be regarded as an important staging post towards it.

The trends towards the boosting of the role of the prime minister in British government have existed at least since Lloyd George. They are part of the era of the extended state. But the effect of modern media and the requirements of fighting elections have made them more intense. The full impact of this style of politics can be seen in the United States, where the emphasis upon personality and negative campaigning, and the disregard of substantive policies, is most marked. Despite the nostalgia for cabinet government and for Parliament as well as for political parties, it is hard to see any future leader of either the Conservatives or Labour being able to give up the increasingly prominent type of role which Thatcher, Major and Blair have played (Heffernan 2005a). Some of the innovations introduced under Blair's premiership, such as the monthly press conferences or the increased size of the Downing Street operation, are hardly likely to be changed. No prime minister can afford not to be accessible to the media, or to dispense with the strategic capability which a larger staff in Downing Street provides. Since the media increasingly expect the prime minister to be responsible for everything that happens in the government, prime ministers react by seeking extra levers to exert some control.

## Conclusion

The future of British politics may well contain something from each of these scenarios, and there will doubtless be something unexpected. The rejection of the European Constitutional Treaty by France and the Netherlands in June 2005 and the London bombings in July 2005 changed the political mood in the UK, and for a time boosted once again the popularity of the government and of Tony Blair, and made an early handover to Gordon Brown less likely.

But whatever the impact of events and whichever of the scenarios sketched above turns out to be closest to the reality, British politics after Blair will also be shaped by the way in which certain deep-seated dilemmas in British politics are resolved, or in many cases not resolved. These include the new challenges which terrorism poses after the London bombings, and how they are best handled. The debate about British national identity and multiculturalism now takes place in a new context, as does the debate on civil liberties. The advance of the security state in response to the terrorist outrages has acquired a new momentum.

After security the biggest domestic policy issue confronting British politicians after Blair is the dilemma over how to reform the welfare state. All parties are moving against the centralist model of the last 60 years, and in favour of experimenting with localist solutions, involving greater autonomy for producers and greater accountability to users of the services through the empowerment of patients and parents, for example. Getting the balance right between a central framework of common standards and rules, and local initiative, choice and autonomy is what all parties now aspire to, but find very hard to achieve in practice. This is because of the inherent complexity of many of the issues, and the incompatibility of some of the objectives which politicians proclaim. The rhetoric from all sides against the centralist state is getting louder but what is not clear is that any party when entrusted with office will actually be bold enough seriously to dismantle the centralist institutions of welfare and public services and install a new localist dynamic. British centralism is under great pressure, but still has formidable powers of resistance and inertia on which it can draw.

A final crucial dilemma concerns Britain's relationship with the European Union and with the United States. The Conservatives increasingly link their new localism with their hostility to the EU, and demand the repatriation of powers to Britain which if followed through would lead to the withdrawal of Britain from the EU (Carswell et al. 2005). The Conservatives seek detachment from Europe and affirmation and consolidation of the links binding Britain to the United States, and to the wider Anglosphere of English-speaking nations (Bennett 2004). British identity is to be found in the cultural and ideological associations of the Anglo-American civilisation with its distinctive view of world order, model of capitalism, and foreign policy. This vision of Britain's future is quite distinct from the view which has its adherents on both right and left and which sees Britain's links with Europe as the priority for its future, and building Britain as a normal European society playing a full part in the

European Union. Tony Blair's way of resolving this dilemma has been to speak of Britain as a bridge between Europe and America, which removes the need to choose either as the priority. But over Iraq the bridge was stretched so thin that it snapped. Finding a way to reconcile Britain's relations with Europe and with America remains elusive.

## Chapter 17

# The Westminster Model and the Distinctiveness of British Politics

PATRICK DUNLEAVY

Around a century and a half ago, it became clear to British commentators that most other liberal constitutional regimes in the world (and not just the United States) would organise their political affairs on different lines from ours. Since then discussion of UK politics has been dominated by a specifically British version of pluralist thought, the Westminster model (Bagehot 1867). It still exercises a very strong grip on how political, administrative and judicial leaders interpret political life:

> The model is an element of the British political tradition which sees governing as a process conducted by a closed elite, constrained by an ethos of integrity with concern for the public good and contained within the framework of a balanced and self-adjusting constitution. (Richards and Smith 2001, 146; see also Tant 1993)

In political science too the Westminster model has dominated accounts of specifically British politics, explaining the unique and apparently unfinished, risky or plain unfair features of the UK's 'unfixed' constitution. Westminster-model exponents often seem to justify these features as well, either on normative grounds (the system is desirable and works well) or on prudential/pragmatic grounds (the system is deep-rooted, works OK and is now too embedded, resilient or costly to alter). At root both the political elite and the academic versions of the model also argue that an underlying stability of political life, combined with the liveliness and apparent dynamism of British public policy, validate the UK's exceptionalist arrangements and institutions. While some problems of course periodically occur, they can be successfully managed or resolved within the accommodating frame of the 'legacy' constitutional doctrines.

Despite the Conservatives' political domination of the twentieth century (when they were in power four fifths of the time), and despite what Marquand (1997, 44) calls a 'constitutional system permeated with monarchical values', the Westminster model has been a surprisingly inclusive approach. Both it and the emergent political science discipline easily accommodated the labour movement's 'collectivist' push from the 1920s to the 1960s (Kavanagh 2003). Successive Labour leaderships were persuaded to leave all the constitution's key elements untouched and to capitalise on the concentrations of power created, so as to implement their own programmes (Harrison 1996). 'Labour politicians have been conditioned, as much as Conservatives, by the Westminster model' (Richards and Smith 2001, 44).

However, this once-dominant intellectual position has now come under severe and unprecedented strain. Popular support for historic arrangements has begun to ebb away in a fashion that has become increasingly hard for their defenders to ignore or deny. Partly as a result of this shift, Westminster-model institutions are increasingly forced to live alongside and compete with new or reformed institutions, founded on a more rationalist constitutional pattern. There are few signs that Westminster-model arrangements are winning out in this period of 'coexistence'. The drift away from them was very rapid from 1997 to 2001 and still continues now, albeit at a slower rate.

To map current debates about the distinctiveness of British politics I first briefly review the Westminster model's core propositions and examine how its exponents have reacted to recent developments. The second section looks at a reformist counter-model that has grown in strength over the last 15 years, calling for the UK to become a more standard-pattern, liberal pluralist state, with a well thought-through and stable constitution. Both the Westminster and reformist positions are liberal views that ascribe strong significance to national constitutional arrangements and formal politics. In the third section I review some positions that deny much relevance to these debates. One stream argues simply that the minutiae of UK politics matter less and less, since power has migrated to other levels, tiers and modes of government at the European, international or global levels. A partly overlapping postmodern stream argues that power has diffused into more complex and pervasive governance networks, channels and processes spread across society, so that 'politics' is no longer hegemonic.

## The Westminster model under pressure

Table 17.1 traces how the Westminster model builds up from plurality-rule elections via strongly nationalised parties to the creation of artificial Commons majorities. From there follow strong, single-party governments, executive dominance of the legislature and Whitehall dominating

**Figure 17.1** *How different groups of UK political scientists view the current applicability and desirability of the Westminster model*

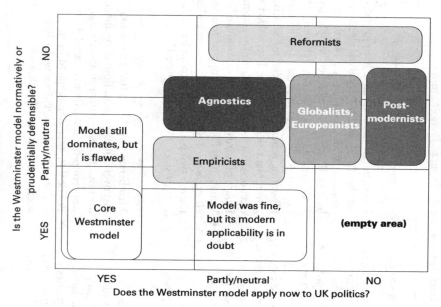

the UK administrative landscape in a closed and elite fashion. However, the table also shows key developments away from the model in the last decade, including the introduction of new voting systems; a fragmentation of popular votes across more parties in PR elections; devolution of powers to constituent nations and to a strong London mayor; more coalition government in all these devolved bodies; some new 'separation of powers' institutions in London; and many measures limiting parliamentary sovereignty and executive discretion, such as the Human Rights Act, freedom of information and the creation of a new Supreme Court. None of these rapid and recent changes seems to fit easily within the Westminster-model orthodoxy.

Political scientists writing on British politics now take a wide range of positions on the Westminster model, shown in summary form in Figure 17.1. The horizontal axis asks whether the model still applies empirically in British politics. An orthodox core group (shown bottom left) still believe that the model fits closely with the key political processes. More radical critics (shown on the right of the figure) deny that the model has much applicability, except as a set of masking elite excuses for exercising power in a fashion that is inadequately controlled. A substantial group of authors takes an intermediate position, arguing

Table 17.1   *The main elements of the Westminster model and the impact of recent changes*

| Element | Conventional Westminster-model arrangements | Developments away from the model |
|---|---|---|
| **Voting and elections** | • All MPs (and local councillors also) are elected in single-member districts using the plurality-rule system (where the top candidate wins, whether they have majority support or not). <br>• Strong nationalised parties compete nationwide on the same issues. <br>• Artificial parliamentary majorities are created for Labour or Conservatives (usually as a result of strong 'leader's bias' for the top party). Around 20–25% of seats go to parties not entitled to them in terms of their national vote share. <br>• Voters in plurality-rule elections are differentially likely to support the top two parties (Labour and Conservative). | • Proportional elections have been introduced for electing MEPs and for devolved elections in Scotland, Wales, London and Northern Ireland. The multi-preference 'Supplementary Vote' method vote is used for choosing the London Mayor and ten other elected mayors. PR voting is being introduced for Scottish local government elections and is likely also for elections to a Second Chamber (or reformed House of Lords) if these are introduced. <br>• Voters in all PR elections support five or six effective parties. Fewer electors are endorsing the top two parties and turnout has fallen sharply since 1992 (see Figure 17.2). |
| **Political parties** | • In the early post-war period, both the Conservatives and Labour still counted as 'mass parties' and had a complex, 'legacy' machinery for policy making and guidance. <br>• They adapted to become 'catch-all' parties and grass-roots influence declined. But, to compensate, leaders are now initially elected by a wider | • Membership in the top two parties has fallen to just over 200,000 each. Both party machines are now professionally run and strongly leadership-dominated on a 'cartel party' model. <br>• Political finance is dominated by major donors and state subsidies. Parties wider links to civil society are now very weak. |

- Increasingly, salient issues lie outside the top two party differences, on other dimensions completely.

base of members. The importance of internal party processes has declined and mass media influence has increased.

- Labour vs Conservative differences encompassed most of the key issues in a restricted 'feasible' spectrum of ideological differences.

- A separated executive and legislature has been set up in London, with a directly elected mayor and PR Assembly.
- Coalition government is the norm there and in devolved institutions in Scotland and Northern Ireland, and occurs in Wales.
- Lords reform has removed hereditary peers and even the all-appointed House has flexed its legislative muscles more. Full reform could further boost its role.
- 'Modernisation' of the Commons has petered out, although Select Committee chairs are now paid and the PM meets the Liaison Committee made up of these chairs every six months.

**Government formation and legislative scrutiny**

- The government is formed out of the legislature on the normal parliamentary model, so that there is no separation of powers between legislature and executive.
- Single-party governments with artificial majorities in the Commons predominate, plus rare hung Parliaments, but there are no coalition governments.
- The unelected Lords has weak powers so there is no meaningful bicameralism.
- There is no significant legislative budgeting in the UK and the largest party's MPs are heavily 'whipped' by the government to deliver 97% of laws unamended.
- Parliamentary oversight works only via Question Time and ritualised opposition in the Commons; backbench rebellions in the majority party; Select Committees scrutinising departments and agencies; parliamentary audit; and the Lords' revising role.

**Table 17.1** *(cont.)*

| Element | Conventional Westminster-model arrangements | Developments away from the model |
|---|---|---|
| **Core-executive structure and top policy making** | • The leader of the largest party becomes PM and appoints the cabinet. The government is 'collectively responsible' for major policy. The PM's media and policy aides exercise tight control of government communications.<br>• Cabinet committees balance out the views of major departments and factions in the majority party but there are no other checks and balances.<br>• The PM dominates foreign policy and 'war/peace' issues and has sway on strategic economic policy (with the Chancellor). PMs can pull in other key issues and use cabinet appointments, rationing scarce legislative time and No. 10 units to enhance their influence elsewhere. | • PM and cabinet ministers often leak or spin against each other via aides.<br>• Critics allege the 'presidentialisation' of policy making, with the PM resolving issues in bilaterals and practising 'sofa government'. |
| **Medium-scale policy making** | • Ministerial responsibility for their department ensures their answerability for key decisions and enhances their power vis-à-vis the civil service. Special advisors add to ministers' capabilities.<br>• The civil service is mainly concerned with | • Ministerial resignations are important for scandals and personal issues. But PMs dump ministers only where doing so tends to boost overall government popularity.<br>• Independent agencies (such as the Bank of England and economic regulators) have |

| | | |
|---|---|---|
| | • service delivery, maintaining the machine, and constitutional propriety.<br>• Policy making is conducted in secret and within a small elite-level community run in 'clubs'. | • increased their roles.<br>• From 2005 freedom of information provisions have been implemented, albeit in a restrictive form. |
| **Allocation of functions and powers within the state apparatus as a whole** | • The UK is highly centralised with much policy on a nationwide scale, covering 60 million people. Ministers and civil servants can pull in issues for central decision and have tended to involve themselves more in local and NHS issues, as other functions drift to EU level.<br>• Local government is relatively weak, with low voting turnout and councils dependent on central finance. | • Devolution to Scotland, Wales and London has removed some issues completely from Westminster. (Northern Ireland remains more problematic.)<br>• The upward transfer of functions to the EU means that in certain policy areas up to 70% of new regulations applying in the UK originate from Brussels. |
| **Key constitutional principles** | • Parliamentary sovereignty means that a government with a Commons majority has a largely unfettered capability to change the constitution, subject only to Lords delays for a year.<br>• Governments can change the law easily to evade judicial control – even retrospectively.<br>• Judges accept that the executive should have discretion and that parliamentary sovereignty limits their role. | • Devolution is de facto irreversible now, while EU membership has created treaty obligations very hard to change, including overview by the European Court of Justice.<br>• The Human Rights Act 1998 also limits parliamentary competence, although its provisions can be and have been suspended again.<br>• In 2004 the government moved to create a Supreme Court and a full separation of the executive and judiciary, removing the Law Lords from the House of Lords. But the change has encountered some judicial resistance. |

that the model's applicability is either indeterminate or partial. The vertical axis in the figure shows whether political scientists see the Westminster model as normatively defensible or desirable. Core exponents (shown at the bottom left) have no doubts that it is. Reformist authors (shown at the top right) see it as without redeeming features (see next section). A substantial intermediate group either make less strong criticisms (on the left), or else see Westminster-model arrangements and reformist alternatives as irrelevant to important current questions (on the right).

Some readers may feel that it is controversial to say that core exponents of the Westminster model not only see it as empirically useful but also defend it normatively, as if this somehow implies that such authors take a less academic or a more slanted view. But in fact this claim does not imply in any way that these authors take a more biased or less professional view than the more neutral authors, any more than reformist political scientists do so. All social science work is inescapably founded at some level on normative alignments and value judgements. In addition some underlying forces seem to sustain the Westminster model for unreflective or unintended reasons. Academics are often slow to adjust well-loved or familiar explanations to fit new facts. Many like to focus on topics that political elites and the media rate as important (like general election voting), not least to win research grants and media coverage. And academic experts often tend to exaggerate the importance of the detailed subjects that they study. All these processes mean that quite a lot of political science presents a pro-status quo, pro-Westminster model view as 'naturally' correct, unless the authors are being more explicit about how they do evaluation (Dunleavy 1990, 2005).

To see how Westminster-model authors have coped with recent developments let's look at some issues in more detail, beginning with party competition. Throughout the period since 1979 successive Conservative and Labour governments have enjoyed solid or landslide Commons majorities with just over two fifths of the vote. Westminster political elites in the top two parties deny outright that anything significant has changed. Consider Table 17.2.

For Jack Straw (2005) any whinging about the fairness of this result should be dismissed out of hand:

Labour won fair and square last Thursday. In more constituencies Labour got more of the popular vote than any other party [at the UK level], which is why we won more seats ... All this is a statement of the blindingly obvious ... We have formed a government because we won more seats, and gained the largest minority of the votes cast as well ... We knew ... the British people preferred strong majority government, rather than some mush in the middle.

**Table 17.2**  *The 2005 general election result in England*

| Party | Votes (thousands) | Seats | % votes share | % seats share |
|---|---|---|---|---|
| Conservatives | 8,102 | 193 | 35.7 | 36.6 |
| Labour | 8,039 | 286 | 35.4 | 54.2 |
| Liberal Democrats | 5,198 | 47 | 22.9 | 8.9 |
| UK Independence Party | 590 | 0 | 2.8 | 0 |
| 79 other named parties | 759 | 2 | 3.4 | 0.4 |
| Total | 22,688 | 528 | 100.0 | 100.1 |

In fact Table 17.2 shows that with 63,000 fewer votes than the Conservatives in England Labour nonetheless secured 93 more MPs. And with nearly a quarter of the votes, the Liberal Democrats were even more severely under-represented than the Tories. In all 21 per cent of seats were misallocated to a party whose tenure was not justified in terms of their national vote share. Thus, within England a huge artificial majority of seats was conferred on the *second-placed* party, with barely more than a third of the votes, at the expense of all its competitors.

Straw also makes clear that for Westminster elites only the balance of Labour and Conservative votes matters – their conflict exhausts the serious ideological space. All third, fourth, or fifth-party voting is somehow irrelevant, or expresses inauthentic or shallow concerns that can be coded as temporary 'protest' voting. For him the Liberal Democrats and the *Independent* newspaper were 'the bad losers in this election' for impugning the legitimacy of the outcome:

> I spent my first 18 years as an MP in opposition ... There were people around then who said that we [Labour] would never, ever, win power – unless we changed the electoral system. Most of my parliamentary colleagues treated this idea with contempt, and recognised that we would win when we deserved to, and meanwhile we would have to take the medicine meted out by a party with more votes than we had ... [T]here are no short cuts in politics, or democracy. It's time the Liberal Democrats learned this too. (Straw 2005)

Orthodox political scientists have often seemed to go along with such views. For example, some authors attack criticisms that plurality-rule elections are unfair, because they 'reflect a narrow understanding of fairness' (Blau 2004; Pinto-Duschinsky 1998). For Blau to even use the language of fairness 'is misleading and overly rhetorical'. Other writers initially dismissed the greater support for smaller parties in devolution elections or European Parliament voting as showing that these were 'secondary elections' and hence less deeply meant or less consequential than general election voting. Votes in general elections are still routinely described as giving positive support for parties, rather than as a conditional preference that voters must express within a limited effective choice set (see Catt 1995 for a critique).

However, the evident drift of support away from the Conservatives and Labour and the advent of different party politics at non-Westminster elections now more generally triggers an admission that something has shifted, albeit without creating any clear alternative yet:

> From having an archetypal two-party system in the early post-war period, the United Kingdom now has a nationwide party system that defies simple classification ... The era of stable two-party politics has since given way to a more complex picture in which the foundations of bipolar party politics have been undermined but not overhauled ... Devolution has brought significant changes. Moderate pluralist party systems operate in Scotland and Wales, where four or more 'relevant' parties compete in the electoral arena. ... At a national level the two-party system has been eroded but not replaced. (Lynch and Garner 2005, 533, 536, 552; and see Heffernan 2003)

Note that again multiparty outcomes in two successive rounds of PR London elections and European Parliament elections are just ignored, and there is a clear reluctance here to let go of the past 'paradigm', even while admitting that it no longer works. (See also O'Neil 2004, where devolution is supposedly discussed with no mention of London government at all, even though its Mayor is certainly the most powerful politician in the UK outside the Cabinet.)

Changes in the main political parties themselves have triggered more internal questioning about what parties are for, especially in the light of simultaneous apparently contradictory trends. Parties seem to have become more democratic because the membership beyond Parliament can now elect their leader. But at the same time, leadership domination of both the top two parties seems to have increased, partly because leaders gain enhanced legitimacy and the need for lengthy electoral contests insulates them from challenges (Quinn 2004). The successful Tory leadership winner in December 2005, David Cameron, will undoubtedly benefit from a similar effect. But in 2003 the choice of Michael Howard as leader by Tory MPs with no membership vote showed that old-style elite manoeuvres could easily subvert party democracy. So did Blair's ill-fated use of Labour's electoral college to swing the Welsh party leadership for

Alun Michael in 1999 (he lasted a year) and the London Mayor candidateship for Frank Dobson in 2000 (he ran a poor fourth, while the rejected Ken Livingstone won as an independent). However, both parties did change back to more open leadership competitions after these lapses, in response to public criticisms (and after the failures of these rigging gambits). The ambivalence surfaced even in the Liberal Democrats though. In January 2006, following Charles Kennedy being forced to step down, some MPs urged the 'coronation' of Menzies Campbell as party leader without a contest – a course of action the party in fact decisively rejected, subsequently electing him in a three-way contest.

The calamitous fall in major-party memberships has produced little questioning of the conventional wisdom about parties' functions in recruiting people to leadership or activism roles and sifting policy options (Webb 2000). Party organisation is still discussed mainly in terms of a shift from 'mass-party' to 'catch-all-party' modes of organising, with less of an ideological core to policies and a more top-down and professionalised political leadership. The problems of much political finance nowadays being raised by very large donations from a few individuals (some of them ministers) and with declining union funding for Labour, have been only episodically discussed. Defenders of the Westminster orthodoxy point out that donations must now be publicly registered and that stricter 'Nolan' rules have been introduced into public appointments.

In Parliament, two-party dominance of the Commons and majority-party control of government have barely been touched by the huge electoral changes of the last three decades. The whips system operates as a duopoly, with the Conservative chief whip and his deputy paid from government funds. The arrival of 62 Liberal Democrat MPs and the presence of MPs from ten other parties in the Commons has not much changed Westminster procedures. Departmental special committees play bigger roles and their chairs are now paid a small amount, but they remain isolated islands of legislative expertise. The 'modernisation' of the House of Commons was also quickly stopped by the conservatism of Labour MPs.

Westminster-model authors focusing on Parliament have always talked up the importance of majority-party dissidents in influencing the policy process. In fact it took eight years for the Blair government to suffer a *single actual defeat* in the Commons. Orthodox authors use the 'rule of anticipated reactions' to insist that this does not necessarily betoken the weakness of parliamentary influence – previously the government may have fine-tuned their proposals to just what their party's MPs would accept (Cowley 2005). Other evidence of Parliament's residual importance is ignored here. For instance, Blair went even further than Thatcher before him in staying away from the Commons (see Dunleavy et al. 1993), concentrating his appearances there to once a week. But in response to pervasive criticisms of remoteness and lack of openness Blair did at least concede a six-monthly appearance before the Commons' Liaison Committee, composed of the chairs of departmental Select Committees, as well as a monthly press conference with the media. These changes are too new and minor to have been much analysed.

The greatest area of debate amongst Westminster-model exponents has been the conduct of government under New Labour. In the 1980s Labour authors opportunistically criticised Thatcher for her dominance over her ministers. In a similar way Conservative commentators have rather predictably lined up to suggest that Blair has wrecked an otherwise perfectly good set of constitutional machinery by ill thought-out 'reforms', plus over-centralisation, cronyism and imperfectly documented 'sofa government' (shown by the Butler Report). For Philip Norton (2003, 543), a Tory peer as well as political scientist:

> The Westminster model of government has been built on relationships characterised by mutual respect and dependence. Recent decades have seen an erosion of the Westminster model through fragmentation and isolation. Fragmentation has occurred as a consequence of major constitutional changes, changes that have been disparate and discrete, falling within no coherent approach to constitutional change. Isolation has taken place as a result of a greater presidentialisation of politics and of [public] ignorance of government. Isolation has reached a new plane under the premiership of Tony Blair with consequences that may appear counter-intuitive. Power is isolated at the centre, rendering the centre vulnerable.

Yet Norton still seems to believe that a reversion to tried and trusted ways (perhaps with a Tory government?) would solve current problems.

Inside departments the Westminster model is still 'the building block from which ministers and [top] civil servants develop narratives that shape and condition their actions' (Richards and Smith 2004, 777) and most orthodox authors are happy to concur. The UK civil service model has consistently remained one of the least corrupt, most studied and best reputed public service systems in the world. British public-sector management has also been exceptionally dynamic, leading the push towards 'new public management' approaches under governments of both the top two parties (Pollitt and Bouckaert 2003). Yet it has also proved capable of evolving in some radically new ways, as with freedom of information and the transition away from life-long career paths. By 2005 nearly one in three entrants to the senior civil service came from the private sector, local authorities or NHS bodies.

In some areas the pull of the Westminster model has been extended, notably in local government with the introduction of local cabinets, which has meant that most councillors' roles have been reduced to constituency work and to serving on 'scrutiny' committees. By leaving plurality-rule elections for councils intact, these supposed 'democratisation' changes in fact created mini-Westminster systems, where previously a somewhat less elitist model (of control by a majority of councillors acting as a 'college') had managed to survive. Meanwhile orthodox authors have attacked the direct election of mayors in London and ten other cities (Rallings et al. 2002). The balance of power between central and local government has continued to oscillate in a pattern familiar throughout the post-war period, where long-lived governments progressively lose control of more local authorities to opposition parties.

The broader changes in the constitutional arrangements under Blair evoke more divergent reactions from Westminster-model exponents. For Norton (2003, see above) the Blair government's changes were introduced ad hoc, without a plan and without any care for their impact on existing arrangements. So they threaten the integrity of the legacy constitutional arrangements. From a more critical perspective Judge (2004, 699) concurs that these are 'challenges to the Westminster model'. But he argues that they 'reveal, paradoxically, the continuing significance of the model' – although he warns too of a possible 'legitimation crisis' ahead.

By contrast, most commentary by political scientists sees these pragmatic changes as stabilising the Westminster-model system without changing its *essential* constitutional operations. On this view devolution has seen off the threat of Scottish secession from the UK, yet without creating new institutions in Edinburgh effective enough to be any threat to Westminster's primacy. The always limited influence of Welsh nationalism has similarly receded. The much famed 'West Lothian Question' (where Scots MPs get to vote on all English laws but English MPs cannot discuss or even raise a question about Scottish or Welsh devolved matters) has flourished in full effect for six years. But no more than minor grumbles have occurred within England about this evidently unfair constitutional anomaly. There is no push for a separate English Parliament to settle English laws. And the possibility of regional assemblies in England was knocked on the head in autumn 2004 when voters in the North East region decisively rejected plans for the first body there, apparently confounding analysts who detected a 'potential for the future growth of regionalism in England' (Bond and McCrone 2004; Giddens 2002, 43–7). The Human Rights Act (HRA) of 1998 tidied up civil liberties law in 2001, but a UK government backed by a Commons majority still has remarkable scope of action free from judicial interference. Parts of the HRA were suspended within months of being legislated, following the 9/11 massacre in New York and Washington DC. From 2005 onwards legislative changes designed to combat terrorism have degraded or suspended long-cherished historical protections for suspects in quite radical ways, suggesting little limitation of the traditional 'flexibility' in the constitution. So from this viewpoint the Blair government has pressed ahead only with a series of diverse, piecemeal and pragmatic changes that increase the stability of the Westminster model. Political elites have backed off from changes that would threaten more fundamental shifts, most notably in the Labour Party's and Conservatives' almost equally strong rejections of proportional elections for the Commons itself and the renewed failure of attempts to reform the House of Lords.

## The reformist critique – normalising British politics

In analysing why any long-lived system of organisation has changed, a key problem is always to understand how the people in control decided to do things differently. Especially in the UK, only the victors can make changes to the rules of the game. But since they are winning, why should they want anything different? Explaining why the first Blair government (with its huge, artificial Commons majority) implemented a major constitutional reform programme between 1997 and 2001 is a classic instance of just such an issue. It is clear from the record so far that Blair himself had little faith in or commitment to the programme enacted:

> Prime Ministers of both parties have been mostly constitutional conservatives, believing in the established institutions and orthodoxies of the 'Westminster model' and supporters of the status quo, not constitutional innovators. Blair's 'modernisation' rhetoric cannot disguise a strong personal attachment to the fundamentals of an executive-dominated parliamentary regime. (Theakston 2005, 38)

> In 2001 the Labour manifesto gave little space to the constitutional reforms that had been enacted and the changes almost seemed to show the Labour leadership acting despite themselves. The existing journalistic accounts of the reform programme's enactment compound this problem by giving very Westminster-model accounts, itemising the manoeuvrings at ministerial level but largely ignoring the cultural, intellectual and academic movements and debates which actually provided the motor of changes from the early 1990s onwards. (Morrison 2001, 129)

Pride of place in these movements went to the Scottish Constitutional Convention. From the early 1990s it brought together all the non-Conservative parties, the labour movement, the churches, legal professionals and many other civil-society groups north of the border to construct a broad consensus – covering not just the powers to be devolved to Edinburgh but also new ways of working in the institutions to be created. South of the border the key group was Charter 88, a network of many different smaller groups founded in 1988 by Stuart Weir (then editor of the *New Statesman*) and Anthony Barnett. Over the next ten years Charter 88 built up a committed membership of more than 15,000 and organised countless meetings, lobbies and conferences on the need for an integrated programme of constitutional reform. Its activities bridged across from the traditional support base of Liberal Democrats to many people and organisations within the Labour and Conservative ranks, especially within the trade unions. Charter 88's work also sifted and sorted constitutional reform alternatives into workable policies suitable for legislation (Barnett et al. 1993). So it secured a well organised media and intellectual profile for its agenda, unrivalled in any other phase of constitutional debates in the twentieth century UK (Kaiser et al. 2000).

The key intellectual grouping backing Charter 88 was the Democratic Audit of the UK, run by Weir and the political theorist David Beetham. Beetham provided a comprehensive blueprint of how a liberal democratic state should be assessed against benchmarks derived from normative philosophical debates. And Weir networked a wide range of academics and intellectuals behind a coherent analysis of all aspects of UK constitutional and political arrangements, resulting in two landmark reformist texts – *The Three Pillars of Liberty* (Klug et al. 1996), and *Political Power and Democratic Control in Britain* (Weir and Beetham 1999), plus the less memorable *Democracy under Blair* (Beetham and Weir 2002). Since imitated in several other countries, the Democratic Audit approach also reflected the influence of the Joseph Rowntree Reform Trust (JRRT), an agit-prop philanthropic trust run for many years by (Lord) Trevor Smith. Along with other Rowntree charitable and research foundations the JRRT subsidised or funded in some way virtually all the activities of the reformist groups from the late 1980s through to the implementation of reforms. For instance, JRRT underwrote the costs of successive 'State of the Nation' surveys that tracked (and still track) public opinion on constitutional issues in ways that most other surveys (sharing the political elite's preoccupations) ignored (see Dunleavy et al. 2001).

All this reformist activity came to a focus in the Cook–Maclennan Pact, negotiated by Robin Cook for the Labour Party and Lord

Maclennan for the Liberal Democrats in March 1997, a few weeks before the general election. Arguably the pact laid a critical foundation for the Tories' loss of power in 1997 and is a key reason why the first Blair government went through with its constitutional reform programme (Cook and Maclennan 2005). In seats where their party could not win and barely campaigned, it produced substantial crossovers of Labour voters to the Liberal Democrats (whose seats jumped from 20 in 1992 to 46 in 1997). And the second preferences of Liberal Democrats swung massively in Labour's favour, helping Blair to win in many marginal seats. This joint deal is an example of how even a third party like the Liberal Democrats can leverage real power in favourable circumstances. In this case they secured implementation of a watertight deal on Scottish, Welsh and London devolution; proportional representation for all these new bodies and for the European Parliament elections; the passing of a (restrictively interpreted) Human Rights Act; and eventually freedom of information. Less successful were clauses which required formal investigations of PR voting for Westminster (the Jenkins Commission) and reform of the House of Lords (the Wakeham Commission). Labour reserved its position on both topics and ultimately did nothing on either of the commissions' reports, beyond removing hereditary peers from the Lords.

The essence of the reformists' critique of the Westminster model and their positive vision of where the constitution should be headed is that lacking a codified conventional liberal-democratic constitution creates major risks, imbalances and unfairnesses which are bad for political life and for public policy. Indeed, at a limit, 'with its extreme concentration of power, the Westminster model has the potential to degenerate into dictatorship (as it did in Singapore and, briefly, in India)' (Shugart 1995, 170). Westminster-model traditionalists trace most of these problems back to the long history of Britain's liberal constitutional evolution from a mediaeval absolute monarchy, followed by the later democratisation of the oligarchical liberal set-up. For this account, it is as if the boundaries of the UK have always been configured as the 'island state' they are now. But the reformists instead ascribe many problems to much more recent history, specifically to the period from 1815 to the 1950s when the UK political elite were simultaneously running a despotic world-empire *and* managing a transition to liberal democracy and a welfare state within the home islands of the Empire (Dunleavy and Beattie 1995; Subrahmanyam 1995, 2004). Like most of the supposedly ancient rituals surrounding the British monarchy, many of the constitutional limits derive chiefly from the exigencies of imperialism. I review how reformists analyse the current development of three key aspects – elections and party politics, Parliament and government, and wider constitutional changes.

Reformists argue that electoral and party politics have changed radically since the 1970s, not just eroding previous patterns but ushering in multiparty competition. In proportional representation elections the Conservative plus Labour share of the vote has consistently fallen to low levels now – 44 per cent in the 2004 London Assembly election; 45 per cent in the 2003 Scottish Parliament election; 48 per cent in the 2004 European Parliament election; and 56 per cent in the 2003 Welsh National Assembly election. Figure 1.1 in Chapter 1 of this book shows that there is a huge difference between the parties winning seats in the most recent PR elections and in the 2005 general election. As a result I argue vigorously that conventional election analysts need to 'face up' to the fact that a multiparty system already exists in every region of the UK, not excepting the metropolitan heartland regions of England:

> Britain is not just a multi-party system – it is, if anything, a set of very closely linked but nonetheless qualitatively different five- or six-party systems. These modern party systems reflect the exhaustion of previous main party and governing elite strategies of attempting to suppress some issues and sublimate others into a limited part of the left–right spectrum. That approach can no longer accommodate what voters want to talk about and vote about. (Dunleavy 2005, 530)

Figure 17.2 shows that the proportion of the electors backing the top two parties has fallen from four fifths in 1951 to two fifths in 2005, while the proportion supporting single-party governments in this period has collapsed from two fifths in 1951 to barely a fifth in 2005. Turnout also fell by 18 percentage points from 1992 to 2001, an unparalleled decline for any established liberal democracy across three consecutive elections. Although turnout apparently increased again in 2005 because of postal-voting rule changes, the underlying rate of turnout actually failed to recover and may have declined further (Curtice 2005).

These trends have deep-seated causes. First, political alignments have been fragmenting in many liberal democracies across the world, with political systems previously organised on left/right lines acquiring extra ideological or issue dimensions. The drift of support from the top two parties charted in Figure 17.2 is mirrored in the sharply diminished numbers of people describing themselves as strong supporters of the top two parties (the phenomenon of 'partisan dealignment'). In every proportional representation election many more voters choose third, fourth or fifth parties instead of the top two. And between a quarter and a third of voters split their votes across several parties wherever the system allows them to do so (Dunleavy 2005). The coexistence of PR and plurality-rule elections has speeded up this fracturing and 'conditionalising' of alignments and

**Figure 17.2**    *The falling proportion of the electorate voting for the top two parties and for the government in the United Kingdom 1945–2005*

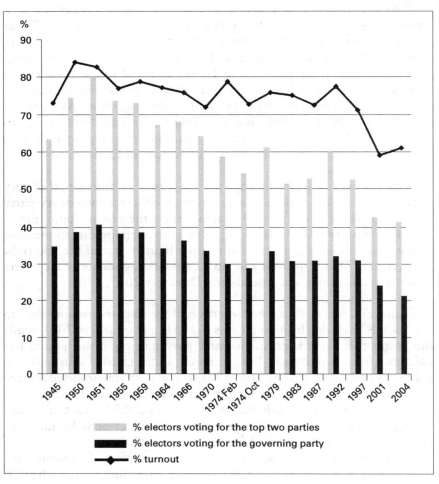

created major problems for party leaders trying to adhere to old Westminster-model tactics of ignoring the 'fringe' or supposedly 'minor' parties – who actually drew more than half of all votes in some PR elections in 2003–04.

Second, the alleged tendency of plurality-rule systems to suppress support for all but the top two parties (often summed up as Duverger's Law) now applies only in the United States. American Congressional elections are the world's last perfect two-party contests, and in fact they operate pretty proportionally. But elsewhere, if Duverger's Law makes any sense at all, it just implies that only two parties should be effective in *any single constituency* (Cox 1997). But it says nothing about how nationalised parties will be, that is whether the same parties will compete everywhere. Strictly interpreted, Cox's reformulation of Duverger means only that in the UK there should never be more than $2 \times 646 = 1,292$ political parties – a fairly safe prediction. Where the nationalisation of parties breaks down, plurality-rule elections can in fact produce any number of parties – as in contemporary India where there are more than 154 organised parties in the legislature (plus many free-floating independent MPs) and where the governing coalition is composed of 18 parties. Even in similar countries to the UK, the days of any 'two-party' system have long passed. Plurality-rule elections have either never applied (in Australia since 1919), or have already switched to PR voting (in New Zealand since 1996), or are being considered for reform (in Canada now).

Third, reformists also draw comfort from the analysis of Josep Colomer (2005) who demonstrates that the number of parties always increases *before* the introduction of PR and not does not change much afterwards – a proposition illustrated quite well in Scotland and Wales, for instance. Reform authors argue that the extent of electoral change in the UK already means that sometime in the next decade either the Labour or Conservative leaderships are likely to decide that their fortunes will be better protected under PR (or some reformed system) than under plurality rule with an ever fragmenting party system (Dunleavy 2005; Dunleavy and Margetts 2001).

On political parties, reformists argue strongly for new controls on political finance to create a level playing field for parties, instead of the top two or three parties being able to de facto exchange honours, places on government 'task forces' and even ministerial positions for large party donations. The top two parties are now so weak as mechanisms for transmitting civil-society views to top policy makers that it makes sense instead to see them as 'cartel parties' (Katz and Mair 1995). They have become extra-parliamentary extensions of the leadership teams in Parliament, increasingly supported by big business or state funding only. They are populated less and less by genuine activists and more and more by career-maximising people from para-party organisations and quasi-government bodies. For example, by 2005 the Labour branches around the country were increasingly being run by younger, ambitious Blairite or Brownite people working for trade unions, other Labour MPs or local authorities, or for think tanks, public affairs consultancies or newspapers. Meanwhile in 2003–05 hundreds of older, more left-wing activists left in disgust over the Iraq war – an ironic reversal of the 'entryism' of the 1970s. In both the top two parties the manifesto doctrine also appears to have been turned from a mechanism for broad electoral and intra-party accountability into a weapon for the leadership to corral their own MPs. Party leaders need policy pledges in writing, in order to hold any dissenting MPs' noses to the grindstone. So specific commitments included in the top two parties' manifestos jumped from an average of 51 in the 1970s to nearly 80 in the 1980s, and to nearly 280 on average from 1992 to 2001 (Bara 2005) – even while these pledges are increasingly disbelieved by voters.

The reformist view is strongly critical of Parliament, where the experience of the failed 'modernisation' reforms suggests that the House of Commons is probably unreformable and incapable of becoming any more effective as a legislature than it is already. MPs seem locked into a spiral of doing more and more parochial constituency work to secure their electoral position, while effectively renouncing their central duty to searchingly scrutinise the executive's actions. For reformists the disastrous British participation in the unprovoked US-led aggression against Iraq in 2003, on the basis of completely wrong or misleading information provided by the Prime Minister, government and intelligence services, is as telling an indication of institutional failure as the strikingly similar Suez invasion. Blair's precise role in this deception remains controversial (compare Stothard 2003 with the views of Lanchester, Parris or Cusick, all 2003) but it is clear that whereas Labour in 1956 carried through their (unpopular) duty of opposing, the Tories in 2003 went along with the executive. And, despite being given two set-piece votes, the fabled Labour dissident MPs proved completely ineffective in surfacing the many gaping holes in the government case for the Iraq war before it was too late. The subsequent failures of the Hutton and Butler government enquiries and several Commons Select Committee investigations to shed any real light on how the miscommitment occurred only compounds the impression of parliamentary ineffectiveness (Butler 2004; Hutton 2004; Runciman 2004).

Moran (2003) points out that an increasing leitmotif of British government has been 'high modernism and hyper-innovation', especially in regulatory areas. He draws on Scott's (1998) argument about why high modernism can lead to policy fiascos. In the 1990s reformists argued that Britain was differentially liable to policy disasters because of four features: the large scale of national policy implementations; the absence or weakness of checks and balances on a government with a Commons majority; political hyperactivism by ministers; and the civil service dominance over other elements of the state (Dunleavy 1995). None of these problems has been resolved or even addressed. After the intermission provided by the popular and genuinely effective first Blair government (1997–2001), there was a striking return to failing form in the core executive's operations. An updated list of eminently foreseeable, large-scale New Labour policy disasters might now include, besides the Iraq war (£5 billion and counting): the failure of tax credits (£0.6 billion); the bankruptcy of Railtrack and the after-costs of Labour ministers propping the company up for four years (many £ billion); the public–private partnerships for the London Tube (several £ billion); the bailouts of the privatised air traffic control system and nuclear waste disposal agencies (£1.2 billion); and the Millennium Dome (£1.1 billion). Upcoming third-term follies look set to include the implementation of a high-tech national ID card scheme (at a minimum cost of £6 billion over ten years) for little clear return (LSE 2005). Still undecided but seeming likely are a replacement for Trident and a return to building nuclear power stations – this last possibly necessary, but possibly not, and likely to cost £16 billion. The reformist case is that a better balance of executive answerability to the public and to Parliament would dramatically thin down these cases and ensure that remedial action was taken before such huge wasted costs are incurred.

Inside government the reformists acknowledge a good deal of welcome change on some elements that are removed from the political elites' interests, like greater openness with less important public information (but not ministerial secrecy, which remains pervasive) and changes to a somewhat more pluralist policy process and civil service culture. But the Commons Public Administration Select Committee has led a so far unavailing campaign for a clear Civil Service Act to specify more precisely the remit of officials' independence from ministers. Progress towards a better balance of central–local relations has also been slow in England, although the new London local government steered through by the reformist minister Nick Raynsford has been a huge success. A directly elected Mayor and small Assembly now supervise one of the most dynamic and successful centres of policy making in the UK. The London governance pattern includes a multipreference system for electing the Mayor, called the Supplementary Vote (Dunleavy and Margetts 1997), also used in ten other towns that directly elect executive mayors. The PR-elected London Assembly would also have been copied in English regional assemblies (had they not failed in the North East). And London has a strong separation of powers between the executive and legislature on US 'strong mayor' lines.

The reformists are most critical of Labour's record in the area of civil liberties, where the Human Rights Act was implemented from the outset in a very restrictive way and now appears to have been comprehensively vandalised within a few years of its implementation, in the name of anti-terror protection. The UK government's apparent compliance with

American illegalism at Guantanamo Bay, and with a rumoured 'gulag archipelago' of hidden detention/torture centres outside the US known as 'extraordinary rendition', has also left a sour taste, especially since British citizens' rights have been invaded as well as those of foreigners. After the suicide bombings in London in July 2005, and failed copycat efforts later that month, Blair staked his personal reputation in the following autumn on securing a 90-days blanket detention of terror suspects without trial or charge. At least this move was actually thrown out by rebel Labour MPs, but a 28-days provision was still agreed.

Reformists once again interpret these events as making the case for a written and codified constitution, a cause strongly promoted within the reformist movement by Barnett (1997) and dallied with by the much more conventional Constitution Unit at University College, London. In fact a written constitution has always remained the poor relation in both the reform movement's practical campaigns and in its intellectual effort. Even at the height of Labour's reform period, ministers clearly proceeded in an ad hoc and piecemeal way, making concessions to the reformists only where they were strictly forced to do so by the weight of informed and public opinion. Tony Wright (2003, 17) famously lamented:

> We do not know anything about constitutions here, at least not in the sense that they are known about elsewhere. We are not even familiar with the basic language of constitutional debate. The British enjoy a marvellous constitutional illiteracy. They think pluralism is a lung disease.

There is little immediate prospect of this situation changing, but reformist groups and authors point out that there is little evidence yet either of the constitutional situation stabilising in some 'post-Westminster-model' configuration.

## The drift of power from the UK state

Both the Westminster model and its reformist critics are chiefly liberal pluralists in their theory of the state. They both believe that formal political processes are and should be central to societal self-guidance and that representative government provides the best (indeed dominant) chance of securing civil-society influence over the nation state's operations (Beetham 2005). Both views also implicitly agree that nation states still matter, although reformists are generally much more Euro-enthusiastic and strong Westminster-model exponents are typically more Euro-sceptical in their attitudes. I turn now to two different but increasingly influential views arguing that focusing on the distinctiveness of British politics in this way is to succumb to liberal illusions of decreasing resonance in the contemporary world. The first camp are globalists and Europeanists, the second postmodernists.

## The globalist and Europeanist view

There has been a huge decline in the volume of books and papers dealing solely with UK politics and a big switch in British political science publications towards EU politics (a few years ago) or globalisation (more recently). In this view, the declining importance of the UK state and how it is formally controlled reflect the displacement of more and more issues to the European or global levels. This shift is compatible with many different positions. But it is strongest amongst practically orientated sociologists who produced concepts like the 'Third Way'. Giddens (1998, 2001, 2002) makes crystal-clear his view that the problems of modern politics are overwhelmingly standard ones for European social democrats, revolving around managing more global economic processes alongside nationally run welfare states. For a time this centrist-welfarist preoccupation was apparently left with a clear field (Leggett 2005). Western Marxism has apparently collapsed into a purely critical position, with things to be against but no positive prescriptions of its own (Callinicos 2001, 2003). At the same time the new right has been eroded as a distinct theory of the state. The Europeanist version of this view points out around 70 per cent of new economic and social regulation in the UK in fact originates from Europe. The globalist view, strongly pushed by David Held, is that the displacement of regulation to the international or global levels and the increase in global competition and interactions have both pushed control of many critical issues far above the level where single-country politics makes sense as a control mechanism (Held and McGrew 2002; Held and Koenig-Archibugi 2003).

## The postmodern turn – social culture, governance and governmentality

In a wide range of disciplines the dispute between modernists and postmodernists has been highly productive of new approaches, but in political science the impact has been less than in the humanities, sociology or cultural studies. Postmodern writers argue that previous political science has been premised on 'grand narratives' that tend towards a totalising view of human nature. Such accounts blur the essential diversity of the human condition and construct mythical sequences and accounts that serve to disguise from us uncomfortable aspects of our social life – such as the lack of progress in combatting social inequality, the hollowing-out of cultural or social life, or continuing environmental unsustainability. In this view, a critical myth in modernist political science is that social development is still controllable, that political leaders are capable of 'running the shop' in a coherent manner via the institutions of the state and political representation. Both Westminster-model exponents and their reformist critics buy into this fundamental assumption to an almost equal degree. By contrast, the central proposition of postmodern writers is that the traditional state institutions and the apparatus of formal politics simply matter less and less in modern Britain. They argue 'against an over-valuation of the "problem of the state" in political debate and social theory ... [T]he analytical language structured by the philosophical opposition of state and civil society is unable to comprehend transformations in modes of exercise of political power' (Rose and Miller 1992, 173). There are three main variants of this line.

A first position stresses cultural politics and social diversification, arguing that Westminster politics, however organised, matters less and less in British society. People vote less because they decreasingly believe in the whole voting-and-parties process. Nor would this attitude change if the barriers to people expressing their actual views (such as plurality-rule elections) were suddenly lifted. Increasing social diversity and changing patterns of social life have had tremendous impacts on formal politics already. Many commentators argue that the Conservatives' prolonged slump in the opinion polls from 1992 onwards reflected their apparent remoteness from urban living conditions. This analysis was strongly accepted by David Cameron, who won the party's 2005 leadership contest largely on a platform of updating the Conservatives' social profile and cultural image. But however important such changes may be in affecting party fortunes, the long-run trend of political engagement is likely to be downwards, with political processes dwindling in salience in media terms or social visibility.

A second postmodern strand focuses on the operations of the state itself and argues that a transition has already taken place to 'governing without government in a differentiated polity' (Rhodes 1997, 200). The key author here is Rod Rhodes who interpreted the results of an ESRC research programme into Whitehall in the closing years of the Tory government as showing that power had diffused away from the core executive and into fragmented policy networks that could only be controlled centrally by the core executive at a cost of unintended consequences. Rhodes concludes that the problems of the Westminster model in the UK are chiefly their irrelevance to contemporary modes of governing in practice, rather than the reformists' diagnoses of insufficient institutionalisation. Bevir and Rhodes

(2003, 215) argue that 'there is no essentialist account of British government, only complex and diverse narratives, and no tool kit for solving problems, only lessons drawn from many stories.' This discourse of multiple narratives has had a fashionable take-up impact in some London think tanks close to New Labour. It has had, however, a restricted impact in the academic world, not least because Rhodes often seems to link very quickly from inadequacies or limitations of managerialism or the Westminster model to a kind of anti-rationalism hostile to any attempt at systematic explanation. For example, elsewhere Bevir and Rhodes (2005, 169) denounce 'misplaced beliefs in the false idols of hard data and rigorous methods'.

A somewhat similar tack is taken by a third postmodern strand, the 'governmentality' literature, whose chief protagonist is the sociologist Nikolas Rose. He declares:

> The investigations of government that interest me ... are those which try to gain a purchase on the forces that traverse the multitudes of encounters where conduct is subject to government: prisons, clinics, schoolrooms and bedrooms, factories and offices, airports and military organisations, the marketplace and the shopping mall, sexual relations and much more. (Rose 1999, 5)

As this long list makes clear, Rose believes that 'governing' is something that is not done by the state or political institutions alone, but is instead an activity that is embedded into a great many (all?) social relations and activities:

> To govern is to cut experience in certain ways, to distribute attractions and repulsions, passions and fears across it, to bring new facets and forces, new intensities and relations into being ... To govern, one could say, is to be condemned to seek an authority for one's authority. (Rose 1999, 27–8, 31)

Governing is about creating 'a governable subject', that is, people who essentially accept that a particular version of rationality and appropriateness should direct their behaviour and reactions. In practice this means that: 'Liberal rule is inextricably bound to the activities and calculations of a proliferation of independent authorities – philanthropists, doctors, hygienists, managers, planners, parents and social workers' (Rose 1999, 49). Top political processes still have some effect here, but more as the icing on a cake long baked by far wider social processes.

## Conclusions

We live in the era of 'the twilight of Westminster' (Norris 2005). But the *Concise Oxford Dictionary* gives two non-literal meanings for 'twilight'. The first is 'a period of decline or destruction', as in Wagner's opera, *The Twilight of the Gods*. The second is 'a state of imperfect knowledge or understanding'. This neat conjunction crystallises my argument here. A period when in Tennyson's words 'the old order changeth, giving way to new' is also ipso facto a time of academic obsolescence and uncertainty of perception. The UK political science literature is now replete with question-mark articles forecasting potential developments like:

- 'a coherent and far-reaching reappraisal of the structure, roles and powers of parliament' (Flinders 2002);
- 'a serious breakdown in the relationship between ministers and civil servants' (Richards and Smith 2004);
- 'a more deep-seated reappraisal of the structure of Whitehall and the dominant values of the British political elite than is currently anticipated' (Flinders 2002);
- 'the whirlwind of a self-generated and self-perpetuated "legitimation crisis"' (Judge 2004).

Yet all these speculations are hedged around with qualifications. And there are many Westminster-model authors who seem to anticipate nothing more than a further period of 'muddling through'.

Roll forward the chronology of British politics ten or twenty years and the different approaches reviewed here currently posit very different scenarios. Westminster-model exponents perhaps look to a revival of two-party politics (which seems unlikely) but most essentially predict politics as usual. Reformists predict that normalisation of the UK constitution on European lines will have proceeded further, with PR for all elections, an elected Lords, a strong Supreme Court, English regions completing a partly federal structure, and a considerable recodification of the constitution. At some stage a possible threat of Scotland's secession may have been faced, or perhaps the question will never seriously arise. Postmodernists predict more complexity and an increasing recognition that formal politics is no longer the 'master' mechanism it once was. Globalists argue that all UK politics will come to be seen (correctly) as essentially local politics within a dominant global level.

The most immediate critical zone of contention will surely be over proportional representation for Westminster itself. The issue may come into play again if an embattled Labour government under Gordon Brown needs to rebuild its shattered links with the Liberal Democrats, in order to fight off a renascent Tory party at or after a general election in 2009–10. Some commentators suspect that Brown himself might seek to short-circuit this possibility by proposing a new constitutional settlement when (and if) he becomes prime minister, sometime between 2006 and 2008. A minimum change to create future stability might perhaps involve the Alternative or Supplementary Vote for electing MPs and the creation of a (mostly) PR-elected House of Lords, an 'Australian-model' solution. Most orthodox political scientists would still dismiss this prospect as reformist wishful thinking, arguing that Brown like Blair before him will turn out to be a constitutional conservative as premier, at least on matters affecting his own power. But even if the short term shows no such shift, in the somewhat longer term the coexistence of PR and plurality-rule systems, combined with the drift of support away from the top two parties, make a further constitutional restabilisation look likely.

# Further Reading

## Chapter 2    The Blair Style of Central Government

Seldon (2005) has provided a thematic biography of Tony Blair, one which draws on elite interviews and private information to consider the way Blair acts as prime minister. Earlier studies by Rawnsley (2001) and Macintyre (2000) also cast considerable light on his style of government. The classic monograph on post-war prime ministers, Hennessy (2001), only discusses the early Blair premiership, but is usefully complemented by Hennessy (2004, 2005a, b). The notion of presidentialisation is explored in Foley (2000, 2004) and by Heffernan (2005b) while the core-executive framework, first developed by Rhodes and Dunleavy (1995) and Smith (1999), is also advanced by Marsh, Richards and Smith (2001, 2003), Richards and Smith (2002) and discussed by Heffernan (2003a). Riddell (2005) discusses Blair's premiership in a wider political context, Burch and Holliday (2004) consider Blair's changes to the centre, and Peston (2005) and Bower (2005) together help uncover some of the complexities of the Tony Blair–Gordon Brown relationship. Additional recent general studies of the prime minister are found in Rose (2001) and Heffernan (2005a). Recent developments at the centre are evidenced on the Number 10 webpage: www.number-10.gov.uk/output/Page1.asp and that of the Cabinet Office: www.cabinetoffice.gov.uk

## Chapter 3    Making Parliament Matter?

For those whose knowledge of Parliament is very limited, there are three excellent introductory texts: Norton (2005), Rush (2005) and Rogers and Walters (2004). An interesting and thought-provoking overview of Parliament in the modern political system is Riddell (2000). Baldwin (2005) contains an eclectic and interesting range of essays, by both practitioners and commentators. A more detailed work of reference is Blackburn and Kennon (2003). The most substantial work on constituency work is Norton and Wood (1993), although a more recent pamphlet is Power (1998). The best summary of the modernisation reforms is Brazier et al. (2005); Robin Cook's published diaries for the period (Cook 2003) are revealing and interesting. For the behaviour of MPs, the most recent study covering the 2001–05 period is Cowley (2005), with Cowley (2002) for the 1997–2001 Parliament. From 2001 to 2005, the journal *Parliamentary Affairs* published annual political updates, which included a chapter on Parliament. Beginning in 2006, a similar volume, including chapters on both Commons and Lords, will be published as the *Palgrave Review of British Politics*. Up-to-date studies of backbench behaviour are published on www.revolts.co.uk. The Parliament website –

which covers both Commons and Lords – is at www.parliament.uk. It contains masses of data and publications, all available free of charge, but is not especially accessible; there are, however, ongoing plans to revamp it. More easily accessible material can be found at www.theyworkforyou.com, which provides useful information on individual MPs.

## Chapter 4   Political Parties and Party Systems

Bartle and King (2005), Geddes and Tonge (2005), Norris and Wlezien (2005) and Kavanagh and Butler (2005) contain studies of the 2005 election and discussion of the parties in the 2001 Parliament. Webb (2000) remains the best introductory text on British parties and the party system, and both Ware (1996) and Maor (1997) apply theoretical approaches to British party politics. Dalton and Wattenberg (2002) contains an excellent collection of essays on the comparative study of parties, which illuminates study of the British case. This is well complemented by the earlier collection by Muller and Strom (1999). The changing British party system is robustly explored by Dunleavy (2005) and by Russell (2005).

## Chapter 5   Elections and Voting

The best introduction to voting behavior and elections studies is Denver (2002) and the most recent studies of the 2005 general election are Bartle and King (2005), Geddes and Tonge (2005), Norris and Wlezien (2005) and Kavanagh and Butler (2005). The Electoral Reform Society also produced a very useful early report and analysis which can be found at www.electoral-reform.org.uk/publications/briefings/gefinal2005.pdf, and King (2006) provides an ingenious and lively account of the 2005 election. Excellent commentaries are also available from MORI, particularly those by Worcester and Mortimore (www.mori.com). Clarke et al. (2004) provide an up-to-date synthesis of British Election Studies prior to the 2005 election while Sanders (2002) and Norris (1997) provide commentary on the changing electoral environment. Farrell (2001) and Dummett (1997) discuss the workings of electoral systems in general.

## Chapter 6   Political Participation beyond the Electoral Arena

The best studies of pressure groups in British politics are Coxall (2001), Grant (1999) and Jordan and Maloney (1997). Parry et al. (1992) write more widely about forms of political participation in Britain, while Pattie et al. (2004) explore the role of participation in creating citizenship. Putnam's edited collection (2002) introduces the reader to the debates on social capital and its impacts on contemporary societies.

## Chapter 7    The Half-hearted Constitutional Revolution

New Labour's approach to the constitution is surveyed in Morrison (2001) and Forman (2002). Foley's (1999) book is strongly recommended, especially in relation to his analyses of 'constitutional fuels'. For a theoretical discussion of why constitutions matter see Berggren, Nergelius and Karlson (2002). The annual reviews published by the Constitution Unit are an invaluable guide to the evolution of specific reforms and Bogdanor (2003) has edited a magisterial volume on constitutional history in the twentieth century. King (2001) and Tomkins (2005) attempt to locate the reforms within a broader theoretical framework and Alexander (1997) provides a lucid and insightful description of the history and background of reforms. For a detailed and sophisticated account of the enduring centrality of Parliament and the importance of the Westminster model see Judge (1993). Blackburn and Plant (1999) and Brazier (1999) provide a detailed account of the constitutional agenda whereas Sutherland (2000) provides an array of provocative and at times polemical essays written by a diverse range of observers.

## Chapter 8    Devolution and the Lopsided State

There is a burgeoning literature on devolution, much of it arising from two major research programmes funded by the Economic and Social Research Council and the Leverhulme Trust. A first port of call is their websites at www.devolution.ac.uk and www.ucl.ac.uk/constitution-unit/nations. The latter hosts quarterly updates on developments in the four nations of the UK which have been maintained since 2000; these provide the outstanding single documentary source on devolution available and are downloadable at www.ucl.ac.uk/constitution-unit/nations/monitoring.php. The two programmes have combined to produce yearbooks on devolution which combine nation-by-nation updates with thematic chapters. The two most recent are Hazell and Trench (2004) and Trench (2005b). Synthetic accounts of devolution in the various nations are beginning to emerge, including the outstanding Rawlings (2003) on Wales, Keating (2005) on Scotland and Tonge (2005) on Northern Ireland. The best overall account of the historical context and introduction of devolution remains Bogdanor (2001). Jeffery and Wincott's (2006) special issue of the journal *Publius: The Journal of Federalism* attempts an assessment of devolution's impact on the UK since 1999.

## Chapter 9    Britain, Europe and the World

The best extended historical account of the tangled relationship between Britain and European integration is Young (1999), whilst Forster (2002) is a very good study of the ways in which Euroscepticism has divided the main political parties. Geddes (2004) provides a comprehensive and accessible introduction to the issues arising in British government and politics as a result of EU membership, with good coverage of policy areas, whilst George (1998) combines both a historical and an analytical approach. Allen (2005) is a concise and penetrating account of the tensions between a Europeanised government and the persistence of cleavages and resistance in British politics. Forster and Blair (2002) provide an analysis of the diplomacy surrounding Britain's EU membership, whilst Gamble (2003) is a very good account of the tensions created by the UK's attempt to remain a 'pivotal power'. The best internet source for broad UK policy is the Foreign and Commonwealth Office Europe site (www.fco.gov.uk), which also has a link to key speeches, and for general EU policies and developments the European Commission's Europa site (www.europa.eu.int). All of the main political parties have websites setting out their European and international stances.

## Chapter 10    Security Policy in an Insecure World

The best historical overview of British foreign policy can be found in Mangold (2001) with a pre-9/11 analysis of New Labour's foreign policy to be found in Little and Wickham-Jones (2000). A good review of Tony Blair's foreign policy can be found in Kampfner (2003) and in the various works by Seldon (2005) and Seldon and Kavanagh (2005). Dickie (2004) provides an excellent account of how British foreign policy is made. The UK–US relationship has been explored in many books with Riddell (2003) being the best guide. Cooper (2003) and Kagan (2003) provide an excellent debate about the future of the transatlantic relationship with Andrews (2005) providing a more detailed and broad-ranging approach. The foreign policy of George Bush has been well documented with the best guide being Daalder and Lindsay (2005). Packer (2005) provides an insightful account of the American intervention in Iraq while Mann (2004) provides a study of neo-conservative influence on the Bush administration. Smith (2003) offers a good introduction to the role of the EU in international affairs. The website of the Foreign and Commonwealth Office at www.fco.gov.uk provides access to a range of speeches and texts on British foreign policy. Plenty of information and analysis can also be found on the websites of the leading British think tanks on foreign and security issues which include Chatham House (the Royal Institute of International Affairs) at www.riia.com, the Centre for European Reform at www.cer.org.uk, the International Institute for Strategic Studies at www.iiss.org, the Royal United Services Institute at www.rusi.org and the Foreign Policy Centre at www.fpc.prg.uk.

## Chapter 11    The Politics of Multicultural Britain

The theoretical debate about the meaning of multiculturalism can be traced in Taylor and Gutmann (1992), Watson (2000) and Parekh (2000b) as well as in Kymlicka (2001) and Alibhai-Brown (2001). The debate about immigration and asylum is well covered in Joppke (1999) and Hansen (2000). Aspects of racial discrimination and racism are covered in McGhee (2005), Hewitt (2005) and Pilkington (2003). Modood (2005) is good on the relationship between Muslims and multiculturalism. Copsey (2004) offers a useful analysis of recent developments on the far right in British politics. Useful websites for following developments in the debate about multiculturalism include that of the Commission for Racial Equality at www.cre.gov.uk. That of Migration Watch at www.migrationwatchuk.org is a useful starting point for following controversies about the demographic issues associated with ethnic diversity. The British National Party's own website at www.bnp.org.uk gives a good flavour of the party's policies and tactics, whilst organisations dedicated to stopping the BNP, such as Stop the BNP, at www.stopthebnp.org.uk, provide additional information on the activities of the far right.

## Chapter 12   The State and Civil Liberties in the Post-9/11 World

The best brief guide to the idea of democracy is Dahl (2000). The relationship between rights and democracy is covered in Beetham (1999). Questions of the protective function of democratic states are covered in Held (1996) and MacPherson (1977). Issues of how democracies should deal with terrorism are considered comprehensively in the Madrid Summit Working Paper Series, available at http://summit.clubmadrid.org.

## Chapter 13   The News Media and the Public Relations State

Curran and Seaton (2003) offer considerable historical insight into the development of the press and broadcasting and McNair (2003) into how politicians have responded through their attempts to influence the media agenda. Street (2001) and Corner and Pels (2003) provide useful analyses of the interrelationship between the media and spin and their impact on political culture more generally. Franklin (2004) critically assesses the role of public relations at various levels of government. Interest in Downing Street 'spin' has spawned a biography of the Prime Minister's former chief spin doctor (Oborne and Walters 2004), an at times sympathetic if candid memoir from one of his retired deputies (Price 2005) and a polemical denunciation by the former's predecessor (Ingham 2003). Whereas Dyke (2004) and Oborne (2005) castigate the impact of official spin on the quality of contemporary debate, Lloyd (2004) defends the government by blaming political journalists for undermining public confidence in democracy. Iraq informs these commentaries and the crisis, the propaganda war, and the media reporting of it are more explicitly considered in other studies (Miller 2003; Tumber and Palmer 2004).

## Chapter 14  Managing Economic Interdependence: the Political Economy of New Labour

A range of alternative characterisations of New Labour's political economy are offered by Arestis and Sawyer (2001), Clift and Tomlinson (2006), Hay (2004, 2006) and Hutton (1999). The clearest statement by a New Labour insider of the content of and rationale behind that political economy is provided by Balls (1998). Coates (2005) offers the most complete and up-to-date assessment of New Labour's social and economic record in office since 1997. The debate on the economic-policy-making latitude afforded to governments in an era of globalisation is reviewed in Hay (2006).

## Chapter 15  Modernising the Public Services

The government's proposals for public-sector reform are set out in papers from the Cabinet Office (Cabinet Office 1999) and the Office of Public Services Reform (Office of Public Services Reform 2002). Important speeches on reform by senior ministers include Blair (2001), Brown (2003), Milburn (2004) and Reid (2005). The Institute for Fiscal Studies is an excellent source of data and analysis on public spending – and much else (www.ifs.org.uk). The case for greater choice and diversity in public service provision is made by Le Grand (2003); and Dixon et al. (2003) is a good starting point for looking at current trends in health policy. The shift to quasi-market governance and private-sector involvement in public-sector reform is critiqued by Pollock (2004). Perri 6 (2003) provides a comprehensive overview of the literature on public-sector reform, in particular regarding greater choice and diversity in provision. Bevir and O'Brien (2001), Flinders (2005b) and Newman (2001) in different ways raise important questions on public-sector reform and the politics of New Labour and UK governance.

## Chapter 16  British Politics after Blair

There is growing flood of books on Blair and the Blair government. Particularly useful are Driver and Martell (2002) and Coates (2005). There is a clutch of early biographies of both Blair and Brown, particularly by Seldon (2005) and Peston (2005), many of them very readable, but many of the judgements in these will change as the period recedes and more papers become available. Bevir and Rhodes (2003) is a provocative essay about ways of understanding contemporary British politics through the construction of narratives. For the political economy context see Hay (1999) and Moran (2002). Perusal of party manifestos on the websites of the political parties at the 2005 election yields much of interest about the present state of political thinking in Britain. See also the websites of Compass, and leading think tanks – the Institute for Public Policy Research

(IPPR), the Fabian Society, Demos, the Institute of Economic Affairs (IEA), Civitas, and the Social Market Foundation. Essays by Crouch (2004), Marquand (2004) and Gamble (2003) offer challenging critiques of the present direction of politics. The political malaise of the Conservative Party is usefully explored by Wheatcroft (2005) and, by looking at the Conservatives in opposition, by Ball and Seldon (2005).

## Chapter 17   The Westminster Model and the Distinctiveness of British Politics

The best overview of the historical perspective embedded in the Westminster model in its pure form is still that given by Harrison (1996), although the author himself seems almost unaware of his strong attachments. A good overview of the reformist view is still Weir and Beetham (1996) and Beetham and Weir (2002). Beetham (2005) provides an accessible introduction to the reformist view of democracy. The literature on constitutional reform in the UK still suffers from many limitations. Morrison (2001) provides an elite-level chronology but has almost no background on the intellectual ideas or the grassroots movements that forced reluctant New Labour ministers into doing anything. Jowell and Oliver (2004) and Oliver (2003) provide a very limited public-law view, but do run through some changes in a basic way. Some of the background on the evolution of British political science can be gleaned from Hayward et al. (2003) and Dunleavy et al. (2000).

# Bibliography

Adams, J., Robinson, P. and Vigor, A. (2003) *A New Regional Policy for the UK*, London, Institute for Public Policy Research.

Admissions to Higher Education Steering Group (2004) *Fair Admissions to Higher Education: Recommendations for Good Practice*, www.admissions-review.org.uk/downloads/finalreport.pdf

Alcock, P (2003) *Social Policy in Britain*, Basingstoke, Palgrave Macmillan.

Alexander, R. (1997) *The Voice of the People: A Constitution for Tomorrow*, London, Weidenfeld and Nicolson.

Alibhai-Brown, Y. (2001) *Who Do We Think We Are? Imagining the New Britain*, London, Penguin.

Allan, T. (2005) 'Opinionated journalists are short-changing the electorate', *Observer*, 4 September.

Allen, D. (2003) 'Great Britain and the future of the European Union: Not quite there yet', in Serfaty, S. (ed.) *The European Finality and its National Dimensions*, Washington, DC, Centre for Strategic and International Studies.

Allen, D. (2005) 'The United Kingdom: A Europeanized government in a non-Europeanized polity', in Bulmer, S. and Lequesne, C. (eds) *The Institutions of the European Union*, Oxford, Oxford University Press.

Allen, D. and Oliver, T. (2006) 'The Europeanisation of the Foreign and Commonwealth Office', in Bache, I. and Jordan, A. (eds) *Britain in Europe and Europe in Britain: The Europeanisation of British Politics*, Basingstoke, Palgrave Macmillan.

Allen, N. (2006) 'A restless electorate: Stirrings in the political system', in Bartle, J. and King, A. (eds) *Britain At The Polls 2005*, Washington, DC, Congressional Quarterly.

Andeweg, R. B. (1997) 'Collegiality and collectivity: Cabinets, cabinet committees, and cabinet ministers', in Weller, P., Bakvis, H. and Rhodes R. A. W. (eds) *The Hollow Crown: Countervailing Trends in the Core Executive*, Basingstoke, Macmillan (now Palgrave Macmillan).

Andrews, M. (ed.) (2005) *The Atlantic Alliance Under Stress*, Cambridge, Cambridge University Press.

Arestis, P. and Sawyer, M. (2001) 'The economic analysis underpinning the "Third Way"', *New Political Economy*, Vol. 6 No. 2 pp. 255–78.

Ashcroft, M. (2005) *Dirty Politics, Dirty Times*, London, Politico's.

Ashdown, P. (2001) *The Ashdown Diaries: 1997–1999*, London, Penguin.

Aspinwall, M. (2003) 'Britain and Europe: Some alternative economic tests', *Political Quarterly*, Vol. 74 No. 2 pp. 146–57.

Bache, I. and Flinders, M. (2004a) *Multi-Level Governance*, Oxford, Oxford University Press.

Bache, I. and Flinders, M. (2004b) 'Multi-level governance and the study of the British state', *Public Policy and Administration*, Vol. 19 No. 1 pp. 31–52.

Back, L., Keith, M., Khan, A., Shukra, K. and Solomos, J. (2002) 'New Labour's white heart: Politics, multiculturalism and the return of assimilation', *Political Quarterly*, Vol. 73 No. 4 pp. 445–54.

Badie, B. (2004) 'Sovereignty and intervention', in Carlsnaes, W., Sjursen, H. and White, B. (eds) *Contemporary European Foreign Policy*, London, Sage.

Bagehot, W. (1867 [1968]) *The English Constitution*, London, Fontana.

Baldwin, N. (1985) 'The House of Lords: Behavioural changes', in Norton, P. (ed.) *Parliament in the 1980s*, Oxford, Basil Blackwell.

Baldwin, N. (ed.) (2005) *Parliament in the 21st Century*, London, Politico's.

Ball, S. and Seldon, A. (2005) *Recovering Power: The Conservatives in Opposition Since 1867*, London, Palgrave Macmillan.

Balls, E. (1998) 'Open macroeconomics in an open economy', *Scottish Journal of Political Economy*, Vol. 45 No. 2 pp. 113–32.

Bara, J. (2005) 'A question of trust: Implementing policy manifestos', *Parliamentary Affairs*, Vol. 58 No. 3 pp. 585–99.

Barnett, A. (1997) *This Time: Our Constitutional Revolution*, London, Vintage.

Barnett, A., Ellis, C. and Hirst, P. (eds) (1993) *Debating the Constitution: New Perspectives*, Cambridge, Polity.

Bartle, J. and King, A. (eds) (2005) *Britain At The Polls 2005*, Washington, DC, Congressional Quarterly.

Beer, S. (1966) 'The British legislature and the problem of mobilising consent', in Frank, E. (ed.) *Lawmakers in a Changing World*, Englewood Cliffs, NJ, Prentice-Hall.

Beetham, D. (1999) *Democracy and Human Rights*, Cambridge, Polity.

Beetham, D. (2005) *Democracy: A Beginner's Guide*, London, Oneworld.

Beetham, D. and Weir, S. (2002) *Democracy under Blair*, London, Polity.

Bennett, J. (2004) *The Anglosphere Challenge: Why the English-Speaking Nations will Lead the Way in the Twenty-First Century*, New York, Rowman and Littlefield.

Berggren, N., Nergelius, J. and Karlson, N. (eds) (2002) *Why Constitutions Matter*, London, Transaction.

Berrington, H. (1968) 'Partisanship and dissidence in the nineteenth century House of Commons', *Parliamentary Affairs*, Vol. 21 No. 4 pp. 338–74.

Bevir, M. and O'Brien, D. (2001) 'New Labour and the public sector in Britain', *Public Administration Review*, Vol. 61 No. 5 pp. 535–47.

Bevir, M. and Rhodes, R. A. W. (2005) 'Interpretation and its others', *Australian Journa of Political Science*, Vol. 40 No. 2 pp. 169–87.

Bevir, M. and Rhodes, R. A. W. (2003) 'Searching for civil society: changing patterns of governance in Britain', *Public Administration*, Vol. 81 No. 1 pp. 41–62.

Bevir, M. and Rhodes, R. (2003) *Interpreting British Governance*, London, Routledge.

Bindman, G. (2005) 'War on terror or war on justice?', OpenDemocracy, 3 March, www.opendemocracy.net/conflict-terrorism/article_2360.jsp

Birch, A. (1964) *Representative and Responsible Government*, London, Unwin.

BIS (2004) *Triennial Central Bank Survey of Foreign Exchange and Derivatives Market Activity in April 2004*, Monetary and Economic Department, BIS.

Blackburn, R. and Kennon, A. (with Wheeler-Booth, M.) (2003) *Parliament: Functions, Practice and Procedures*, London, Sweet and Maxwell.

Blackburn, R. and Plant, R. (1999) *The Labour Government's Constitutional Reform Agenda*, London, Longman.

Blair, T. (1998) Hansard Official Report, House of Commons, 28 July 1998.

Blair, T. (1999) 'Doctrine of the international community', speech delivered in Chicago, 24 April.

Blair, T. (2001) Speech on public service reform, 16 October. www.number-10.gov.uk/output/Page1632.asp

Blair, T. (2001a) Speech to the Labour Party Conference, 2 October.

Blair, T. (2002) 'Rebalancing the criminal justice system', www.number-10.gov.uk/output/Page1717.asp

Blair, T. (2004) 'Strengthening Britain's alliances with Europe and America', Speech delivered at the Lord Mayor's Banquet, Mansion House, London, 15 November.

Blair, T. (2005) Prime Minister's press conference, 12 May, www.number-10.gov.uk/output/Page7481.asp

Blau, A. (2004) 'Fairness and electoral reform', *British Journal of Politics and International Relations*, Vol. 6 No. 2 pp. 165–81.

Blick, A. and Weir, S. (2005), 'The rules of the game: Britain's counter-terrorism strategy', OpenDemocracy, 10 November, www.opendemocracy.net/conflict-terrorism/defeat_3015.jsp

Bogdanor, V. (2001) *Devolution in the United Kingdom*, updated edition, Oxford, Oxford University Press.

Bogdanor, V. (ed.) (2003) *The British Constitution in the Twentieth Century*, Oxford, Clarendon.

Bogdanor, V. (2005a) 'Footfalls echoing in the memory: Britain and Europe: The historical perspective', *International Affairs*, Vol. 81 No. 4 pp. 689–702.

Bogdanor, V. (2005b) 'Foreign policy', in Seldon, A. and Kavanagh, D. (eds) *The Blair Effect 2001–5*, Cambridge, Cambridge University Press.

Bond, R. and McCrone, D. (2004) 'The growth of English regionalism? Institutions and identity', *Regional and Federal Studies*, Vol. 14 No.1 pp. 1–25.

Bower, T. (2005) *Gordon Brown*, London, Perennial.

Bradbury, J. and Russell, M. (2005) 'Learning to live with pluralism? Constituency and regional members and local representation in Scotland and Wales', *ESRC Devolution Briefings* No. 28, www.devolution.ac.uk/Briefing_papers.htm

Brazier, A., Flinders, M. and McHugh, D. (2005) *New Politics, New Parliament? A Review of Parliamentary Modernisation since 1997*, London, Hansard Society.

Brazier, R. (1999) *Constitutional Practice: The Foundations of British Government*, Oxford, Oxford University Press.

Bromley, C. and Curtice, J. (2003) 'Devolution: Scorecard and prospects', in Bromley, C., Curtice, J., Hinds, K. and Park, A. (eds) *Devolution – Scottish Answers to Scottish Questions*, Edinburgh, Edinburgh University Press.

Bromley, C., Curtice, J. and Seyd, B. (2004) *Is Britain Facing a Crisis of Democracy?*, London, Constitution Unit.

Brown, G. (2001) Speech to Transport and General Workers Union conference, www.hm-treasury.gov.uk/newsroom_and_speeches/press/2001/press_77_01.cfm

Brown, G. (2003) 'A modern agenda for prosperity and social reform', speech to Social Market Foundation, Cass Business School, 3 February, www.hm-treasury.gov.uk/newsroom_and_speeches/press/2003/press_12_03.cfm

Bryce, Lord (1921) *Modern Democracies*, London, Macmillan (now Palgrave Macmillan).

Burch, M. and Gomez, R. (2002) 'The English Regions and the European Union', *Regional Studies*, Vol. 36 No. 7 pp. 767–78.

Burch, M. and Holliday, I. (1996) *The British Cabinet System*, London, Prentice-Hall.

Burch, M. and Holliday, I. (1999) 'The Prime Minister's and Cabinet Offices: An Executive Office in all but name', *Parliamentary Affairs*, Vol. 52 No. 1 pp. 32–45.

Burch, M. and Holliday, I. (2004) 'The Blair government and the core executive', *Government and Opposition*, Vol. 39 No. 1 pp. 1–21.

Bush, G. W. (2001) Address to a Joint Session of Congress and the American People, www.whitehouse.gov/news/releases/2001/09/20010920-8.html

Butler, D. and Kavanagh, D. (1984) *The British General Election of 1983*, Basingstoke, Macmillan (now Palgrave Macmillan).

Butler, D. and Kavanagh, D. (2002) *The British General Election of 2001*, Basingstoke, Macmillan (now Palgrave Macmillan).

Butler, R. (2004) *The Butler Report: Review of Intelligence on Weapons of Mass Destruction*, London, TSO, www.thebutlerreview.org.uk

Butt, R. (1967) *The Power of Parliament*, London, Constable.

Byrne, I. and Weir, S. (2004) 'Democratic audit: Executive democracy in war and peace', *Parliamentary Affairs*, Vol. 57 No. 2 pp. 453–68.

Cabinet Office (1999) *Modernising Government*, Cm 4310, London, TSO.

Cabinet Office/Department of Transport, Local Government and the Regions (DTLR) (2002) *Your Region, Your Choice. Revitalising the English Regions*, Cm 5511, London, TSO.

Callinicos, A. (2001) *Against the Third Way*, Cambridge, Polity.

Callinicos, A. (2003) *An Anti-Capitalist Manifesto*, Cambridge, Polity.

Carswell, D. (and other Conservative MPs) (2005) *Direct Democracy: An Agenda for a New Model Party*, www.direct-democracy.co.uk

Castells, M. (2000) *The Rise of the Network* Society, Oxford, Blackwell.

Catt, H. (1996) *Voting Behaviour: A Radical Critique*, Leicester, Leicester University Press.

Chaney, P., Hall, T. and Pithouse, A. (eds) (2001) *New Governance – New Democracy? Post-Devolution Wales*, Cardiff, University of Wales Press.

Chatham House (2005) *Security, Terrorism and the UK*, ISP/NSC Briefing Paper, July.

Childs, S. (2003) 'The Sex Discrimination (Election Candidates) Act and its implications', *Representation*, Vol. 39 No. 2 pp. 83–92.

Childs, S., Lovenduski, J. and Campbell, R. (2005) *Women at the Top: Changing Numbers Changing Politics*, London, Hansard Society.

Chote, R., Emmerson, C. and Oldfield, Z. (2004) *The IFS Green Budget 2004*, London, Institute for Fiscal Studies, www.ifs.org.uk/budgets/gb2004/index.php

Clarke, H. D., Sanders, D., Stewart, M. and Whiteley, P. (2004) *Political Choice in Britain*, Oxford, Oxford University Press.

Clarke, M. (2004) 'Does my bomb look big in this? Britain's nuclear choices after Trident', *International Affairs*, Vol. 80 No. 1 pp. 49–62..

Clift, B. and Tomlinson, J. (2006) 'Credible Keynsianism: New Labour macroeconomic policy and the political economy of coarse tuning', *British Journal of Political Science*, forthcoming.

Coates, D. (1980) *Labour in Power? A Study of the Labour Government 1974–79*, London, Longman.

Coates, D. (2003) *The Hutton Inquiry*, London, Tim Coates.

Coates, D. (2005) *Prolonged Labour: The Slow Birth of New Labour in Britain*, London, Palgrave Macmillan.

Coates, D. and Krieger, J. (2004) *Blair's War*, Cambridge, Polity

Cole, A. and Storer, A. (2002) 'Political dynamics in the Assembly', in Osmond, J. and Jones, J. (eds), *Building a Civic Culture: Institutional Change, Policy Development and Political Dynamics in the National Assembly*, Cardiff, Institute of Welsh Affairs.

Colomer, J. (2005) 'It's parties that choose electoral systems (or, Duverger's Laws upside down)', *Political Studies*, Vol. 53 No.1 pp. 1–21.

Commission for Racial Equality (2005) *The Police Service in England and Wales: Final Report of the Commission of Inquiry*, London, CRE.

Commission on Public–Private Partnerships (2001) *Building Better Partnerships*, London, Institute for Public Policy Research.

Commission on Social Justice (1994) *Social Justice: Strategies for National Renewal*, London, Vintage.

Cook, R. (2003) *The Point of Departure*, London, Simon and Schuster.

Cook, R. and Maclennan, R. (2005) *Looking Back, Looking Forward: The Cook–Maclennan Agreement Eight Years On*, London, New Politics Network.

Cooke, P. (2003) 'Varieties of devolution: Visionary and precautionary economic policy formulation in Scotland and Wales', *ESRC Devolution Policy Papers* No. 7, www.devolution.ac.uk/Policy_Papers.htm

Cooper, R. (2003) *The Breaking of Nations: Order and Chaos in the Twenty-First Century*, London, Atlantic.

Copsey, N. (2004) *Contemporary British Fascism: The BNP and the Search for Legitimacy*, London, Palgrave Macmillan.

Corner, J. and Pels, D. (2003) *Media and the Restyling of Politics: Consumerism, Cynicism, Celebrity*, London, Sage.

Cowley, P. (ed.) (1998) *Conscience and Parliament*, London, Frank Cass.

Cowley, P. (2000) 'Legislatures and assemblies', in Dunleavy, P., Gamble, A., Heffernan, R., Holliday, I. and Peele, G. (eds) *Developments in British Politics 6*, London, Palgrave Macmillan.

Cowley, P. (2002) *Revolts and Rebellions: Parliamentary Voting Under Blair*, London, Politico's.

Cowley, P. (2005) *The Rebels: How Blair Mislaid His Majority*, London, Politico's.

Cowley, P. and Green, J. (2005) 'New leaders, same problems: The Conservatives', in Geddes, A. and Tonge, J. (eds) *Britain Decides: The UK General Election 2005*, London, Palgrave Macmillan.

Cowley, P. and Stuart, M. (2004) 'Still causing trouble? The Parliamentary Party', *Political Quarterly*, Vol. 75 No. 4 pp. 356–61.

Cowley, P. and Stuart, M. (2005a) 'Parliament', in Seldon, A. and Kavanagh, D. (eds) *The Blair Effect 2001–5*, Cambridge, Cambridge University Press.

Cowley, P. and Stuart, M. (2005b) 'Parliament: Hunting for votes', *Parliamentary Affairs*, Vol. 58 No. 2 pp. 258–71.

Cox, A. (1997) *Making Votes Count: Strategic Co-ordination in the World's Electoral Systems*, Cambridge, Cambridge University Press.

Cox, M. (2005) 'Beyond the West: Terrors in Transatlantia', *European Journal of International Relations*, Vol. 11 No. 2 pp. 203–33.

Coxall, B. (2001) *Pressure Groups in British Politics*, London, Longman.

Cracknell, D. (2004) 'Blair's own spin gurus savage No. 10', *Sunday Times*, 26 September.

Crenson, M. A. and Ginsberg, B. (2002) *Downsizing Democracy: How American Sidelined Its Citizens and Privatized Its Public*, Baltimore, MD, Johns Hopkins University Press.

Crewe, I. (1996) '1979–1996', in Seldon, A. (ed.) *How Tory Governments Fall*, London, Fontana.

Crewe, I. (2006) 'New Labour's hegemony: Erosion or extension', in Bartle, J. and King, A. (eds) *Britain At The Polls 2005*, Washington, DC, Congressional Quarterly.

Crouch, C. (2004) *Post-Democracy*, Cambridge, Polity.

Curran, J. and Seaton, J. (2003) *Power Without Responsibility: The Press and Broadcasting in Britain*, sixth edition, London, Routledge.

Curtice, J. (2006) 'A stronger or weaker Union? Public reactions to asymmetric devolution in the United Kingdom', *Publius: The Journal of Federalism*, Vol. 36 No. 1 pp. 95–113.

Curtice, J. (2005) 'Turnout: Electors stay home – again', in Norris, P. and Wlezien, C. (eds) *Britain Votes 2005*, Oxford, Oxford University Press.

Curtice, J., Fisher, S. and Steed, M. (2005) 'Appendix 2: The results analysed', in Kavanagh, D. and Butler, D. (eds) *The British General Election of 2005*, Basingstoke, Palgrave Macmillan.

Cusick, J. (2003) 'The madness of King Tony', *Sunday Herald*, 22 June.

Daalder, I. and Lindsay, J. (2005) *America Unbound: The Bush Revolution in Foreign Policy*, London, John Wiley.

Dahl, R. (2000) *On Democracy*, New Haven, CT, Yale University Press.

Dalton, R. J. and Wattenberg, M. (2002) *Parties Without Partisans*, Oxford, Oxford University Press.

Danchev, A. (2005) 'Story development or Walter Mitty the Undefeated', in Danchev, A. and Macmillan, J. (eds) *The Iraq War and Democratic Politics*, London, Routledge.

Deacon, D. and Golding, P. (1994) *Taxation without Representation*, London, John Libbey.

Deacon, D. and Wring, D. (2005) 'Election Unspun? The mediation of the campaign', in Geddes, A. and Tonge, J. (eds) *Britain Decides: The UK General Election 2005*, London, Palgrave Macmillan.

Deakin, N. and Parry, R. (2000) *The Treasury and Social Policy: The Quest for Control of Welfare Strategy*, London, Palgrave Macmillan.

Denver, D. (2003) *Elections and Voters in Britain*, London, Palgrave Macmillan.

Denver, D., Hands, G. and MacAllister, I. (2004) 'The electoral impact of constituency campaigning in Britain', *Political Studies*, Vol. 52 No. 2 pp. 289–306.

Department for Constitutional Affairs (2001) *The House of Lords: Completing the Reform*, Cm 5291, London, TSO.

Department of Health (2005) *Treatment Centres: Delivering Faster, Quality Care and Choice for NHS Patients*, London, Department of Health, www.dh.gov.uk/assetRoot/04/10/05/24/04100524.pdf

Diamond, P. and Giddens, A. (eds) (2005) *The New Egalitarianism*, Cambridge, Polity.

Dickie, J. (2004) *The New Mandarins: How British Foreign Policy Works*, London, IB Tauris.

Dixon, J. (2001) 'Health care: Modernising the Leviathan', *Political Quarterly*, Vol. 72 No. 3 pp. 30–8.

Dixon, J., Le Grand, J. and Smith, P. (2003) *Shaping The New NHS: Can Market Forces Be Used For Good?*, London, King's Fund, www.kingsfund.org.uk/resources/publications/can_market.html

Dolowitz, D. P. (2004) 'Prosperity and fairness? Can New Labour bring fairness to the 21st century by following the dictates of endogenous growth?', *British Journal of Politics and International Relations*, Vol. 6 No. 2 pp. 213–30.

Dorling, D. (2005) 'Why Trevor is wrong about race ghettos', *Observer*, 25 September.

Dowding, K. (2005) 'Is it rational to vote? Five types of answer and a suggestion', *British Journal of Politics and International Relations*, Vol. 7 No. 3 pp. 443–56.

Driver, S. and Martell, L. (2002) *Blair's Britain*, Cambridge, Polity.

Dummett, M. (1997) *Principles of Electoral Reform*, Oxford, Oxford University Press.

Dunleavy, P. (1990) 'Mass political behaviour: Is there more to learn?', *Political Studies*, Vol. 38 No. 3 pp. 453–69.

Dunleavy, P. (1991) *Democracy, Bureaucracy and Public Choice: Economic Explanations in Political Science*, Hemel Hempstead, Harvester Wheatsheaf.

Dunleavy, P. (1995) 'Policy disasters: Explaining the UK's record', *Public Policy and Administration*, Vol. 10 No. 2 pp. 52–70.

Dunleavy, P. (2005) 'Facing up to multi-party politics', *Parliamentary Affairs*, Vol. 58 No. 3 pp. 503–32.

Dunleavy, P. and Beattie, A. (1995) 'Imperial government and the formation of the British ministerial state', in Lovenduski, J. and Stanyer, J. (eds) *Contemporary Political Studies, 1995: Volume I*, Belfast, UK Political Studies Association.

Dunleavy, P., Jones, G. W. and Burnham, J. (1993) 'Leaders, politics and institutions: Prime Ministerial accountability to the House of Commons', *British Journal of Political Science*, Vol. 23 No.2 pp. 267–98.

Dunleavy, P., Kelly, P. and Moran, M. (eds) (2000) *British Political Science: Fifty Years of Political Studies*, Oxford, Blackwell.

Dunleavy, P. and Margetts, H. (1997) *Electing the London Mayor and the London Assembly: Report Commissioned by the Government Office for London*, London, LSE Public Policy Group.

Dunleavy, P. and Margetts, H. (2001) 'From majoritarian to pluralist democracy: Electoral reform in Britain since 1997', *Journal of Theoretical Politics*, Vol. 13 No. 3 pp. 295–319.

Dunleavy, P. and Margetts, H. (2005) 'The impact of UK electoral systems', *Parliamentary Affairs*, Vol. 58 No. 4 pp. 854–70.

Dunleavy, P., Margetts, H., Smith, T. and Weir, S. (2005) *Voices of the People: Popular Attitudes to Democratic Renewal in Britain*, London, Politico's.

Dunleavy, P. and Rhodes, R. A. W. (1990) 'Core executive studies in Britain', *Public Administration*, Vol. 68 No. 2 pp. 3–28.

Dunne, T. (2004) 'When the shooting starts: Atlanticism in British security strategy', *International Affairs*, Vol. 80 No. 5 pp. 893–909.

Duvell, F. and Jordan, B. (2003) 'Immigration control and the management of economic migration in the United Kingdom: Organizational culture, implementation, enforcement and identity processes in public services', *Journal of Ethnic and Migration Studies*, Vol. 29 No. 2 pp. 299–336.

Dyke, G. (2004) *Inside Story*, London, Harper Collins.

Economist (2004) 'PFInancing new hospitals', *Economist*, 10 January.

Economist (2005) 'New blood for the health service', *Economist*, 23 April.

Electoral Commission (2004) *The Funding of Political Parties*, London, Electoral Commission.

Elster, J. and Slagstad, R. (eds) (1988) *Constitutionalism and Democracy*, Cambridge, Cambridge University Press.

Emmerson, C. and Frayne, C. (2005) *Public Spending*, London: Institute for Fiscal Studies, Election Briefing Notes BN56, www.ifs.org.uk/publications.php?publication_id=3354

European Council (2003) *A Secure Europe in a Better World: The European Security Strategy*, Brussels, Europa.

Evans, G. and Andersen, R. (2005) 'The impact of party leaders: How Blair lost Labour votes', in Norris, P. and Wlezien, C. (eds) *Britain Votes 2005*, Oxford, Oxford University Press.

Evans, M. (2003) *Constitution-making and the Labour Party*, Basingstoke, Palgrave Macmillan.

Falconer, Lord (2003) 'Constitutional reform', Speech at University College, London, 8 December.

Falconer, Lord (2004a) 'Human rights and constitutional reform', Speech at Law Society and Human Rights Lawyers Association, London, 17 February.

Falconer, Lord (2004b) 'Constitutional reform: Strengthening democracy and rights', Inaugural Leslie Falconer WS Memorial Lecture, Signet Library, Edinburgh, 20 February.

Farrell, D. M. (2001) *Electoral Systems: A Comparative Introduction*, Basingstoke, Palgrave Macmillan.

Farrell, D. M. and Webb, P. (2000) 'Political parties as campaigning organizations', in Dalton, R. J. and Wattenberg, M. P. (eds) *Parties Without Partisans: Political Change in Advanced Industrial Democracies*, Oxford, Oxford University Press.

Fawcett, H. (2005) 'Social exclusion in Scotland and the UK: Devolution and the welfare state', *ESRC Devolution Briefings* No. 22, www.devolution.ac.uk/Briefing_papers.htm

Fielding, S. (2003) *The Labour Party: Continuity and Change in the Making of New Labour*, Basingstoke, Palgrave Macmillan.

Fisher, J. (2004) 'Money matters: The financing of the Conservative Party', *Political Quarterly*, Vol. 75 No. 4 pp. 405–10.

Fisher, J. and Clift, B. (2004) 'Comparative party finance reform: The cases of France and Britain', *Party Politics*, Vol. 10 No. 6 pp. 677–99.

Flinders, M. (2000a) 'The politics of accountability: A case study of freedom of information legislation in the United Kingdom', *Political Quarterly*, Vol. 71 No. 4 pp. 422–36.

Flinders, M. (2000b) 'The enduring centrality of individual ministerial responsibility within the British constitution', *Journal of Legislative Studies*, Vol. 6 No. 3 pp. 73–91.

Flinders, M. (2001) *The Politics of Accountability in the Modern State*, London, Ashgate.

Flinders, M. (2002a) 'Governance in Whitehall', *Public Administration*, Vol. 80 No. 1 pp. 51–75.

Flinders, M. (2002b) 'Shifting the balance? Parliament, the Executive and the British Constitution', *Political Studies*, Vol. 50 No. 2 pp. 23–42.

Flinders, M. (2003) 'New Labour and the constitution', in Ludlam, S. and Smith, M. (eds) *New Labour: Politics and Policy Under Blair*, London, Palgrave Macmillan.

Flinders, M. (2005a) 'Majoritarian democracy in Britain', *West European Politics*, Vol. 28 No. 1 pp. 62–94.

Flinders, M. (2005b) 'The politics of public–private partnerships', *British Journal of Politics and International Relations*, Vol. 7 No. 3 pp. 215–39.

Flynn, D. (2003) *Tough as Old Boots: Asylum, Immigration and the Paradox of New Labour Policy*, London, JCWI.

Foley, M. (1999) *The Politics of the British Constitution*, Manchester, Manchester University Press.

Foley, M. (2000) *The British Presidency*, Manchester, Manchester University Press.

Foley, M. (2002) *John Major, Tony Blair and a Conflict of Leadership*, Manchester, Manchester University Press.

Foley, M. (2004) 'Presidential attribution as an agency of prime ministerial critique in a parliamentary democracy', *British Journal of Politics and International Relations*, Vol. 6 No. 3 pp. 292–311.

Forman, N. (1992) *Constitutional Change in the UK*, London, Routledge.

Forster, A. (2002) *Euroscepticism in Contemporary British Politics: Opposition to Europe in the British Conservative and Labour Parties Since 1945*, London, Routledge.

Forster, A. and Blair, A. (2002) *The Making of Britain's European Foreign Policy*, London, Longman.

Foster, C. (2005) *British Government in Crisis*, Oxford, Hart.

Franklin, B. (2004) *Packaging Politics: Political Communications in Britain's Media Democracy*, London, Arnold.

Gaber, I. (2000) 'Government by spin: An analysis of the process', *Media, Culture and Society*, Vol. 22 No. 4 pp. 507–18.

Gaber, I. (2004) 'Alastair Campbell exit stage left: Do the Phillis recommendations represent a new chapter in political communications or is it business as usual?', *Journal of Public Affairs*, Vol. 4 No. 4 pp. 365–73.

Gamble, A. (2000) 'Policy agendas in a multi-level polity', in Dunleavy, P., Gamble, A., Heffernan, R., Holliday, I. and Peele, G. (eds) *Developments in British Politics 6*, Basingstoke, Palgrave Macmillan.

Gamble, A. (2003) *Between Europe and America: The Future of British Politics*, Basingstoke, Palgrave Macmillan.

Garnett, M. (2004) 'The free economy and the schizophrenic state', *Political Quarterly*, Vol. 75 No. 4 pp. 367–72.

Geddes, A. (2004) *The European Union and British Politics*, Basingstoke, Palgrave Macmillan.

Geddes, A. (2005) 'Getting the best out of both worlds? Britain, the EU and migration policy', *International Affairs*, Vol. 81 No. 4 pp. 723–40.

Geddes, A. and Tonge, J. (eds) (2005) *Britain Decides: The UK General Election 2005*, London, Palgrave Macmillan.

George, S. (1998) *An Awkward Partner: Britain in the European Community*, Oxford, Oxford University Press.

Giddens, A. (1998) *The Third Way*, Cambridge, Polity.

Giddens, A. (ed.) (2000) *The Third Way and its Critics*, Cambridge, Polity.

Giddens, A. (ed.) (2001) *The Global 'Third Way' Debate*, Cambridge, Polity.

Giddens, A. (2002) *Where Now for New Labour?*, Cambridge, Polity and Fabian Society.

Giegerich, B. and Wallace, W. (2004) 'Not such a soft power: The external deployment of European forces', *Survival*, Summer.

Glazer, N. (1997) *We Are All Multiculturalists Now*, Cambridge, MA, Harvard University Press.

Golding, P. and Middleton, S. (1982) *Images of Welfare*, Oxford, Oxford University Press.

Gordon, P. and Klug, F. (1986) *New Right, New Racism*, London, Searchlight.

Grant, W. (1978) 'Insider groups, outsider groups and interest group strategies in Britain', *University of Warwick Department of Politics Working Paper*, No. 19.

Grant, W. (1999) *Pressure Groups and British Politics*, London, Palgrave Macmillan.

Grant, W. (2003) 'Economic policy', in Dunleavy, P., Gamble, A., Heffernan, R. and Peele, G. (eds) *Developments in British Politics 7*, Basingstoke, Palgrave Macmillan.

Greer, S. (2006) 'The fragile divergence machine: Citizenship, policy divergence and devolution', in Trench, A. (ed.) *Devolution and Power*, Manchester, Manchester University Press.

Greenslade, R. (2003) 'Their Master's Voice', *Guardian*, 17 February.

Greenwald, B. and Stiglitz, J. (1993) 'New and Old Keynesians', *Journal of Economic Perspectives*, Vol. 7 No. 1 pp. 23–44.

Hague, W. (1998) 'Thinking creatively about the constitution', Speech at the Centre for Policy Studies, 24 February.

Hall, P. A. (2002) 'Great Britain: The role of government in the distribution of social capital', in Putnam, R. D. (ed.) *Democracies in Flux: The Evolution of Social Capital in Contemporary Society*, Oxford, Oxford University Press.

Hallward, P. and MacDonald, R. (2005) 'The economic case for fiscal federalism', in Coyle, D., Alexander, W. and Ashcroft, B. (eds) *New Wealth for Old Nations: Scotland's Economic Prospects*, Princeton, NJ, Princeton University Press.

Halpin, T. (2005) 'State pupils suffer as private schools take university places', *The Times*, 22 September.

Ham, C. (2005) *Health Policy in Britain*, Basingstoke, Palgrave Macmillan.

Hamilton, D. S. and Quinlan, J. P. (2005) 'Deep integration: How Transatlantic markets are leading globalization', London, Centre for Transatlantic Studies.

Hampshire, J. (2005) *Citizenship and Belonging: Immigration and the Politics of Demographic Governance in Post-War Britain*, Basingstoke, Palgrave Macmillan.

Hansard Society (2001) *The Challenge for Parliament: Making Government Accountable*, London, Hansard Society.

Hansen, R. (2000) *Citizenship and Immigration in Post-War Britain: The Institutional Origins of a Multicultural Nation*, Oxford, Oxford University Press.

Harrison, B. (1996) *The Transformation of British Politics, 1865–95*, Oxford, Oxford University Press.

Hay, C. (1999) *The Political Economy of New Labour: Labouring under False Pretences?*, Manchester, Manchester University Press.

Hay, C. (ed.) (2002) *British Politics Today*, Cambridge, Polity.

Hay, C. (2004) 'Credibility, competitiveness and the business cycle in third way political economy: A critical evaluation of economic policy in Britain since 1997', *New Political Economy*, Vol. 9 No. 1 pp. 39–57.

Hay, C. (2006) 'Towards a global political economy?', in Lee, D., Steans, J., Hay, C., Hudson, D. and Watson, M. (eds) *International Political Economy*, Oxford, Oxford University Press.

Hay, C., Smith, N. and Watson, M. (2006) 'Beyond prospective accountancy: Reassessing the case for British membership of the Single European Currency comparatively', *British Journal of Politics and International Relations*, Vol. 8 No. 1 pp. 101–21.

Hayward, J., Barry, B. and Brown, A. (2003) *The British Study of Politics in the Twentieth Century*, Oxford, Oxford University Press/ British Academy.

Hazell, R. (2000) 'Conclusion: The state of the nations after one year of devolution', in Hazell, R. (ed.) *The State of the Nations: The First Year of Devolution in the United Kingdom*, Thorverton, Imprint Academic.

Hazell, R. (2001) 'Reforming the constitution', *Political Quarterly*, Vol. 72 No. 1 pp. 39–49.

Hazell, R. (2003) 'Conclusion: The devolution scorecard as the devolved assemblies head for the polls', in Hazell, R. (ed.) *The State of the Nations 2003: The Third Year of Devolution in the United Kingdom*, Thorverton, Imprint Academic.

Hazell, R. and Trench, A. (2004) *Has Devolution Made a Difference? The State of the Nations 2004*, Thorverton, Imprint Academic.

Healey, J., Gill, M. and McHugh, D. (2005) *MPs and Politics in Our Time*, London, Hansard Society.

Heald, D. and McLeod, A. (2002) 'Fiscal autonomy under devolution: Introduction to symposium', *Scottish Affairs*, Vol. 41 No. 2 pp. 5–25.

Heath, A., Jowell, R., Curtice, J. and Taylor, B. (eds) (1994) *Labour's Last Chance? The 1992 Election and Beyond*, Aldershot, Dartmouth.

Heath, A., Rothon, C. and Jarvis, L. (2002) 'English to the core?', in Park, A., Curtice, J., Thomson, K., Jarvis, L. and Bromley, C. (eds) *British Social Attitudes: The 19th Report*, London, Sage.

Heffernan, R. (2001) *New Labour and Thatcherism: Political Change in Britain*, Basingstoke, Palgrave Macmillan.

Heffernan, R. (2003a) 'Prime ministerial predominance? Core executive politics in the UK', *British Journal of Politics and International Relations*, Vol. 5 No. 3 pp. 347–72.

Heffernan, R. (2003b) 'Political parties and the party system', in Dunleavy, P., Gamble, A., Heffernan, R. and Peele, G. (eds) *Developments in British Politics 7*, Basingstoke, Palgrave Macmillan.

Heffernan, R. (2005a) 'Exploring (and explaining) the Prime Minister', *British Journal of Politics and International Relations*, Vol. 7 No. 4 pp. 605–20.

Heffernan, R. (2005b) 'Why the Prime Minister cannot be a president: Comparing institutional imperatives in Britain and the US', *Parliamentary Affairs*, Vol. 58 No. 1 pp. 53–70.

Held, D. (1996) *Models of Democracy*, 2nd edition, Cambridge, Polity.

Held, D. and McGrew, A. (2002) *Globalization and Anti-globalization*, Cambridge, Polity.

Held, D. and Koenig-Archibugi, M. (2003) *Taming Globalization: Frontiers of Governance*, Cambridge, Polity.

Hennessy, P. (2000a) 'The Blair style and the requirements of twenty-first century premership', *Political Quarterly*, Vol. 70 No. 4 pp. 386–95.

Hennessy, P. (2000b) *The Prime Minister: The Office and its Holders Since 1945*, London, Penguin.

Hennessy, P. (2004) *Rulers and Servants of the State: The Blair Style of Government 1997–2004*, London, Office of Public Management.

Hennessy, P. (2005a) 'Informality and circumscription: The Blair style of government in war and peace', *Political Quarterly*, Vol. 76 No. 1 pp. 3–11.

Hennessy, P. (2005b) 'The Blair style of government', *Parliamentary Affairs*, Vol. 58 No. 1 pp. 6–18.

Hewart, Lord (1929) *The New Despotism*, London, Macmillan (now Palgrave Macmillan).

Hewitt, R. (2005) *White Backlash and the Politics of Multiculturalism*, Cambridge, Cambridge University Press.

House of Commons (2004) *Judicial Appointments and a Supreme Court: First Report of the Constitutional Affairs Committee*, Session 2003–2004, London, TSO.

Hill, C. (2004) 'Renationalising or regrouping? EU foreign policy since 11 September 2001', *Journal of Common Market Studies*, Vol. 42 No. 1 pp. 143–63.

Hill, C. (2005) 'Putting the world to rights: Tony Blair's foreign policy mission', in Seldon, A. and Kavanagh, D. (eds) *The Blair Effect 2001–5*, Cambridge, Cambridge University Press.

Hills, J. (2004) *Inequality and the State*, Oxford, Oxford University Press.

Hirst, P. (1994) *Associative Democracy*, Cambridge, Polity.

Hirst, P. and Thompson, G. (1999) *Globalisation in Question*, 2nd edition, Cambridge, Polity.

Hiskett M. (1992) 'Democracy or theocracy?', *Salisbury Review*, Vol. 10 No. 2 pp. 23–7.

Hocking, B. and Spence, D. (eds) (2003) *Integrating Diplomats: Foreign Ministries in the European Union*, Basingstoke, Palgrave Macmillan.

Hollis, C. (1946) *Can Parliament Survive?*, London, Hollis and Carter.

Home Affairs Select Committee (2005) *Counter-Terrorism and Community Relations in the Aftermath of the London Bombings, 2005–2006*, London, TSO.

Home Office (1998) *Fairer, Faster and Firmer: A Modern Approach to Immigration and Asylum*, Cm 4018, London, TSO.

Home Office (1999) *Inquiry into the Death of Stephen Lawrence* (The Macpherson Report), Cm 4262-I, London, TSO.

Home Office (2002a) 'International Terrorism', unpublished briefing paper circulated to MPs.

Home Office (2002b) *Secure Borders, Safe Haven: Integration and Diversity in Modern Britain*, Cm 5387, London, TSO.

Home Office (2005) *Controlling Our Borders: Making Migration Work for Britain*, Cm 6472, London, TSO.

Hood, C. (1983) *Tools of Government*, Basingstoke, Macmillan (now Palgrave Macmillan).

Hooghe, E. and Marks, G. (2001) *Multi-Level Governance and European Integration*, Lanham, MD, Rowman and Littlefield.

Hussein, D. (2004) 'The impact of 9/11 on British Muslim identity', in Geaves, R., Gabriel, T., Haddad, Y. and Idleman Smith, J. (eds) *Islam and the West Post 9/11*, Aldershot, Ashgate.

Hutton Report (2004) *Report of the Committee of Inquiry into the Circumstances Surrounding the Death of Dr David Kelly*, www.the-hutton-inquiry.org.uk

Hutton, W. (1996) *The State We're In*, London, Vintage.

Hutton, W. (1999) 'New Keynesianism and New Labour', *Political Quarterly*, Vol. 70 No. 1 pp. 97–102.

Huysmans, J. (2005) *What is Politics?*, Edinburgh, Edinburgh University Press and the Open University.

IMF (2004) *Foreign Direct Investment: Trends, Data Availability, Concepts, and Recording Practices*, Washington, DC, IMF.

Ingham, B. (2003) *The Wages of Spin*, London, John Murray.

IPPR (2001) *Building Better Partnerships*, London, Institute for Public Policy Research.

Irvine, Lord. (1998) Lecture to the Constitution Unit, 8 December.

James, S, (1992) *British Cabinet Government*, London, Routledge.

Johnson, B. (2004) 'How not to run a country', *Spectator*, 11 December.

Johnson, N. (2001) 'Taking stock of the constitution', *Government and Opposition*, Vol. 36 No. 3 pp. 331–49.

Jeffery, C. (2003a) 'The politics of territorial finance', *Regional and Federal Studies*, Vol. 13 No. 4 pp. 183–96.

Jeffery, C. (2003b) 'The English regions debate: What do the English want?', *ESRC Devolution Briefings*, No. 3, www.devolution.ac.uk/Briefing_papers.htm

Jeffery, C. (2004) 'Judgements on devolution? The 2003 elections in Scotland, Wales and Northern Ireland', *Representation*, Vol. 40 No. 4 pp. 302–15.

Jeffery, C. (2005a) 'Devolution and divergence: Public attitudes and institutional logics', in Adams, J. and Schmuecker, K. (eds) *Devolution in Practice II: Public Policy Differences in the UK*, London, Institute for Public Policy Research.

Jeffery, C. (2005b) 'Devolution and the European Union: Trajectories and futures', in Trench, A. (ed.) *The Dynamics of Devolution: The State of the Nations 2005*, Thorverton, Imprint Academic.

Jeffery, C. (2006) 'Devolution and local government', *Publius: The Journal of Federalism*, Vol. 36 No. 1 pp. 57–73.

Jeffery, C. and Hough, D. (2003) 'Elections in multi-level systems: Lessons for the UK from abroad', in Hazell, R. (ed.) *The State of the Nations 2003: The Third Year of Devolution in the United Kingdom*, Thorverton, Imprint Academic

Jeffery, C. and Wincott, D. (eds) (2006) *Devolution in the United Kingdom: Statehood and Citizenship in Transition*, Special Issue of *Publius: The Journal of Federalism*, Vol. 36 No. 1 pp. 3–18.

Johnston, R. and Pattie, C. (2003) 'Local battles in a national landslide', *Political Geography*, Vol. 22 No. 2 pp. 381–414.

Johnston, R., Pattie, C., Dorling, D. and Rossiter, R. (2001) *From Votes to Seats: The Operation of the UK Electoral System Since 1945*, Manchester, Manchester University Press.

Jones, N. (1999) *Sultans of Spin: Media and the New Labour Government*, London, Weidenfeld and Nicolson.

Joppke, C. (1999) *Immigration and the Nation State: The United States, Germany and Great Britain*, Oxford, Oxford University Press.

Jordan, G. and Maloney, W. A. (1997) *The Protest Business: Mobilizing Campaigning Groups*, Manchester, Manchester University Press.

Jordan, G. and Maloney, W. A. (forthcoming 2006) *Interest Groups and Democracy: Enhancing Participation?*, Basingstoke, Palgrave Macmillan.

Jowell, J. and Oliver, D. (eds) (2004) *The Changing Constitution*, Oxford, Oxford University Press.

Judge, D. (1993) *The Parliamentary State*, London, Sage.

Judge, D. (2004) 'Whatever happened to parliamentary democracy in the United Kingdom?', *Parliamentary Affairs*, Vol. 57 No. 3 pp. 682–701.

Kagan, R. (2003) *Paradise and Power: America and Europe in the New World Order*, London, Atlantic.

Kaiser, W., Catterall, P. and Walton-Jordan, U. (eds) (2000) *Reforming the Constitution*, London, Cass.

Kalestsky, A. (2005) 'Educashun, ejucation, edication: All parties can say it but none is able to get it right', *The Times*, 22 April.

Kampfner, J. (2003) *Blair's Wars*, London, Free Press.

Katz, R. and Mair, P. (1995) 'Changing models of party organization and party democracy: The emergence of the cartel party', *Party Politics*, Vol. 1 No. 1 pp. 5–28.

Katz, R. and Mair, P. (2002) 'The ascendancy of the party in public office: Party organisational change in twentieth century democracies', in Gunther, R., Montero, J. R. and Linz, J. (eds) *Political Parties: Old Concepts and New Challenges*, Oxford, Oxford University Press.

Kavanagh, D. (2003) 'British political science in the inter-war years: The emergence of the founding fathers', *British Journal of Politics and International Relations*, Vol. 5 No. 4 pp. 594–613.

Kavanagh, D. and Butler, D. (2005) *The British General Election of 2005*, London, Palgrave Macmillan.

Keating, M. (2004) 'How distinctive is Holyrood? An analysis of legislation in the first Scottish Parliament', *ESRC Devolution Policy Papers*, No. 10, www.devolution.ac.uk/Policy_Papers.htm

Keating, M. (2005) *The Government of Scotland: Public Policy Making after Devolution*, Edinburgh, Edinburgh University Press.

Kelly, G. and Lissauer R. (2000) *Ownership for All*, London, Institute for Public Policy Research.

Kelly, R., Gay, O. and Cowley, P. (2006) 'The House of Commons in 2005: Turbulence ahead?', in Rush, M. and Giddings, P. (eds) *Palgrave Review of British Politics 2005*, Basingstoke, Palgrave Macmillan.

Kelso, A. (2003) 'Where were the massed ranks of parliamentary reformers? "Attitudinal" and "contextual" approaches to parliamentary reform', *Journal of Legislative Studies*, Vol. 9 No. 1 pp. 57–76.

Kerr, P. (2001) *Post-War British Politics: From Conflict to Consensus*, London, Routledge.

King, A. (1993) 'The implications of one-party government', in King, A. (ed.) *Britain at the Polls 1992*, Chatham, NJ, Chatham House.

King, A. (2001) *Does the United Kingdom Still Have a Constitution?*, London, Sweet and Maxwell.

King, A. (2006) 'Why Labour won – yet again', in Bartle, J. and King, A. (eds) *Britain At The Polls 2005*, Washington, DC, Congressional Quarterly.

King, D. (2000) *Making Americans: Immigration, Race and the Making of the Diverse Democracy*, Cambridge, MA, Harvard University Press.

King's Fund (2003) 'New freedoms of foundation trusts to be welcomed, but robust evaluation is key, says Kings Fund', London, King's Fund.

Kirchner, J. (1999) 'Inflation: Paper dragon or Trojan Horse?', *Review of International Political Economy*, Vol. 6 No. 4 pp. 609–18.

Klein, R. (2005) 'Transforming the NHS: The story in 2004', in Powell, M., Bauld, L. and Clarke, K. (eds) *Social Policy Review 17*, Bristol, Policy Press.

Klug, F., Weir, S. and Beetham, D. (1996) *The Three Pillars of Liberty*, London, Routledge.

Krieger, J. (1999) *British Politics in the Global Age*, Cambridge, Polity.

Kuhn, R. (2003) 'The media and politics', in Dunleavy, P., Gamble, A., Heffernan, R. and Peele, G. (eds) *Developments in British Politics 7*, Basingstoke, Palgrave Macmillan.

Kymlicka, W. (2001) *Politics in the Vernacular: Nationalism, Multiculturalism and Citizenship*, Oxford, Oxford University Press.

Labour Party (1997) *Because Britain Deserves Better*, London, The Labour Party.

Labour Party (2001) *Ambitions for Britain*, London, The Labour Party.

Labour Party (2005) *Britain Forward Not Back*, London, The Labour Party.

Lanchester, J (2003) 'Unbelievable Blair', *London Review of Books*, 10 July.

Lambert, D. and Navarro, M. (2005) 'The nature and scope of the legislative powers of the National Assembly for Wales', *ESRC Devolution Briefings*, No. 13, www.devolution.ac.uk/Briefing_papers.htm

Laws, D. and Marshall, P. (2004) *The Orange Book: Reclaiming Liberalism*, London, Profile.

Lawson, N. (1992) *The View From No. 11: Memoirs of a Tory Radical*, London, Bantam.

Lawson, N. and Sherlock, N. (2001) *The Progressive Century: The Future of the Centre-Left in Britain*, Basingstoke, Palgrave Macmillan.

Layton-Henry, Z. (1994) 'Britain: The would-be zero immigration country', in Cornelius, W., Martin, P. L. and Hollifield, J. F. (eds) *Controlling Immigration: A Global Perspective*, Stanford, CA, Stanford University Press.

Le Grand, J. (1998) 'The third way begins with cora', *New Statesman*, 6 March.

Le Grand, J. (2003) *Motivation, Agency and Public Policy: Of Knights and Knaves, Pawns and Queens*, Oxford, Oxford University Press.

Lea, R. (2005) *The NHS Since 1997*, London, Centre for Policy Studies, www.cps.org.uk/pdf/pub/412.pdf

Lee, D., Steans, J., Hay, C., Hudson, D. and Watson, M. (2006) *International Political Economy*, Oxford, Oxford University Press.

Lee, J. M., Jones, G. W. and Burnham, J. (1998) *At the Centre of Whitehall: Advising the Prime Minister and Cabinet*, Basingstoke, Macmillan (now Palgrave Macmillan).

Leggett, S. (2005) *After New Labour*, Basingstoke, Palgrave Macmillan.

Lewis, J. and Brookes, R. (2003) 'Reporting the war on British television', in Miller, D. (ed.) *Tell me Lies: Propaganda and Media Distortion in the Attack on Iraq*, London, Pluto.

Lewis, J. and Brookes, R. (2004) 'British TV news and the case for war in Iraq', in Allan, S. and Zelizer, B. (eds) *Reporting War: Journalism in Wartime*, London, Routledge.

Lijphart, A. (1999) *Patterns of Democracy*, New Haven, CT and London, Yale University Press.

Little, R. and Wickham-Jones, M. (2000) *'New Labour's Foreign Policy: A New Moral Crusade?*, Manchester, Manchester University Press.

Lloyd, J. (2004) *What the Media Are Doing to Our Politics*, London, Constable.

Loescher, G. (2005) ' "Asylum crisis" in the UK and Europe', OpenDemocracy, posted 22 May, www.opendemocracy.net/people-migrationeurope/article_1291.jsp

Loughlin, J. and Sykes, S. (2004) 'Devolution and policy-making in Wales: Restructuring the system and reinforcing identity', *ESRC Devolution Policy Papers*, No. 11, www.devolution.ac.uk/Policy_Papers.htm

Lovenduski, J. (2005) *Feminizing Politics*, Cambridge, Polity.

Low, S. (1904) *The Governance of England*, London, Fisher Unwin.

Lowe, R. (2005) *The Welfare State in Britain Since 1945*, Basingstoke, Palgrave Macmillan.

Lowell, A. L. (1924) *The Government of England, Volume 2*, New York, Macmillan (now Palgrave Macmillan).

LSE (2005) *The Identity Project: An Assessment of the UK Identity Cards Bill and its Implications*, London, London School of Economics and Political Science.

Lucas, C. and Woodin, M. (2004) *Green Alternatives to Globalisation*, London, Pluto.

Ludlam, S. (2004) 'New Labour, "vested interests" and the union link', in Ludlam, S. and Smith, M. J. (eds) *Governing as New Labour: Policy and Politics under Blair*, Basingstoke, Palgrave Macmillan.

Lynch, P. and Garner, R. (2005) 'The changing party system', *Parliamentary Affairs*, Vol. 58 No. 3 pp. 533–54.

MacGinty, R. (2003) 'A breathing space for devolution: public attitudes to constitutional issues in a devolved Northern Ireland', *ESRC Devolution Policy Papers*, No. 2, www.devolution.ac.uk/Policy_Papers.htm

Macintyre, D. (2000) *Peter Mandelson and the Making of New Labour*, London, HarperCollins.

Maclean, I., Spirling, A. and Russell, M. (2003) 'None of the above: The UK House of Commons votes on reforming the House of Lords', *Political Quarterly*, Vol. 74 No. 3 pp. 298–310.

MacPherson, C. B. (1977) *The Life and Times of Liberal Democracy*, Oxford, Oxford University Press.

Maddison, A. (1987) 'Growth and slowdown in advanced capitalist economies: Techniques of quantitative assessment', *Journal of Economic Literature*, Vol. 25 No. 2 pp. 649–98.

Maer, L. et al. (2004) 'Dragging the constitution out of the shadows', *Parliamentary Affairs*, Vol. 57 No. 2 pp. 253–68.

Major, J. and Heathcoat-Amory, D. (2003) *The Erosion of Parliamentary Government*, London, Centre for Policy Studies.

Maloney, W. A. and van Deth, J. W. (2005) 'Assessing the associational impact on members: Associations as schools of democracy', Paper prepared for delivery at the Joint Sessions of the European Consortium for Political Research, Granada, April 2005.

Mandelson, P. and Liddle, R. (2002) *The Blair Revolution Revisited*, London, Politico's.

Mangold, P. (2001) *Success and Failure in British Foreign Policy: Evaluating the Record, 1900–2000*, London, Palgrave Macmillan.

Mann, J. (2004) *The Rise of the Vulcans: The History of Bush's War Cabinet*, Harmondsworth, Penguin.

Maor, M. (1997) *Political Parties: Comparative Approaches and the British Experience*, London, Routledge.

Margetts, H. (2005) 'The 2004 London GLA Elections Study', *ESRC Devolution Briefings*, No. 33, www.devolution.ac.uk/Briefing_papers.htm

Marquand, D. (1997) *The New Reckoning*, Cambridge: Polity.

Marquand, D. (1999) 'Populism or Pluralism? New Labour and the Constitution', Misheon Lecture, University College London, May.

Marquand, D. (2004) *The Decline of the Public: The Hollowing Out of Citizenship*, Cambridge, Polity.

Marsh, D. (1992) *The New Politics of British Trade Unionism: Union Power and the Thatcher Legacy*, Basingstoke, Macmillan (now Palgrave Macmillan).

Marsh, D., Buller, J., Hay, C., Johnston, J., Kerr, P., McAnnulla, S. and Watson, M. (1999) *Postwar British Politics in Perspective*, Cambridge, Polity.

Marsh, D., Richards, D. and Smith, M. J. (2001) *Changing Patterns of Governance in the United Kingdom: Reinventing Whitehall?*, London, Palgrave Macmillan.

Marsh, D., Richards, D. and Smith, M. J. (2003) 'Unequal plurality: Towards an asymmetrical power model of British politics', *Government and Opposition*, Vol. 38 No. 3 pp. 306–32.

Massey, A. (2001) 'Policy, management and implementation', in Savage, S. and Atkinson, R. (eds) *Public Policy under Blair*, Basingstoke, Palgrave Macmillan.

McGhee, D. (2005) *Intolerant Britain? Hate, Citizenship and Difference*, Milton Keynes, Open University Press.

McKenzie, R. T. (1964) *British Political Parties*, London, Heinemann.

McConnell, A. (2004) *Scottish Local Government*, Edinburgh, Edinburgh University Press.

McLeish, H. (2004) *Scotland First: Truth and Consequences*, Edinburgh, Mainstream.

McNair, B. (2003) *Introduction to Political Communication*, London, Routledge.

Meade, J. (1964) *Efficiency, Equality and the Ownership of Property*, London, Allen and Unwin.

Messina, A. (1989) *Race and Party Competition in* Britain, Oxford, Clarendon.

Metropolitan Police Authority (2004) *Independent Inquiry into Professional Standards and Employment Matters* (chaired by Sir William Morris), London, MPA.

Meyer, C. (2005) *DC Confidential*, London, Weidenfeld and Nicolson.

Micklethwait, J. and Wooldridge, A. (2004) *The Right Nation: Conservative Power in America*, London, Penguin.

Milburn, A. (2004) 'Power to the people', Speech to the Social Market Foundation, London, 8 December.

Miliband, D. (ed.) (1994) *Beyond Left and Right: The Future of Radical Politics*, Cambridge, Polity.

Miller, D. (ed.) (2003) *Tell me Lies: Propaganda and Media Distortion in the Attack on Iraq*, London, Pluto.

Miller, W. L., Clarke, H., Harrop, M., LeDuc, L. and Whiteley, P. (1990) *How Voters Change: The 1987 British Election Campaign in Perspective*, Oxford, Clarendon.

Mitchell, J. (2003) 'Spectators and audiences: The politics of UK territorial finance', *Regional and Federal Studies*, Vol. 13 No. 4 pp. 7–21.

Mitchell, J. (2004) 'Scotland: Expectations, policy types and devolution', in Trench, A. (ed.) *Has Devolution Made a Difference? The State of the Nations 2004*, Thorverton, Imprint Academic.

Mitchell, J. (2006) 'Evolution and devolution: Citizenship, institutions and public policy', *Publius: The Journal of Federalism*, Vol. 36 No. 1 pp. 153–68.

Monbiot, G. (2004) *The Age of Consent*, London, Perennial.

Modood, T. (2005) *Multicultural Politics: Racism, Ethnicity and Muslims in Britain*, Minneapolis, MN, University of Minnesota Press.

Moran, M. (1991) *The Politics of the Financial Services Revolution*, Basingstoke, Macmillan (now Palgrave Macmillan).

Moran, M. (2002) *The British Regulatory State*, Oxford, Oxford University Press.

Morgan, K. (2001) *Britain Since 1945: The People's Peace*, Oxford, Oxford University Press.

Morgan, K. and Upton, S. (2005) 'Culling the quangos', in Osmond, J. (ed.) *Welsh Politics Comes of Age: Responses to the Richard Commission*, Cardiff, Institute of Welsh Affairs.

Morgan, P. (2005) *The Insider: The Private Diaries of a Scandalous Decade*, London, Ebury.

Morgan, R. (2004) Speech by the First Minister to ESRC Conference, Cardiff, 24 June.

Morrison, J. (2001) *Reforming Britain: New Labour, New Constitution?*, London, Reuters.

Moss, M. (2005) 'Spin-doctors now cost us £5.5 million', *Tribune*, 29 July.

Moxon, S. (2004) *The Great Immigration Scandal*, Exeter, Imprint Academic.

Mulgan, G. (1993) 'Reticulated organisations: The birth and death of the mixed economy', in Crouch, C. and Marquand, D. (eds) *Ethics and Markets: Cooperation and Competition Within Capitalist Economies*, Oxford, Blackwell/Political Quarterly.

Mulgan, G. (2004) 'The media's lies poison our system', *Guardian*, 7 May.

Mullard, M. and Swaray, R. (2006) 'The politics of public expenditure from Thatcher to Blair', *Policy and Politics*, forthcoming.

Muller, W. and Strom, K. (1999) *Policy, Office or Votes? How Political Parties in Western Europe Make Hard Decisions*, Cambridge, Cambridge University Press.

Nairn, T. (2000) 'UKania under Blair', *New Left Review*, Vol. 30 No. 1 pp. 69–103.

National Audit Office (2005) *Returning Failed Asylum Seekers*, HC 76 (2005–2006), London, TSO.

Naughtie, J. (2002) *The Rivals: The Intimate Story of a Political Marriage*, London, Fourth Estate.

Newman, J. (2001) *Modernising Governance: New Labour, Policy and Society*, London, Sage.

Norris, P. (1997) *Electoral Change in Britain Since 1945*, Oxford, Basil Blackwell.

Norris, P. (2001) 'The twilight of Westminster? Electoral reform and its consequences', *Political Studies*, Vol. 49 No. 5 pp. 877–900.

Norris, P. and Wlezien, C. (eds) (2005) *Britain Votes 2005*, Oxford, Oxford University Press.

Norton, P. (1975) *Dissension in the House of Commons 1945–1974*, London, Macmillan (now Palgrave Macmillan).

Norton P. (2003) 'Cohesion without discipline: Party voting in the House of Lords', *Journal of Legislative Studies*, Vol. 9 No. 4 pp.57–72.

Norton, P. (2003) 'Governing alone', *Parliamentary Affairs*, Vol. 56 No. 4 pp. 543–59.

Norton, P. (2005) *Parliament in British Politics*, Basingstoke, Palgrave Macmillan.

Norton, P. and Wood, D. M. (1993) *Back From Westminster*, Lexington, KT, University of Kentucky Press.

Oborne, P. (2005) *The Rise of Political Lying*, London, Free Press.

Oborne, P. and Walters, S. (2004) *Alastair Campbell*, London, Aurum.

Office of Public Services Reform (2002) *Reforming our Public Services: Principles into Practice*, London, www.pm.gov.uk/files/pdf/Principles.pdf

Oliver, D. (2003) *Constitutional Reform in the United Kingdom*, Oxford, Oxford University Press.

O'Neil, M. (ed.) (2004) *Devolution in British Politics*, London, Longman.

O'Sullivan, J. (2003) 'How not to think about immigration', *Salisbury Review*, Vol. 21 No. 3 pp. 6–11.

Osmond, J. (ed.) (2005) *Welsh Politics Comes of Age: Responses to the Richard Commission*, Cardiff, Institute of Welsh Affairs.

Owen, D. (1981) *Face the Future*, London, Cape.

Owen, D. (1984) *A Future That Will Work*, London, Penguin.

Owen, G. (1999) *From Empire to Europe: The Decline and Revival of British Industry Since the Second World War*, London, HarperCollins.

Owens, J. E. (2003) 'Explaining party cohesion and discipline in democratic legislatures: Purposiveness and contexts', *Journal of Legislative Studies*, Vol. 9 No. 4 pp. 12–40.

Packer, G. (2005) *The Assassin's Gate: America In Iraq*, New York, Farrar, Strauss and Giroux.

Page, A. and Batey, A. (2002) 'Scotland's other Parliament: Westminster legislation about devolved matters in Scotland since devolution', *Public Law*, Autumn, pp. 501–23.

Page, B. (2003) *The Murdoch Archipelago*, London, Simon and Schuster.

Parekh, B. (2000a) *The Future of Multi-Ethnic Britain* (The Parekh Report), London, Profile.

Parekh, B. (2000b) *Rethinking Multiculturalism: Cultural Diversity and Political Theory*, Basingstoke, Palgrave Macmillan.

Parker, G. (2004) 'Will the Big Three give Europe fresh impetus – Or just deepen its divisions?', *Financial Times*, 16 February.

Parker, G. (2005) 'Europe's budget barons get ready to fight', *Financial Times*, 16 June.

Parris, M. (2003) 'Are we witnessing the Madness of Tony Blair?', *The Times*, 29 March.

Parry, G., Moyser, G. and Day, N. (1992) *Political Participation and Democracy in Britain*, Cambridge, Cambridge University Press.

Paterson, L., Brown, A. and Curtice, J. (2001) *New Scotland, New Politics?*, Edinburgh, Edinburgh University Press.

Pattie, C., Seyd, P. and Whiteley, P. (2004) *Citizenship in Britain: Values, Participation and Democracy*, Cambridge, Cambridge University Press.

Paul, K. (1997) *Whitewashing Britain: Race and Citizenship in the Postwar Era*, Ithaca, NY, Cornell University Press.

Paxton, W. (ed.) (2003) *Equal Shares? Building a Progressive and Coherent Asset-based Welfare Policy*, London, Institute for Public Policy Research.

Pearce, N. and Paxton, W. (eds) (2005) *Social Justice: Building a Fairer Britain* London, Institute for Public Policy Research.

Perri 6 (2003) 'Giving consumers of British public services more choice: What can be learned from recent history', *Journal of Social Policy*, Vol. 32 No. 2 pp. 239–70.

Peston, R. (2005) *Brown's Britain*, London, Short Books.

Peters, B. G. and Pierre, J. (2000) *Governance, Politics and the State*, Basingstoke, Palgrave Macmillan.

Phillips, D. (2005) *Losing Iraq: Inside the Postwar Reconstruction Fiasco*. Westview, CO, University of Colorado Press.

Phillips, T. (2004) 'Britishness and the "M" word', *Connections*, Spring.

Phillips, T. (2005) 'Equality in our lifetime: Talking about a revolution', Speech at the University of Northampton, 28 October.

Phillis, B. (2004) *An Independent Review of Government Communications* (The Phillis Report), London, TSO.

Pierre, J. and Stoker, G. (2000) 'Towards multi-level governance', in Dunleavy, P., Gamble, A., Heffernan, R., Holliday, I. and Peele, G. (eds) *Developments in British Politics 6*, Basingstoke, Palgrave Macmillan.

Pilkington, A. (2003) *Racial Disadvantage and Ethnic Diversity in Britain*, Basingstoke, Palgrave Macmillan.

Pinto-Duschinsky, M. (1998) 'Send the rascals packing: Defects of proportional representation and the virtues of the Westminster model', *Times Literary Supplement*, September.

Poguntke, T. and Webb, P. (eds) (2005) *The Presidentialization of Politics: A Comparative Study of Modern Democracies*, Oxford, Oxford University Press.

Pollard, S. (2004) *David Blunkett*, London, Hodder and Stoughton.

Pollitt, C. and Bouckaert, G. (2003) *Public Management Reform: A Comparative Analysis*, Oxford, Oxford University Press.

Pollock, A. (2003) 'Foundation hospitals will kill the NHS', *Guardian*, 7 May.

Pollock, A. (2004) *NHS plc: The Privatisation of our Health Care*, London, Verso.

Posen, A. S. (1993) 'Why Central Bank independence does not cause low inflation', in O'Brien, R. (ed.) *Finance and the International Economy 7*, Oxford, Oxford University Press.

Posen, A. S. (1998) 'Do better institutions make better policy?', *International Finance*, Vol. 1 No. 1 pp. 173–205.

Power, G. (1996) *Reinventing Westminster*, London, Charter 88.

Power, G. (1998) *Representing the People: MPs and their Constituents*, London, Fabian Society.

Power, M. (1997) *The Audit Society: Rituals of Verification*, Oxford, Oxford University Press.

Price, L. (2005) *The Spin Doctor's Diary: Inside Number 10 with New Labour*, London, Hodder and Stoughton.

Public Administration Committee (2003) *Government by Appointment*, HC 165 (2002–03), London, TSO.

Putnam, R. D. (1993) *Making Democracy Work*, Princeton, NJ, Princeton University Press.

Putnam, R. D. (1995) 'Bowling alone: America's declining social capital', *Journal of Democracy*, Vol. 6 No. 1 pp. 65–78.

Putnam, R. D. (2000) *Bowling Alone: Collapse and Revival of American Community*, New York, Simon and Schuster.

Putnam, R. D. (ed.) (2002) *Democracies in Flux: The Evolution of Social Capital in Contemporary Society*, Oxford, Oxford University Press.

Quinn, T. (2004) 'Electing the leader: The British Labour Party's electoral college', *British Journal of Politics and International Relations*, Vol. 6 No. 3 pp. 333–52.

Rallings, C. and Thrasher, M. (2005) 'Why the North East said "No": The 2004 referendum on an elected regional assembly', *ESRC Devolution Briefings*, No. 19, www.devolution.ac.uk/Briefing_papers.htm

Rallings, C., Thrasher, M. and Cowling, D. (2002) 'Mayoral referendums and elections', *Local Government Studies*, Vol. 28 No. 4, pp. 67–90.

Rawlence, B. (2004) 'Blair is the original neo-con', *Guardian*, 23 October.

Rawlings, R. (2003) *Delineating Wales: Constitutional, Legal and Administrative Aspects of National Devolution*, Cardiff, University of Wales Press.

Rawnsley, A. (2001) *Servants of the People: The Inside Story of New Labour*, London, Penguin.

Rawnsley, A. (2003) 'Duelling monarchs of Downing Street', *Observer*, 18 May.

Rawnsley, A. (2005) 'The nice party no longer', *Observer*, 18 December.

Reid, J. (2005) 'Social democratic politics in an age of consumerism', Speech at Paisley University, 27 January.

Reif, K. and Schmitt, H. (1980) 'Nine second-order national elections: A conceptual framework for the analysis of European election results', *European Journal of Political Research*, Vol. 8 No. 1 pp. 3–44.

Rentoul, J. (2001) *Tony Blair*, London, Time Warner.

Rhodes, R. A. W. (1997) *Understanding Governance*, Buckingham, Open University Press.

Rhodes, R. A. W. and Dunleavy, P. (eds) (1995) *Prime Minister, Cabinet and Core Executive*, London, Macmillan (now Palgrave Macmillan).

Richard Commission (2004) *Report of the Richard Commission*, London, TSO.

Richards, D. and Smith, M. J. (2001) 'New Labour, the constitution and reforming the state', in Ludlam, S. and Smith, M. J. (eds) *New Labour in Government*, Basingstoke, Palgrave Macmillan.

Richards, D. and Smith, M. J. (2002) *Governance and Public Policy in the United Kingdom*, Oxford, Oxford University Press.

Richards, D. and Smith, M. J. (2004) 'Interpreting the world of political elites', *Public Administration*, Vol. 82 No. 4 pp. 777–800.

Richards, P. (1959) *Honourable Members*, London, Faber and Faber.

Richards, S. (2005) 'Look Back at Power', broadcast on BBC Radio Four, 5 September.

Richardson, J. and Jordan, G. (1979) *Governing Under Pressure: The Policy Process in a Post-Parliamentary Democracy*, Oxford, Martin Robertson.

Riddell, P. (1993) *Honest Opportunism*, London, Hamish Hamilton.

Riddell, P. (2000) *Parliament Under Blair*, London, Politico's.

Riddell, P. (2003) *Hug Them Close: Blair, Clinton, Bush and the 'Special Relationship'*, London, Politico's.

Riddell, P. (2005) *The Unfulfilled Prime Minister: Tony Blair's Quest for a Legacy*, London, Politico's.

Robinson, N. (2005) 'Why I hate this absurd row between politicians and the media', *Observer*, 28 August.

Robison, R. (2006) *The Neoliberal Revolution: Forging the Market State*, Basingstoke, Palgrave Macmillan.

Rogers, R. and Walters, R. (2004) *How Parliament Works*, London, Pearson Longman.

Rokkan, S. and Urwin, D. (1982) *The Politics of Territorial Identity*, London, Sage.

Rometsch, D. and Wessels, W. (eds) (1996) *The European Union and Member States: Towards Institutional Fusion?*, Manchester, Manchester University Press.

Rosamond, B. (2002) 'Britain's European future', in Hay, C. (ed.) *British Politics Today*, Cambridge, Polity.

Rose, N. (1999) *Powers of Freedom: Reframing Political Thought*, Cambridge, Cambridge University Press.

Rose, N. and Miller, P. (1992) 'Political power beyond the state: Problematics of government', *British Journal of Sociology*, Vol. 4 No. 2 pp. 173–205.

Rose, R. (2001) *The Prime Minister in a Shrinking World*, London, Polity.

Rosenblum, N. (1998) *Membership and Morals: The Personal Uses of Pluralism in America*, Princeton, NJ, Princeton University Press.

Roy, O. (2004) *Globalised Islam: The Search for a New Ummah*, London, Hearst.

Royal Commission on the Reform of the House of Lords (The Wakeham Commission) (2000) *A House for the Future*, Cm 4535, London, TSO.

Runciman W. G. (2004) *Hutton and Butler: Lifting the Lid on the Workings of Power*, London, British Academy.

Runnymede Trust (1997) *Islamophobia: A Challenge for Us All*, London, Runnymede Trust.

Rush, M. (2005) *Parliament Today*, Manchester, Manchester University Press.

Russell, A. (2005) 'The party system in 2004', *Parliamentary Affairs*, Vol. 58 No. 2 pp. 351–65.

Russell, A. and Fieldhouse, E. (2005) *Neither Left nor Right? The Liberal Democrats and the Electorate*, Manchester, Manchester University Press.

Russell, M. (2005) *Building New Labour*, Basingstoke, Palgrave Macmillan.

Russell, M. and Sciara, M. (2006) 'The House of Lords in 2005: A more representative and more assertive Chamber', in Rush, M. and Giddings, P. (eds) *Palgrave Review of British Politics 2005*, Basingstoke, Palgrave Macmillan.

Ryle, M. (2005) 'Forty years on and a future agenda', in Giddings, P. (ed.) *The Future Of Parliament: Issues for a New Century*, Basingstoke, Palgrave Macmillan.

Sanders, D. (1993) 'Why the Conservative Party won – again', in King, A. (ed.) *Britain at the Polls 1992*, Chatham, NJ, Chatham House.

Sanders, D. (2002) 'Electoral competition in contemporary Britain', in Hay, C. (ed.) *British Politics Today*, Cambridge, Polity.

Sanders, D. (2005) 'The political economy of UK party support, 1997–2004: Forecasts for the 2005 General Election', *Journal of Elections, Public Opinion and Parties*, Vol. 15 No. 1 pp. 47–71.

Savage, S. and Atkinson, R. (eds) (2001) *Public Policy under Blair*, Basingstoke, Palgrave Macmillan.

Saward, M. (1998) *The Terms of Democracy*, Cambridge, Polity.

Schattschneider, E. E. (1960) *Semisovereign People*, New York: Holt, Rinehart and Winston.

Scott, D. (2004) *Off Whitehall*, London, IBTauris.

Scott, J. (1998) *Seeing like a State: How Certain Schemes to Improve the Human Condition Have Failed*, New Haven, CT, Yale University Press.

Scottish Constitutional Convention (1995) *Scotland's Parliament, Scotland's Right*, Edinburgh, Scottish Constitutional Convention.

Scottish Parliament (2004) *The Holyrood Enquiry: A Report by the Rt Hon. Lord Fraser of Carmyllie QC on his Inquiry into the About Holyrood Project*, SP Paper 205, Edinburgh, The Scottish Parliament.

Searle, G. R. (1995) *Country Before Party: Coalition and the Idea of National Government in Modern Britain, 1885–1987*, London, Longman.

Seldon, A. (1997) *Major: A Political Life*, London, Weidenfeld and Nicolson.

Seldon, A. (2005) *Blair*, London, Free Press.

Seldon, A. and Kavanagh, D. (eds) (2005) *The Blair Effect 2001–2005*, Cambridge, Cambridge University Press.

Select Committee on the Constitution (2002) *Devolution: Inter-Institutional Relations in the United Kingdom*, HL 28 (2002–03), London, TSO.

Select Committee on the Office of the Deputy Prime Minister (2005) *The Draft Regional Assemblies Bill* HC 61-I (2004–05), London, TSO.

Seyd, P. (1999) 'New parties/New politics', *Party Politics,* Vol. 5 No. 3 pp. 383–406.

Seyd, P and Whiteley, P. (2004) 'British party members: An overview', *Party Politics*, Vol. 10 No. 4 pp. 355–66.

Seymour-Ure, C. (2003) *Prime Ministers and the Media: Issues of Power and Control*, Oxford, Blackwell.

Shaw, E. (2004) 'What matters is what works: The Third Way and the case of the Private Finance Initiative', in Hale, S., Leggett, W. and Martell, L. (eds) *The Third Way and Beyond*, Manchester, Manchester University Press.

Shugart, M. (1995) 'Parliaments over President', *Journal of Democracy*, Vol. 6 No.2 pp. 168–72.

Smith, J. (2005) 'A missed opportunity? New Labour's European policy, 1997–2005', *International Affairs*, Vol. 81 No. 4 pp. 703–22.

Smith, K. (2003) *European Union Foreign Policy in a Changing World*, Cambridge, Polity.

Smith, M. J. (1999) *The Core Executive in Britain*, London, Macmillan (now Palgrave Macmillan).

Stanyer, J. (2004) 'Politics and the media: A crisis of trust?', *Parliamentary Affairs*, Vol. 57 No. 2 pp. 420–34.

Stephens, P. (2005) 'Blair's bridge needs a strong Europe', *Financial Times*, 7 June.

Stewart, J. (1994) 'Reply to William Waldegrave', in Flynn, N. (ed.) *A Reader: Change in the Civil Service*, London, Public Finance Foundation.

Stewart, J. D. (1958) *British Pressure Groups*, Oxford, Oxford University Press.

Stothard, P. (2003) *Thirty Days: A Month at the Heart of Blair's War*, London, HarperCollins.

Straw, J. (2005) 'There are no shortcuts to democracy: Our people want strong majority government, not the mush of PR', *Guardian*, 12 May.

Street, J. (2001) *Mass Media, Politics and Democracy*, London, Palgrave Macmillan.

Subrahmanyam, G. (1995) 'Effortless rule and imperial realities: The British imperial state in 1891', in Lovenduski, J. and Stanyer, J. (eds) *Contemporary Political Studies, 1995: Volume I*, Belfast, UK Political Studies Association.

Subrahmanyam, G. (2004) *Bringing the Empire Back In: Patterns of Growth in the British Imperial State, 1860–1960*, unpublished PhD thesis, London School of Economics.

Sutherland, K. (ed.) (2000) *The Rape of the Constitution*, Thorverton, Imprint Academic.

Tant, A. P. (1993) *British Government: The Triumph of Elitism*, Aldershot, Dartmouth.

Taylor, C. (1994) *Multiculturalism: Examining the Politics of Recognition*, Princeton, NJ, Princeton University Press.

Taylor, C. and Gutmann, A. (1992) *Multiculturalism and the Politics of Recognition*, Princeton, NJ, Princeton University Press.

Taylor, J. (Lord) (2001) 'Winning back the people', *Reformer Magazine*, Summer.

Taylor, S. (1982) *The National Front in English Politics*, Basingstoke, Macmillan (now Palgrave Macmillan).

Theakston, K. (2005) 'Prime ministers and the constitution: Attlee to Blair', *Parliamentary Affairs*, Vol. 58 No. 1 pp. 17–37.

Tickell, A., John, P. and Musson, S. (2005) 'The referendum campaign: Issues and turning points in the North East', *ESRC Devolution Briefings*, No. 20, www.devolution.ac.uk/Briefing_papers.htm

Tiltman, D. (2005) 'Government adspend up to record level of £203m', *Marketing*, 26 October.

Timmins, N. (1995) *The Five Giants: A Biography of the Welfare State*, Basingstoke, Palgrave Macmillan.

Tomkins, A. (2005) *Our Republican Constitution*, London, Hart.

Tonge, J. (2005) *The New Northern Irish Politics?*, Basingstoke, Palgrave Macmillan.

Toynbee, P. and Walker, D. (2005) *Better or Worse: Has Labour Delivered?*, London, Bloomsbury.

Travers, T. (2003) *The Politics of London: Governing an Ungovernable City*, Basingstoke, Palgrave Macmillan.

Trench, A. (2001) 'Intergovernmental relations a year on', in Trench, A. (ed.) *The State of the Nations 2000: The Second Year of Devolution in the United Kingdom*, Thorverton, Imprint Academic.

Trench, A. (2005a) 'The Assembly's future as a legislative body', in Osmond, J. (ed.) *Welsh Politics Comes of Age: Responses to the Richard Commission*, Cardiff, Institute of Welsh Affairs.

Trench, A. (ed.) (2005b) *The Dynamics of Devolution: The State of the Nations 2005*, Thorverton, Imprint Academic.

Tumber, H. and Palmer, J. (2004) *Media at War: The Iraq Crisis*, London, Sage.

Turnbull, A. (2005) Professionalising public management in an era of choice, www.cabinetoffice.gov.uk/about_the_cabinet_office/speeches/turnbull/html/index.asp

Tyrie, A. (2004) *Mr Blair's Poodle Goes to War*, London, Centre for Policy Studies.

UK Government (2003) *The Government's Response to the Second Report of the Select Committee on the Constitution, Session 2002–2003: Devolution: Inter-Institutional Relations in the United Kingdom*, Cm 5780, London, TSO.

Verba, S., Schlozman, K. L. and Brady, H. (1995) *Voice and Equality: Civic Voluntarism in American Politics*, Cambridge, MA, Harvard University Press.

Waldegrave, W. (1993) 'The reality of reform and accountability in today's public service', Lecture to the Public Finance Foundation, 5 July.

Waldron, J. (2003) 'Security and liberty: The image of balance', *Journal of Political Philosophy*, Vol. 11 No. 2 pp. 191–210.

Wales Office (2005) *Better Governance for Wales*, Cm 6582, London, TSO.

Wallace, W. (2005) 'The collapse of British foreign policy,' *International Affairs*, Vol. 81 No. 1 pp. 54–68.

Wallace, W. and Oliver, T. (2005) 'A Bridge Too Far: The United Kingdom and the transatlantic relationship', in Andrews, D. (ed.) *Alliance Under Stress: Atlantic Relations After Iraq*, Cambridge, Cambridge University Press.

Wanless, D. (2002) *Securing our Future Health: Taking a Long Term View* (The Wanless Report), www.hm-treasury.gov.uk/Consultations_and_Legislation/wanless/consult_wanless_final.cfm

Ward, S., Gibson, R. and Lusoli, W. (2003) 'Online participation and mobilisation in Britain: Hype, hope and reality', *Parliamentary Affairs*, Vol. 56 No. 4 pp. 652–68.

Ware, A. (1996) *Political Parties and Party Systems*, Oxford, Oxford University Press.

Warren, M. (2000) *Associations and Democracy*, Princeton, NJ, Princeton University Press.

Watson, C. W. (2000) *Multiculturalism*, Buckingham, Open University Press.

Watson, M. (2003) 'The politics of inflation management', *Political Quarterly*, Vol. 74 No. 3 pp. 285–97.

Watson, M. and Hay, C. (2003) 'The discourse of globalisation and the logic of no alternative: Rendering the contingent necessary in the political economy of New Labour', *Policy and Politics*, Vol. 31 No. 3 pp. 289–305.

Webb, P. (2000) *The Modern British Party System*, London, Sage.

Webb, P. (2002) 'Parties and party systems: More continuity than change', *Parliamentary Affairs*, Vol. 55 No. 2 pp. 363–76.

Webb, P. (2003) 'Parties and party systems: Prospects for realignment', *Parliamentary Affairs*, Vol. 56 No. 2 pp. 283–96.

Weir, S. and Beetham, D. (1999) *Political Power and Democratic Control in Britain*, London, Routledge.

Wheatcroft, G. (2005) *The Strange Death of Conservative England*, London, Penguin.

White, S. (2002) *The Civic Minimum*, Oxford, Oxford University Press.

Whitman, R. and Benford, J. (2005) *Opportunity in Crisis? Prospects for the UK EU Presidency 2005*, Munich, Centre for Applied Policy Research/Bertelsmann Foundation.

Winder, R. (2004) *Bloody Foreigners: The Story of Immigrants to Britain*, London, Abacus.

Wright, T. (1996) *Socialisms Old and New*, London, Routledge.

Wright, T. (2003) *British Politics: A Very Short Introduction*, Oxford, Oxford University Press.

Wright, T. (2004) 'Prospects for parliamentary reform', *Parliamentary Affairs*, Vol. 57 No. 4 pp. 867–76.

Wring, D. (2005a) 'Politics and the media: The Hutton Inquiry, the public relations state, and crisis at the BBC', *Parliamentary Affairs*, Vol. 58 No. 2 pp. 380–93.

Wring, D. (2005b) 'The Labour campaign', in Norris, P. and Wlezien, C. (eds) *Britain Votes 2005*, Oxford, Oxford University Press.

YouGov (2005) Survey of British Muslims, released 25 July 2005. www.yougov.com/archives/pdf/TEL050101030_1.pdf

Young, H. (1999) *This Blessed Plot: Britain and Europe from Churchill to Blair*, London, Papermac.

# Index